C000265088

THE YPRES SALIENT

THE YPRES SALIENT

A Guide to the Cemeteries
and Memorials of the Salient

MICHAEL SCOTT

Gliddon Books
Norwich   Norfolk
1992

First published in 1992

ISBN 0 947893 28 8

Printed and bound in Great Britain by
Biddles Ltd., Guildford and King's Lynn
and published by Gliddon Books,
The Reading Room, Brooke, Norwich, Norfolk

CONTENTS

Introduction   1

Glossary   2

Ypres – Ieper   3

Cemeteries   5

Map   between pages 99 and 100

Commonwealth War Graves Commission   145

The Ypres Salient   147

Order of Battles   151

Cemetery Dead   174

Victoria Cross Holders   179

Bibliography   181

Military Index   183

People and Places Index   188

INTRODUCTION

A war that ended in 1918 and in which most of the men who fought are now dead is even today of great historical interest for many British people. The Ypres Salient was an area of particularly intense fighting during that 'Great War'. Every one who visits the cemeteries and memorials to the men who died defending Ypres will be affected in some way, and many of today's pilgrims return to the battlefields of Flanders again and again.

Each year I take groups to the battlefields of World War One. In trying to provide these groups with as much information about the area as possible I found that there was no straight forward guide available. The books that did exist did not answer the questions that my parties most frequently asked such as "Why is this cemetery here and what happened?"

Therefore, I decided to create a simple but informative guide to the cemeteries of the Ypres Salient which would also include information on other features such as the fighting near each cemetery, the towns and the memorials.

Defining the Ypres Salient was an arbitrary decision with which some readers may disagree but I had to set some markers and mine serve the purpose that I need. Hence, the southern boundary is the A25 autoroute and the northern edge of Armentieres. The western limit is the French border from Steenvoorde to Hondschoote. The eastern boundary is the D945 from Armentieres to Wervik, the N303 from Wervik to Westrozebeke and then a line directly north to Staden. This leaves the northern limit as a line from Staden to Hondschoote. With the exception of three German cemeteries and Ledeghem Military Cemetery all the burial grounds in this book are within this area.

All the graveyards are accessible though it is not possible to get a car right up to the entrance of each one and sometimes great care will have to be taken when using/driving larger vehicles.

I have included each British cemetery alphabetically using the names as spelt by the Commonwealth War Graves Commission and given each one a number from 1 to 171. Following these are the Belgian, French and German cemeteries containing graves dating from the Great War. These are numbered 172 to 176. Finally a miscellaneous group of cemeteries have been included and numbered 177 to 186. At the end of each entry I have included the C.W.G.C. reference number as marked on their own map, a copy of which can be found in the centre pages of this book, this is the C.W.G.C. overlay of the Michelin 1 cm to 2 km series No. 51. The reference number consists of two parts, the first is the section of the map (which is divided into twenty sections each with a number); and the second part is the number that is overprinted.

In order to use this book you should firstly identify the cemetery and then refer to the C.W.G.C. number and locate it upon the map, the 'Location' details will be of assistance. The other information about each cemetery tells you the history and local events or features. Journey times are calculated from the Grote Markt in Ypres and are very generous.

I have used the Flemish spellings. Hence, Messines is Mesen, Menin is Menen and so on. This means that the original spelling of some cemetery names is different from the spelling of the village, for example, Locre Churchyard is in Loker, the Messines Ridge is now the Mesen Ridge and the Menin Road is the Menen Road. I have also kept to the original spelling for the titles of the Battle of the Menin Road and the Battle of Messines. In addition, I could not bring myself to change Ypres to Ieper except for the information under 'Location'. I do not believe that this will cause confusion.

So, I hope you find the book useful and have as much enjoyment reading it as I did in writing it.

GLOSSARY

The Argyll and Sutherland Highlanders (Princess Louises's)

The Black Watch (Royal Highlanders)

The Buffs (East Kent Regiment)

The Queen's Own Cameron Highlanders

The Cameronians (Scottish Rifles)

The Duke of Wellington's Regiment (West Riding)

The King's Regiment (Liverpool)

The King's Own Royal (Lancaster) Regiment

The Prince of Wales's Leinster Regiment (Royal Canadians)

The Middlesex Regiment (Duke of Cambridge's Own)

The North Staffordshire Regiment (Prince of Wales's)

The Queen's Royal Regiment (West Surreys)

The Rifle Brigade (The Prince Consort's Own)

The Royal Berkshire Regiment (Princess Charlotte of Wales's

The Royal Fusiliers (City of London Regiment)

The Royal Irish Fusiliers (Princess Victoria's)

The Royal Scots (Lothian Regiment)

The Queen's Own (Royal West Kent Regiment)

The King's Own Scottish Borderers

The Seaforth Highlanders (Ross-shire Buffs, The Duke of Albany's)

The Sherwood Foresters (Nottinghamshire and Derbyshire Regiment)

The King's Shropshire Light Infantry

The Somerset Light Infantry (Prince Albert's)

The South Lancashire Regiment (Prince of Wales's Volunteers)

The West Yorkshire Regiment (Prince of Wales's Own)

The Wiltshire Regiment (Duke of Edinburgh's)

The King's Own Yorkshire Light Infantry

The Yorkshire Regiment (Alexandra, Princess of Wales's Own)

A.D.S. – Advanced Dressing Station

A.I.F. – Australian Imperial Force

A.N.Z.A.C. – Australian and New Zealand Army Corps

Aust – Australia

B.E.F. – British Expeditionary Force

Bel – Belgian/Belgium

Bt – Baronet

Btn – Battalion

BWI – British West Indies Regiment

Can – Canada

C.W.G.C. – Commonwealth War Graves Commision

D.C.L.I. – Duke of Cornwall's Light Infantry

D.C.M. – Distinguished Conduct Medal

D.S. – Dressing Station

D.S.O. – Distinguished Service Order

Fr – France/French

Ger – Germany

H.A.C. – Honourable Artillery Company

Hon. – Honourable

hr – hour

I.W.G.C. – Imperial War Graves Commission

K.C.V.O. – Knight Commander of the Victoria Order

KUG – Known Unto God

M.C. – Military Cross

M.M. – Military Medal

mins – minutes

N.A. – New Army

No. – Number

N.C.O. – Non-Commissioned Officer

NF – Newfoundland

NZ – New Zealand

O.B.E. – Order of the British Empire

R.A.M.C. – Royal Army Medical Corps

R.E. – Royal Engineers

S Afr – South Africa

SM – Special Memorial

sq mts – square metres

sq yds – square yards

T.F. – Territorial Force

UK – United Kingdom (British)

US – United States of America

V.C. – Victoria Cross

WWII – World War Two

Y.M.C.A. – Young Men's Christian Association

YPRES – IEPER

During the First Battle of Ypres in October and November 1914 the German Kaiser demanded of his troops that they "Take Ypres or die". They died as Ypres did not fall. It remained in Allied hands, a symbol of defiance to the German Army who tried to capture the town in a series of monumental battles. Even so, many men from Britain, Ireland, Canada, New Zealand, Australia, South Africa, India, the U.S.A., Belgium, France and the Caribbean will forever defend the town of Ypres and the Salient as they died and are buried in the Salient.

Ypres was created in 962 A.D. though there is some archeological evidence of an earlier settlement at the site of the Lille Gate. The town became one of the main textile trading centres in Flanders and Europe during the Middle Ages, centre of a population of over 200,000. As Ypres became less important as a commercial centre it grew more strategically important and was regularly besieged, particularly in the years 1383, 1584, 1689-92, 1713, 1744 and 1792-4. Ypres became a pawn of the European powers, coming under the dominance of the Spanish, Austrians, French and Dutch.

The fortifications were begun by the Spanish before 1670, but following the Peace of Nijmegen, when Ypres was ceded to the French, the walls were made stronger notably with a citadel at the Antwerp (Menin) Gate, the most ornate of the four gates of Ypres. The defences, partially dismantled during the French rule which lasted from 1744-92, were rebuilt under the Austrians in the next year and taken down again by the French in 1794. The Antwerp Gate was re-named the Napoleon Gate in 1804 and the defences rebuilt, just before the Battle of Waterloo in 1815, by the British. From 1815-38 Belgium and Holland were one country and the defences were built up against the French, at which time the Menin Gate acquired its name. In 1838 Belgium achieved its independence and Ypres began to dismantle its defences once more, including the Menin Gate, for the building of railways and general growth of the town. As a result, when the Great War began in August 1914, only the Lille Gate was still standing.

The 3rd Cavalry Division of the German IV Cavalry Corps entered Ypres on 13 October 1914 but they retreated when the British Expeditionary Force arrived the next day. The civilians did not leave Ypres until the bombardment during the Second Battle of Ypres in 1915, but the town nearly fell during the German Spring Offensive in 1918 when the Germans reached its outskirts. The Salient was broken in September and October 1918.

FEATURES

GROTE MARKT – This is one of the grandest market squares in Flanders. If you are lucky there will be one of the numerous fairs held when you visit but it is important to remember that the weekly market is in the square on Saturday mornings, therefore no parking areas are available at that time. The planners have not yet completed rearranging the roads in the town which may affect your access to the Grote Markt.

CLOTH HALL – The original Cloth Hall was built over a period of forty-five (1260-1304) years, though the Nieuwkerke at the east end was not added until 1609. The only surviving section of the pre-1914 hall is now beneath the Belfry around the 'Donkerspoort' where you can see the coats of arms.

Externally the building appears to be as it was prior to 1914, when it was destroyed by German shelling, particularly by incendiary devices which were specifically aimed at damaging the ancient town. There are now modern offices in the building, including the main Tourist Office on the ground floor at the east end where the staff are always willing to help with any enquiry. You will find the Flemish people open and friendly, I am always impressed by their linguistic ability. The first time that I visited the Tourist Office the young lady helping me was doing so in English, while holding a conversation with another man in Flemish and answering a telephone call in French – I felt very inadequate with my limited schoolboy French.

On the first floor is the 1914-1918 Ypres Salient War Museum, its entrance being next to the Tourist Office. It provides an excellent introduction to the War, particularly the fighting on the Salient. The museum is open from 1 April to mid November from 9.30 am to 12.00 pm and 1.30 pm to 5.30 pm but can also be opened out of season by arrangement.

On the outside walls of the Cloth Hall are several plaques and Memorials to:

Earl Baldwin IX and Queen Margaret of Champagne.
King Albert and Queen Elizabeth.
Our Lady of Thuyne.
The Sacred Heart.
The French killed during 1914-18 on the Salient.

St. MARTIN'S CATHEDRAL – situated north of the Cloth Hall. The first church was built in 1073 and the cathedral in the Thirteenth Century. It was destroyed in the War and later rebuilt in the Gothic style, a spire which had been part of the original blueprint, but had not been built, was also added. Within the cathedral a number of features include Memorial windows to King Albert, the R.A.F., the B.E.F., and the 5th (Princess Charlotte of Wales's) Dragoon Guards, Memorial plaques to the British Commonwealth dead and the French dead on the Salient and the graves of several personalities from the history of Ypres.

Behind the cathedral are the cloisters containing original fragments of the cathedral destroyed in the War and a Memorial to the men of Munster who fell in the War. Just outside the south exit of the cathedral are some original pre-war cobblestones. The road in front of the cathedral is the Vandenpereboomplein which was formerly a canal to the Cloth Hall for transporting wool and materials.

St. GEORGE'S MEMORIAL CHURCH – on the corner of the Vandenpereboomplein and Elverdingsestraat. Designed by Sir Reginald Blomfield, who designed many of the cemeteries on the Salient including Tyne Cot, it was built after Field Marshal Lord French had the idea of a church for the large numbers of British still living in Flanders, as well as for pilgrims to the Salient. Sir John French led the original B.E.F. and was Commander-in-Chief of the British Army until December 1915. He was made the First Earl of Ypres in 1921. The foundation stone was laid by Field Marshal Lord Plumer on 24 July 1927 and a service of dedication led by the Lord Bishop of Fulham on 24 March 1929. Plumer led the V Corps at Ypres from January – May 1915 and was then commander of the Second Army until the end of the War. He planned and led the British victory at the Battle of Messines in June 1917 for which he was highly regarded. Known to the troops as 'Daddy' or 'Plum' he was made a Field Marshal in 1919 and Viscount, the 1st Baron Plumer of Messines, in 1929. There was also an Eton Memorial School, for

the children of workers of the I.W.G.C. and other officials near the church, that lasted to 1948. In the church each chair is an individual memorial and there are many Regimental plaques, banners and a bust of Lord French.

MENIN GATE – see the section devoted to this.

BELGIAN MEMORIAL – near the Cloth Hall across the road at the west end of the hall.

RAMPARTS CEMETERY – see the section for this that also deals with the Lille Gate, Lion Tower, moat, walk and Powder Magazine.

RIJSELSTRAAT – this is the road to the Lille Gate that I have recommended for a walk to Ramparts Cemetery. There are a number of interesting buildings, for example, at No. 38 the Belle Alms House or Belle Godhuis has some of the original Sixteenth Century structure remaining. Founded in 1279 and rebuilt in 1616, there is a plaque to Master Jan Yperman, the 'father' of Flemish surgery who worked here from 1304-29.

No. 70, the old Post Office, is a replica of a Fourteenth Century house that was possibly owned by the Knights' Templar. The St. John's Alms House was founded in 1277 and is now an art gallery. St. Peter's Church, near the Lille Gate, was built in the Twelfth Century in the Romanesque style and was rebuilt after the War.

SALVATION CORNER – this is found at the Ypres end of the N369 road to Dixmuide. It gained this name because of the Salvation Army hut that was situated on the corner here throughout the War. Nearby, at the town end of the Ypres – Ijzer canal, is a bend known to the British as TATTENHAM CORNER, one of many similarly named junctions on the Western Front.

There are other places of interest in Ypres that you may consider worth visiting. I do not claim this to be a definitive list, merely some of the more relevant features for someone interested in the Ypres Salient and the Great War.

HISTORY

The cemetery was begun by the French during the Battles of the Lys when they buried ninety-nine of their fallen here, with four British officers on the south-east side. It was taken over by British units, who created seventy-five graves, during July and August of 1918. At this time eighty-four American soldiers were also buried here. The French and American dead were removed after the Armistice, while twenty-five British dead of April to August 1918, who had been buried in Boeschepe Church-yard (about 3 km south-east of L'Abeele), were moved here.

INFORMATION

Located at the site of a Royal Flying Corps Aerodrome, the men who landed planes in the fields near this cemetery must have been taking their lives in their hands with each landing on such rough ground. The cemetery is technically in a no man's land between France and Belgium with good views of the Monts des Flandres.

UK – 104

Area – 1033 sq yds

LOCATION

Abeele Aerodrome Cemetery is situated south of L'Abeele village west of the new Poperinge – Steenvoorde road. This is reached most easily from the Poperinge by-pass by taking the right turn just south of a large crossroads with the L'Abeele – Bailleul road (D10).

Journey Time – 30 mins

C.W.G.C. Reference – 4/20

AEROPLANE CEMETERY, POTIJZE　　　　*No. 2*

HISTORY

Until 31 July 1917 this site was in no man's land when, during the first day of Third Battle of Ypres, the 15th (Scottish) and 55th (West Lancashire) Divisions took Verlorenhoek and Frezenberg. On the following day the cemetery was begun as the New Cemetery, Frezenberg, by the 15th and 16th (Irish) Divisions. It had gained its present name by October 1917 due to the presence of the wreck of a British aeroplane, near the site of the Cross of Sacrifice that we can see today. It was used until March 1918, when occupied by the Germans, and again in September 1918. After the Armistice nearly 1,000 graves were concentrated here.

INFORMATION

From 8 to 11 May 1915 the front-line had been withdrawn from the Zonnebeke side of Frezenberg and formed here 800 m east of Potijze Chateau. On 12 May the 1st Cavalry Brigade took over this section of line with the 2nd (Queen's Bays) Dragoon Guards north of the road. South of the road to Hooge the 6th and 7th Cavalry Brigades held the line.

On 13 May the Germans launched a heavy bombardment which inflicted severe casualties on the Queen's Bays, especially 'B' Squadron on the left flank towards Wieltje. This was followed by an infantry attack.

The 8th Cavalry Brigade was the divisional reserve from a point in Wieltje to the Menen Road. The 10th (Prince of Wales's Own Royal) Hussars, north of the road, and Essex Yeomanry on the road, were sent up as reinforcements but could not successfully take the front-line. The limited section of line that they managed to occupy was exposed and their hold tenuous, in addition their rifles soon began to jam. South of the road the Royal Horse Guards (the Blues) were ordered to counter-attack. Although the regiment on the Queen's Bays' left flank withdrew, the German artillery's accurate fire on these trenches meant that the German infantry could not occupy them. This, combined with counter-attacks by the 8th Cavalry Brigade saw the German advance falter. The Queen's Bays suffered sixty casualties out of 250 men who had gone into the line. The 10th Hussars were reduced to four officers and ninety-eight men. The Blues lost eleven officers (including Viscount Lieutenant Albert Wendover who died of his wounds on 19 May) and 112 men out of 277 ranks who went into action. With them a detachment of the 19th London Sanitary Section, Royal Army Medical Corps, had gone into action. All thirteen men were killed.

On 15 July 1915 a line from here south to Railway Wood was held by the 1st North Staffordshires (17th Brigade, 6th Division) when the Germans launched a surprise attack after a period of quiet. No help could come from either flank as the Germans were also attacking there. Hence, the North Staffords counter-attacked on their own which in turn surprised the Germans. As a result the line was held.

On 26 July 1915 five men were executed on the ramparts of Ypres in what became the largest single execution by the British Army during the War. They were all men of the 3rd Worcesters (7th Brigade, 3rd Division) who had deserted in late 1914 or early 1915. They were originally buried on the ramparts and their graves were moved after the War. Privates John Robinson, Alfred D. Thompson and Bert Hartells were concentrated here while Corporal Ives and Private Fellows were moved to Perth Cemetery.

Concentrated here were:

Bedford House Cemetery (Enclosure No. 2), Zillebeke – a little east of the Ypres – Wijtschate Road. The enclosure was separate from the others now forming the Bedford House Cemetery. It contained fourteen men of the 1st Duke of Cornwall's Light Infantry and six men of the 1st Devonshires who fell in April 1915.
Lock 8 Cemetery, Voormezele – in a field about 200 m north of Lock 8 on the Ypres – Comines canal. It contained nineteen British, two Australian and two German soldiers who fell during July to September 1917.

UK – 825	Aust – 204	NZ – 17	Can – 47
NF – 1	S Afr – 1	KUG – 1	Unnamed – 637

Special Memorials to four British men and one Australian buried among the unnamed.

Area – 4974 sq yds

LOCATION
Aeroplane Cemetery is on the south side of the Potijze – Zonnebeke road 1.2 km from the roundabout in Potijze and 300 m from the French cemetery.

Journey Time – 15 mins

C.W.G.C. Reference – 5/36

ARTILLERY WOOD CEMETERY, BOEZINGE   *No. 3*

HISTORY
The graveyard was begun by the Guards Division shortly after they had taken the wood that used to be just south of here between the burial ground and the former railway next to the Boezinge – Langemark road. Used as a front-line cemetery until March 1918, when it contained 141 graves, it was enlarged after the Armistice by the concentration of over 1,150 graves from the battlefields surrounding Boezinge.

INFORMATION
The Guards took an almost empty German front-line on the first day of the Third Battle of Ypres. The Royal Engineers had to cut through the canal banks to lay bridges over the canal for this attack on 31 July 1917. The Germans, learning from the experience of the Battle of Messines only a month before, thought that the noise was being made by tunnellers laying mines and, hence, evacuated the front-line moving back to a second line 200 m to the east. As a result, only a skeleton force held the positions when the Guards attacked.

This point marks the northern limit of the British sector of the front. From here to the sea, the Belgians and French held the line.

Several interesting features can be found in the area:
1 – At the crossroads 250 m south of the cemetery are a group of monuments. The 'Carrefour des Roses' are memorials to the 87th French Territorial Infantry Division (Les Peperes) and the 45th Infantry Division (Les Joyeux) who defended this area during the first gas attack in April 1915. An orientation table and map stand next to the Breton Calvary from Brittany.
2 – The largest German bunker still standing in the Salient can be reached by turning towards Langemark at the crossroads by the French Memorials. In 1 km you will come to a small crossroads at which you turn left. By following the road to the left as it crosses the now disused railway line you will come to the bunker which stands in fields to the left of the road. By turning right at each junction that follows you can return to the Boezinge-Langemark road.

Concentrated here:

Boezinge Chateau Grounds Cemetery – on the southwest side of the road between the village and the former railway station, now the old road. It contained nineteen British soldiers, mainly of the

Guards Division, who fell from June to August 1917. There were other British graves elsewhere in the Chateau grounds as well as a French cemetery that have all been removed.

Brissein House Cemetery, Bikschote – 2 km north of Langemark. A French cemetery in which twenty-two British soldiers were buried from December 1917 to March 1918.

Captain's Farm Cemetery, Langemark – 3 km west of Langemark. A group of graves in which sixty-three soldiers, mainly of the Guards and 29th Divisions, were buried from July 1917 to March 1918.

UK – 1243	Aust – 5	NZ – 2	Can – 30
S Afr – 1	KUG – 5		Unnamed – 506

Special Memorials to twelve British men buried with the unnamed.

Area – 5312 sq yds

LOCATION
Artillery Wood Cemetery is on the east side of the canal near Boezinge. It is about 250 m north of the Boezinge – Langemark road and is reached most easily from the crossroads at the French Memorial. Turn left at the junction 200 m north of the cemetery to return to the canal.

Journey Time – 20 mins

C.W.G.C. Reference – 5/4

BAILLEUL COMMUNAL CEMETERY   *No. 4*

HISTORY
The Town Cemetery was first used for British burials, at the eastern end, in October 1914. It was closed in April 1915 when the available space had been filled; a new area was set aside at the east end of the cemetery as the Extension.

INFORMATION
Bailleul was an ancient lace-making and linen centre and a military base for most of the War. The town fell to the Germans in early October 1914 but was taken by the 19th Brigade and 4th Division on 14 October 1914. It was an important railhead, air depot and rest and recuperation centre.

The 2nd, 3rd, 8th, 11th, 53rd, 1st Canadian and 1st Australian Casualty Clearing Stations were located here near to a well known clinic and asylum. Dr. J. S. Haldane and Professor H. B. Baker were sent to Bailleul by the British Government on 26 April 1915 to report on the effects of the German gas attack. Their report was highly publicised in Britain and caused revulsion towards the Germans.

The Germans had a numerical advantage here of four to one in April 1918. The advantage was enhanced by the fact that most of the British troops in the area had just arrived for rest from the German onslaught on the Somme so they were battle-weary and depleted in strength. The Germans reached Bailleul by 11 April and the Battle of Bailleul, one of the Battles of the Lys, lasted from 13-15 April. Among the defenders were the 29th, 31st, 34th and 59th (North Midland) Divisions, and the 4th Guards and 147th (West Riding) Brigades who were forced to withdraw having suffered heavy casualties. Some units were reduced to twenty or thirty men, for example, Lieutenant Chicken withdrew with the three survivors of his two platoons of 'C' Company of the 1st Borders. The Germans took the ruins on the evening of 15 April and Bailleul remained in German hands until it was retaken by the 25th Division who found it empty on 30 August.

John Laffin in his book *On The Western Front* tells the possibly apocryphal story of a group of Australians who were waiting in Bailleul to move to the front in the early months of 1916. They shared memories and passed around photographs with an officer of the Guards who had stopped to talk. He apologised for not having a photo of his family but as he left he handed them a coin saying "That is my father". The Australians suddenly realised that they had been talking to the Prince of Wales.

The stone obelisk Memorial to the 25th Division is in the town, and can be reached by passing through the town square on the main road to Hazebrouck (D933). There is also a municipal War Memorial, a copy of a tower and belfry forming part of the Church of St. Armand, unveiled in 1925 by the Lord Mayor of Bradford, just off the square behind the Town Hall.

The British graves are separated from, and surround, a French military cemetery. Many of the headstones have two or three names inscribed upon them.

UK – 586   Can – 21   India – 4   Fr – 1
Bel Civilians – 2   Unnamed – 10
Ger – 8 (Concentrated here during 1939-45 War)

Special Memorials to seventeen graves, including the four Indian, destroyed by shell-fire.

Area – 707 sq yds

LOCATION
Bailleul Communal Cemetery is located on the north side of the town which lies in northern France. Bailleul can be reached by taking the N375 through Dikkebus turning right in Loker on to the D23 to Belle and Bailleul. Just before the square in Bailleul is a C.W.G.C. sign, part of several local direction signs, pointing to a side street on the left. A narrow road leads to the main entrance at a fork in the road, though the entrance you want is 150 m down the left fork. When you enter the cemetery the British graves are to your left.

Journey Time – 50 mins

C.W.G.C. Reference – 5/89

BAILLEUL COMMUNAL CEMETERY EXTENSION   *No. 5*

HISTORY
This was begun as the space in the Communal Cemetery was filled. Hence, burials started in the Extension in April 1915 and continued throughout the British occupation, halting only during the German offensive in 1918. It was enlarged after the Armistice with the concentration of 300 graves from the neighbouring battlefields.

INFORMATION
For general information please refer to Bailleul Communal Cemetery. There are some interesting features here such as the Special Memorials in a raised area next to the pavilions at the eastern end.

There are three men buried in the Extension who suffered less honourable deaths than their comrades as they were executed after Courts Martial. Private William W. Roberts of the 4th Royal Fusiliers (9th Brigade, 3rd Division) was injured at Hooge in June 1915 when his battalion suffered 369 casualties. He returned to duty in September 1915 but deserted soon after during heavy fighting again at Hooge. One can only imagine what must have been going through Roberts' mind. He surrendered to the authorities on 4 May 1916 at Brandhoek and was tried at Loker on 20 May before his execution on 29 May 1916.

Lance-Corporal William A. Moon of the 11th Cheshires (75th Brigade, 25th Division) deserted from his battalion during the Battle of the Somme but was not tried until the winter. He was executed near Bailleul on 21 November 1916.

Private John Rodgers of the 2nd South Lancashires (75th Brigade, 25th Division) was shot on 9 March 1917 for desertion while under fire.

V.C. – Sergeant T. Mottershead, D.C.M., V.C..
20 Squadron, Royal Flying Corps.
From Widnes, Lancashire.
His aeroplane was attacked at 9000 ft on 7 January 1917, and though it was in flames he landed behind British lines saving his observer, Lieutenant W. Gower. The plane then collapsed, trapping Mottershead. He died of his wounds on 12 January 1917. Sergeant Mottershead was the only non-commissioned officer on air operations to win the Victoria Cross.

Concentrated here:

Pont de Nieppe German Cemetery – on the south side of the hamlet. It was used in summer 1918 and included two British graves.
Reningelst Chinese Cemetery – in a field a little south of the Poperinge Road. It contained thirty men of the Chinese Labour Corps killed from November 1917 to March 1918.

UK – 3411   Aust – 396   NZ – 252   Can – 290
NF – 1   S Afr – 1   BWI – 3   Guernsey – 1
India – 4   Chinese Labour Corps – 31
Fr – 2 (1 interpreter with 41st Battalion, AIF)
Russian Labour Corps – 1 Ger – 111 Unnamed – 181

Special Memorials to eleven British soldiers buried here in 1918 whose graves were destroyed by shell-fire.

Area – 11323 sq yds

LOCATION
As for the Communal Cemetery.

BARD COTTAGE CEMETERY, BOEZINGE   *No. 6*

HISTORY
The cemetery was begun in June 1915 and used until October 1918. We can tell the units that held parts of the northern sector of the Salient during the Third Battle of Ypres in that many graves here are of the 49th (West Riding) and 38th (Welsh) Divisions showing that those units were nearby at that time. Later, the artillery that moved into this area as the front-line moved forward to the east in 1917, buried their dead here. The graveyard was increased in size after the Armistice.

INFORMATION
Bard Cottage was a house that stood opposite the site of the present cemetery close to a bridge over the canal (now gone) called the Bard's Causeway. The house and the cemetery were protected from observation from the canal by a high bank that can still be seen.

Nearly 200m to the south of this cemetery stood Marengo Farm from which most of the graves concentrated into Bard Cottage Cemetery came. It was used from June 1915 to August 1916 and, like many farms in this area of the Salient, was originally named by the French Army who were stationed here first.

UK – 1615   Can – 9   NF – 6
S Afr – 2   BWI – 3   Ger – 4

Special Memorials to three soldiers known/believed to be buried here in unnamed graves.

Area – 6535 sq yds

LOCATION
Bard Cottage Cemetery can be found on the west side of the road to Boezinge about 2km north of Ypres.

Journey Time – 10 mins

C.W.G.C. Reference – 5/20

HISTORY

The Chateau Rosendal that stood on this site was taken over by the British Army early in the War as headquarters for many units including Dressing Stations and Field Ambulances. As a consequence, the grounds of the chateau were used for burials.

By the end of the War the grounds had become covered by a series of burial sites which were combined into this one cemetery. It was enlarged after the Armistice with the concentration of many graves from the surrounding battlefields.

INFORMATION

The Chateau Rosendal was a country house in a wooded, moated park, and though house and wood have gone the moats and some ruins can still be seen. It was in British hands throughout the War, though the front-line ran through what is now the cemetery after the German advance in 1918.

Deceptively large, much of it cannot be seen from the road, the cemetery is, in effect, several enclosures linked by a common name and boundary. This is a place that invites you to explore though the bridge to Enclosure No. 6 needs to be crossed with care.

Of the five enclosures that existed at the Armistice, No. 1 was removed to White House Cemetery, St. Jan, and No. 5 to Aeroplane Cemetery.

Enclosure No. 2 was begun in December 1915 and used until October 1918. It was enlarged after the Armistice with the concentration of graves from the Ecole de Bienfaisance and Asylum Cemeteries in Ypres. There are two Special Memorials to men buried in Ypres but whose graves were destroyed by shell-fire.

Enclosure No. 3, the smallest, was used from February 1915 to December 1916. Of the graves, twenty-two are men of the 7th East Yorkshires (50th Brigade, 17th (Northern) Divison). One Belgian soldier has been removed.

Enclosure No. 4, the largest, was used from June 1916 to February 1918, mainly by the 47th (2nd London) Division, and, again, after the Armistice for the concentration of 3,300 graves. There are Special Memorials to twenty men known or believed to be buried here among the unnamed. There are also twenty-five Special Memorials to men whose graves in cemeteries concentrated here have been lost.

Enclosure No. 6 was rediscovered after the War. Most of the graves are unidentified.

Among those buried here Private Frederick Turner of the 1/6th Northumberland Fusiliers (149th Brigade, 50th (Northumbrian) Division) had deserted from his unit in August 1917 while they were near Arras in France. After capture he escaped before recapture and trial. He was executed on 23 October 1917.

V.C. – Temporary Second Lieutenant Rupert Price Hallowes, M.C., V.C..
4th Middlesex (The Duke of Cambridge's Own), 8th Brigade, 3rd Division.
From Port Talbot.
Died – 30 September 1915.
Won – at Hooge on 25-30 September 1915 for his encouragement of, and example to, his men. He went back to get supplies, reconnoitred German positions and stood on the trench parapet without regard to the danger. He was killed in action.

Concentrated here:

Asylum Cemetery – in the grounds of the mental hospital on the Poperinge Road. It was used from February 1915 to November 1917 for 265 British, nine Canadian, seven Australian graves and two men of the British West Indies Regiment.
Boezinge French Cemetery No. 2 – a little south of Bard Cottage. It contained one British soldier.
Droogenbroodhoek German Cemetery, Moorslede – it contained one British soldier who fell in October 1914.
Ecole de Bienfaisance, Ypres – on the north side of the Poperinge Road near the Asylum. It was used from 1915 to 1917 for 133 British, three Canadian, three Australian graves and one man of the British West Indies Regiment.
Kerkhove Churchyard – it held five British men, with seven Germans, who fell in October and November 1918.
Poelkapelle German Cemetery No. 4 – on the St. Juliaan Road. It held fifty-two British men who fell from 1914 to 1916.
Zonnebeke British Cemeteries No.'s 1 & 3 – these (and two others) were made by the Germans on either side of the Zonnebeke – Broodsiende road on what was known as Devil's Hill. No. 1 contained thirty-one British men (mainly 2nd East Surreys) who fell in April 1915, and No. 3 had sixty-nine British men who fell in April and May 1915.

DEAD BURIED IN BEDFORD HOUSE CEMETERY

	No. 2	No. 3	No. 4	No. 6	Total
UK	673	55	3188	35	3951
Aust	22		179		201
NZ	5		25		30
Can	21	5	309		335
S Afr			17		17
BWI	5		1		6
Guernsey			3		3
India			20		20
Russia			1		1
Ger	1		1		2
KUG			2	499	501
TOTAL	727	60	3746	534	5067
Unnamed	33		2478 (60%)		2511
S.M.'s	2		45		47

LOCATION

Bedford House Cemetery can be found south of Ieper on the road to St. Eloi and Lille (Rijsel). It is 1.1km south of Shrapnel Corner on the left hand side of the road.

Journey Time – 5 mins

C.W.G.C. Reference – 5/57

BELGIAN BATTERY CORNER CEMETERY, IEPER   *No. 8*

HISTORY

This cemetery was begun by the 8th Division at the start of the Battle of Messines in June 1917 and was used until October 1918. It was mainly for burials from the nearby Dressing Station.

INFORMATION

Belgian Battery Corner was the name given by the Army to the point where the Dikkebus Road bends sharply to the south and forks from a road to Brandhoek. It is believed that the Battery after which the corner was named was the 1st Groupe Regiment d'Artillerie Provisoire (97, 98 and 99 Batteries) that was posted near here in 1915, though it is not certain.

Artillery units account for 206 of the men buried here which reflects the type of activity in the area during the War, this was behind the front-line but the artillery pieces were an obvious target for the German guns.

UK – 430	Aust – 123	NZ – 8
Can – 7	India – 2	KUG – 9

Special Memorials to two Australians whose graves have been lost.

Area – 4006 sq yds

LOCATION
Belgian Battery Corner Cemetery lies in the southern suburbs of Ieper about 300 m west of the point where the N375 bends sharply to the south. A road to Brandhoek leaves the N375 at this point, at the first crossroads of which is a C.W.G.C. sign directing to the cemetery. Turn right and the cemetery is soon on your right. Don't try any track to the right at the south end of the cemetery as they lead to private property.

Journey Time – 5 mins

C.W.G.C. Reference – 5/45

(ROYAL) BERKSHIRE CORNER CEMETERY EXTENSION   *No. 9*

HISTORY
The cemetery was opened in June 1916 and remained in use until September 1917.

INFORMATION
This is directly opposite Hyde Park Corner Cemetery, which was started by the Royal Berkshire Regiment, and dominates the other because of the large Memorial to the Missing.

The Memorial records the names of 11,447 missing from the Battles of Armentieres in 1914; Aubers Ridge, Loos and Fromelles in 1915; Estaires in 1916; Hazebrouck, Scherpenberg and Outersteene Ridge in 1918. As most of these are not strictly in the Salient I will not deal with them in too much detail. The Memorial takes the form of a circular temple, 22 m in diameter and 12 m high, with the names on panels within the interior. At the entrance there are two huge stone lions, the most memorable feature for many people whom I have spoken to. The Memorial was designed by H. Charlton Bradshaw, sculptured by Sir Gilbert Ledward and unveiled by the Duke of Brabant on 7 June 1931.

There are three men commemorated on the Memorial who were executed under the terms of the British Army Act in 1914 and 1915 but whose graves were lost. Private Archibald Browne of the 2nd Essex (12th Brigade, 4th Division) was the fourth British soldier to be executed in the War and the last in 1914. Having deserted from his battalion in November 1914 he was found guilty of desertion, plundering and escaping arrest before his execution on 19 December 1914.

Private A. Pitts of the 2nd Royal Warwickshires (22nd Brigade, 7th Division) deserted near Zonnebeke on 24 October 1914 but was captured at Boulogne on 12 January 1915. Pitts was executed on 8 February 1915.

Private Thomas Hope of the 2nd Leinsters (17th Brigade, 6th Division) deserted on 23 December 1914. He was captured, disguised as a Military Policeman, on 9 February 1915 and was executed on 2 March 1915.

In addition, four men commemorated on the Memorial were awarded the Victoria Cross:

Sapper W. Hackett, V.C..
    254th Tunnelling Company, Corps of Royal Engineers.
    Won – 22 – 23 June 1916, at Givenchy.
    Died – 27 June 1916.
Captain (later Major) William Henry Johnstone, V.C..
    59th Field Company, Corps of Royal Engineers, 5th Division.
    Won – 14 September 1914, at Missy.
    Died – 8 June 1915.
Private James MacKenzie, V.C..
    2nd Scots Guards, 20th Brigade, 7th Division.
    Won – 19 December 1914, at Rouges Bancs.
    Died – 19 December 1914.
Acting Captain Thomas Tannatt Pryce, M.C. and Bar, V.C..
    4th Grenadier Guards, Special Reserve, 4th (Guards) Brigade, 31st Division.
    Won – 11 April 1918, at Vieux Berquin.
    Died – 13 April 1918.

UK – 295	Aust – 51	NZ – 45	Can – 3

Area – 3738 sq yds

LOCATION

Royal Berkshire Corner Cemetery lies on the east side of the Armentieres road, about 1 km north of Ploegsteert, and at the foot of Hill 63, which is approximately 13 km south of Ieper.

Journey Time – 35 mins

C.W.G.C. Reference – 5/96

BERTENACRE MILITARY CEMETERY, FLETRE   *No. 10*

HISTORY

The cemetery was begun by the French when it was named the 'Cemetiere du Calvaire de Bertenacre' after a crucifix on the road nearby. It was used by the British Army during the War only by the 36th (Ulster) Division after the Battles of the Lys in July to September 1918. After the Armistice all 115 French and two German graves were removed. In their place came over forty British graves.

INFORMATION

This is one of the most isolated cemeteries included in this book and one of the most difficult to reach. The views of the Monts des Flandres make the journey worthwhile but the noise from the motorway by which this graveyard stands can be intrusive.

The Royal West Surrey Cemetery was situated 500 m to the south. It contained the graves of forty-two men who were killed in an air raid on their camp on 18 August 1917, of whom thirty-eight belonged to the 10th (Battersea) Queen's Regiment; and one Canadian who fell in June 1918. They were concentrated here after the War.

UK – 108   Can – 2   Area – 857 sq yds

LOCATION

Bertenacre Cemetery lies 2 km south of Godewaersvelde and south-west of Ieper. The easiest route is via the Poperinge by-pass and the new road to Steenvoorde, leaving the latter at the crossroads with the D10, and following the directions for Bailleul and then Godewaersvelde. Pass through the village and you will soon come to a sharp left bend just after which the road forks, take the right fork to Hazebrouck. Just before the road crosses the motorway you find the old road on the left at a C.W.G.C. sign. This ends at a farm track that leads to the path to the cemetery.

Journey Time – 50 mins

C.W.G.C. Reference – 4/23

BETHLEEM FARM EAST, MESEN   *No. 11*

HISTORY

The cemetery was begun as the farm was captured on 7 June 1917, the first day of the Battle of Messines, and remained in use until September though most burials were made during June.

INFORMATION

The farm was captured by the 3rd Australian Division. Most of the burials are of men from that Division who fell in action on 8 or 10 June 1917.

It is clear from this spot how the Mesen Ridge

dominates the countryside and, therefore, how important it was to hold it. You can imagine how difficult it must have been to fight up its sides which is what the Germans had to do in 1914 and 1918. On 31 October 1914 the position was held by the 57th (Wilde's) Rifles of the Indian Army. They were being relieved by the 2nd Royal Inniskilling Fusiliers when the Germans attacked. The British were forced to withdraw into the village where a new line was held with the help of the 5th (Princess Charlotte of Wales's) Dragoon Guards. (See Messines Ridge Cemetery)

As you pass through the square the Town Hall is on the left within which is an excellent small museum founded in 1972 by the Mayor. The curator, Albert Ghukiere has a wealth of stories about the area and his life. He will show you around the museum and the church, rebuilt in 1928 (in which Adolf Hitler spent some time at a German Dressing Station, he also made a painting of the Church which is now found in the museum). The crypt, the only one in the area, in Roman style, dates from the Eleventh Century and contains the grave of Countess Adela of France, mother-in-law of William the Conqueror, who died at the Abbey of Messines in 1079. The tower, from which you can get possibly the best view of the Salient, features a tough and daunting climb for those who have any fear of heights – it is made worse when the church bells start to play as you are climbing the open steps to the tower just above the bells; these are part of the Peace Carillon of which the largest bell, named Pax, was blessed by Pope John Paul in 1985. The only thing that M. Ghukiere asks in return is a small donation to help in the purchase of bells for the Peace Carillon. I take groups of children every year, Albert and the Church always leave a lasting impression upon them.

| UK – 1 | Aust – 42 | Unnamed – 8 |

Special Memorial to one Australian soldier known to be buried among the unnamed.

Area – 405 sq yds

LOCATION
Bethleem Farm East Cemetery is south-east of Mesen. In the town square there are C.W.G.C. signs to the Bethleem Farm cemeteries directing you through the south-east corner of the square out of the village passing housing for 200m until you reach open space from which you can see the cemeteries in the fields below. The entrance to this cemetery is 100m from the road and 100m to the left of the farm track from the road. It is just possible to get cars to the path to the cemetery if you are adventurous, but it would be safer to park and walk the final 200m.

Journey Time – 30 mins

C.W.G.C. Reference – 5/86

BETHLEEM FARM WEST CEMETERY, MESEN   *No. 12*

HISTORY
This cemetery was begun at the start of the Battle of Messines, when the area was captured by the 3rd Australian Division on 7 June 1917, and remained in use until December.

INFORMATION
This was mainly used by the 14th (Light) Division. For other information please refer to the East Cemetery.

| UK – 24 | Aust – 114 | NZ – 26 | Unnamed – 2 |

Special Memorial to one New Zealander whose grave was destroyed by shell-fire.

14

Area – 753 sq yds

LOCATION
Directions are as for the East Cemetery except that the entrance is on the right 50 m south of that for the East Cemetery. Then you have a walk of 200 m to the path to the cemetery which is next to the farm.

You could take a car down here but it is private and I would not recommend it.

Journey Time – 30 mins

C.W.G.C. Reference – 5/86

BIRR CROSSROADS CEMETERY, ZILLEBEKE   *No. 13*

HISTORY
Begun in August 1917, next to a Dressing Station, the cemetery was used, creating what is now Plot I, until the Germans took this point in the spring of 1918. It was enlarged after the Armistice when over 650 graves were concentrated here.

INFORMATION
Birr Crossroads is at the eastern corner of the cemetery, and was named by the 1st Leinsters, after the name of their depot in Ireland, when they were stationed here in 1915. The line of the road changed after the War such that the northern part of the crossroads, Cambridge Road, is about 100 m to the east along the Menen Road.

On 16 June 1915 an attack by the Honourable Artillery Company (7th Brigade, 3rd Division) was made from trenches opposite this cemetery in the direction of 'Y' Wood and the Bellewaerde Spur near the site of R.E. Grave. 'Y' Wood was a small copse that use to exist between here and the Bellewaerde Spur which got its name from its shape in the form of the letter 'Y'. The trenches at the wood were undefended but the H.A.C. found Germans buried alive by the British artillery bombardment along with parts of bodies blown to pieces by the shelling.

To reach the cemetery you may have passed one of the many 'White Chateaux' in the Salient. This is one of the more famous as it was the site of Sir Douglas Haig's (q.v.) headquarters during the First Battle of Ypres and was then in use constantly throughout the War by various units. It came into the front-line during the German advance of Spring 1918. The Chateau is now a restaurant.

The large crossroads west of the cemetery known as Hellfire Corner is one of the most infamous locations of the War. The point at which the Zillebeke – St. Jan Road crossed the Menen Road as did the Railway to Zonnebeke, the junction was one of the most important crossroads as nearly all munitions, men and equipment passed through it. The junction was exposed to almost constant German artillery fire as the enemy knew the exact distance to its position. The Germans reached the crossroads during their advance in 1918, taking Birr Crossroads for the only time, the closest that they got to Ypres. This is signified by the demarcation stone in the middle of the junction of the Potijze Road with the Menen Road.

The view of the slope of the Menen Road gives us a good idea of the advantage that the Germans had in holding the ridges near Hooge. You also get a good view towards St. Charles and the Bellewaerde Ridge, with R.E. Grave on the spur, across the Menen Road to the north-east. But the road is very intrusive and dangerous because of the speed of cars coming down the hill from Hooge.

V.C. – Temporary Captain Harold Ackroyd, M. C., V.C..
Royal Army Medical Corps, attached 6th Royal Berkshire Regiment (Princess Charlotte of Wales's), 53rd Brigade, 18th (Eastern) Division.
Died – 11 August 1917.
Won – at Hooge on 31 July 1917 to 1 August 1917. Ackroyd tended the wounded in the open under heavy fire, rescuing many men from no man's land. Twenty-three recommendations were made that he should receive the Victoria Cross.

Concentrated here:

Bellewaarde Ridge Military Cemetery, Zonnebeke – was a little north-east of the lake on the spur north of the Menen Road. It contained eleven British men and seventeen Australians who fell in September and October 1917.

Birr Crossroads Cemetery No. 2 – 75m south of here. It contained eighteen British men who fell in July and August 1917.

Union Street Graveyards No.'s 1 & 2, Zillebeke – these were north of the village in a major trench formation south of Hellfire Corner. They contained nineteen British men who fell in August and September 1915.

UK – 625	Aust – 140	NZ – 12	Can – 15
NF – 1	S Afr – 1	BWI – 1	KUG – 11
Unnamed – 336			

Special Memorials to five British men and three Australians known/believed buried among the unnamed.

Special Memorials to eighteen British men buried in Birr Crossroads No. 2 Cemetery and Union Street Graveyards whose graves were destroyed by shellfire.

Special Memorial to a Belgian interpreter whose grave is also lost.

Area – 3243 sq yds

LOCATION
Birr Crossroads Cemetery is on the south side of the Menen Road, east of Ieper, 900m beyond Hellfire Corner.

Journey Time – 10 mins

C.W.G.C. Reference – 5/37

BLAUWEPOORT FARM CEMETERY, ZILLEBEKE   *No. 14*

HISTORY
This cemetery was begun by a French Regiment of Chasseurs Alpins (Mountain Hunters) in November 1914. The British Army did not begin to make burials until they moved here in February 1915 and it then remained in use for a year until February 1916.

INFORMATION
The cemetery, entered by a very stiff gate, is in a small valley next to a private house, Blauwepoort Farm, whose owners do not want visitors to the cemetery wandering beyond the C.W.G.C. area. The majority of the men buried here served in the Staffordshire, Norfolk or Scottish Highland Regiments. The French graves have been removed.

UK – 83   KUG – 7

Area 1312 sq yds

LOCATION
Blauwepoort Farm Cemetery is near the road to Comines, south of Ieper, 350m beyond the railway crossing and the entrance to Zillebeke Lake. It lies 200m to the west of the road at the end of a track which has a C.W.G.C. sign at the road.

Journey Time – 10 mins

C.W.G.C. Reference – 5/58

HISTORY

The cemetery was begun in preparation for the Flanders Offensive of 1917. In use from June to December 1917 it served the Dressing Station in the farm.

INFORMATION

Many of the graves, 148, are of men of the Guards or Guards Machine Gun Regiments. The cemetery was enlarged after the Armistice with the addition of two isolated graves from the surrounding battlefields. At the same time a French grave was also removed. A further nine graves were made during World War II.

A light railway ran along the road from Elverdinge to the front-line. The village had become a major centre during the war for railways, hospitals, stores and camps. Elverdinge chateau was used as an headquarters for several units until it was accidentally burnt down by British cooks!

There are three men buried in this cemetery who were executed by the British Army. They had committed offences during the Third Battle of Ypres and were tried afterwards when their battalions were in camps near here at the rear of the Salient. Private Thomas Hawkins of the 7th Queen's (55th Brigade, 18th (Eastern) Division) was already under a suspended sentence of death when he deserted. He was executed on 22 November 1917.

Private Arthur Westwood of the 8th East Surreys (55th Brigade, 18th (Eastern) Division) deserted during the Battle of Poelkapalle. He was executed on 23 November 1917.

Private Frederick W. Slade of the 2/6th (2nd City of London Rifles) Londons (174th Brigade, 58th (2/ 1st London) Division) refused to go into action during the Battle of Passendale on 26 October 1917. He was executed for disobedience on 14 Decemeber 1917.

UK – 437	Can – 1	NF – 1
S Afr – 3	Ger – 1	WWII – 9

Area – 2534 sq yds

LOCATION

Bleuet Farm Cemetery is found west of Elverdinge, north of Ieper, on the Elverdinge – Boezinge road. The cemetery is in the fields next to the farm 150 m from the road.

Journey Time – 15 mins

C.W.G.C. Reference – 5/11

BOEZINGE CHURCHYARD   *No. 16*

HISTORY

In 1914 two British officers were buried here but one grave was moved. There remains :

Captain Edward Frederick Maltby Urquhart.
1st Black Watch.
Killed in action – 23 October 1914. Aged 37.

INFORMATION

The church, St. Michael's, was rebuilt after the War and now contains four Seventeenth Century tapestries that depict the life of St. Franciscus Xaverius (1506-52), one of the earliest missionaries to China and India. There is also a plaque to the French 87th Territorial Infantry who suffered so greatly nearby during the first gas attack in 1915. They have another Memorial on the other side of the canal. (See Artillery Wood Cemetery)

The 2nd Royal Sussex were stationed here while the rest of their Division were involved in the fighting just over the canal in 1914. (See Ruisseau Farm Cemetery) There are also fourteen soldiers who fell during World War II buried in the churchyard just a little apart from Captain Urquhart. All the British graves are on the far side of the church from the road.

UK – 1   WWII – 14

LOCATION
Boezinge churchyard is in the centre of the village which lies just west of the main road from Ieper to Diksmuide.

Journey Time – 20 mins

C.W.G.C. Reference – None

BRANDHOEK MILITARY CEMETERY, VLAMERTINGE   *No. 17*

HISTORY
This cemetery was begun in May 1915 next to a Dressing Station and used until the field was full in July 1917. It was replaced by the New Military Cemetery as the Third Battle of Ypres began.

INFORMATION
Brandhoek was considered to be within a safe area, out of range of German artillery, during much of the War. As a result it became a centre for supplies, camps, hospitals, and naturally, burial grounds. This is, therefore, one of three cemeteries in this small hamlet.

UK – 601   Aust – 4   Can – 63   Bermuda – 2
Ger – 2

Area – 3600 sq yds

LOCATION
The three Brandhoek cemeteries lie west of

Vlamertinge and just south of the new road to Poperinge. They are visible from the new road.

Journey Time – 20 mins

C.W.G.C. Reference – 5/42

BRANDHOEK NEW MILITARY CEMETERY,   *No. 18*
VLAMERTINGE

HISTORY
This was begun as the Military Cemetery became full and because the number of casualties from the Third Battle of Ypres was expected to be high. It was used by the 32nd, 44th and 3rd Australian, Casualty Clearing Stations until closed in August as the space available was filled and another cemetery opened close by.

INFORMATION
Among the men who lie here one has become well known for the reason that he was the only man to fall in the Great War to win the Victoria Cross and Bar. His headstone is unique in that it has two Victoria Crosses carved upon it.

V.C. – Captain Noel Godfrey Chavasse, M.C., D.S.O., V.C. and Bar.
Royal Army Medical Corps, attached 1/10th (Liverpool Scottish) King's (Liverpool Regiment), 166th Brigade, 55th (West Lancashire) Division.
From Liverpool – Son of the Bishop of Liverpool and identical twin of Christopher Chavasse O.B.E., M.C. and Croix de Guerre.

M.C. – won at Hooge in 1915.
V.C. – won at Guillemont on the Somme on 9 August 1916. During an attack he tended the wounded in the open all day under heavy fire. He was injured in bringing wounded back from the front-line but still went out that night to rescue more men from near to the German trenches. He also collected the identity disks of the dead and buried fallen officers.
Bar – won at the start of the Third Battle of Ypres when he was severely wounded while carrying casualties to Dressing Stations. He then worked, almost without any food, for two days tending the injured. Although extremely fatigued, he rescued many men from the appalling conditions. He died of wounds in Brandhoek Military Hospital on 4 August 1917.

UK – 514	Aust – 11	Can – 6	Ger – 28

Area – 1500 sq yds

LOCATION
Directions are as for the Military Cemetery except that as soon as you leave the new Poperinge road turn right to this cemetery which is behind the houses on the right and is reached by a path from the road.

Journey Time – 20 mins

C.W.G.C. Reference – 5/42

BRANDHOEK NEW MILITARY CEMETERY No. 3, VLAMERTINGE

No. 19

HISTORY
Opened as the New Military Cemetery became full, this cemetery was used until May 1918 and was linked to the many Casualty Clearing Stations in the vicinity.

INFORMATION
The gates were presented by Mr. G. H. Strutt. His son, Lieutenant Anthony Harold Strutt of the 16th (Chatsworth Rifles) Sherwood Foresters, who died of wounds on 27 April 1918, is buried here. Of the graves here, 286 (25%), are those of artillerymen due to the large number of gun positions that were nearby. Four French graves have been removed.

UK – 849	Aust – 46	NZ – 18	Can – 46
S Afr – 5	BWI – 1	Chinese Labour Corps – 1	

Area – 3500 sq yds

LOCATION
Directions to this cemetery are exactly as for the New Military Cemetery, except for the walk back!

Journey Time – 20 mins

C.W.G.C. Reference – 5/42

HISTORY

Begun at the end of September 1917, shortly after this area was taken by the British, the cemetery was used almost exclusively by the 59th (North Midland) Division. This was to bury their dead who fell in the Battle of Polygon Wood in the three days from 26 – 28 September 1917.

INFORMATION

All bar five graves are of the 59th Division and all except one fell in the Battle of Polygon Wood. Bridge House was the name given to the farmhouse close by.

The single monument to the 1/1st Monmouths, and Second Lieutenant Henry Anthony Birrell-Anthony of that Regiment who was killed in action on 8 May 1915, is 700m to the east of Bridge House Cemetery on the south side of a road that leads to the junction where the St. Jan road (N313) joins the St. Juliaan road.

This ground was fought over before the cemetery was created. On 8 May 1915 the 84th Brigade held the line which passed through the present location of the monument to the 1/1st Monmouths. South of the road the line ran to Frezenberg and north of the road to Mousetrap Farm. In the German attack the 2nd Cheshires were wiped out losing all three front-line companies and their battalion headquarters; the 1st Suffolks lost their commanding officer, eleven officers and 432 men. The 1/1st Monmouths, mainly miners, could only muster 120 men that night. The 1/12th (Rangers) Londons were sent up to reinforce the line but only a few men reached the Monmouths and only fifty-three out of 200 men were left by nightfall. This Territorial battalion had ceased to exist.

UK – 45   Unnamed – 4   Area – 223 sq yds

LOCATION

Bridge House Cemetery lies about 1 km south of St. Juliaan, north-east of Ieper and could prove difficult to find. As you enter St. Juliaan on the N313 from Ieper turn right at the junction with C.W.G.C. signs on the corner. This passes St. Julien D.S. Cemetery immediately and comes to a junction, in about 1 km, from which you can see the cemetery almost directly opposite.

Journey Time – 20 mins

C.W.G.C. Reference – 5/15

BUFFS ROAD CEMETERY, St. JAN   *No. 21*

HISTORY

Begun on 31 July 1917 just after this piece of no man's land had been captured, the cemetery was used until the German Spring Offensive of March 1918. Then it was enlarged after the Armistice with the concentration of graves from the surrounding battlefields.

INFORMATION

Buffs Road, now called Hoge Zeikenweg, was the name given to the road that runs parallel to, and north of, the new road in the valley. The road ran from the cemetery, through the crossroads 200m to the east where Admiral's Road (Mortelweg) passed through Admiral's Corner, to the next crossroads, with Boundary Road (Briekestraat), at the corner of New Irish Farm Cemetery.

The cemetery was mainly used by the 11th, 12th and 13th Royal Sussex (1st, 2nd and 3rd South Downs) battalions during the 1917 Flanders Offensive. One Belgian soldier has been removed while one British officer was brought here from Brielen Churchyard when others were concentrated from the battlefields.

On 29 April 1915 the 2nd Lancashire Fusiliers took over the line here at Mousetrap Farm which you can see on the ridge to the west and watched an attack by the Sirhind Brigade of the Lahore Division, Indian Army fail. (See Track 'X' Cemetery) On 2 May incendiary shells and gas, a green yellowish fog, were employed against the British here, causing the Lancashire Fusiliers to abandon the front-line and make their way to Ypres. However, the trenches were not taken by the

Germans due to the lingering gas. Hence, the British were the first to re-occupy the line. The Fusiliers began the day with thirty-three officers and 1,070 men, they ended it with eight officers and eighty men.

During the German attack Private John 'Jack' Lynn won the Victoria Cross by manning his machine-gun for several hours without a gas mask; machine-gunners were not part of the chain of command so he would probably not have received the order to withdraw and gas masks were not standard issue at that time. He halted the German advance saving his comrades and was found, barely alive in the trenches, by the battalion that was sent to re-occupy the line. He had been awarded the Distinguished Conduct Medal and Order of St. George (Russia) for his actions at Le Touquet. Jack Lynn died of the effects of gas and is buried at Grootebeek Cemetery.

By 24 May the 2nd Royal Dublin Fusiliers had taken over the line here. When the Germans attacked, again using gas, the Fusiliers, and the 1/9th (Dumbartonshire) Argyll and Sutherland Highlanders stood firm. At the end of the day the Dubliners were ordered to retire, which they did with just one officer and twenty men out of seventeen officers and 650 men.

This cemetery has good views of the Salient and would be a pretty, peaceful little cemetery but for the end of the motorway that intrudes upon the environment.

UK – 265	Aust – 13	Can – 10
S Afr – 1	Unnamed – 86	

Special Memorials to ten men whose graves were destroyed.

Area – 1275 sq mts

LOCATION
Buffs Road Cemetery lies north-east of Ieper just north of the end of the motorway (A19) and is easily reached via the northern by-pass. Turn off the N38 at the small crossroads just west of the motorway junction onto Mortelweg, reaching the crossroads from which you can see the cemetery to the east.

Journey Time – 20 mins

C.W.G.C. Reference – 5/22

BUS HOUSE CEMETERY, VOORMEZELE   *No. 22*

HISTORY
This cemetery was begun at the start of the Battle of Messines in June 1917 and remained in use until the end of the Flanders Offensive in November 1917. A soldier who fell in January 1915 was brought here together with four more in April 1918.

INFORMATION
The farm next to the cemetery was named after a local wartime estaminet which was in turn named after a London Omnibus that had broken down here as it was taking troops to the nearby front-line during the frantic days of the First Battle of Ypres in October and November 1914. This was one of 300 London General Omnibus Company B-Type buses in use in France and Flanders in 1914. By comparison the French sent troops to the battle-front in taxis from Paris during the Battle of the Marne in September 1914. The cost was as on the meter. It is thought that the bus was carrying the 1/14th (London Scottish) Londons to Wijtschate where they

were to become the first full battalion of Territorial troops in action in the War.

St. Eloi, 200 m to the west, was bitterly fought over many times because of its strategic position in controlling the crossroads and the routes to the Mesen Ridge and Lille. Mines were blown at 'The Mound' on several occasions.

In February 1915 the 3rd and 4th King's Royal Rifle Corps (80th Brigade, 27th Division) took part of the German trench system at St. Eloi but lost it soon after. On 14 March the 1st Leinsters (82nd Brigade, 27th Division) briefly retook the trenches suffering heavy casualties of sixteen officers and 257 men. They were mentioned in dispatches on St. Patrick's Day, 17 March. Even so, on the next day the 4th Rifle Brigade and Princess Patricia's Canadian Light Infantry (both 80th Brigade, 27th Division) had to attack from Bus House and Bedford House Cemeteries respectively.

With support from the 2nd King's Shropshire Light Infantry (also of the 80th Brigade) they cleared the Germans from St. Eloi. By October the 1st North Staffordshires (72nd Brigade, 24th Division) had to retake the trenches at 'The Mound' which they did with only slight losses.

From 27 March to 16 April 1916 the 12th West Yorkshires, 8th East Yorkshires, 4th Royal Fusiliers and 1st Northumberland Fusiliers (all 3rd Division) had to take the craters again. For this attack six mines using 73,000 lbs of explosive enabled the battalions to capture parts of St. Eloi though they suffered heavy casualties, for example, the Royal Fusiliers lost forty officers and 809 men in the action. Captain, the Reverend, temporary Chaplain, Edward Noel Mellish tended the wounded and rescued men from 27 to 29 March for which he was awarded the Victoria Cross.

At the start of the Battle of Messines on 7 June 1917, the 4th Division attacked from Bus House towards their second objective of the 'Dammstrasse' which is east of the village. They were accompanied by two tanks, as were most of the Divisions during the attack. The 'male' had a gun for shells while the 'female' was armed with machine-guns.

On 20 September 1918, Sergeant Louis McGuffie, of the 1/5th King's Own Scottish Borderers, won the Victoria Cross by capturing a large number of German positions and prisoners. He thus made the British advance here easier so that they incurred a low number of casualties. He was later killed by a shell and is buried in Zantvoorde Military Cemetery.

| UK – 190 | Aust – 10 | NZ – 1 | Can – 2 |
| BWI – 1 | Unnamed – 12 | | |

Special Memorials to two British men known to be buried among the unnamed.

Area – 1863 sq yds

LOCATION
Bus House Cemetery is located on the south side of the St. Eloi – Voormezele road, 400 m west of the crossroads in St. Eloi, which is south of Ieper. The turn at the crossroads, from the road to Mesen and Armentieres, is almost hidden but there is a C.W.G.C. sign on the corner.

Journey Time – 15 mins

C.W.G.C. Reference – 5/64

BUTTES NEW BRITISH CEMETERY, POLYGON WOOD, *No. 23* ZONNEBEKE

HISTORY
This cemetery was not begun until after the Armistice when it was used for the concentration of graves from the battlefields of Zonnebeke and Polygon Wood.

INFORMATION
In a beautiful and peaceful location hidden in, and surrounded by, the wood, the cemetery is reached by a cool, dark, walled avenue leading to the contrasting bright island of sunlight that is the large burial ground and Memorial. It is possible to walk through the wood, which is owned by the state and now called 'Dien Doel', but I wouldn't stray too far from the paths.

Before 1914 the wood was the Belgian Army's firing range, the Butts providing the cemetery with its name and one of its most distinctive features, the large mound that dominates the cemetery. The wood was also the site for a riding school and a racecourse that can still be made out.

At the south-east corner of the wood, on the Reutal Ridge, on 24 October 1914, the 2nd Wiltshires were overwhelmed with only a Quarter Master Sergeant-Major and 170 men surviving. Once the Germans were in the wood the 2nd Royal Warwickshires counter-attacked with a squadron of the Northumberland Hussars Yeomanry in support, the first men of a Territorial unit to see action in the Salient. These were followed by the 2nd Highland Light Infantry and the 2nd Worcesters who fought north and east through the wood to the position of this cemetery clearing the wood of Germans. The Worcesters were warned not to use bullets, as no trench line existed and they might kill British troops, so they mounted a bayonet charge through the wood instead.

By the end of October men of eleven battalions and five Brigades had fought to hold the wood. The 2nd Royal Warwickshires had lost their commanding officer, Lieutenant-Colonel Walter Latham Loring, killed in action on 23 October, one of three brothers killed in the early months of the War. By the end of the First Battle of Ypres the 2nd Royal Warwickshires numbered one officer, Lieutenant Richard Francis Richardson (who died of wounds recieved at Loos in September 1915) and 100 men despite having received a draft of 200 men on 26 October.

In May 1915, the battalions holding the wood withdrew as the British line was drawn back after the German gas attack in April. The 2nd King's Own, 1st King's Own Yorkshire Light Infantry and 1/3rd Monmouths left the wood so quietly that the Germans were still shelling it the next day.

The wood was retaken by the 5th Australian Division, whose Memorial now surmounts the Butts, during the Third Battle of Ypres in September 1917. At the south-west end of the cemetery is the New Zealand Memorial to the Missing, which honours 383 men, who fell from September 1917 to May 1918 in this area and who have no known graves.

By the end of the War the wood had been destroyed. As a result the final resting places of many men who had fallen in the wood were lost.

UK – 1317	Aust – 564	NZ – 167	Can – 50
KUG – 30	Unnamed – 1673 (over 80% of the total)		

Special Memorials to twenty-three New Zealanders and twelve British men known/believed to be buried among the unnamed.

Area – 18030 sq yds

LOCATION
Buttes New Cemetery is on the north-east edge of Polygon Wood which lies east of Ieper and north of the Menen Road and motorway. You can leave the Menen Road at the junction just east of the Bellewaerde Pleasure Park known in the War as Clapham Junction where a C.W.G.C. sign indicates to the left to the Princess Patricia's Canadian Light Infantry Monument.

Journey Time – 20 mins

C.W.G.C. Reference – 6/6

CABIN HILL CEMETERY, WIJTSCHATE   *No. 24*

HISTORY
Begun by the 11th Division in June 1917 during the Battle of Messines, the burial ground was used as a front-line cemetery until the German Spring Offensive in March 1918.

INFORMATION
The site is in a small valley near the source of the Blauwepoortebeek on the edge of the Mesen Ridge. The 9th (Queen's Royal) Lancers held the line here in late October 1914, though at that point they numbered only 150 men, when the Germans attacked with a numerical advantage of six to one. The Lancers were pushed back, with the other units here, such as 'J' Battery, Royal Horse Artillery, suffering heavy casualties.

On 10 April 1918 the 10th Royal Warwickshires were in the front-line nearby when they were forced to withdraw by the German attack suffering casualties over the next few days of 450 men.

UK – 42	Aust – 25	Area – 453 sq yds

LOCATION
Cabin Hill Cemetery is about 2km south-east of Wijtschate and 1km north-west of Mesen. It is reached from the Mesen Road in Wijtschate by taking the turn for Torreken Farm Cemetery and continuing for 1.2km to a crossroads reached as you start to descend off the ridge. The cemetery is to the left past the farm and 75m from the road in a small hollow.

Journey Time – 30 mins

C.W.G.C. Reference – 5/85

CALVAIRE (ESSEX) MILITARY CEMETERY, PLOEGSTEERT   *No. 25*

HISTORY
Begun in November 1914 the cemetery remained in use until July 1916. This is a good example of a number of cemeteries used in 1914 and 1915 by one or two regiments at a time. As such each Plot is constituted almost entirely of burials from one battalion. The order of burials also gives us an insight into the order in which units were posted to the area. It's dual name comes from the fact that the first burials made in the cemetery were the dead of the 2nd Essex battalion.

INFORMATION
The burials here are:

Plot I, Rows A to M	–	2nd Essex and 1/2nd Monmouths.
Plot I, Row O	–	9th Royal Fusiliers and 11th Middlesex.
Plot II	–	7th Suffolk and 9th Essex.
Plot III	–	6th Buffs.
Plot IV, Rows A to C	–	1/7th and 1/8th Worcesters.
Plot IV, Rows D to M	–	11th (Lambeth) Queen's and 10th (Kent County) Royal West Kents.

UK – 218

Area – 1850 sq yds

See Gunners' Farm Cemetery

LOCATION
Calvaire Cemetery is about 1.5km south-east of Ploegsteert, south of Ieper. Approximately 1.4km south of Ploegsteert square you will find, on the east side of the road, near a supermarket, a tree of C.W.G.C. signs. The road to the left leads to Calvaire cemetery, which is on the south side of the road beyond Gunners Farm Cemetery.

Journey Time – 35 mins

C.W.G.C. Reference – 5/107

HISTORY

The cemetery was begun at the start of the Battle of Messines in June 1917 and used until the end of the Flanders Offensive. It was mostly used for the burials of men who died at the Casualty Clearing Station in the farm. A few graves were added after the offensive.

INFORMATION

The farm after which this cemetery is named was used as Dressing Station from June to September 1917. The graveyard stands in open ground on a slight rise. Most of the men buried here are either of the Royal Artillery (438), or from the Guards Division (144) who fell in the opening attack of the Third Battle of Ypres.

V.C. – Corporal James Llewellyn Davies, V.C..
13th (1st North Wales Pals) Royal Welsh Fusiliers, 113th Brigade, 38th (Welsh) Division.
Killed in action – 31 July 1917. Age 31.
From Nantymoel, Glamorgan.
Won – on 31 July 1917 when he single-handedly attacked a machine-gun position after others had been killed trying to take it. He captured it and then led an attack killing a sniper hidden in a nearby house. Corporal Davies died of his wounds at the Dressing Station.

UK – 879   Can – 5   NF – 4   BWI – 19

Area – 4093 sq yds

LOCATION

Canada Farm Cemetery is about 2 km west of Elverdinge and north of Ieper. The road to Poperinge (N333), that forks left from the main road to Veurne just north of the Elverdinge traffic lights, passes Ferme Olivier Cemetery before reaching the right turn opposite a C.W.G.C. sign to Canada Farm Cemetery.

Journey Time – 20 mins

C.W.G.C. Reference – 5/10

CEMENT HOUSE CEMETERY, LANGEMARK   *No. 27*

HISTORY

Cement House Cemetery was begun in August 1917 once this area had been captured during the Third Battle of Ypres. It was used by front-line units and Field Ambulances until April 1918 when the Germans retook the area. The original burial ground comprises Plot I of this large cemetery while the rest was made after the Armistice with the concentration of graves from the surrounding battlefields. It is still in use as the cemetery into which remains found on the Salient today are brought. Small cemeteries are also concentrated here when the need arises.

INFORMATION

Cement House was the name used by the British Army for the building at the east end of the present cemetery, a bunker that can still be seen.

This site saw much fighting in the War particularly in August 1917. On 14 August the 10th and 11th Rifle Brigade attacked from either side of the road towards Langemark. They had to cross the Steenbeek, running almost north – south 400 m east of here, a 'stream', swollen by rain and a wide marsh by this time. The battalions suffered heavy casualties in reaching the mill 200 m further on, but as they could not take this heavily defended position they withdrew.

On 16 August another attempt was made by the Rifle Brigade with the support of men from the 83rd Field Company, Royal Engineers, who went to deal with the bunker. Through careful planning and preparation the bunker was taken by the 12th Rifle Brigade which enabled the rest of the 60th and 61st Brigades to attack Langemark though the attack was halted by machine-guns in blockhouses on the edge of the village. In the attack Private Wilfred Edwards (later Captain) of the 7th King's Own Yorkshire Light Infantry and Sergeant Edward Cooper (later Major) of the 12th King's Royal Rifle Corps displayed such courage that they were to be awarded the Victoria Cross.

To the south of this attack on a line to St. Juliaan, the 29th Division was attacking across the Steenbeek during which two men of the 1st King's Own Scottish Borderers won the Victoria Cross. Acting Company Quarter-Master Sergeant William Henry Grimbaldston from Lancashire attacked a pill-box from the rear, capturing it, thirty-six defenders and six machine-guns, opening the way for his company. The other recipient was Company Sergeant-Major John Skinner who was later killed and is buried in Vlamertinge New Military Cemetery. The ground gained in this attack was limited and the cost high. From 15 to 18 August the 29th Division lost eighty-eight officers and 2,024 men.

Approximately 400 m to the east of this cemetery on the road to Langemark is the Memorial to the 20th (Light) Division who captured the village on 16 August 1917. It is 600 m from the traffic lights in Langemark. Closer to this cemetery, on the bridge over the Steenbeek, is the small Memorial to the Belgian forces who captured the village in 1918. A French Memorial can be seen on the road to Boezinge. (See Artillery Wood Cemetery)

It is important to remember that this cemetery is still in use. For example, a group of eighteen graves were brought here in the early 1970's, from a graveyard in Maiseires, near Mons, to make way for a new road. Among them was the grave of Captain Jonathan Edward Knowles of the Middlesex Regiment, who was one of the earliest British officer casualties in the War. As such, I put a caveat on the statistics below.

UK – 3415 (2282 unnamed)	Aust – 19 (15 unnamed)
NZ – 10 (8 unnamed)	Can – 57 (30 unnamed)
NF – 14 S Afr – 1	Guernsey – 5 Fr – 1
Ger – 1 KUG – 1	

Special Memorials to five British men and three Newfoundlanders believed to be buried among the unnamed.

Special Memorials to three men of the 15th (Nottingham Pals) Sherwood Foresters (105th Brigade, 35th Division) buried in Pheasant Trench Cemetery but whose graves are lost.

WWII – 22 (UK – 20 Aust – 1 Can-1)

Area – 11607 sq yds

LOCATION
It is easiest to visit this cemetery as part of a circuit through Langemark and Boezinge, passing St. Juliaan and Vancouver Corner on route. The cemetery is on the south side of the Langemark – Boezinge road about 600 m west of the centre of Langemark. The traffic lights in Langemark should be treated with caution as the turn is tight, coaches and trucks will swing wide hitting cars that have pulled up too close to the junction.

Journey Time – 35 mins

C.W.G.C. Reference – 5/5

CHESTER FARM CEMETERY, ZILLEBEKE   *No. 28*

HISTORY
This cemetery was begun in March 1915 and used as a front-line cemetery until November 1917.

INFORMATION
Most of the dead are from fighting in the wooded area across the road on the hill next to the old Ypres – Comines Canal, the hill being known as 'The Bluff'. It is now possible to take a pleasant walk along the old canal and 'The Bluff' to Pallingbeek Park. (See Larch Wood Cemetery) For further information about the fighting on 'The Bluff' please refer to 1st D.C.L.I. Cemetery.

This is an example of the regimental cemeteries in use early in the War as men of the same regiment are buried in the same Plot even though they may have died months apart. For example, there are ninety-two men of the 2nd Manchesters in Plot I.

UK – 306	Aust – 21	Can – 87	Ger – 4

Special Memorials to five British men and one Canadian known/believed to be buried here but whose graves were lost.

LOCATION
Chester Farm Cemetery is located south of Ieper, west of the Comines road between Zillebeke and St. Eloi. The cemetery is on the right 1.3 km from the Comines road.

Journey Time – 15 mins

C.W.G.C. Reference – 5/59

COLNE VALLEY CEMETERY, BOEZINGE   *No. 29*

HISTORY
The oldest of three graveyards in the vicinity, Colne Valley Cemetery was begun by Territorial battalions of the 49th (West Riding) Division. They held a trench here from which the cemetery gets its name, in July 1915, and the burial ground was used until February 1916. By July 1917 this area was in no man's land until it was captured at the start of the Third Battle of Ypres.

INFORMATION
An example of the fact that the Salient still has some surprises today was provided in February 1992. A farmer ploughing a field on his tractor just west of the cemetery fell into a World War I British communications centre eight metres below the surface. The telephone exchange had twelve rooms containing tables and chairs, bayonets and rifles, communications equipment and a tool machine room. This type of exciting find is becoming increasingly rare though smaller finds are not yet uncommon.

The Germans reached the site of this cemetery by the evening of 22 April 1915 on the day of the first German gas attack as they exploited a gap of 5000 m in the line from Colne Valley to St. Juliaan. At one point on the night of 22 April a Staff officer from the 1st Canadian Division's headquarters found a French machine-gun crew at Fusilier Farm, just south of here, who claimed that they were the front-line – this was probably close to being the truth!

A British attack on 23 April through the position of this cemetery failed to regain any ground but cost heavy casualties for the 1st York and Lancasters who lost their commanding officer and 425 men, and the 2nd East Yorkshires who lost seven officers and 280 men.

Those buried here come from three regiments, the Duke of Wellington's who fell in July and August 1915, the Rifle Brigade who were killed in December 1915 and January 1916, and King's Royal Rifle Corps dead of January and February 1916. This gives a good reflection of the units holding the front-line here during that period.

UK – 47   Area – 381 sq yds

LOCATION
Colne Valley Cemetery lies north of Ieper, southeast of Boezinge, and east of the canal. It is reached most easily by taking the road south from the French Memorial on the Boezinge – Langemark road. The cemetery is on the right below the level of the road but beware of the deep roadside ditch.

Journey Time – 25 mins

C.W.G.C. Reference – 5/12

HISTORY

The cemetery was named after a shrine that was nearby and begun by the Burial Officer of the 19th (Western) Division in June 1917. Begun after this part of no man's land had been captured during the Battle of Messines, the burial ground remained in use until November 1917 though two graves were added later, one in April 1918 and one after the Armistice.

INFORMATION

Where the path to the cemetery leaves the road there is a Memorial to both Lieutenant Lasnier and the dead of the French 1st Battalion of Light Infantry who fell in 1914.

On 31 October 1914 the French pushed back the Bavarians into the wood nearby. A Captain Hoffman lay wounded in the open in front of the wood so a young Corporal crawled out of the wood to rescue him. The Captain died of his wounds but the Corporal developed a sense of his own infallibility, immortality and destiny. He received the Iron Cross from the Kaiser for his actions, the first of two he was to win in the War. He was Adolf Hitler. There were fifty-one of his fellow Germans, who were killed in the Battle of Messines, buried here but they were removed after the Armistice.

About 100 m to the south-east Hollandescheschur Farm had been turned into a German machine-gun redoubt under which a mine was exploded on the first day of the Battle of Messines.

UK – 74   Chinese Labour Corps – 1   Unnamed – 7

Area – 544 sq yds

LOCATION

Croonaert Chapel Cemetery is found south of Ieper, about 2 km north of Wijtschate on the road to Voormezele which leaves Wijtschate town square from the north-west corner.

Journey Time – 30 mins

C.W.G.C. Reference – 5/67

DERRY HOUSE CEMETERY No. 2, WIJTSCHATE *No. 31*

HISTORY

This cemetery was begun by the 11th (Northern) Division in June 1917, during the Battle of Messines, after this area was captured from the Germans. It was used as a front-line cemetery until December 1917, and then again in October 1918 by the 2/14th (2nd London Scottish) Londons.

INFORMATION

The cemetery, the second of two created in the vicinity though Derry House No. 1 Cemetery no longer exists, has two distinct sections separated by a neck of land in which stands the Cross of Sacrifice. Recent work in the cemetery, including tree-felling, means that the area is now a much starker environment than the shaded burial ground that it was in 1991.

The 1st Wiltshires held the line nearby until forced to withdraw on 10 April 1918 when the Germans attacked. There are twenty-nine Australians buried here who were from the 47th Battalion.

UK – 126   Aust – 37   Area – 2001 sq yds

LOCATION
Derry House Cemetery is south of Ieper and southeast of Wijtschate. It is reached from a crossroads on the Armentieres road in Wijtschate with C.W.G.C. signs on the corner. Turn east and follow the signs at the next fork. As you crest the ridge you can see the cemetery to your left 100 m away.

Journey Time – 30 mins

C.W.G.C. Reference – 5/73

DICKEBUSCH OLD MILITARY CEMETERY, DIKKEBUS   *No. 32*

HISTORY
Begun as a front-line cemetery and used from January to March 1915, it was closed once the space was filled. The New Cemetery and the Extension, which are situated close by, provided extra space for burials in the village.

INFORMATION
At first view, one wonders why it was considered that the available space in this cemetery was used, and why there was a need for new cemeteries as early as they were begun, but seventy-eight French graves have been removed which accounts for the space now visible. Some of this space was taken up by the burial of ten British men who fell in the 1939-45 war.

Dikkebus churchyard used to contain British War Graves but most were removed shortly after the Armistice. One Canadian and three British officers who fell in 1915 were not removed until February 1962.

The village was used for a number of base camps, for example the 1/16th (Queen's Westminster Rifles) Londons were here in 1917 before moving to the front during the Third Battle of Ypres.

UK – 41   Can – 3   Ger – 1   WWII – 10

Area – 995 sq mts

LOCATION
The cemeteries in Dikkebus are on the eastern edge of the village south of Ieper. The Old Cemetery is located behind the church 100 m from the N375 to Loker.

Journey Time – 20 mins

C.W.G.C. Reference – 5/54

DICKEBUSCH NEW MILITARY CEMETERY, DIKKEBUS   *No. 33*

HISTORY
This cemetery was begun in February 1915, as the Old Cemetery was considered to be full, and used until May 1917 when the space here was also filled and the Extension begun. However, four more burials were made in March and April 1918.

INFORMATION
Of the men buried here ninety-two are from artillery units reflecting the nature of activity in the village for much of the War as Dikkebus was usually well behind the front-lines. The New Cemetery contains the War Stone while the Extension opposite contains

the Cross of Sacrifice.

Lance-Corporal Joseph Stanley Victor Fox of the 1st Wiltshires (7th Brigade, 3rd Division) was executed on 20 April 1915 after being convicted of desertion. He is now buried in this cemetery.

Lyn Macdonald in *They Called it Passchendaele*, page 30, tells us that Pastor van Walleghem, of Dikkebus church, visited a scale model of the Mesen Ridge which had been made on the slopes of the Scherpenberg to train officers involved in the attack at the start of the Battle of Messines. He toured this model with the Dean of De Klijte church without any challenge by the British, so much for security!

The 19th and 248th Machine Gun Companies of the 33rd Division moved from billets in Dikkebus and Watou to various front-line positions at the beginning of the Battle of the Menin Road on 20 September 1917. At the start of the attack two sections of the 248th were wiped out. Even so, the machine-gun companies helped in taking Inverness Copse, Dumbarton Lakes and Tower Hamlets on 20 and 21 September.

UK – 528   Aust – 11   Can – 84

Area – 4880 sq yds (with the extension)

LOCATION

Directions for this cemetery are the same as those for the Old Cemetery until you pass the church at which point continue on the road to Vierstraat. The two cemeteries are on either side of the road 100m from the church.

Journey Time – 20 mins

C.W.G.C. Reference – 5/54

DICKEBUSCH NEW MILITARY CEMETERY EXTENSION, *No. 34*
DIKKEBUS

HISTORY
The extension was used from May 1917 until January 1918 as the space in the New and Old Cemeteries had been filled.

INFORMATION
Dickebusch New Military Cemetery Extension lies opposite to the New Cemetery. The two are usually considered to be one, for example the Extension has the Cross of Sacrifice and the New Cemetery has the War Stone. They are only a short distance from the church and the Old Cemetery.

Of the men buried here 260 were from artillery units. 'C' Battery, of the 2nd City of Edinburgh Brigade Royal Artillery, were resting nearby in 1917 when a shell landed in the middle of their unit as they fed their horses. Nine men were killed, many wounded and the Battery ceased to exist.

UK – 520   Aust – 24   Can – 2
S Afr – 1   Ger – 1

Area – 4480 sq yds (with the New Cemetery)

LOCATION
Directions are as for the New Cemetery in Dikkebus.

Journey Time – 20 mins

C.W.G.C. Reference – 5/54

HISTORY

Begun in 1914 the cemetery was used by British units from April 1915 until May 1916. It was used again during the Flanders Offensive in 1917 when mainly men of artillery units were buried here.

INFORMATION

There are twenty-three men of the Duke of Wellington's (West Riding) Regiment, who fell in the German gas attack at Hill 60 on 5 May 1915, buried in Row C, grave 18. (See Larch Wood Cemetery) Three Belgian graves have been removed.

UK – 188   NZ – 65   Can – 26   Bermuda – 1
KUG – 1   Area – 1718 sq yds

LOCATION

Divisional Cemetery lies in a housing/industrial area in the suburbs west of Ieper. There are clear C.W.G.C. signs directing you from the old road to Poperinge (N308) to the cemetery.

Journey Time – 5 mins

C.W.G.C. Reference – 5/44

DIVISIONAL COLLECTING POST (AND EXTENSION), St. JAN *No. 36*

HISTORY

The original cemetery was begun by the 48th (South Midland) and 58th (2/1st London) Divisions in August 1917 during the Third Battle of Ypres, and was closed in January 1918. The Extension is, in fact, a concentration cemetery created in the 1920's.

INFORMATION

The two cemeteries are bounded by the same wall and are considered to be one, certainly it is difficult to see any physical distinction between the wartime cemetery and the post-war additions. However, the original burials, now forming Plot 1, Rows A to E, are near the Cross of Sacrifice furthest from the road and facing the Cross. The concentrated burials that form the Extension face the War Stone and the road and in the opposite direction to the War burials. There are Special Memorials next to the Cross to two men buried in Westrozebeke Church whose graves have been lost.
    The burial grounds get their name from the Collecting Post for casualties that was here during the Third Battle of Ypres situated on a main trench to the rear called Coney Street.

Concentrated here :

Deerlijk Churchyard – it contained twenty British men (mostly 31st Division) who fell in October and November 1918.
De Voorstraat German Cemetery (No. 50) – 800 m south-east of Zandvoorde containing two British men who fell in 1914-15.
Houthulst Forest Chateau West Cemetery – a German cemetery in the middle of the forest including two British men who fell in 1914.
Westrozebeke Churchyard – it contained nine British men buried by the Germans.

UK – 86 + 493 = 579   Aust – 102   NZ – 5   Can – 73
NF – 2   S Afr – 1   Ger – 1   Unnamed – 512 (80%)

Area – 600 + 2622 sq yds = 3222 sq yds

LOCATION

The Divisional Collecting Post Cemetery lies north of Ieper and 300 m north of the northern by-pass (N38) on a road that runs parallel to the by-pass from which it is reached easily. There are two other graveyards nearby, the New Irish Farm Cemetery being clearly signed from the N38.

Journey Time – 15 mins

C.W.G.C. Reference – 5/21

HISTORY

This cemetery is a concentration cemetery created after the Armistice to contain bodies found in isolated graves and small burial grounds in this area.

INFORMATION

The farm after which this cemetery is named was captured by the 4th New Zealand Brigade on 4 October 1917 during the Battle of Broodseinde and was situated down the slope across the main road. There is a Memorial to the New Zealanders that you can see across the road and valley to north-east. An obelisk in a small copse, the Memorial can be reached from the nearby crossroads called Kansas Cross. You can also see Tyne Cot Cemetery across the area that was fought over in October 1917 by the New Zealanders, known as the Abraham Heights.

The cemetery has a very formal layout which shows clearly that it was not here during the fighting as this ridge was an important objective for the British in the Third Battle of Ypres.

Before 1917, in the German gas attack in April 1915, the 85th and 11th Brigades were stationed along this ridge as far as the Canadian Memorial at Vancouver Corner and the French at Langemark.

On 23 April 1915, St. George's Day and possibly one of the most important days of the Second Battle of Ypres, British regiments were trying to re-establish the line that had been damaged the day before. Divisional reserves had been deployed with some companies helping the Canadians on the left, filling the line vacated by the French from Lange-mark to Boezinge, and some near this cemetery. Colonel A. Geddes, of the Buffs, was put in charge of a formation of companies from several units, used as an early form of 'Rapid Reaction Corps', which fought wherever it was needed, to hold the German advance. It comprised elements of the 3rd Middlesex, 4th Rifle Brigade, 2nd King's Shropshire Light Infantry, 2nd Buffs, 1/9th (Highlanders) Royal Scots, 1st York and Lancasters, 1/5th King's Own and 2nd Duke of Cornwall's Light Infantry but despite their efforts the British were forced to pull back from this ridge and all along the front.

To reach this cemetery you could have come through Zonnebeke which was also a centre of fierce fighting on many occasions throughout the War. On 19 – 21 October 1914 the Germans tried to break the flank of the British 7th Division but the 22nd Brigade held the line until forced to pull back on 22 October. The French reoccupied Zonnebeke on the following day before the British 2nd Division took over the line from here to Reutal in late October.

The Germans occupied Zonnebeke in May 1915 after the British 'consolidation' of their line during the German offensive. Zonnebeke was taken by the British on 26 September 1917 during the Third Battle of Ypres but lost in the German Spring Offensive in April 1918. The Belgians finally captured Zonnebeke on 28 September 1918 by which time there was very little of the town left standing.

There are now several places to visit in the town including the Streekmuseum, the church and the Bremen Redoubt. A plaque on the west outer wall of the church is a Memorial to D/21 Battery, Canadian Field Artillery who were stationed in the churchyard and almost the only defenders of the Frezenberg Ridge in April 1915.

Surgeon-Captain Martin-Leake (later Lieutenant-Colonel) of the Royal Army Medical Corps, won a Bar to the Victoria Cross which he had won in South Africa (1902) in action near Zonnebeke Church in late October and early November 1914.

On 25 July 1915 Captain Lanoe George Hawker of 6th Squadron, Royal Flying Corps gained a Victoria Cross for bringing down three German planes in one morning before crashing into the lines at Zonnebeke. Captain Hawker, formerly of the Royal Engineers, was later promoted to Major and also awarded the Distinguished Service Order but died on 23 November 1916.

A line from Frezenberg to this cemetery was an objective of the first day of the Third Battle of Ypres. The first objective, the German front-line north and south of Verlorenhoek, along the line of the modern motorway, fell at 3.45 am and Frezenberg was taken by the 9th Black Watch and 8/10th Gordon Highlanders by 6.00 am. The Potsdam Redoubt, where the road to Zonnebeke crosses the Hannebeek, was captured next, under heavy fire, by the 7/8th King's Own Scottish Borderers. The final objective for that day was a line from Potsdam Redoubt to Kansas Cross near this cemetery, taken by the 6/7th Royal Scots Fusiliers and 6th Cameron Highlanders with the 11th Argyll and Sutherland Highlanders and 13th Royal Scots. However, the battalions suffered severe casualties including the commanding officer of the Camerons. The 12th Highland Light Infantry were sent up to support and consolidate the line during the night.

On the next morning the Germans attacked a gap in the line north of the road to Zonnebeke. The Royal Scots were forced back from the line during which there were many examples of heroism in holding the Germans long enough for the battalion to withdraw under controlled conditions. Colonel Hanway, at his headquarters just north of Frezenberg, ordered his Staff and the 46th Company, Machine Gun Corps to counter-attack with the remaining 130 men of the Royal Scots Fusiliers and the Argyll and Sutherland Highlanders. They retook the lost ground and held it.

UK – 523   Aust – 305   NZ – 98   Can – 81
NF – 1 S Afr – 17 KUG – 412 Unnamed – 958 (60%)

Special Memorials to one British soldier and one Australian man believed to be among the unnamed.

Area – 5412 sq yds

LOCATION
Dochy Farm Cemetery is located on the ridge north-west of Zonnebeke, about 1.5 km from the village, on the west side of the road to Vancouver Corner and Langemark. The simplest route to Zonnebeke is via Hellfire Corner and Potijze.

Journey Time – 30 mins

C.W.G.C. Reference – 5/16

DOZINGHEM MILITARY CEMETERY, WESTVLETEREN *No. 38*

HISTORY
In preparation for the British Flanders Offensive in 1917 many Casualty Clearing Stations were put into position in the rear of the Salient at locations such as Brandhoek, Proven and the '-Vleterens'. The cemeteries that grew up associated with some of them were named by the soldiers Bandaghem, Mendinghem and Dozinghem, which played ironically upon the Flemish language and spelling for their apt description of the function of the Casualty Clearing Stations near each cemetery. The 4th, 47th and 61st Casualty Clearing Stations were located here and the cemetery which grew up next to them remained in use until March 1918.

INFORMATION
On route to this cemetery you could have passed the La Lovie Chateau, now a private school and hospital. King George V stayed there in July 1917 and it was used as a British headquarters from May 1915 by:
May 1915 – February 1916 : VI Corps
February 1916 – July 1916 : XIV Corps
July 1916 – June 1917 : VIII Corps
June – November 1917 : 5th Army
November 1917 – April 1918 : II Corps
April – August 1918 : 34th, 41st and 49th (West Riding) Divisions
August – November 1918 : II Corps

Also nearby is the St. Sixtus Abbey in which the monks produce a strong beer. It is sign-posted from the cemetery and can be visited as part of your tour.

Some later burials in the War took place at Dozinghem and some British graves were concentrated here from the former French cemeteries at Hoogstade, Hoogbrug and Krombeke. There were 118 Belgian graves within the cemetery near the entrance but these have been removed. The space vacated has been used for the burial of seventy-three men who fell during World War II.

UK – 3021	Aust – 6	NZ – 14	Can – 61
NF – 19	S Afr – 15	BWI – 34	KUG – 1
Chinese Labour Corps – 3	Ger – 65	WWII – 73	

Area – 14721 sq yds

LOCATION
Dozinghem is one of the hardest cemeteries to find on the Salient. It is included in very few maps and it took me a morning to find it on the first occasion that I tried. As such, this cemetery more than most was the catalyst for putting this book together. It is possible to get here from Krombeke or by car from Proven or most easily from Poperinge. The cemetery is in a wood on the east side of the Poperinge – Krombeke road about 4 km from the crossroads at Poperinge. It is 250 m from the main road on a dirt track.

Journey Time – 35 mins

C.W.G.C. Reference – 5/6

HISTORY

This cemetery was opened by the 13th (1st North Wales Pals) Royal Welsh Fusiliers on 9 August 1917 and remained in use until October 1917.

INFORMATION

The cemetery is very small with good views of this part of the Salient. It is peaceful because of its distance from the road which means a long walk for visitors.

Dragoon Camp was a German camp until the start of the Third Battle of Ypres when this area was taken on 31 July 1917. Captured by the 38th (Welsh) Division, Dragoon Camp was a name used by the soldiers, its official name being House 10, or Villa Gretchen Cemetery. Of the known graves only six are not of Royal Welsh Fusiliers (thirty-nine) or Royal Field Artillery (fifteen).

UK – 66   Unnamed – 6   Area – 636 sq yds

LOCATION

Dragoon Camp Cemetery lies north of Ieper, east of the canal, about 1 km east of Boezinge. Turn towards Ieper at the French Memorials on the Boezinge – Langemark road and in 400 m you come to a C.W.G.C. sign directing along a track to the cemetery in the middle of fields. For the adventurous, you can drive a car almost to the cemetery, but you will have to walk the last 100 m along a neat grass path that seems out of place in the middle of the fields.

Journey Time – 25 mins + 5 mins walk

C.W.G.C. Reference – 5/7

HISTORY

The churchyard was used from the start of fighting in this area in October 1914 until the Military Cemetery nearby was opened in July 1915.

INFORMATION

Several small plots were made within the churchyard some of which still exist though nineteen graves were moved to the Military Cemetery in 1923 as the church was being rebuilt.

UK – 79   Unnamed – 2

LOCATION

Dranoutre Churchyard is in the centre of the village which lies south of Ieper. It is difficult to miss the church from whichever direction you enter Dranouter, though the easiest route is the N375 through Dikkebus and Loker.

Journey Time – 40 mins

C.W.G.C. Reference – 5/78

HISTORY

Begun in July 1915, as burials in the churchyard were ended, the cemetery was used until the German advance in March 1918. The graves in Plot III were added in September and October 1918. In addition, nineteen graves were moved here from the churchyard in 1923 during rebuilding operations.

INFORMATION

Many of the burials were made by the 72nd Brigade of the 24th Division from April to June 1916. The cemetery contains one member of the Australian Y.M.C.A.. Private Frederick Broadrick of the 11th Royal Warwickshires (112th Brigade, 37th Division) deserted from billets at Loker on 1 July 1917. As this was his second offence he was executed in Dranouter on 1 August and is buried in this cemetery.

UK – 421	Aust – 17	NZ – 1	Can – 19
Ger – 1		KUG – 3	

Area – 4554 sq yds

LOCATION

Dranoutre Military Cemetery lies on the southern edge of the village. The cemetery is reached from the Dranouter – Loker road, at the point at which a C.W.G.C. sign indicates off the main road, by means of a track that seems to be leading into a lumber yard. The cemetery can be seen on the left once you are past the buildings. There is a path to the cemetery next to a drainage ditch which can be fairly aromatic in the summer!

Journey Time – 40 mins

C.W.G.C. Reference – 5/78

DUHALLOW ADVANCED DRESSING STATION (A.D.S.) CEMETERY, IEPER *No. 42*

HISTORY

The cemetery was begun on the first day of the Third Battle of Ypres, 31 July 1917, next to the Advanced Dressing Station, and remained in use until the end of the War in November 1918. After the Armistice the cemetery was almost doubled in size with the concentration of many graves.

INFORMATION

The name of the cemetery is believed to have been taken from a Southern Irish hunt. The Dressing Station was located next to the canal, and the 11th, 36th and 44th Casualty Clearing Stations were posted here in October and November 1918.

Of the original 875 burials, which make up Plots I to IV, 215 were artillerymen and seventy-seven engineers. There are forty-one men of the 13th Company, Labour Corps, buried in Plot II, who were killed in the destruction of an ammunition truck, when it was bombed by a German plane on 9 January 1918.

One man who fell in World War II is buried in Plot V, six American and one Belgian graves have been removed. Also buried here is Private John Seymour of the 2nd Royal Inniskilling Fusiliers (96th Brigade, 32nd Division) who was executed for desertion nearby on 24 January 1918.

Both cemeteries concentrated here were badly shelled in 1918 and many graves were destroyed. Hence, Duhallow A.D.S. Cemetery contains Special Memorials to ten soldiers buried in Malakoff Farm Cemetery and twenty-nine buried at Fusilier Wood Cemetery whose graves have been destroyed. The Special Memorials are located near the entrance with the French and Belgian graves at the canal end of the cemetery. There is another Special Memorial to a man of the Loyal North Lancashire Regiment who is believed to be buried here.

Concentrated here:

Malakoff Farm Cemetery, Brielen – between Solferino Farm Cemetery and Dawson's Corner, it contained thirty-three graves, including thirteen men of the 1/4th (Hallamshire) York and Lancasters, (148th Brigade, 49th (West Riding) Division) who were killed from April 1915 to July 1917.

Fusilier Wood Cemetery, Hollebeke – it contained sixty-six British men and one Australian who fell from September 1917 to January 1918.

UK – 1442	Aust – 13	NZ – 6	Can – 26
NF – 12	S Afr – 3	BWI – 2	Indian – 2
Bel – 1	Fr – 2	Ger – 54	WWII – 1
Special Memorials – 41		Area – 6057 sq yds	

LOCATION
Duhallow A.D.S. Cemetery is in the northern suburbs of Ieper on the eastern side of the N369 between the road and the canal.

Journey Time – 10 mins

ELSENWALLE BRASSERIE CEMETERY, VOORMEZELE *No. 43*

HISTORY
This cemetery was opened in February 1915 and used as a front-line cemetery until June 1917. From that time it was used by units holding the new front-line won in the Battle of Messines until November 1917.

INFORMATION
The Brasserie is situated opposite the graveyard. The cemetery is a series of regimental burial grounds that reflect the battalions that held the front-line at the time the burials were made. As such, the cemetery lacks a formal pattern, which invites you to explore the graves.

On route you may have passed the Chateau Elsenwalle just north of the cemetery. This is a fascinating design in that the owner has incorporated the war damage in the rebuilding of the chateau. It lies in the remains of Scottish Wood and is, in my opinion, one of the most beautiful chateaux on the Salient.

UK – 106	Can – 41	BWI – 2	Unnamed – 5

Area – 2183 sq yds

LOCATION
Elsenwalle Brasserie Cemetery lies about 3 km south of Ieper on the west side of the road to Kemmel.

Journey Time – 10 mins

C.W.G.C. Reference – 5/55

ESSEX FARM CEMETERY, BOEZINGE   *No. 44*

HISTORY
The cemetery was begun in April 1915, next to a Dressing Station, and remained in use until August 1917.

INFORMATION
This is one of the most visited sites on the Salient because it has almost everything the tourist wants within a small area. It has the last resting place of one of the youngest to die in the War, the grave of a holder of the Victoria Cross, Memorials and a set of dug-outs.

The cemetery gets its name from the small farm building that was here in the War in which the Dressing Station was established in April 1915. One of the Doctors who worked here was Lieutenant-Colonel John McCrae, Royal Canadian Medical Corps, who was trying to save lives in the dug-outs

that can be found at the north end of the burial ground. One day, when he emerged from a particularly arduous session within the Dressing Station, he found that the cemetery had burst into colour and life with a field of poppies surrounding the graves. He then wrote one of the most famous poems of the War, *In Flanders Fields*, as he sat on the bank that separates the canal from the cemetery. McCrae died of pnemunomia and meningitis on 28 January 1918 and is buried in Wimmereaux Cemetery in France. There is a Memorial to him at the roadside.

Another Memorial, a tall obelisk on the canal bank, can be reached from Essex Farm Cemetery. It is a Monument to the 49th (West Riding) Division who have men buried in Plot I. The 38th (Welsh) Division have men buried in Plot III who fell during the autumn of 1916. Buried in the cemetery is one of the youngest known casualties of the War, Private Valentine Joe Strudwick of the Rifle Brigade who died on 14 January 1916, aged 15.

On the first day of the Third Battle of Ypres, 31 July 1917, the 1/9th (Highlanders) Royal Scots were waiting beside the cemetery before attacking as part of the second wave. Two officers were stood on the canal bank watching the progress of the rest of the 51st (Highland) Division particularly the 1/4th Gordon Highlanders. They ignored the advice of other officers to come off the bank when a shell exploded next to them killing one officer and blowing an arm off the other who was then placed in an ambulance that was hit by a shell and destroyed.

The track by the side of the cemetery leads to the canal bank at a point where there was a bridge during the War. This is now a popular spot with the inhabitants of Ypres for their Sunday afternoon relaxation.

V.C. – Private T. Barrett, 17114, V.C..
  7th South Staffordshire Regiment, 33rd Brigade, 11th (Northern) Division.
  Died – 27 July 1917. Age 22.
  Won – 27 July 1917. Private Barrett killed two German snipers and helped a patrol to return safely from no man's land. He was killed by a shell later in the day.

Special Memorials to nineteen British men who are believed/known to be buried here.

Area – 6059 sq mts

LOCATION
Essex Farm Cemetery lies north of Ieper and just north of the by-pass on the N369 to Boezinge between the road and the canal.

Journey Time – 10 mins

C.W.G.C. Reference – 5/28

FERME OLIVIER CEMETERY, ELVERDINGE   *No. 45*

HISTORY
This cemetery was used from 9 June 1915 to 5 August 1917 for burials from Dressing Stations located nearby in the Chateau.

INFORMATION
The 62nd, 16th, 9th, 11th, 129th and 130th Field Ambulances were posted successively to the Dressing Stations that this cemetery served. The burials in Plots I and II are not grouped in order of date but those in Plot III are, reflecting the order of postings to the area and the occupation of the Chateau in Elverdinge by the 38th (Welsh) and Guards Divisions as well as units of the Royal Artillery.

Plot II, Row E contains many graves of forty-one men of the 1/3rd Monmouths (49th (West Riding) Division Pioneers). They were killed while on parade in December 1915 by a single shell from a large German gun sited in Houthulst Forest.

Also buried here are two men who were executed when their units were in camp in Elverdinge. Private George Watkins of the 13th (2nd Rhondda Pals) Welsh Regiment (114th Brigade, 38th (Welsh) Division) deserted in the Salient in December 1916 and was caught in March 1917. He was executed and buried here on 15 May 1917.

Private Robert Hope, who enlisted as Hepple, which is the name on his headstone, of the 1st Royal Inniskilling Fusiliers (87th Brigade, 29th Division) deserted near Arras. He was tried after his battalion had moved north to the Salient and was executed on 5 July 1917.

The 1st Hampshires (11th Brigade, 4th Division), were stationed in the Chateau having lost 650 men on the first day of the Battle of the Somme. Though the battalion was gradually moved towards the front-

line it did not go over the top again until it was back on the Somme later in the year.

In Elverdinge churchyard, which can be found in the centre of the village, ten British soldiers were buried in late 1914 and early 1915. The church and churchyard were severely damaged by shell-fire, the village (though not Ferme Olivier Cemetery) being just inside the range of German guns until the British advance in the Flanders Offensive of 1917. The graves were removed to Cement House Cemetery in 1973.

UK – 407   Ger – 3

LOCATION
Ferme Olivier Cemetery lies on the northern edge of Elverdinge north of Ieper. It is located on the south side of the N333 Poperinge road about 1 km from its junction with the N8, which is just north of the traffic lights in Elverdinge.

Journey Time – 20 mins

C.W.G.C. Reference – 5/17

1st D.C.L.I. CEMETERY, THE BLUFF, ZILLEBEKE   *No. 46*

HISTORY
The cemetery dates from April to July 1915. Twenty-three graves were concentrated in Row D.

INFORMATION
This small cemetery, one of three in the area, is in

the fields some distance from the road on the path to the Hedge Row Cemetery. The two smaller graveyards are particularly tranquil. 1st D.C.L.I. Cemetery contains fifty-one men of the 1st Duke of Cornwall's Light Infantry who fell in defending 'The Bluff' in early 1915 as well as men from other units who fell in that action.

'The Bluff' was at the edge of the Ypres – Comines canal on a ridge and was probably created out of spoil from the excavations for the canal. The 2nd Manchesters held 'The Bluff' for eighty-seven consecutive days from 15 April to 25 July 1915 during which time Lieutenant Arthur Brooks Close-Brooks won the Military Cross for rescuing his Sergeant from no man's land after they had both been on patrol on 10 June. However, the Sergeant was found to be dead when they got to the British lines and Close-Brooks died of wounds in January 1917 having been promoted to Captain.

'The Bluff' was lost on 14/15 February 1916, when it was held by the 10th Lancashire Fusiliers (52nd Brigade, 17th (Northern) Division), after the Germans had blown a mine. A counter-attack by 'A' Company, 7th York and Lancasters, (17th Division Pioneers), failed to retake it though 'The Bluff' was recaptured on the night of 2/3 March by the 2nd Suffolks who attacked next to the canal through, and around, the crater. To their left the 8th King's Own and 1st Gordon Highlanders (all 76th Brigade, 3rd Division) attacked the line between 'The Bluff', through the position of this cemetery, and Woods Cemetery situated in what was known as 'The Ravine'. The attack was so successful that much of the original German line was taken with the old British trenches, but the Suffolks suffered 50% casualties. The Germans failed to over-run 'The Bluff' in July even after blowing a mine under the position. It fell to the Germans in their Spring Offensive in 1918 but was finally recaptured by the 14th (Light) Division on 28 September 1918.

UK – 99   Unnamed – 15

Area – 474 sq mts

LOCATION
1st D.C.L.I. Cemetery is about 5 km south of Ieper lying in fields halfway between the Comines and Warneton roads south-west of Zillebeke near Hill 60. There is a turn from the Comines road to several cemeteries about 200 m south of the turn to Zillebeke. Near Chester Farm Cemetery is a left turn, at C.W.G.C. signs, on to a narrow road leading to the three cemeteries on 'The Bluff' that you can see in the fields to the south of the road.

Journey Time – 20 mins + 5 mins walk

C.W.G.C. Reference – 5/65

GODEWAERSVELDE BRITISH CEMETERY   *No. 47*

HISTORY
The cemetery was begun in July 1917 during the lull in fighting between the Battle of Messines and the Third Battle of Ypres. It remained in use until August 1918.

INFORMATION
This is a very pleasant cemetery, situated on rising ground between the valley and the Mont des Cats, with an unusual raised area for the Cross of Sacrifice.

Three Casualty Clearing Stations were posted here in July 1917 and the cemetery grew up servicing them. The 37th and 41st remained until November 1917 while the 11th stayed until the German advance in April 1918. Burials during the German Offensive were then carried out by fighting units and Field Ambulances.

The nurses at No. 11 Casualty Clearing Station suffered from the effects of a gas attack on 12 July

1917 as the substance was brought in on the clothes of the wounded soldiers. Some of the nurses later in the month went on to the Mont des Cats to watch the bombardment that was the prelude to the Third Battle of Ypres.

The French made a large Plot at the higher end of the cemetery in May and June 1918 but the graves were removed after the Armistice. At that time five graves of men of the 110th Brigade Royal Field Artillery were brought from the slopes of the Mont des Cats and four graves, consisting of one British body, one Canadian soldier and two Indians, were concentrated from the churchyard in the village. One Sister of the Territorial Nursing Force is also buried here.

UK – 985	Aust – 65	NZ – 2	Can – 5
S Afr – 2		India – 3	Ger – 19

Area – 3163 sq yds

LOCATION

Godewarsvelde Cemetery lies on the northern edge of the village south-west of Ieper and south of Poperinge. It is situated on the slopes of the Mont des Cats just east of the road into the village on a dead-end. The easiest route is via Poperinge and the new road to Steenvoorde leaving this by taking the D10 towards Bailleul before turning to Godewaersvelde.

Journey Time – 45 mins

C.W.G.C. Reference – 4/22

GODEZONNE FARM CEMETERY, KEMMEL   *No. 48*

HISTORY

The cemetery was used from February to May 1915 though three graves were added in 1916. Then it was enlarged after the Armistice by the concentration of fifty-nine graves which were added to the twenty made during the War.

INFORMATION

This little cemetery has good views of the Salient, especially of the Kemmelberg. The seventeen original graves made in 1915 and making up Plot I, Rows A and B, were of men of the 4th Middlesex and the 2nd Royal Scots (both 8th Brigade, 3rd Division). It was created in the garden of a farm on the edge of a road known as 'Cheapside'.

South of the cemetery, past the next junction, is the Memorial to the men of the French 32nd Infantry Division who fell in 1914 and 1918.

UK – 74	Aust – 1	Can – 1	S Afr – 3

Area – 915 sq yds

LOCATION

Godezonne Farm Cemetery is located south of Ieper, about 1 km north of Kemmel. It is reached by taking the Kemmel road from Shrapnel Corner for 3.5 km to the crossroads in Vierstraat distinguished by two extremely large warehouses. Turn right to a small crossroads at a C.W.G.C. sign and left to the cemetery which is on the left after 500 m.

Journey Time – 15 mins

C.W.G.C. Reference – 5/63

GROOTEBEEK BRITISH CEMETERY, RENINGELST   *No. 49*

HISTORY

This cemetery was begun in April 1918 during the Battles of the Lys and used at intervals until the end of September.

INFORMATION

This is a beautiful little burial ground set away from the road behind a hop field and on the edge of open fields. The Grootebeek stream surrounds the cemetery making it an island reached by a small stone bridge which also contains the register.

Burials from this area, which was under British occupation throughout the War, were carried out in the cemeteries in Reningelst. But at the start of the Battles of the Lys the Field Ambulances stationed here created a new burial ground known as Ouderdom Military Cemetery which was later renamed after the stream which runs either side of it.

Grootebeek absorbed a small Indian Cemetery that had been made in April 1915. The graves of three French soldiers have been removed and replaced by those of two men who fell in World War

II buried in Row G. There is a Special Memorial to Private J. Lynn whose grave in Vlamertinge Church-yard was destroyed by shell-fire.

V.C. – Private John Lynn V.C., D.C.M., Cross of the Order of St. George, 4th Class (Russia). 2nd Lancashire Fusiliers, 12th Brigade, 4th Division.
From Forest Hill, London.
Died – 2 May 1915.
Won – 2 May 1915. In the German attack at Mousetrap Farm Private Lynn kept his machine-gun firing and stopped the German advance. He saved many of his comrades' lives but gave his own life in the attack as he had no gas mask. He died later from his wounds. (See Buffs Road Cemetery)

UK – 97	NZ – 1	S Afr – 1	Bermuda – 1
India – 7	WWII – 2		Unnamed – 1

Special Memorials to two graves destroyed by shell-fire.

Area – 2026 sq yds

LOCATION
Grootebeek Cemetery lies in the village of Ouder-dom about 5 km south-west of Ieper. It can be reached either from Vlamertinge or from the Halle-bast Restaurant crossroads 1 km south of Dikkebus on the N375 to Loker. The path to the cemetery is well marked.

Journey Time – 30 mins

C.W.G.C. Reference – 5/52

GUNNERS' FARM MILITARY CEMETERY, PLOEGSTEERT *No. 50*

HISTORY
This cemetery was begun in July 1915 and remained in use until June 1916 except for three British, and four German, burials made later. It is a good example of a number of cemeteries used in 1914 and 1915 by a few regiments at a time, as such, each Plot consists of burials of one or two battalions. The order of the burials also gives us an insight into the succession of postings to this area.

INFORMATION
The cemetery gets its name from the farm opposite. It is a pleasant cemetery except for the noise from the dogs in the farm. The burials here are :

Rows A to C – 9th Essex and 7th Suffolks.

Rows D to J – 9th Loyal North Lancashires and 11th Lancashire Fusiliers.

Rows J to Q – 9th (Scottish) Division.

Rows R to W – 11th (Lambeth) Queen's and 10th (Kent County) Royal West Kents.

UK – 163	Aust – 2	NZ – 1	S Afr – 9
Ger – 4	Area – 1700 sq yds		

See Calvaire Cemetery

LOCATION
Gunners Farm Cemetery is about 1.5 km south-east of Ploegsteert, south of Ieper. Approximately 1.4 km south of Ploegsteert square you will find, on the east side of the road, near a supermarket, a tree of C.W.G.C. signs. The road to the left leads to this cemetery, which is on the north side of the road.

Journey Time – 35 mins

C.W.G.C. Reference – 5/107

HISTORY

Begun early in July 1917, in the period between the Battle of Messines and the Third Battle of Ypres, the cemetery remained in use until the end of fighting on the Salient in September 1918.

INFORMATION

Situated on a rise in the middle of fields, Gwalia Cemetery is a fitting resting place for those who gave their lives for their country. The graveyard gets its name from the farm by which you walk to reach the cemetery, known to the Army as 'Gwalia Farm'. The farm and burial ground were situated among the camps in the rear of the Salient.

Of those buried here, 179 were from artillery units, thirty from the Royal Engineers and thirty from Labour Corps of the Royal Army Service Corps. One American and two French graves have been removed.

In Plot I, Row H, fourteen men of the 9th Lancashire Fusiliers are buried. They were killed in an air raid over Dirty Bucket Camp, which was near to Hospital Farm Cemetery, in the early morning of 4 October 1917.

UK – 444	Aust – 2	NZ – 5	S Afr – 1
BWI – 14	Chinese Labour Corps – 4		Ger – 3

Area – 1434 sq yds

LOCATION

Gwalia Cemetery lies in open fields north-west of Ieper and about 2.5 km north-east of Poperinge. It is approximately 250 m north of the road from Poperinge to Elverdinge (N333) nearly halfway between the two towns. A C.W.G.C. path leads from a lay-by at the roads' edge past the farm to the cemetery which can be seen from the road.

Journey Time – 35 mins

C.W.G.C. Reference – 5/110

HAGLE DUMP CEMETERY, ELVERDINGE   *No. 52*

HISTORY

Begun next to the camp of the same name in April 1918 during the Battles of the Lys, the cemetery remained in use until October and was then greatly enlarged after the Armistice.

INFORMATION

This cemetery was within British lines throughout the War and replaced Ferme Olivier and Hospital Farm cemeteries as they were filled. The graves of twenty-six Americans, who fell from July to September 1918, and two French soldiers, have been removed.

There are two men buried here who deserted from their units during the German Spring Offensive in 1918. Private Walter Dossett of the 1/4th (Hallam-shire) York and Lancasters (148th Brigade, 49th (West Riding) Division) was executed nearby on 25 June 1918. Private George Ainley of the 1/4th King's Own Yorkshire Light Infantry (147th Brigade, 49th Division) had deserted three times in 1918 and was executed here on 30 July 1918.

Concentrated here:

Brielen Military Cemetery – on the south side of the village, and used from April 1915 to September 1917, it contained thirty-one French, sixteen British and four Canadian soldiers.

UK – 397	Aust – 26	Can – 14	Ger – 2
Unnamed – 142		Area – 2174 sq yds	

LOCATION

Hagle Dump Cemetery is found about 1 km north of the old road to Poperinge (N308), west of Ieper, and about 3 km west of Vlamertinge. The turn to the 'Dump' from the N308 is clearly marked.

Journey Time – 25 mins

C.W.G.C. Reference – 5/24

HARINGHE (BANDAGHEM) BRITISH CEMETERY   *No. 53*

HISTORY

Haringhe was one of several cemeteries, set up in preparation for the Flanders Offensive of 1917, and attached to Casualty Clearing Stations. It remained in use until October 1918. The cemetery acquired its ironic name, Bandaghem, with two other local cemeteries, Dozinghem and Mendinghem, from the soldiers, who were playing upon the Flemish language to describe the job of the Dressing Stations, though this graveyard has now been renamed after the town by which it stands.

INFORMATION

The Casualty Clearing Stations posted here in 1917 were the 62nd and 63rd with the 36th arriving in 1918. The 62nd was designated to receive all 'N.Y.D.N.' (Not Yet Diagnosed Nervous) cases, who we might today call 'battle fatigue', 'shell-shock' or 'post traumatic stress syndrome'. These were usually evacuated to base hospitals but for the Third Battle of Ypres the British commanders had decided that they would be held at Haringhe for one month to sort out the genuine cases.

During the Offensive No. 62 Casualty Clearing Station dealt with 5,000 cases. Only 16% were eventually evacuated to base hospitals in Rouen or Etaples; this breaks down as 4% who were not 'N.Y.D.N.' but had been sent to Haringhe by mistake, 12% psycho-neurotic and 4% psycho-neurotic with physical complications. 55% were immediately returned to their units and 29% went to work for four weeks on farms away from the front-line before returning to their units.

Four British Plots and four French were removed after the Armistice as were a Plot of German, two American and two Belgian graves, whereas five British men were buried here during World War II.

UK – 732	Aust – 2	NZ – 11	Can – 1
NF – 5	S Afr – 7	BWI – 4	Bermuda – 1
KUG – 5	Chinese Labour Corps – 4		Ger – 39
Fr Civilian – 1	WWII – 5	Area – 2708 sq yds	

LOCATION

Haringhe Cemetery is north-west of Ieper and about 12 km north-west of Poperinge. Lying 2 km south-west of Roesbrugge on the southern edge of the village of Haringe, just east of the border with France, it is reached most easily via the Poperinge by-pass and the N308 through Proven.

Journey Time – 45 mins

C.W.G.C. Reference – 4/17

HISTORY
Previously known as Ravine Wood Cemetery this was opened in March 1915 and used until August 1917.

INFORMATION
This is the furthest from the road of the three cemeteries on 'The Bluff'. It stands high on the crest of the ridge and can only just be seen from the road.

The cemetery suffered from the effects of very severe shell-fire later in the War so that after the Armistice the individual graves could not be identified. Hence, the headstones are arranged symmetrically in a pattern around the Cross of Sacrifice. Further information about 'The Bluff' can be found by referring to 1st D.C.L.I. Cemetery.

UK – 94   Can – 2   KUG – 2

Area – 679 sq mts

LOCATION
Hedge Row Trench Cemetery is about 5 km south of Ieper lying in fields halfway between the Comines and Warneton roads south-west of Zillebeke near Hill 60. There is a turn from the Comines road to several cemeteries about 200 m south of the turn to Zillebeke. Near Chester Farm Cemetery is a left turn, at C.W.G.C. signs, on to a narrow road leading to the three cemeteries on 'The Bluff' that you can see in the fields to the south of the road.

Journey Time – 20 mins + 5 mins walk

C.W.G.C. Reference – 5/65

HOOGE CRATER CEMETERY, ZILLEBEKE   *No. 55*

HISTORY
Hooge Cemetery lies on the site which the German front-line occupied at the start of the British Flanders Offensive in 1917 and it was created in October 1917 once this land had been taken by the British 8th Division. Opened by the Burial Officer of the 7th Division it held seventy-six graves until the German Spring Offensive in 1918 when the area was again lost to the Germans. The burial ground was enlarged after the Armistice with the concentration of 5,800 graves from the battlefields of Zillebeke, Zandvoorde and Geluveld.

INFORMATION
The cemetery, which has a formal layout with good views of Sanctuary Wood, is entered across the route of the former light railway that ran by the side of the Menen Road. The circular depression at the entrance represents the crater blown in 1915.

Hooge Chateau, opposite the site of this cemetery, was the headquarters for various units including at times Sir John French (q.v.) and Sir Douglas Haig (q.v.) before French was removed and Haig promoted. On 31 October 1914, during the First Battle of Ypres, the Staffs of the 1st and 2nd Divisions were in conference at Hooge Chateau when a shell fell on the meeting. Only one officer was unhurt and most were killed. The dead have been buried in Ypres Town Cemetery.

The Chateau was defended against German attacks in June 1915 but fell on 30 June. On 16 June the 3rd Division had advanced here taking 3,500 casualties including the then Major A. P. Wavell who went on to become Commander-in-Chief in North Africa, and then moved to the South Pacific, during World War II. A huge mine was blown, after the 175th Tunnelling Company had laid 3,500 lbs of Amonal under the grounds of the Chateau, on 18 July 1915 killing 145 Germans. The 3rd Division again attacked, with the objective of taking the ridge from Bellewarde Farm to Hooge, and the 4th Middlesex, of the 8th Brigade, attacked the mine crater though the mine explosion had already killed ten men of their battalion. The action here to take the crater and trenches turned into a prolonged bombing fight with the Middlesex holding as much trench as they could with dwindling supplies of ammunition. They consolidated their position at the lip of the crater and in some German trenches, repulsing all attacks, until handing over to the 1st Gordon Highlanders in the morning. The distance between the trenches was in places only 15 m and this action saw the first use of tin hats in the war by the British.

In August the trenches here were held by the 2nd Leinsters (17th Brigade, 6th Division). The ground was littered with the corpses of dead Germans killed in the blowing of the crater. Amongst them were the dead of the 2nd Durham Light Infantry (18th Brigade, 3rd Division) who had died in the fighting of early August. The attack by the Durham Light Infantry had been particulary violent as this had been their first opportunity to gain revenge for the German attacks on the British town of Hartlepool where many of the Durhams had families. The Germans attacked on 12 August and, although the site of this cemetery was exposed to fire from north of the Menen Road, the line held. On 18 and 19 August the Leinsters buried the dead of the Durham Light Infantry in graves of three and four men. The Germans retook the area in June 1916 during the Battle of Mount Sorrel.

On 31 July 1917 the plan was for the 30th Division, led by the 90th Brigade, to capture Inverness Copse, Clapham Junction and Glencorse Wood having crossed the valley next to this cemetery. The 18th (Eastern) Division would capitalise on this by taking Polygon Wood and the 8th Division would attack north of the Menen Road through Hooge Chateau Wood. The 30th Division got lost and went straight through the position of Hooge Cemetery into Hooge Chateau Wood, already captured by the 8th Division. They then reported that they had taken Glencorse Wood at which point the reserve of the 18th Division and 53rd Brigade advanced along the valley here to take Polygon Wood believing that the first objectives had fallen, but instead they walked in to a storm of fire from the untouched German line on the Menen Road. Even so, they persevered into impossible conditions.

Lieutenant G. B. W. Hill of the 8th Suffolks and Lieutenant-Colonel B. G. Clay of the 6th Royal Berkshires urged their men forward with the 79th Company, Royal Engineers, helping on the flanks. The Menen Road was taken by the Suffolks at 9.00 am at the same time as five tanks arrived only to become stuck in the valley. A link-up with the 8th Division was achieved, though not in Polygon Wood. During the desperate fighting on this day Captain Harold Ackroyd, Royal Army Medical Corps, Medical Officer of the 6th Royal Berkshires was awarded the Victoria Cross after twenty-three separate recommendations were made about his actions. He was killed in action on 11 August 1917 and is believed to be buried at Birr Crossroads Cemetery.

On 26 August 1917, just before the cemetery was created, the 280th Brigade, Royal Field Artillery were stationed at the southern edge of this location. When a shell fell in 'A' Battery, Gunner Harding was the only man left alive, but he continued to fire the gun in support of an infantry attack.

The position was lost for the last time in April 1918 as the Germans surged down the Menen Road towards Ypres reaching Hellfire Corner. It was retaken in the advance by the 9th (Scottish) and 29th Divisions on 28 September 1918.

The number of burials in Plot II, Row G is not known but it is assumed to be twenty-three. There are Special Memorials to twelve British men buried at La Chappele Farm and two British men buried in Kruiseeke German Cemetery whose graves were destroyed by shell-fire.

Just to the east of the cemetery is the large Bellewaerde Pleasure Park which is open in the summer. Near the park there is a small cross at the roadside which is the Memorial to the King's Royal Rifle Corps. Beyond the Park at the top of the rise is Clapham Junction. On either side of the Menen Road near the junction are Memorials to the 18th (Eastern) Division and the Gloucester Regiment, the 1st battalion of which fought here in 1914 and the 2nd battalion in 1915. Between Clapham Junction and Geluveld village there are locations such as Chateau Herentage, Dumbarton Lakes, Stirling Castle, the Tower Hamlets Ridge and Inverness Copse that became infamous during the War. In Geluveld village you can find Memorials to the 1st South Wales Borderers and 2nd Worcesters who fought valiantly to hold the village in October 1914.

V.C. – Private Patrick J. Bugden, V.C..
     31st Battalion, (Queensland and Victoria)
     Australian Imperial Force, 8th Australian
     Brigade, 5th Australian Division.
     From New South Wales.
     Died – 28 September 1917.
     Won – 26–28 September 1917. In Polygon
     Wood the advance was held up by pill-boxes.
     Bugden led small parties taking them and
     releasing a Corporal captured by the
     Germans. He also rescued wounded men on
     five occasions. He was always first to
     volunteer for dangerous missions, during one
     of which he died.

Concentrated here:

Bass Wood Cemeteries No.'s 1 & 2, Zillebeke – on the east side of the Bassevillebeek south of Herentage Wood. It was used from December 1917 to March 1918 and contained forty-eight British graves.
Koelenberg German Cemeteries, Gheluwe – south of

the Menen Road near the village. They contained 163 British men, four Canadians and one Australian.

King's Own Scottish Borderers Cemetery, Gheluwe – on the Menen Road, 1km west of the village. Eighteen British men, ten of them from the 1/5th King's Own Scottish Borderers, were buried here in October 1918 after the capture of Gheluwe by the 34th Division.

La Chapelle Farm, Zillebeke – next to Chester Farm Cemetery at the road junction where seventeen British men were buried in February and March 1915.

Menin Road Pill-box Cemetery, Zillebeke – between Herentage Chateau and Geluveld where twenty British soldiers who fell in October 1917 were buried.

Nieuwe Kruiseeke Cabaret Cemetery, Geluveld – at the main crossroads east of Geluveld. The cemetery was on the south-west corner of the junction where twenty-one British men and one Canadian were buried in October 1918.

Pill-box Cemetery, Zonnebeke – 450m north-east of Westhoek. It was used in October 1917 for the burial of twenty-six British, thirty-four Australian, two Canadian soldiers and one man of the British West Indies Regiment.

Sanctuary Wood Old British Cemetery, Zillebeke – sited within the wood north-east of the present cemetery where fifty British men and four Canadians were buried from 1915 to 1917.

Tower Hamlets Cemetery, Geluveld – south of the Menen Road on the eastern edge of Herentage Wood by the side of a row of pill-boxes known as Tower Hamlets. Thirty-six British men who fell in the winter of 1917-1918 were buried there.

Westhoek Ridge Small Cemetery, Zonnebeke – in Westhoek village. It was used in autumn 1917 for the burial of one British soldier and sixteen Australian servicemen.

UK – 5182	Aust – 513	NZ – 121	Can – 105
BWI – 2		Unnamed – 3580 (60% of total)	

Special Memorials to six British men, four Australians, one New Zealander and eight Canadians known/believed to be buried among the unnamed.

Special Memorials to fourteen graves destroyed by shell-fire in other cemeteries.

Area – 14329 sq yds

LOCATION
Hooge Cemetery is on the south side of the Menen Road, at the top of a rise, about 3km from Ieper.

Journey Time – 15 mins

C.W.G.C. Reference – 5/38

HOP STORE CEMETERY, VLAMERTINGE

HISTORY
The cemetery was opened in May 1915 and remained in use until the end of the War. However, the majority of burials here date from 1915 and 1917.

INFORMATION
Vlamertinge was, for most of the War, at the edge of the range of German artillery. The Hop Store and its cemetery was in the 'safe' area, but remained small because of the limited space available. The site was drained by the Royal Engineers in 1917 and a moat has been created to keep the ground dry.

The large red building by which you turn to get here is the Hop Store which was used as a Casualty Clearing Station in the War. There are fifty-eight men of the Royal Artillery buried here reflecting the fact that many of the men who died in the local dressing stations were from nearby artillery units, the target of German shelling. One French grave has been removed.

UK – 247   Can – 1

LOCATION
Hop Store Cemetery is situated 70 m north of the old road to Poperinge (N308) approximately 1 km west of Vlamertinge and west of Ieper. Access is by a private road at the west end of the Hop Store, an imposing red brick building on the north side of the N308.

Journey Time – 20 mins

C.W.G.C. Reference – 5/26

HOSPITAL FARM CEMETERY, ELVERDINGE   *No. 57*

HISTORY
This cemetery was in use for much of the War but particularly in 1915 and 1917 by the regiments fighting close to Ypres.

INFORMATION
The cemetery is reached by a small bridge from the field through which you must walk to reach the graveyard. The farm, and the field which is in use, do not entirely contribute to the atmosphere – just the aroma! The nearby pond, stagnant in summer, and ditch surrounding the cemetery, also detract from the area. The entry to the field and cemetery is through a turnstile so the cemetery is really not accessible to those in wheelchairs. Hospital Farm, from which this cemetery gets its name, was the name given in the War to a nearby farm which was used as a Dressing Station.

UK – 115   Fr Civilian – 1   Unnamed – 4

Area – 1248 sq yds

LOCATION
Hospital Farm Cemetery is found west of Ieper and 2 km north-west of Vlamertinge. The road from the Poperinge road (N308) leads north from the centre of Vlamertinge at the church, and has C.W.G.C. signs on the corner. The cemetery, next to a field which contains a wide avenue of trees, is 150 m west of the road behind the farm. There is no C.W.G.C. path through the field and a distribution of cow-pats must be avoided.

Journey Time – 20 mins

C.W.G.C. Reference – 5/23

HUTS CEMETERY, DIKKEBUS   *No. 58*

HISTORY
The cemetery was made at the start of the Third Battle of Ypres in July 1917 and used until November 1917. This accounts for most of the burials though Plots XI and XV were added in the winter of 1917-18 before the German Spring Offensive in April 1918 almost reached this area, at which point the cemetery was closed.

INFORMATION
Enclosed by a high brick wall, which gives it the feel of an english country garden, Huts Cemetery is isolated with good views of the Mont des Flandres.

In the War there were a line of huts at the roadside housing Field Ambulances from which the cemetery gets its name. The cemetery was near a series of gun positions for much of the time that it was in use. Hence, 687 of the burials, nearly 70%, were of artillerymen who were killed by enemy shelling of their positions.

As this area was usually well behind the front-lines a number of camps were located nearby. Breaches of discipline were normally matters dealt with when units were in camp in the rear. Therefore, two men are buried here, near each other in Plot XV, who were executed for their indiscipline. Private Victor M. Spencer of the 1st Otago Regiment, New Zealand Expeditionary Force, deserted for the second time in August 1917 and was not captured until 2 January 1918. He was executed on 24 February 1918.

Private Henry Hughes of the 1/5th York and Lancasters (148th Brigade, 49th (West Riding) Division) deserted while under a suspended sentence of death. He was the first man from the 49th Division to be executed when he was shot on 10 April 1918.

On the day that the Germans achieved the limit of their advance, at Dikkebus Lake, on 8 May 1918, the line here was held by the 10th Royal Warwickshires.

UK – 815	Aust – 243	NZ – 19	Can – 5
S Afr – 4	BWI – 1	India – 1	KUG – 6
Ger – 6	Area – 5626 sq yds		

LOCATION
Huts Cemetery is south-west of Ieper about 1 km west of Dikkebus in open fields. It is clearly signed from the village and is difficult to miss as you can see it across the fields once you leave Dikkebus.

Journey Time – 20 mins

C.W.G.C. Reference – 5/53

HYDE PARK CORNER (ROYAL BERKS) CEMETERY, *No. 59*
PLOEGSTEERT

HISTORY
Begun by the 1/4th Royal Berkshire Regiment (145th Brigade, 48th (South Midland) Division) in April 1915, the cemetery remained in use until November 1917.

INFORMATION
Hyde Park Corner is the original of the two cemeteries here that face each other across the main road. It is an attractive small cemetery dominated by the one that faces it, though both are overshadowed by Hill 63.

One man buried here suffered a less than honourable death. Rifleman Samuel McBride of the 2nd Royal Irish Rifles (74th Brigade, 25th Division) was executed for desertion at Hope Farm near Prowse Point Cemetery on 7 December 1916. He is now buried next to the entrance.

| UK – 81 | Aust – 1 | Can – 1 | Ger – 4 |

Area – 907 sq yds

LOCATION
Hyde Park Cemetery lies on the west side of the

Armentieres road, about 1 km north of Ploegsteert, at the foot of Hill 63, and approximately 13 km south of Ieper. The imposing Memorial opposite this cemetery is difficult to miss.

Journey Time – 35 mins

C.W.G.C. Reference – 5/96

HISTORY

This cemetery was opened in June 1917 for the Battle of Messines though it was a little behind the front-line on 7 June. It remained in use until September 1918 with the exception of the period from April to August 1918 when the area was in German hands.

INFORMATION

This isolated little cemetery lies in a valley, sombre and dark under the shelter of the trees. The cemetery gets its name from a farm that was 100m to the west, though this is not the farm that you can see nearby today.

The cemetery was begun by the 16th (Irish) Division. Row A contains the graves of thirty-three men of the 1st Gordon Highlanders killed in an attack on Wijtschate by the 3rd Division. They were reburied here by the 11th (South Antrim Volunteers) Royal Irish Rifles in June 1917.

The attack by the Gordon Highlanders, with the 2nd Royal Scots (both 8th Brigade) in support, was launched from here on 15 December 1914 against the German line at Petit Bois next to the site of the present Wytschaete Military Cemetery. Their impossible task was to attack uphill across a muddy ploughed field covered with barbed wire. Even so, the 2nd Royal Scots reached the Petit Bois taking two machine-guns and thirty-five prisoners but losing eight officers and 157 men. Some of the Gordon Highlanders reached the German trenches but failed to hold them suffering, in the process, casualties of nine officers and 250 men. The Highlanders were only saved by hiding in the deep furrows of the ploughed field until they were able to return to the British trenches at night. However, a German sniper killed eighteen men in one furrow during the day that must have seemed endless to the Highlanders. This attack was reported as a British success in the newspapers on the next day!

Only three days before on 12 December, two other battalions from the 3rd Division, the 1st Lincolns and 1/10th (Liverpool Scottish) King's had been ordered to attack Petit Bois from positions near Irish House Cemetery. Four volunteers, Corporal John Williams and three Sappers from the Royal Engineers, supported by twelve men of the Lincolns, had been sent out at night to cut wire. While in no man's land Corporal Williams was mistaken for a dog by the Germans who threw rubbish at him, but he also found, and cut, the wires of the German telephone system. The attack started prematurely while he and his men were still in no man's land armed with no more than a pair of wire cutters. He spent the day rescuing wounded and taking them back to dressing stations. The attack succeeded and Corporal Williams was awarded the Distinguished Conduct Medal.

UK – 103   Aust – 13   Ger – 4   Unnamed – 40

Special Memorial to one Australian soldier known to be buried among the unknown.

Area – 681 sq yds

LOCATION

Irish House Cemetery is south of Ieper. It lies 80m from a small side road, reached by a small path next to a farm building, that leaves the Wijtschate – Kemmel road about midway between the two villages.

Journey Time – 35 mins

C.W.G.C. Reference – 5/75

KANDAHAR FARM CEMETERY, NIEUWKERKE *No. 61*

HISTORY

This cemetery was in use throughout most of the time that British troops were on the Salient. It was begun in November 1914 and used until the German Spring Offensive, when they took Wulvergem for the only time, in April 1918. The cemetery was used again when the British had retaken the village in September and October 1918.

INFORMATION

The front-line ran nearby from Wulvergem until June 1917 when it was moved to the east following the British successes during the Battle of Messines. The Germans created a small cemetery on the south side of the farm in Spring 1918 but it has been removed. Many of the British buried here were from the 14th (Light) Division.

UK – 211	Aust – 186	NZ – 33
Can – 6	KUG – 7	Ger – 3

C.W.G.C. Reference – 5/117

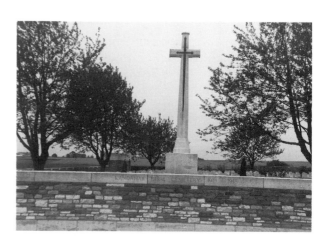

Special Memorial to one Australian soldier whose grave has been lost.

Area – 3360 sq yds

LOCATION
Kandahar Farm Cemetery lies on the east side of the road from Wulvergem to Nieuwkerke about 1 km south of Wulvergem. This is approximately 10 km south of Ieper and reached either through Kemmel or Mesen.

Journey Time – 50 mins

KEMMEL CHATEAU MILITARY CEMETERY, KEMMEL *No. 62*

HISTORY
The cemetery was begun in December 1914 and used until March 1918 when the Germans captured the village. It was used again in September and October 1918 when the area had been retaken.

INFORMATION
The entrance to this attractive cemetery represents the old chateau that was destroyed and the trees make a wide avenue to the Cross of Sacrifice. The road upon which this cemetery stands was known as Sackville Street. Kemmel was behind the front-lines for much of the War and many cemeteries were created nearby.

The village saw bitter fighting in Spring 1918 as the Germans tried to capture the Mont des Flandres in their 'Big Gamble'. German troops took the village, from the South African Brigade, on 25 April 1918 after a short battle in which the Germans also used ninety-six aeroplanes to drop 700 bombs on Kemmel and nearby villages. Though the Germans also took the Kemmelberg their gamble failed and the village was evacuated on 31 August 1918. While they held the village it was heavily shelled, the chateau was destroyed and Kemmel Chateau Cemetery was damaged.

There are two men buried here who were executed in Kemmel by the British Army. Private Stanley Stewart of the 2nd Royal Scots Fusiliers (90th Brigade, 30th Division) had been conscripted back into service having been invalided out of the Army in 1914. He deserted on 25 July 1917 and later escaped from custody before his execution on 29 August 1917.

Private James C. Smith of the 17th (1st Liverpool Pals) King's (89th Brigade, 30th Division) was executed for desertion and disobedience on 5 September 1917. Also here are sixty-six burials in Row E of men of the Sherwood Foresters (Nottingham & Derbyshire Regiment) and fifty-eight in Row N of men from Irish Regiments.

UK – 1030	Aust – 24	NZ – 1	Can – 80
WWII – 21 UK and 1 Fr		Area – 6585 sq yds	

LOCATION
Kemmel Chateau Cemetery can be found on the northern edge of Kemmel village which is south of Ieper. It is reached from the village by taking the road opposite the church in the centre of Kemmel.

Journey Time – 20 mins

C.W.G.C. Reference – 5/71

HISTORY

The churchyard was used for the burial of British dead from October 1914 to March 1915.

INFORMATION

The churchyard is up a flight of steps from the road. Most of the graves are found on the right from the steps though a small number are on the far side of the church from the road.

On 19 February 1917 Colonel Rowland Feilding, who was billeted in the 'Doctors House' in Kemmel, led an attack by nine officers and 190 men of the 6th Connaught Rangers (47th Brigade, 16th (Irish) Division), towards Mesen. An armistice was agreed by the Germans after the attack so that the Rangers could venture into no man's land to retrieve their wounded. After all the injured had been recovered the truce was ended though one officer who was last seen near the German lines carrying a revolver, had been taken prisoner. His price for not following 'the rules of the game'.

UK – 23   Unnamed – 3

Special Memorials to 15 graves destroyed by shell-fire.

LOCATION

Kemmel Church is on the south side of the N304 in the centre of Kemmel village which is south of Ieper and reached by taking the road from Shrapnel Corner.

Journey Time – 20 mins

C.W.G.C. Reference – None

HISTORY

The history of this cemetery is unknown. It was found after the Armistice by the French Graves Service who then removed the French graves to the Ossuary on the Kemmelberg or their cemetery at Potijze. In their place British graves were brought from the surrounding battlefield to add to those already here. Some German graves were also identified within the cemetery.

INFORMATION

The cemetery stands high above the road and is entered by means of a steep flight of steps. However, a side road at the west end of the burial ground provides a rear access if you cannot deal with the steps at the main entrance. There are excellent views of the Salient from the towers of Ypres to the Kemmelberg.

It is strange to think that a cemetery can be forgotten, as it was behind the lines for much of the War and only saw fighting during the German advance in Spring 1918 when the line came just east of here, and amazing that it was not found again until after the War. This gives us an indication of what the fighting must have been like in 1918 and how much shelling must have gone on in the area to obliterate a burial ground.

The number of Germans in the mass grave in German Row A is not known. However, the C.W.G.C. assess the number of Germans in the cemetery to be 253. These are represented by a small number of headstones in two rows.

UK – 277	Aust – 12	NZ – 3	Can – 3
Ger – 253	KUG – 1		Unnamed – 259

Area – 4692 sq yds

LOCATION

Kemmel No. 1 French Cemetery can be found on the south side of the road from Vierstraat to Hallebast which is south of Ieper and about 3 km north of Kemmel. This is best reached from the Kemmel road leaving it at the two unmistakeable warehouses in Vierstraat.

Journey Time – 15 mins

C.W.G.C. Reference – 5/114

KLEIN VIERSTRAAT BRITISH CEMETERY, KEMMEL *No. 65*

HISTORY
The cemetery was begun in January 1917, used until January 1918 and then again in April 1918. After the Armistice it was enlarged with the concentration of graves from two smaller cemeteries and from the surrounding battlefields.

INFORMATION
This cemetery was behind the lines for most of the War, but the fighting came to this area, as indicated by the Demarcation Stone only 300 m east of here, in April 1918. Hence, Klien Vierstraat was promptly closed. However, it was not lost like the cemetery next to it. (See Kemmel No. 1 French Cemetery) This burial ground is located at the site of the Klein Vierstraat (Little Crossroads) Cabaret from which it gets its name. Of the original burials, 188 (45%) were of artillerymen. One American grave has been removed.

Concentrated here:

Ferme Henri Pattyn-Vanlaeres, Poperinge – fifty-eight British men, and one Canadian who fell in May-July 1915, with one British soldier from April 1918, were buried there.
Mont Vidaigne Military Cemetery, Westouter – sited on the west slope of the Vidaignberg near Rodeberg. It contained seventeen British men who fell in July and August 1918. Seventeen French graves from April and May 1918 were moved elsewhere.

UK – 777	Aust – 8	NZ – 7	Can – 8
S Afr -1	BWI – 1	Chinese Labour Corps – 1	

Area – 3636 sq yds

LOCATION
Klien Vierstraat Cemetery can be found on the south side of the road from Vierstraat to Hallebast which is south of Ieper and about 3 km north of Kemmel. This is best reached from the Kemmel road leaving it at the two unmistakeable warehouses at Vierstraat.

Journey Time – 15 mins

C.W.G.C. Reference – 5/114

HISTORY

This cemetery was used in February and March 1916 by the 10th and 11th King's Royal Rifle Corps (both 59th Brigade, 20th (Light) Division). It was used again in July and August 1917.

INFORMATION

Sited on one of the main trenches to the front, Coney Street, the cemetery was named after the farmhouse and shrine here that were both destroyed in the War and never rebuilt. The exact number buried here is unknown but eight men of the 7th South Staffordshires (33rd Brigade, 11th (Northern) Division), are thought to be buried in Row D.

UK – 60   Unnamed – 10   Area – 350 sq mts

LOCATION

La Belle Alliance Cemetery lies north of Ieper and 300 m north of the N38 on a road that runs parallel to the by-pass. It is reached easily from the by-pass by taking the Pilkemsweg and Zwaanhofweg (Buffs Road) past New Irish Farm cemetery, which is clearly signed from the N38. The cemetery is 70 m from the Zwaanhofweg at the end of a short path.

Journey Time – 15 mins

C.W.G.C. Reference – 5/21

LA BRIQUE MILITARY CEMETERY No. 1, St. JAN   *No. 67*

HISTORY

The cemetery was used from May to December 1915.

INFORMATION

This burial ground, and its partner the No. 2 Cemetery that faces it across the road, derive their name from the brickworks that used to stand nearby. This is the smaller of the two and stands below the level of the other on the east side of the road. You can see the White House Cemetery across the field from here.

On 5 June 1915 the 6th Division took over the line here from the 4th Division as the 2nd Leinsters relieved the 1st Royal Irish Fusiliers. The officers of the Leinsters claimed that they could still smell the gas that had been used two months before in the German attack at the start of the Second Battle of Ypres.

UK – 90   Unnamed – 4   Area – 726 sq mts

LOCATION

The cemeteries lie in the suburbs of north-east Ieper on the edge of a new industrial park. They can be reached by a number of routes, but possibly the easiest is via Salvation Corner and Tattenham Corner taking the Brugseweg towards St. Jan until you reach a set of traffic lights at the top of the rise. Turn left on the road to the motorway into the new industrial area. As soon as you have turned left take the right fork where there are a series of C.W.G.C. signs. Having turned right it is 600 m to the two cemeteries on either side of the road, No. 1 is on the right as you arrive.

Journey Time – 10 mins

C.W.G.C. Reference – 5/30

HISTORY

From February 1915 until March 1918 the irregular group of graves in Plot I was created. The cemetery was enlarged after the Armistice with the concentration of graves from the surrounding battlefields.

INFORMATION

The cemetery, and its partner the No. 1 Cemetery, derive their name from the brickworks that used to stand nearby. This is the larger of the two cemeteries and stands above the level of the other on the west side of the road.

The original cemetery had 383 graves. One soldier was brought here from Kemmel No. 2 French Cemetery when the French graves were concentrated in larger cemeteries.

V.C. – Corporal Alfred George Drake, S/107, V.C.. 8th Rifle Brigade (The Prince Consort's Own), 25th Brigade, 8th Division. From Stepney, London.
Died – 23 November 1915. Age 22.
Won – 23 November 1915 at La Brique. He gave his life saving an officer when they were on patrol near the German lines and came under fire. The rest of the patrol withdrew but Drake stayed with the wounded officer. They were found later, Drake's body full of bullets and the officer, still alive, beside him.

| UK – 788 | Aust – 18 | NZ – 9 | Can – 23 |
| S Afr – 7 | KUG – 2 | | Unnamed – 387 |

Special Memorials to four men known/believed to be buried among the unnamed.

Area – 3270 sq mts

LOCATION

Directions for this cemetery are the same as for the No. 1 Cemetery.

Journey Time – 10 mins

C.W.G.C. Reference – 5/30

LA CLYTTE MILITARY CEMETERY, DE KLIJTE   *No. 69*

HISTORY

Opened on 1 November 1914 this cemetery remained in use until April 1918. La Clytte was almost doubled in size after the Armistice with the concentration of graves from isolated positions and small cemeteries from around De Klijte, Reningelst and Loker.

INFORMATION

The cemetery is deceptively large as it is positioned on the crest of a small rise with part of the burial ground hidden from the road. It has good views of the Salient from Ypres to the Monts des Flandres.

The original Plots consisted of nearly 600 graves with the concentration adding over 450. The wartime burials included 250 artillerymen and sixty-six engineers reflecting the nature of the activity in the rear of the Salient. Post-war burials included 185 unnamed graves with Special Memorials to twenty-

four men who are known to be buried among them.

Private Leonard Mitchell of the 8th York and Lancasters (70th Brigade, 23rd Division) was executed in the village on 19 September 1917 and buried here. He had deserted while under a suspended sentence of death for a previous desertion attempt.

In De Klijte church there are murals dedicated to the French who fell in the fighting at De Klijte and on the Scherpenberg. The church is in the village 100 m south of the roundabout on the road to Loker. However, you may find the church locked.

| UK – 813 | Aust – 12 | NZ – 3 | Can – 51 |
| S Afr – 6 | BWI – 7 | | Unnamed – 190 |

Special Memorials to twenty-four men known to be buried among the unnamed.

Area – 4436 sq mts

LOCATION
La Clytte Cemetery is on the south side of the N304, 100m west of the roundabout on the N375, just south of De Klijte. This is about 10km south-west of Ieper.

Journey Time – 25 mins

C.W.G.C. Reference – 5/62

LA CRECHE COMMUNAL CEMETERY, LA CRECHE   *No. 70*

HISTORY
For most of the War La Creche was behind the front-line and of limited importance. It was in German hands only during the Battles of the Lys in 1918.

INFORMATION
There are three British soldiers who died in 1915 buried here. They are on the left hand side of the cemetery as you enter, one near the gate and two further away.

UK – 3

LOCATION
La Creche Cemetery is found 600m south of the Bailleul – Armentieres road (D933) in France. On the north side of the village and clearly signed from the D933, it is on the east side of the Rue du Cemetiere.

Journey Time – 50 mins

C.W.G.C. Reference – None

LA LAITERIE MILITARY CEMETERY, KEMMEL   *No. 71*

HISTORY
This cemetery was in use throughout most of the War having been open from November 1914 until October 1918. It was enlarged after the Armistice with the concentration of 200 graves from the surrounding battlefields.

INFORMATION
Much of the cemetery was developed in the same way as the regimental burial grounds common in the early part of the War. Several Plots are composed almost entirely of men from one unit. For example,

Plots X, III and II are made up of the fallen of the 24th, 25th and 26th Canadian Infantry Battalions respectively and Plot VIII contains those of the 5th Northumberland Fusiliers (149th Brigade, 50th (Northumbrian) Division).

The road here was known as York Road. On it can be found, 800m to the north, the Memorial to the U.S. 27th and 30th Divisions who fought on the Salient in 1918.

UK – 468	Aust – 7	Can – 197	NF – 1
KUG – 78	Area – 6586 sq yds		

LOCATION
La Laiterie Cemetery is on the west side of the road to Kemmel about 1km north of the Kemmel crossroads and approximately 6km south of Ieper. It is easy to miss as it is set behind a new wall below the level of the road.

Journey Time – 15 mins

C.W.G.C. Reference – 5/66

LANCASHIRE COTTAGE CEMETERY, PLOEGSTEERT *No. 72*

HISTORY
This cemetery was begun by the 1st East Lancashires, who have eighty-four graves here, and the 1st Hampshires, who have fifty-six, in November 1914 and remained in use until March 1916. A few later burials were made and the Germans created a cemetery nearby when they were here in 1918.

INFORMATION
You can see several farms, such as Hampshire Farm in the fields to the north, from here that were important in the War. In the fields to the south is Lawrence Farm, painted by Winston Churchill when he was a Lieutenant-Colonel commanding the 6th Royal Scots Fusiliers in the winter of 1915-16. Churchill, who was responsible for the Gallipoli campaign, had been forced to resign from the British Government after criticism of his plans. Recalled by the Prime Minister, Lloyd George, as Minister of Munitions in July 1917, he later became Prime Minister during World War II and again in the 1950's.

Approximately 1km east of the cemetery is the crossroads in Le Gheer, held by the 1st East Lancashires in November 1914 when, on the morning of 2 November, the Germans attacked killing all of the officers. Drummer Spencer John Bent took command winning the Victoria Cross by holding the line and halting the German advance. The crossroads was estimated to be the northern limit of the famous 'Christmas Truce' of 1914, called by the British headquarters the 'fraternization episode'.

North of Le Gheer is the small hamlet of Le Pelerin on the edge of Ploegsteert Wood. Of the mines laid for the start of the Battle of Messines on 6 June 1917, two did not explode. The one at Le Pelerin finally did so in 1955, thirty-eight years late to the month, when a tree was hit by lightening. No-one was hurt. The other mine may be in the area of, or under, the Mesen – Ploegsteert road in the valley of the Douve. I had a coach driver stop exactly above where it may be and then proceeded to tell all the children on the coach what was possibly under us. The driver pulled away with astounding speed to get his new coach moved once he realised what I had said.

UK – 229   Aust – 23   Can – 2   Unnamed – 5

Special Memorials to two men buried among the three British unnamed graves.

Area – 2541 sq yds

LOCATION
Lancashire Cottage Cemetery lies about 1.2km east of the town square in Ploegsteert, south of Ieper, and on the south side of the old road to Warneton.

Journey Time – 35 mins

C.W.G.C. Reference – 5/106

HISTORY

Opened in April 1915 by the 48th (South Midland) Division the cemetery remained in use until May 1918 when the Germans captured the valley during their Spring Offensive.

INFORMATION

Located next to the impressive farm from which it gets its name the cemetery has good views of the valley as well as of Hill 63 and the Mesen Ridge. It is possible to imagine the cavalry charges in the valley during the early parts of the War and also the importance of holding the ridge.

The two sizable farms, La Plus Douve and La Petite Douve, have both been rebuilt next to each other, La Plus Douve being the nearer to this cemetery. The farm was within the British lines for most of the War and was often used as a battalion headquarters. Hence, it was also known as Ration Farm because the battalion transport could only get this close to the front-lines at night with rations.

In November 1914 the German Guards Cavalry Corps were ordered to take the farm. However, two Companies of the 2nd Royal Inniskilling Fusiliers managed to hold the line with nothing more than rifles.

UK – 101	Aust – 86	NZ – 61	Can – 88
Ger – 9	Area – 3618 sq yds		

LOCATION

La Plus Douve Cemetery lies in the valley of the Douve about 8 km south of Ieper, south-west of Mesen and approximately 2 km south-east of Wulvergem. It is reached by means of a well signed farm track from the Mesen – Wulvergem road and is found on the edge of an attractive tree-lined avenue that leads south from the farm to Hill 63.

Journey Time – 40 mins

C.W.G.C. Reference – 5/116

LARCH WOOD (RAILWAY CUTTING) CEMETERY, ZILLEBEKE   *No. 74*

HISTORY

This cemetery was begun in a small plantation of larches in April 1915 and used until the German advance in April 1918. It was enlarged after the Armistice by the concentration of 250 graves from the battlefields of the Salient and some German cemeteries that have been removed.

INFORMATION

Approximately 150 m east of the Comines road and situated right next to the railway, the cemetery is entered by means of a path through shrubs, though the tranquility is regularly shattered by passing trains.

This cemetery was used particularly by the 46th (North Midland) Division and the 1st Dorsets, who served in the 5th Division until 1916 and then in the 32nd Division. Unusually, it contains the grave of a Canadian Merchant Seaman as well as Special Memorials to four British men and one Canadian buried in German cemeteries whose graves have been lost. One French and one Belgian grave have been removed. The tunnels in the wood were used as a battalion headquarters in 1917.

There are three features close to this cemetery that played a major role in the War. Two can be reached by continuing on the road to Comines for 700 m to the left turn to Zwarteleen and Hill 60.

THE CATERPILLAR: Now private land this feature can not be visited but with Hill 60, this was a key position and can be found on the north of the road west of the railway cutting. It seems insignificant today, but the slight rise here was enough of a feature on the landscape to be considered an important objective. Hence, many men died there.

On 6 November 1914 the line was held by the 1st Irish Guards, 2nd Grenadier Guards, 1st Royal Sussex and 1/1st Oxford and Bucks Light Infantry. They were losing the position when men of the 1st and 2nd Life Guards and the Royal Horse Guards (the Blues) arrived in support to turn the German advance by means of a cavalry charge led by General Moussy. The next day, Lord Cavan took the 4th (Guards) Brigade into action pushing the Germans to the south.

In 1915 the 1/5th Leicesters (138th Brigade, 46th

(North Midland) Division) held the line when on 23 June the Germans blew a mine killing many men. The day was only saved by the arrival of men from the same Brigade in the form of the 1/4th Leicesters.

For much of the winter of 1916 – 1917 the 47th (2nd London) Division held the trenches. On 15 February 1917 the 1/6th (London Rifles) Londons carried out one of the most successful raids on the Salient. Having staged a dummy attack the battalion, with sappers of the 520th Royal Engineers and Australian Tunnelling Company, raided German trenches almost unopposed, capturing an officer and 117 men with five machine-guns and a large amount of valuable documents.

HILL 60: This is also on the north of the road but it is on the east side of the railway. Hill 60 is preserved so that you can have access to one of the more infamous sites in the Salient. It is a strange feeling to stand on a small mound upon which so many men died and within which so many still lie, undiscovered and undisturbed.

Hill 60 was created at the end of the last century as a spoil heap dug from the railway cutting. It is not a real hill at all, and as such is a microcosm of the whole Salient, being somewhere at which the Generals decided they would make their stand, of little significance at the start of the War but it was to increase in importance as time passed.

The hill was captured on 10 December 1914 by the German 39th Division. Tunnelling to lay mines was begun almost immediately by the Monmouth Engineers and the task was completed by the new 171st Tunnelling Company. The mine blown at 7.00pm on 17 April 1915 used approximately 10,000lbs of explosive and killed over 150 soldiers including two men of the Royal Engineers. An infantry attack by the 1st Royal West Kents, 2nd King's Own Scottish Borderers and 1/9th (Queen Victoria's Rifles) Londons (all of the 13th Brigade, 5th Division) then suffered few casualties.

A counter-attack by the Germans at night inflicted heavy casualties forcing the British off the hill, though the next day, 18 April 1915, the 2nd Duke of Wellington's and 2nd King's Own Yorkshire Light Infantry, both of the 13th Brigade, took the hill in a new attack. The 15th Brigade relieved the 13th Brigade on 19 April, the 1st Norfolks, 1st Cheshires, 1st Bedfords and 1st Dorsets taking over the line with the 1/6th (Liverpool Rifles) King's in reserve. They repulsed a German attack with the help of the 1st East Surreys of the 14th Brigade, 5th Division.

During the attack Lieutenant (later Brigadier) George Roland Patrick Roupell, C.B., 1st East Surreys, won the Victoria Cross on 20 April for holding his post though wounded several times. On the same day Private (later Corporal) Edward Dwyer, also 1st East Surreys, a greengrocer's son from Fulham, aged 19, found himself alone in a trench attacked by Germans but managed to single-handedly hold the position. He was wounded on 27 April and awarded the Victoria Cross which he received from King George V on 28 June 1915. The spot at which he won the Cross is now the highest point on Hill 60. In the same battle Second Lieutenant (later Captain) Geoffrey Harold Woolley, O.B.E., M.C., of the 1/9th (Queen Victoria's Rifles) Londons became the first officer of a Territorial unit to be awarded the Victoria Cross when, at times during 20 and 21 April, he was the only officer remaining on Hill 60. Second Lieutenant (later Major) Benjamin Handley Geary attached to the 1st East Surreys was awarded the Victoria Cross during the same action for conspicuous bravery.

The hill remained in British hands while the Germans were busy with their gas attack in the north and east of the Salient but they then brought gas here on 1 May 1915. The 1st Devons, 1st Bedfords, 1st Dorsets and 59th Field Company, Royal Engineers, suffered heavy losses but held the hill.

Another gas attack by the Germans was made on 5 May 1915 causing the 2nd Duke of Wellington's, 1st Bedfords and 1/6th King's to fall back from the hill. The 2nd King's Own Scottish Borderers and the 2nd King's Own Yorkshire Light Infantry tried to retake the hill but suffered very heavily. Hill 60 was now in German hands. In the struggle for possession of Hill 60 the 5th Division had lost 100 officers and 3,000 men.

Between the fall of Hill 60 and the first day of the Battle of Messines on 6 June 1917 fighting here went on above and below ground. New tunnels were dug which were finished by July 1916 though the British commanders did not use them to blow mines until June 1917 and, therefore, they had to be defended and protected from German tunnellers and infantry. This task fell consecutively to 175th, 3rd Canadian and 1st Australian Tunnelling Companies.

On 6 June 1917 the mines were blown as part of the start of the Battle of Messines. 125,000lbs of explosive was used to create a crater 60ft deep and 260ft across killing nearly 700 men. The 11th West Yorkshires and 12th Durham Light Infantry attacked the hill taking it with ease. Those Germans who survived the explosion were too dazed to fight. It must come as no surprise that Hill 60 became known as Mount Calvary or 'the blood soaked hill of death'.

There are a number of interesting features at Hill 60:-

1 – A German bunker.
2 – Memorial to the Queen Victoria's Rifles.
3 – Memorial to the 14th (Light) Division moved here from Railway Wood in 1978.
4 – Memorial to 1st Australian Tunnelling Company, this includes an account of the events here.
5 – Queen Victoria's Rifles Cafe and Museum.

PALLINGBEEK PARK: On the road to Comines and Hollebeke at the top of the rise 400m beyond the turn to Hill 60, are two single track roads between an avenue of trees leading south-west to the park. There is a large sign so it is difficult to miss. There is a cafe/restaurant, information centre and short walks amongst the woods. Many large and important trenches, such as International, Impudence and Imperial trenches, were situated in the area of the Park.

The longer walks lead, through the woods, along the disused canal. East is Lock 6 at the point where the canal meets the Hollebeke road. More interestingly, the walk to the west, ending at Spoilbank Cemetery, will take you through the front-lines at 'The Bluff' which saw much fighting throughout the War. (See 1st D.C.L.I. Cemetery) I have enjoyed the peace and tranquillity of the walks to reflect on the events on the Salient.

Concentrated in Larch Wood Cemetery:

America Crossroads German Cemetery, Wervik – named after a cabaret on the road to Kruiseeke. It contained five British men who fell in October 1914.
Bruges General Cemetery, St. Michel – it contained thirty-two British men and one Canadian Merchant seaman.
Eerneghem German Cemetery – a little east of the village which contained one Royal Flying Corps officer.
Ghistelles Churchyard – there was a German aerodrome near the village. The Germans used a Plot in the churchyard for burials which included two British men who fell in July 1917.
Groenenberg German Cemetery, Zandvoorde – on the south side of Shrewsbury Forest it contained four British soldiers who fell in February 1915.
Handzaeme German Cemetery – on the north side of the village. It contained two Canadian soldiers who fell in May 1915.
Ichtegem German Cemetery – a little west of the village. It contained two unidentified Royal Air Force officers.
Kortemark German Cemetery No. 1 – a little north-west of the village which contained two Royal Flying Corps officers.
Leffinghe German Cemetery – on the north side of the village. It contained one Royal Flying Corps officer killed in July 1917 and three unidentified British soldiers.
Markhove German Cemetery, Kortemark – it contained ten British soldiers and airmen who died in 1918.
Oudenburg Churchyard – it contained two British soldiers who fell in 1917.
Ten-Brielen Communal Cemetery German Extension – it contained six British soldiers who fell in 1914.
Thourout German Cemetery No. 2 – seven British soldiers and one Canadian serviceman were buried there.

Vladslo German Cemetery – situated near the church it contained two Royal Flying Corps officers killed in 1917.
Warneton Sud-et-Bas German Cemetery – it contained two British unidentified soldiers who fell in 1918.
Wervik Communal Cemetery and Extensions – on the Belgian side of the Lys. It contained sixty-two British and six Canadian men.
Wijnendale German Cemetery, Torhout – it contained two Royal Flying Corps and one Canadian Flying Corps men.
Zandvoorde German Cemetery – also known as De Voorstraat No. 49. It contained eleven British men who fell in 1914.

UK – 614	Aust – 35	Can – 86
BWI – 1	KUG – 33	Unnamed – 321

Special Memorials to eighty-one British men and one Australian known/believed to be buried among the unnamed.

Special Memorials to four British men and one Canadian whose graves have been lost.

Area – 3272 sq yds

LOCATION
Larch Wood Cemetery lies south-east of Ieper, 150m east of the road to Comines, next to the railway line, at the end of a farm track clearly marked by C.W.G.C. signs.

Journey Time – 15 mins

C.W.G.C. Reference – 5/49

HISTORY

This cemetery was made and used by the 29th Division in October 1918.

INFORMATION

I include this cemetery because I consider that with the fall of Ledegem the Salient had been broken. Ledegem was used throughout the War as a base for the Germans who had several hospitals located here. From October 1914 to September 1918 they buried over 2,400 men including thirty-four British soldiers in cemeteries in the town.

Ledegem was almost captured by the 10th (Prince of Wales's Own Royal) Hussars on 19 October 1914. As it was they met the large German force advancing on Ypres and had to retire. They and the 22nd Brigade had already taken the nearby village of Dadizele but were forced to withdraw with the 1st Royal Welsh Fusiliers suffering heavy casualties. It can be said that with the fall of Dadizele the Salient had begun to be shaped. Therefore, the beginning and the end of the Salient are both found within a very short distance of one another.

On 1 October 1918 Lieutenant Robert Vaughan Gorle of the 50th Brigade Royal Field Artillery led his unit in destroying the German guns in Ledegem for which he gained the Victoria Cross.

The village was taken on 14 October 1918 by the 9th (Scottish), and 29th Divisions, the 12th Royal Scots led the way into the village with the 2nd Leinsters close behind. Private Martin Moffat, of the 2nd Leinsters, gained a Victoria Cross for capturing 120 prisoners, while another Leinster, Sergeant (later Lieutenant) John O'Neal, won the Victoria Cross four days later after hearing of the death of his brother. Also involved in the attack on 14 October was Thomas Ricketts, D.C.M., of the 1st Royal Newfoundland Regiment, aged 15. King George V invested him as the youngest Victoria Cross in the Army for his efforts at Ledegem.

In the centre of Ledegem the Churchyard contains fourteen British graves of soldiers who fell in October 1914 and from September to October 1918. One grave was destroyed by shell-fire and is represented by a Special Memorial.

Dadizele contains two cemeteries. The Communal

Cemetery contains twenty-seven British men, mostly of the 36th (Ulster) Division. There are also the graves of two German soldiers though approximately 100 German graves have been removed. Dadizele New British Cemetery was made after the Armistice with the concentration of graves from the battlefields in this area. Most of these men served in the 9th, 35th and 36th Divisions. The New British Cemetery now contains 998 British, twenty Newfoundland and one Canadian graves. In the cemetery there are Special Memorials to seven British men who are believed to be buried among the 158 unnamed graves, and to three British men buried in German cemeteries whose graves have been lost. There are also the graves of two men who fell in 1940.

UK – 65   Unnamed – 14

Special Memorials to two British men believed to be buried among the unnamed.

Area – 259 sq yds

LOCATION

The cemeteries are in the centre of each village which are clearly signed from the Menen – Roeselare road about 20 km east of Ieper.

Journey Time – 50 mins

C.W.G.C. Reference – 6/8

LE TOUQUET RAILWAY CROSSING CEMETERY, *No. 76*
WARNETON

HISTORY

The cemetery was in use for much of the War from October 1914 until June 1918.

INFORMATION

This graveyard was begun near the point where the

railway used to cross the road to Le Bizet and includes twenty-eight graves of men of the 1st Rifle Brigade who fell in October and November 1914.

The 2nd Lancashire Fusiliers were in the line to the east of the cemetery during the Christmas Day Truce in 1914. A German messenger who crossed no man's land under a white flag was kept as a Prisoner of War as he had seen behind the British lines and therefore could not be allowed to return.

On 10 February 1918 a trench raid was launched at Warneton by 204 men of the 3rd Australian Division which took thirty-three prisoners. Like all things in the War the statistics had grown larger as time passed.

There are several cemeteries in this area that contain the graves of men who fell in World War II. These are:

1) Frelinghien Communal Cemetery – near the centre of the village. It contains six men who fell in May 1940.
2) Bas-Warneton Communal Cemetery – on the edge of the village behind a new housing estate. It contains fifty-three British men who fell in May and June 1940.
3) Comines Communal Cemetery – the cemetery is on the old road from Bas-Warneton to Comines about 200m from Comines town square. The graves of 100 British men who fell in May and June 1940 are by the entrance.

UK – 71   KUG – 21

Special Memorials to three men known to be buried here.

Area – 1040 sq yds

LOCATION
Le Touquet Cemetery is found south of Ieper about 4km south-east of Ploegsteert. 1.4km south of the square in Ploegteert you can find on the east side of the road, near a supermarket, a tree of C.W.G.C. signs on the corner. The road to the left and then the tree-lined avenue to the right will take you past Motor Car Corner Cemetery to a junction at which you turn left before passing Tancrez Farm Cemetery and factories. As you reach the flyover the cemetery is on the north side of the old road.

Journey Time – 40 mins

C.W.G.C. Reference – 5/108

LIJSSENTHOEK MILITARY CEMETERY, POPERINGE   *No. 77*

HISTORY
The cemetery was begun in 1914 by the French who had a Casualty Clearing Station, the 15th Hopital d'Evacuation, at Remi Farm on the boundary of the cemetery near the new road. Therefore, the earliest burials here are of French 'Poilu'.

The British began to use Lijssenthoek Cemetery in June 1915 and by the time of the Armistice it had become the largest cemetery in the Salient, though that dubious honour now belongs to Tyne Cot. Some graves were concentrated here after the War.

INFORMATION
Despite its size I still find this one of my favourite cemeteries in the Salient and one that I try to get to on each visit to Ypres.

Remi Farm still exists much as it was in the War. In the great barn the graffiti inscribed by French and British soldiers waiting for treatment at the Casualty Clearing Stations can still be seen. However, ask permission of the farmer, it is his property!

The cemetery lay outside the range of even the largest German guns for most of the War, except during the Battles of the Lys in 1918, which explains how it became so large. It served the many Casualty

Clearing Stations and hospitals in the area and the fallen from many countries were buried here. Hence, there are French, German, Chinese, Algerian graves and the only American men to still lie buried on the Salient. These are a Sergeant and Private from New York and a Lieutenant from Tennessee buried in the semi-circle of graves near the War Stone. However, forty-seven of their countrymen have been removed.

The last British officer to fall in the Salient, Lieutenant-Colonel George Ernest Beaty-Pownall, D.S.O., of the 2nd Borders (20th Brigade, 7th Division) is buried here. He died of wounds on 10 October 1918, aged 41, and is buried with his men who fell in September and October 1918. One I.W.G.C. worker is also buried here.

Among the men from many nations buried here one suffered a dishonourable death under the terms of the British Army Act. Private William Baker of the 26th (Bankers) Royal Fusiliers (124th Brigade, 41st Division) was executed in Poperinge on 14 August 1918 as the result of several desertions during the German Spring Offensive. Unusually, he was not buried in Poperinge New Military Cemetery with seventeen other executed men.

There is a large nursery garden for the C.W.G.C. that can be seen and visited but again, ask first. In spring the flower beds are very attractive. This is far preferable to the three inches of snow under which I have also seen it.

V.C. – Lieutenant (later Major) Frederick Harold
    Tubb, V.C..
    7th Battalion (Victoria), Australian
    Imperial Force, 2nd Australian Brigade, 1st
    Australian Division.
    From St Helena, Victoria, Australia.
    Died of Wounds – 20 September 1917.
    Won – at Lone Pine Trenches, Gallipoli in
    repulsing a German attack during which he
    was wounded in the head and arm on 9
    August 1915.

UK – 7350	Aust – 1131	NZ – 291	Can – 1053
NF – 5	S Afr – 29	BWI – 21	India – 2
KUG – 3	Fr – 658	US – 3	IWGC – 1
Chinese Labour Corps – 3		Ger – 223	

LOCATION
Lijssenthoek Cemetery is south-west of Ieper and about 2 km south of the Poperinge by-pass. It is just west of the new road to Steenvoorde from which it is clearly signed.

Journey Time – 30 mins

C.W.G.C. Reference – 5/40

LINDENHOEK CHALET MILITARY CEMETERY, KEMMEL   *No. 78*

HISTORY
Begun in March 1915 as British units came to this part of the Salient, the cemetery remained in use until October 1917. It was enlarged after the Armistice with the concentration of 130 graves.

INFORMATION
A new chalet is now opposite the cemetery on the site of the old one which was destroyed in the fighting in 1918 when the Germans took the hill at great cost to both sides. The Kemmelberg was then shelled almost constantly until the Allied advance in the autumn.
The Battle Book of Ypres, page 110, tells us that in November 1914 a Battery of the 5th Division Royal Field Artillery was in reserve on the west side of the Kemmelberg when a Major stationed on the Lindenhoek – Wijtschate road called for their assistance. The subaltern in command of the Battery decided that the situation was so urgent that he should take his guns over the hill and down the slopes through the point of this cemetery. He helped the Division to hold the line by his actions.
   In my opinion, one of the best Youth Hostels on the Salient, the Centre de Lork, is situated nearby on the slopes of the Kemmelberg.

UK – 282	Aust – 10	NZ – 8
Can – 15	Ger – 2	Unnamed – 67

Special Memorials to four Australians and two

British men known/believed to be buried among the unnamed.

Area – 1410 sq mts

LOCATION
Lindenhoek Chalet Cemetery can be found about 1 km south of Kemmel, south of Ieper, on the eastern slope of the Kemmelberg. It lies 200 m west of the road from Kemmel to Nieuwkerke from which it is clearly signed.

Journey Time – 30 mins

C.W.G.C. Reference – 5/80

HISTORY
The churchyard was used by the British from December 1914 until June 1917.

INFORMATION
The graves are in two Plots one on either side of the church. An interesting feature of the churchyard is that three men buried here were executed by the British Army within a ten-day period in early 1915 and yet the churchyard was never again used for the burial of executed men. Privates Andrew Evans and Joseph Byers, aged 16, both of the 1st Royal Scots Fusiliers (9th Brigade, 3rd Division) were tried for desertion on 31 January and then executed together in the village on 6 February 1915. They are buried side by side near the entrance to the Plot on the west side of the church. In the next row lies Private George E. Collins of the 1st Lincolns, also of the 9th Brigade, who was executed in the village for desertion on 15 February 1915.

The village was in British hands for most of the War. In November 1914 the 1st Grenadier Guards were sent to rest here after defending Ypres. The battalion was by this time only a company strong under the command of a Captain. The 2nd Scots Guards, a Captain and sixty-nine men, joined them.

Loker was at the limit of the German advance during their Spring Offensive in 1918 though they failed to take all of the village. The British 21st, 25th and 49th (West Riding) Divisions were supporting the French in defending Loker and, though the Germans occupied part of the settlement for one day on 25 April, it was retaken by the French on 26 April. The Germans entered Loker again on 29 April but were forced out by the French on 30 April. During the course of this battle the village was completely destroyed.

The 84th Battery, Royal Field Artillery was stationed above the village on the Rodeberg during April 1918 manned by one officer and several cooks. The guns had to be abandoned but in the evening teams of artillerymen rescued them by moving them off the hill in the direction of Loker, directly in front of the enemy lines. The Germans were too shocked by this boldness to fire upon the British soldiers.

There are three Memorials to French units involved in the fighting here in 1918. They were formerly on the walls of the Town Hall opposite the church but have been moved and are now on one stone at the south corner of the churchyard near the town War Memorial at the junction with the Kemmel road. The Memorials are to the 2nd Brigade of Cavalerie Legere (Light Cavalry) Francaise (17th and 18th Cavalry); 4th and 12th Regiments of French Dragoons; and the 23rd Regiment of French Infantry.

UK – 184	Can – 31	Unnamed – 2

Area – 1887 sq yds

LOCATION
Locre Church is in the centre of the village on the north side of the main road. Loker is south of Ieper and is reached most easily by the N375.

Journey Time – 30 mins

C.W.G.C. Reference – 5/70

HISTORY
Begun at the start of the Battle of Messines in June 1917, the cemetery remained in use until April 1918. Four graves were brought here after the Armistice from the garden of Loker Convent.

INFORMATION
The cemetery lies in fields about 100m from the Hospice, which was the scene of bitter fighting in 1918. It fell to the Germans in April and was only retaken in July despite a concentrated attack upon it by the French on 20 May 1918. This imposing building, still in use as School, Convent and Hospice, is hard to miss from most roads in the area of Loker, so that if you can reach the Hospice you can see the cemetery.

There are two men buried here who were executed by the British Army. Private Denis Jetson Blakemore of the 8th North Staffordshires (57th Brigade, 19th (Western) Division) deserted from the trenches near Wijtschate on the eve of the Battle of Messines. This was his second offence. He was shot on the Kemmelberg on 9 July 1917. Private William Jones of the 9th Royal Welsh Fusiliers (58th Brigade, 19th Division) was the last deserter to escape across the Channel to the United Kingdom. He absconded on 5 June 1917 and surrendered in Bristol on 4 September. He was shot at the same place as Private Blakemore on 25 October 1917.

Buried just outside the walls of the cemetery is Major William Hoey Kearney Redmond of the 6th Royal Irish Regiment. He was wounded in the attack by the II Corps at Wijtschate on 6 June 1917, and was taken to the 36th (Ulster) Division Dressing Station at Dranouter where he died. His body was then moved to the 16th (Irish) Division base at Loker Hospice and buried in the garden in a grave just beyond the walls of the Convent. A Southern Irishmen, one of the very few to fight with the 36th Division, he was a Nationalist M.P. for Ireland who believed firmly in a United Ireland. Beyond the fighting age he had persuaded his commander to let him go to the front where he was killed. His grave is beneath a Memorial Cross and can be reached by a path from the cemetery entrance.

| UK – 238 | Aust – 2 | NZ – 1 | Can – 1 |
| BWI – 1 | Ger – 2 | | Unnamed – 12 |

Special Memorials to ten men whose graves have been destroyed by shell-fire.

Area – 1018 sq yds

LOCATION
Loker Hospice Cemetery lies in fields on the southwest edge of the village, south of Ieper. A road from the east corner of the church in the centre of the village leads past the Hospice to a small single building on the south side of the road. A C.W.G.C. path leads from the building to the cemetery 50 m from the road. It is a pleasant stroll from Loker church to the cemetery, but as you walk remember that you are traversing the front-line positions of 1918 where many men died.

Journey Time – 30 mins

C.W.G.C. Reference – 5/74

LOCRE No. 10 CEMETERY, LOKER   *No. 81*

HISTORY
This was one of several cemeteries made in the area by the French during the German offensive in April 1918. It was taken over by the British after the Armistice when the French graves were removed and British and German graves from the battlefields nearby were concentrated here.

INFORMATION
The British graves are mainly of men of the 2/14th (2nd London Scottish) Londons, 2/16th (2nd Queen's Westminsters) Londons and 2nd South Lancashires, all part of the 89th Brigade, 30th Division at the end of the War after they had been transferred from other Divisions. The 248 French graves were removed and the Germans are in a mass grave at the west end of the cemetery.

John Laffin in *On the Western Front*, page 33 tells of the following event. In late 1914 Captain W. G. Padstow was travelling in a Staff car past this cemetery in heavy rain when he came upon a convoy of trucks that soon came to a stop. They were facing a unit of French cavalry still dressed in their bright blue uniforms with metal breast-plates who also refused to leave the narrow road. The Army Service Corps Sergeant shouted at the French Cuirassier who then gave way – a shining example of British diplomacy!

| UK – 55 | Unnamed – 14 | Ger – 150 |

Area – 871 sq yds

Loker No. 10 Cemetery lies south of Loker, south-west of Ieper, on the south side of the Loker – Dranouter road, about 1 km from Loker church.

Journey Time – 35 mins

C.W.G.C. Reference – 5/77

LONDON RIFLE BRIGADE CEMETERY, PLOEGSTEERT   *No. 82*

HISTORY
Begun by the 4th Division in December 1914, the cemetery remained in use until it fell into German hands in March 1918. It was used by the Germans in April and May 1918 before the British took over the graveyard again in October.

INFORMATION
The cemetery acquired its name when twenty-two men of the London Rifle Brigade were buried here in the early months of 1915. A group of them are buried near to the Cross of Sacrifice.

Lieutenant-General Sir H. F. M. Wilson unveiled a tablet on the wall at the north corner of the cemetery, in June 1927. The plaque commemorates the dedication of the cemetery, on Easter Day 1915, by the Bishop of London and is in memory of the ninety-one officers and 1,831 men of the London Rifle Brigade who fell in the War.

UK – 263	Aust – 38	NZ – 34	Ger – 18
Unnamed – 1	Area – 2196 sq yds		

LOCATION
London Rifle Brigade Cemetery is situated 500 m south of the square in Ploegsteert, south of Ieper, on the west side of the road to Armentieres.

Journey Time – 35 mins

C.W.G.C. Reference – 5/105

LONE TREE CEMETERY, SPANBROEKMOLEN,   *No. 83*
WIJTSCHATE

HISTORY
Nearly all the graves in this cemetery are of men who fell on the first day of the Battle of Messines, 7 June 1917.

INFORMATION
This cemetery lies in what was formerly no man's land next to the German line that ran through the farm and along the edge of the Pool of Peace. The Royal Irish Rifles of the 36th (Ulster) Division, who fought in this area on the first day of the Battle of Messines, have sixty men buried here.

The Spanbroekmolen mine that formed the nearby crater was placed by 171st Tunnelling Company of the Royal Engineers. It was blown at 3.10 am, with eighteen others, signalling the start of the British offensive in Flanders in 1917. The 36th (Ulster) Division had been rebuilt from its near annihilation on the first day of the Battle of the Somme nearly twelve months before and now contained nine battalions of Royal Irish Rifles who attacked in an easterly direction through the site of this cemetery making rapid progress and taking the Wijtschate – Mesen road. Some of the men buried in this cemetery were killed by the fall-out of the Spanbroekmolen mine which exploded fifteen seconds late, by which time the 8th (East Belfast) Royal Irish Rifles were already in no man's land. The 36th Division was positioned next to the 16th (Irish) Division, the first time that men from the north and south of Ireland had fought together.

All you can see from the road of the crater is a raised copse and mound of earth, but enter the gate, climb the steps and the largest crater blown on 7 June 1917, made by 91,000 lbs of explosive, comes into view. It was called Lone Tree Crater and was bought by Lord Wakefield for the Toc H organisation who have preserved it as a Pool of Peace. A solemn place, but pleasant in summer, the site is potentially muddy, and therefore dangerous, particularly in wet weather as the pool is 27 m deep with a high rim. A path exists so that you can walk round the copse.

This position had seen action before 1917. On 30 April 1916 the Germans had used gas on a front from St. Eloi to Mesen. The 10th Royal Welsh Fusiliers (76th Brigade, 3rd Division), were located here. The attack had limited success.

UK – 88   KUG – 6   Area – 737 sq yds

LOCATION
Lone Tree Cemetery is found in open fields, south of

Ieper, about 2.5 km south-west of Wijtschate, and approximately 600 m south of the Wijtschate – Kemmel road. The side road to the cemetery is signposted. There is parking space at the Pool of Peace from which you can walk the short distance to the cemetery. Take care to remember to close and secure all gates as you pass through the farmer's field.

Journey Time – 30 mins

C.W.G.C. Reference – 5/84

MAPLE COPSE CEMETERY, ZILLEBEKE   *No. 84*

HISTORY
Burials in this cemetery took place mostly in 1916, but particularly during the Battle of Mount Sorrell in June.

INFORMATION
This is one of the prettiest cemeteries on the Salient, lying below the level of the road in a quiet copse. The importance of Hill 62 becomes clear when you stand within the grounds.

This cemetery was associated with the Advanced Dressing Stations located in this copse close to Sanctuary Wood and Hill 62. Most of the graves were destroyed so that of the 256 men known to be buried here, only twenty-six could be identified, and located, when the cemetery was officially created at the end of the War.

On 7 November 1914 the 1st Gloucesters, 2nd Queen's and 1st South Staffordshires attacked from here south and east towards Armagh Wood across the road from Zillebeke. The Staffordshires were led by Captain John Franks Vallentin, who had insisted on rejoining them from hospital in Ypres, and was then killed in leading the successful attack. He won the Victoria Cross and is commemorated on the Menin Gate.

Another Victoria Cross was won close by by Sergeant John Carmichael, M.M., of the 9th North Staffordshires on 8 September 1917 who tried to protect his men from a German grenade by standing on his helmet placed over the grenade. He was severely injured but survived.

UK – 114 Can – 142 Unnamed – 40 UK and 12 Can

Special Memorials to 230 men known to be buried here.

Area – 4881 sq mts

LOCATION
Maple Copse Cemetery can be found east of Ieper, about 2 km east of Zillebeke, and 2 km south of the Menen Road. There are C.W.G.C. signs from Zillebeke.

Journey Time – 15 mins

C.W.G.C. Reference – 5/113

MAPLE LEAF CEMETERY, LE ROMARIN, NIEUWKERKE *No. 85*

HISTORY
This cemetery was begun in December 1914 and used until December 1917 for British burials. Nine German graves were made here in April 1918 when this village was in German hands.

INFORMATION
The small cemetery has pleasant views of the valley of the Lys though the immediate area of the burial ground could be improved. The 3rd Canadian Field Ambulance Advanced Dressing Station was stationed here from July 1915 to April 1916 when the cemetery gained its present name.

Private Albert Parry of the 2nd West Yorkshires (23rd Brigade, 8th Division) was executed nearby for desertion and buried here on 30 August 1917.

UK – 80	Aust – 4	NZ – 43	Can – 39
S Afr – 1	Ger – 9		Area – 1295 sq yds

LOCATION
Maple Leaf Cemetery lies on the French border south of Ieper and about 3 km south-east of Nieuwkerke in the small hamlet of Le Romarin which is at the point of a sharp bend on the Nieuwkerke – Ploegsteert road. The cemetery is behind the cafe in Le Romarin. If you cross the border, marked by the large speed limits sign, then you have missed the turn for the cemetery.

Journey Time – 55 mins

C.W.G.C. Reference – 5/101

MENDINGHEM BRITISH CEMETERY, PROVEN *No. 86*

HISTORY
Begun in June 1916 when the 46th (1/1st Wessex) Casualty Clearing Station was located here, the first burials did not take place until August 1916, and the cemetery then remained in use until September 1918. The ironic name was given to the cemetery by the soldiers who were treated in the Dressing Stations here. The name humourously plays upon the Flemish language to describe the function of the Casualty Clearing Stations.

INFORMATION
No. 46 Casualty Clearing Station had 200 beds but this was increased to 1,300 in preparation for the Third Battle of Ypres. After a German gas attack on 12 July 1917 the Casualty Clearing Station took more than 100 casualties for treatment over the next few days even though it was trying to clear the beds for the coming battle. Four more Casualty Clearing Stations were stationed at Proven when the cemetery gained its present name along with those known

as Bandaghem and Dozinghem. One of the Clearing Stations, No. 61, was staffed by Americans from Philadelphia. Three others, No.'s 12, 46 and 64, remained in the area until 1918.

Some French burials were made from May to July 1918 in an area that had been set aside for them since this cemetery had been created. These have since been removed.

There are three men buried here who were executed by the British Army. Private John J. Hyde of the 10th King's Royal Rifle Corps (59th Brigade, 20th (Light) Division) was shot for desertion on 5 September 1917. Private Charles Britton of the 1/5th Royal Warwickshires (143rd Brigade, 48th (South Midlands) Division) had deserted at the start of the British Flanders Offensive in 1917 and was arrested while his battalion were fighting on the first day of the Battle of Langemark. He was executed on 12 September 1917. Private David Gibson of the 12th Royal Scots (27th Brigade, 9th (Scottish) Division) had failed to return from leave and was arrested in the United Kingdom. He was executed on 24 September 1918.

The nearby village of Proven was one of the main railheads for the Salient during the preparations for the Flanders Offensive. Troops massed in the fields near the village for the assault including one, detailed below, who gained the Victoria Cross and died in a Casualty Clearing Station at Mendinghem.

In Proven churchyard, on the Alexisplein, three British and one Canadian graves dating from 1915 and 1916, were removed to Cement House Cemetery in August 1916. Now there remain five World War II graves made in late May 1940.

V.C. – Captain (temporary Lieutenant-Colonel)
    Bertram Best-Dunkley, V.C..
    Commanding Officer, 2/5th Lancashire
    Fusiliers, 164th Brigade, 55th (West
    Lancashire) Division.
    Died of Wounds 5 August 1917.

Won – 31 July 1917. In the attack his battalion became disorganised so he went forward and rallied his men to take their objectives. The Fusiliers sustained heavy losses but his leadership helped the battalion to succeed. In the evening he took the battalion headquarters into battle to defeat a German counter-attack during which he was mortally wounded.

UK – 2272	Aust – 15	NZ – 12	Can – 28
NF – 3	S Afr – 33	BWI – 26	Ger – 51
Chinese Labour Corps – 8		Area – 7589 sq yds	

LOCATION
Mendinghem Cemetery can be found 150 m west of the N308 from Poperinge to Roesbrugge, west of Ieper, approximately 8 km north-west of Poperinge and on the northern outskirts of Proven. A track leads from the N308 to the cemetery which is next to a private house.

Journey Time – 35 mins

C.W.G.C. Reference – 4/16

MENIN GATE MEMORIAL, IEPER   *No. 87*

HISTORY
During the War there was no gate on this site, just two carved lions, one on either side of the road. The gate was designed by Sir Reginald Blomfield (who designed many of the cemeteries for the I.W.G.C.) and was inaugurated by Field Marshal Plumer (q.v.) on 24 July 1927.

INFORMATION
I accept that this is not a cemetery in the true sense, but it is the last resting place for the names of many of the men who died on the Salient. Other Memorials are included elsewhere in this book as they are part of cemeteries, but as this is one of the most important places of remembrance on the Salient I feel that it deserves separate inclusion.

The I.W.G.C. decided that four Memorials would be set up to commemorate those who had fallen on the Salient and who had no known graves. There were about 40,000 unnamed graves in cemeteries in the area, a further 50,000 bodies had simply disappeared. These 90,000 men needed suitable Monuments.

New Zealand troops were to be included at Tyne Cot or on Memorials at Messines Ridge and Buttes New Cemeteries. All other men of the Empire and its Dominions were to be inscribed on the Memorials at Tyne Cot or here. The Menin Gate was a logical place for a Memorial as many of the men whose names are upon it would have passed through the gate on the way to the trenches.

It bears the names, engraved on panels of Portland Stone, of nearly 55,000 officers and men who were killed, and have no known grave, between the start of the War and the night of 15 August 1917 when the Battle of Langemark began. Those who were lost after that date are listed on the Tyne Cot Memorial. Above the central arches of the Menin Gate can be found a lion facing out to the front-lines, and facing the town a sarcophagus with a flag and wreath.

Among the many names on the Memorial are those of three men who were executed by the British Army but whose graves have since been lost. For Private William Scotton please refer to Suffolk Cemetery and for Corporal George H. Povey please refer to Wulvergem Churchyard. The third, Driver Thomas Moore of No. 197 Company, Army Service Corps, was executed on 26 February 1916 at Busseboom, south-east of Poperinge. He had murdered Sergeant James Pick of his unit on 11 February 1916 while in camp near Busseboom. Pick is now buried in Poperinge New Military Cemetery where the largest group of executed soldiers to be buried in any cemetery on the Western Front can also be found.

The Memorial is on the site of the old Hangoart or Antwerp Gate. On either side of it are well kept gardens which you can reach by the steps leading from the road. It is possible to walk along the old ramparts to the Lille Gate about 800m away. The ramparts were built, upon the original fortifications dating from the Twelth Century, by Vauban who was the military architect for the French King, Louis XIV.

The casements beneath the ramparts were some of the safest places in Ypres during the War as not even the heaviest German guns could cause serious damage. They were almost the only thing standing in Ypres at the Armistice. The 'Wipers Times' was printed in one of the casements while others were used as bedrooms, a signal headquarters, cinema and hospital.

On the evening of the inauguration of the Gate the Last Post was sounded by buglers from the Somerset Light Infantry, and the Ypres Fire Brigade then took over the task. With the exception of the period of German occupation in World War II the Ceremony has taken place at 8.00pm each evening, the Last Post being sounded by between one and six men of the Ypres Fire Brigade using bugles provided by the Royal British Legion.

This is a very emotional ceremony and can affect young and old alike. I claim this based upon years of attending the ceremony with a wide range of companions. I have seen school children, a company of soldiers and my parents, both ex-Royal Navy, affected by the simple ceremony. I would suggest strongly that on some evening during your visit you attend and take part in the experience.

There are seven men who won the Victoria Cross in World War I, and one other holder of the award, commemorated on the Menin Gate:

Lance-Corporal Frederick Fisher, V.C..
13th Battalion, Quebec Regiment (Royal Highlanders of Canada), 3rd Canadian Brigade, 1st Canadian Division, Canadian Expeditionary Force.
Won – St. Juliaan, 23 April 1915.
Died – 24 April 1915.

Company Sergeant-Major F. W. Hall, V.C..
8th Battalion, Manitoba Regiment, 2nd Canadian Brigade, 1st Canadian Division, Canadian Expeditionary Force.
Won – Ypres, 24 April 1915.
Died – 25 April 1915.

Second Lieutenant Dennis George Wyldbore Hewitt, V.C..
2nd Hampshire Regiment attached 14th (1st Portsmouth Pals) Hampshire Regiment, 116th Brigade, 39th Division.
Won – Ypres, 31 July 1917.
Died – 31 July 1917.

Lieutenant Hugh McKenzie, D.C.M., V.C..
7th Company, Canadian Machine Gun Corps, 7th Canadian Brigade, 3rd Canadian Division, Canadian Expeditionary Force.
Won – Passendale, 30 October 1917.
Died – 30 October 1917.

Captain John Franks Vallentin, V.C..
1st South Staffordshire Regiment, 22nd Brigade, 7th Division.
Won – Zillebeke, 7 November 1914.
Died – 7 November 1914.

Private Edward Warner, V.C..
1st Bedfordshire Regiment, 15th Brigade, 5th Division.
Won – Hill 60, 1 May 1915.
Died – 2 May 1915.

Second Lieutenant Sidney Clayton Woodroffe, V.C..
8th Rifle Brigade (The Prince Consort's Own), attached 2nd Rifle Brigade, 41st Brigade, 14th (Light) Division.
Won – Hooge, 30 July 1915.
Died – 30 July 1915.

Captain (later Brigadier-General) Charles Fitzclarence, V.C..
Staff (Late of the Royal Fusiliers and Irish Guards), Commanding 1st Brigade, 1st Division.
Won – South Africa, 1899.
Died – 12 November 1914.

UK – 40244	Aust – 6198	Can – 6983
S Afr – 564	BWI – 6	India – 421

LOCATION
The simplest way to get to the Gate is to walk from the town square. Leave by the eastern exit diagonally opposite the Cloth Hall and tourist office and you can see the Memorial from the square.

Journey Time – 2 mins

C.W.G.C. Reference – 5/32

MENIN ROAD SOUTH MILITARY CEMETERY, IEPER   *No. 88*

HISTORY

Opened in January 1916 the cemetery remained in use until the summer of 1918. It was enlarged after the Armistice with the concentration of 200 graves from the Menin Road North Cemetery and isolated locations in the battlefields nearby.

INFORMATION

This cemetery was always within the British lines though during the German advance in April 1918 it came close to the front-line. The 8th South Staffordshires (51st Brigade, 17th (Northern) Division) and 9th East Surreys (72nd Brigade, 24th Division) had begun this cemetery.

By September 1918 the line south of here was just a series of posts held by the 29th Division, as the trenches had been destroyed.

V.C. – Second Lieutenant (acting Captain) Thomas Riversdale Colyer-Fergusson, V.C..
2nd Northamptonshire Regiment, 24th Brigade, 8th Division.
From Sevenoaks, Kent.
Died – 31 July 1917. Age 21.
Won – 31 July 1917 at Bellewaerde. In the attack by the 8th Division from Sanctuary Wood his battalion could not keep to their plan encountering problems with the ground and the enemy wire. With a Sergeant and five men he continued the attack capturing enemy trenches and killing many Germans. Colyer-Fergusson then resisted a counter-attack capturing a German machine-gun. Later he attacked again with his Sergeant and captured a second machine-gun before being joined by his men who consolidated the position. Captain Colyer-Fergusson was killed soon after by a sniper.

Concentrated here:

Menin Road North Cemetery, Ypres – on the north

side of the Menen Road opposite this cemetery. It was used mainly from May 1915 to August 1916 but also in 1917 and 1918. It contained 130 British men, three Canadians and three Newfoundlanders.

UK – 1051   Aust – 263   NZ – 52   Can – 145
BWI – 3   Ger – 1   KUG – 65   Unnamed – 121

Special Memorials to twenty British men and four Australians known/believed to be buried among the unnamed.

Special Memorials to fifty-two British men and three Newfoundlanders buried in Menin Road North Cemetery whose graves were destroyed by shell-fire.

Area – 7589 sq yds

LOCATION

Menin Road South Cemetery is situated in the western suburbs of Ieper, on the south side of the Menen Road 100m from the junction with the southern ring road.

Journey Time – 5 mins

C.W.G.C. Reference – 5/35

HISTORY
This cemetery was created after the Armistice with the concentration of graves from the battlefields of Mesen.

INFORMATION
The importance of holding the Mesen Ridge is clear when you visit this cemetery, you can see how it dominates the plain below and how difficult it must have been to attack. The entrance to the area is guarded by the New Zealand Memorial to the 840 missing of the battles in the south of the Salient. A pavilion in the cemetery is like that at Buttes New Cemetery, where there is another New Zealand Memorial. A system of bunkers and tunnels bore the name of the Institution Royale, to which the ground used to belong and the Cross of Sacrifice is on the site of the Institution's windmill.

On route to Mesen you may have passed the Memorial to the 1/14th (London Scottish) Londons 800m north of the crossroads in Mesen. They were the first full Territorial battalion to see action in the Salient when they were rushed to Wijtschate in London buses and were then thrown into action on the Mesen Ridge north of the village during the First Battle of Ypres at the end of October 1914.

Another Monument to the men from New Zealand who fought in the battles at Mesen can be found west of the road to Ploegsteert, in the New Zealand Park. South of the village, it was unveiled by King Albert on 1 August 1924, and is now the location of a service of remembrance on A.N.Z.A.C. Day, 25th April. The park has an obelisk, two German bunkers and a good view west from the ridge.

Mesen saw much fighting throughout the War. On 31 October 1914 the German 26th Division attacked the village. The 9th (Queen's Royal) Lancers, 2nd Royal Inniskilling Fusiliers, and 57th (Wilde's) Rifles of the Indian Army were forced to pull back to the ridge forming a new line through the village. This was held by the 10th (Prince of Wales's Own Royal) and 11th (Prince Albert's Own) Hussars, 2nd (Queen's Bays), 4th (Royal Irish) and 5th (Princess Charlotte of Wales's) Dragoon Guards. These units were reinforced, after a new German attack, by the battle-weary and depleted 2nd King's Own Yorkshire Light Infantry and 2nd King's Own Scottish Borderers who launched a counter-attack in which the London Scottish were deployed, but the tired and outnumbered force failed.

Mesen fell to the Germans on 1 November 1914. As French troops failed to recapture it on 6 and 7 November 1914 the village was abandoned to the Germans until 1917. It was captured by troops of the New Zealand Division on 6 June, the first day of the Battle of Messines.

The Germans took the village and the ridge during their offensive in 1918 when it fell on 10-11 April after a stubborn defence by the South African Brigade. The British over-ran Mesen for the last time on 28 to 29 September 1918 when it was attacked by the 34th Division.

There were four German cemeteries made at Mesen after the Armistice but these have been removed.

Concentrated here:

Bell Farm Cemetery, Wijtschate – by the side of the road leading to Spanbroekmolen from opposite this cemetery. It contained thirty-two British men of the 25th Division who fell in June 1917.

Blauwepoortebeek Cemetery, Wijtschate – north-east of Mesen. It contained seven British graves and sixteen Australians who were buried from August to October 1917.

Bousbecques East German Cemetery – on south side of a village in France. It contained four British men who were buried by a German Field Hospital in November 1914.

Bristol Castle Military Cemetery, Mesen – on the Mesen – Wulvergem road near Wulvergem. It contained thirty-two British men of the 36th (Ulster) and 14th (Light) Divisions who fell in September and October 1918.

Lumm Farm Cemetery, Wijtschate – a little east of the Mesen road. It contained thirteen British graves and two Australians who died in June to September 1917.

Middle Farm Cemetery, Wijtschate – near the road to Wijtschate, 450m north of Mesen. It contained fourteen British, sixteen Australian and four New Zealand graves made from July to December 1917.

Onraet Farm Cemetery, Wijtschate – 400m north of the crossroads at the turn to Somer Farm Cemetery on the road to St. Eloi. It contained twenty-nine British men of the 36th (Ulster) Division buried during June to August 1917.

Queensland Cemetery, Warneton – on the road from Mesen to Warneton. It contained three British graves and thirty Australians who fell in June and July 1917.

River Douve Cemetery, Mesen – also called Snitchel Farm, on the river bank south of Mesen. It contained four British men and twenty-four Australians who fell from June to November 1917.

UK – 986   Aust – 332   NZ – 115   Can – 1
S Afr – 56   KUG – 1   Unnamed – 954 (65% of total)

Special Memorials to four British, ten Australian, thirteen New Zealand and one South African men known/believed to be buried among the unnamed.

Special Memorials to thirteen British men buried in other cemeteries whose graves were destroyed by shell-fire.

Area – 6212 sq mts

LOCATION
Messines Ridge Cemetery lies on the south side of the Mesen – Wulvergem road 500m west of the crossroads in Mesen. It is difficult to miss as the Memorial dominates the area.

Journey Time – 25 mins

C.W.G.C. Reference – 5/88

METEREN MILITARY CEMETERY, METEREN   *No. 90*

HISTORY
This cemetery was created in 1919 by the French authorities to concentrate graves from the battlefields and small cemeteries in the area.

INFORMATION
The British burial ground is on the edge of the Communal Cemetery on the north-western border of Meteren. You must pass through the Town Cemetery to reach the Military one.

The 210 German graves that were concentrated here have been removed. There are six World War II graves set apart on a small terrace below the rest of the graveyard. The Communal Cemetery was created as the church and churchyard were destroyed during the Battles of the Lys in 1918.

Meteren was involved in fighting at the beginning and end of the War. In 1914 the German advance was repelled by means of a bayonet charge by the 2nd Seaforth Highlanders. The Germans occupied the village in early October but their positions were captured by the 10th Brigade of the 4th Division on 13 October 1914. Lieutenant Bernard Montgomery of the 1st Royal Warwickshires was wounded twice in capturing the village during the advance by the III Corps on 13 October 1914. He was promoted to Captain and awarded the Distinguished Service Order. He is better known as the saviour of the 8th Army in North Africa during World War II and for his exploits in Europe following D-Day.

The next fighting that the village saw was in the German Spring Offensive in April 1918. The following story is recorded on page 138 of the book *Machine Gunner 1914-1918* edited by C. E. Crutchley. On 12 April 1918 Lieutenant-Colonel Graham Seton Hutchison, commanding officer of the 33rd Battalion Machine Gun Corps, had patrols south of Meteren who found men of the 31st Division in full retreat ahead of the enemy just 600m away. He immediately rallied them and formed a new line. After trips to the Divisional headquarters in

Meteren he was given extra machine-guns which stopped the German advance by midday. Hence, this village was at the limit of the German advance during the Battles of the Lys.

The 33rd Division held the village until it was lost on 16 April and, though the French took the area briefly, they were forced to withdraw. It was not until 19 July that the 9th (Scottish) and 1st Australian Divisions attacked the sector with the South African Composite Battalion capturing the village.

Concentrated here:

Berthen Churchyard – it contained thirteen British men, two Canadians and one Newfoundlander who were buried in 1916 and 1918.
Le Roukloshille Military Cemetery – south of the little hamlet on the road to Godewaersvelde. Twenty-six British men, thirty-eight Australians and one French soldier were buried here from April to August 1918.
Meteren Churchyard – it contained eleven British men who were buried in 1914 and 1917.
Mont des Cats British and Indian Cemeteries – on the hill south-east of the monastery. The British cemetery contained nine British men and two Canadians buried in April 1915 while the Indian burial ground contained sixteen men buried in April 1915. Another six British men, buried in the grounds of the monastery were also brought to Meteren.

UK – 583	Aust – 104	NZ – 22	Can – 5
NF – 1	S Afr – 31	India – 15	Fr – 65
WWII – 6	Unnamed-181		

Special Memorials to five British men believed to be buried among the unnamed.

Special Memorial to one British soldier buried in Meteren Churchyard whose grave was destroyed by shell-fire.

Special Memorial to an Indian buried in Mont des Cats Indian Cemetery whose grave was destroyed by shell-fire.

Area – 3507 sq yds

LOCATION
Meteren is south-west of Ieper in northern France 4 km west of Bailleul. The cemetery lies on the west side of the Meteren – Godewaersvelde road (D18) about 300 m from the town square. Meteren can be reached either through Bailleul or via the Rodeberg and Mont Noir on the N372/D318. It would be much easier to park in the town square and walk the short distance to the cemetery than park and try to turn your vehicle.

Journey Time – 1 hr

C.W.G.C. Reference – 5/79

MINTY FARM CEMETERY, St. JAN   *No. 91*

HISTORY
The cemetery was used from October 1917 until April 1918.

INFORMATION
The farm from which the cemetery gets its name was used as a German blockhouse until captured during the Third Battle of Ypres, and it was then used for a British Company headquarters. It is thought that the name 'Minty Farm' originates from the period when the blockhouse was occupied by a unit from Wiltshire.

The 1/6th (Banff and Donside) Gordon Highlanders of the 51st (Highland) Divison took the farm on 31 July 1917. The Division continued towards the Steenbeek and dug in about 250 m short of the river during which time the Highlanders came under fire from two machine-guns across the stream. Private (later Flight-Sergeant) George Imlach Macintosh dealt with them for which he was awarded the Victoria Cross.

On route to the cemetery it is possible to detour to the Memorial to the 38th (Welsh) Divison at Goumier Farm. At the junction 500 m before this cemetery take the left to Langemark and in 400 m you come to a junction with a farm to the right. Just beyond the farm is a large bunker in the fields, on the wall of which is the Memorial plaque to the Welsh. It is possible to get to the bunker if you ask permission.

UK – 188   Ger – 1   Unnamed – 4

Area – 1185 sq yds

LOCATION
Minty Farm Cemetery is found about 5 km north-east of Ieper, 2 km west of St. Juliaan. It is most easily reached via the Ieper northern by-pass and the Mortelweg known in the War as Admiral's Road which runs north-west from the N38 at the small crossroads just west of the motorway. About 1.5 km from the N38 turn north at another crossroads, where there are C.W.G.C. signs on the wall of the house on the corner. This brings you to the cemetery, which lies 30 m from the road, in about 1 km.

Journey Time – 20 mins

C.W.G.C. Reference – 5/8

HISTORY

Mont Noir Cemetery was begun in April 1918, during the fighting here in the German offensive, and remained in use until September. It was enlarged after the Armistice with the concentration of British and French graves from the surrounding battlefields.

INFORMATION

This cemetery is in a disused sand-pit, cut into the side of Mont Noir which stands 426 ft above sea level, and sunk below the level of the track by which you get to it from the main road. The hill was captured by the British Cavalry Corps on 13 October 1914 and remained in Allied hands until the end of the War.

Nearby is the Memorial to the 34th Division. The Germans had tried to take Mont Noir having overrun Kemmel but were thrown back by the 34th Division who had their headquarters at the summit of the hill. Should you wish to visit the 34th Division Memorial, or just have an excellent view of the Salient, stay on the main road to the summit of Mont Noir passing the turn to Bailleul and Mont Noir Cemetery. At the summit the Hotel du Mont Noir has a large picnic area at the rear from which you get an impressive view of the Salient, and next to the hotel is the Memorial.

In reaching this cemetery, you may have passed my favourite hotel in the area, situated on the summit of the Rodeberg. I have always been made very welcome at the Hotel Kosmos and I would recommend it to anyone who wants to have a comfortable, and affordable, stop in the Salient. At the very least try the restaurant.

The Monts des Flandres are used by cyclists to practice hill climbing. The numbers can be substantial in summer as they can attempt three steep climbs in quick succession onto the Rodeberg, Vidaigneberg and the Zwaarteberg (Mont Noir). Between the Vidaigneberg and Zwaarteberg, in the village of Rodeberg, is a border post that I have never seen manned. There are a number of tourist attractions worth visiting and several cafes and restaurants.

The thirty-two French graves in the cemetery at the Armistice were of men of the 26th Dragoons or 88th Infantry Regiment who fell in April and May 1918. The concentrated French graves are of men who fell from March to May 1915.

Concentrated here:

Wolfheok British Cemetery, St. Jans-Cappel – 200 m south-west of the hamlet, containing twenty-three British men. It was used from August to September 1918, mostly by the 36th (Ulster) Division.

UK – 146	Aust – 1	NF – 2
Fr – 84	Unnamed – 15	WWII – 2

Area – 1573 sq yds

LOCATION

Mont Noir Cemetery is found south of Ieper on the southern edge of the village of Rodeberg, in northern France on the northern slopes of the Mont Noir. It lies at the end of a dirt track leading from the D223 Mont Noir – Bailleul road and is clearly signed from Rodeberg.

Journey Time – 55 mins

C.W.G.C. Reference – 5/76

MOTOR CAR CORNER CEMETERY, PLOEGSTEERT *No. 93*

HISTORY

Begun at the start of the Battle of Messines in June 1917, the cemetery remained in use until the German advance in March 1918.

INFORMATION

The Germans extended the cemetery in 1918 when they were in control of the area but their graves have been removed. The name derives from the fact that this was the closest to the front that Army vehicles were permitted.

UK – 36	Aust – 9	NZ – 84	KUG – 2
Ger – 1	Area – 767 sq yds		

LOCATION

Motor Car Corner Cemetery is found south of Ieper about 4 km south-east of Ploegsteert. 1.4km south of Ploegteert square you will find on the left a tree of C.W.G.C. signs. Turn left and then right onto a tree-lined avenue leading to Motor Car Corner Cemetery on the right.

Journey Time – 40 mins

C.W.G.C. Reference – 5/109

MUD CORNER CEMETERY, WARNETON   *No. 94*

HISTORY

This cemetery was begun at the start of the Battle of Messines on 7 June 1917, when the New Zealand Division captured this site, and it remained in use until December 1917.

INFORMATION

In the tranquility of this small area you can imagine the cavalry charges of 1914 when this old fashioned style of warfare came to an end. It is easy to understand how Mud Corner got its name because in the winter this low-lying spot must have been a morass of mud in which it would have been almost impossible to fight.

UK – 1	Aust – 31	NZ – 53

Area – 616 sq yds

LOCATION

Mud Corner Cemetery lies at the northern edge of Ploegsteert Wood, south of Mesen and about 2km north-east of Ploegsteert. It is reached most easily from the crossroads at the summit of Hill 63 on the Armentieres road. A dirt track 50m east of Prowse Point Cemetery leads to Mud Corner Cemetery in the valley below.

Journey Time – 35 mins

C.W.G.C. Reference – 5/94

NEW IRISH FARM CEMETERY, St. JAN   *No. 95*

HISTORY

The cemetery was opened in August 1917 once this territory, which had been near the front-line, was considered to be safe. It was used until November 1917 and again in April and May 1918. After the Armistice the cemetery was enlarged with the concentration of 4,560 graves adding to the 70 already here.

INFORMATION

The cemetery is situated on what was known as Boundary Road next to the farm from which it gets its name. The crossroads at the northern corner was called Hammond's Corner.

Hill Top Farm, on Buffs Road by the crossroads, was, by 1917, just a series of trenches. A tree, on the edge of a trench, was turned into an observation post by hollowing it out and lining it with steel. The post was then used to guide shell-fire on to German positions. The 39th Division attacked through the site of Hill Top Farm on the first day of the Third Battle of Ypres, 31 July 1917.

Concentrated here:

Admiral's Cemetery, Boezinge – at the junction of Admiral's and Boundary Roads near No Man's Cot Cemetery. It contained nineteen British soldiers who fell in 1917 and 1918.
Canopus Trench Cemetery, Langemark – a little south-west of the village. It contained twelve British men of the 1/5th Gloucesters who fell in August 1917.
Comedy Farm Cemetery, Langemark – south of the village near the Steenbeek. It contained twenty-nine British men who fell from June to September 1915.
Crossroads Cemetery, St. Jan – two groups of graves at the crossroads in the village. They contained nineteen British men who fell in June and July 1915.
Ferdinand Farm Cemetery, Langemark – near the Steenbeek on the way to St. Juliaan. It contained fifteen British men who fell from July to October 1917.
Francois Farm Cemetery, Langemark – near a farm directly south of Cement House Cemetery. It contained twenty-three British men who fell from July to October 1917.
Fusilier Farm Cemetery, Boezinge – on the Ypres – Pilkem road south-west of No Man's Cot Cemetery. It contained seventeen British men of the 38th (Welsh) Division who fell on 31 July 1917.
Fusilier Farm Road Cemetery, Boezinge – 400m north-west of Fusilier Farm Cemetery near Colne Valley Cemetery. It contained fourteen British men of the 38th (Welsh) Division who fell from 31 July to 2 August 1917.
Glimpse Cottage Cemetery, Boezinge – just south of Colne Valley Cemetery. It contained eighteen British men of the 38th (Welsh) Division who fell in July and August 1917.
Irish Farm Cemetery, St. Jan – immediately south of this cemetery. Begun by 1st Royal Fusiliers in May 1915, it was used regularly until September 1915 and at intervals until January 1918 by which time it contained fifty-four British graves.
La Miterie German Cemetery, Lomme – a little north of La Miterie. It contained eight British men who fell in September 1918.
Manor Road Cemetery, Zillebeke – situated where the railway crosses the road near the village. It contained nineteen British men of the 1st Royal Irish Fusiliers who fell in August 1916.
Mirfield Cemetery, Boezinge – sited between the canal and the Ypres – Pilkem road. It contained sixteen British men, fifteen of the 51st (Highland) Division, who fell from June to August 1917.
Paratonnier's Farm Cemetery, Boezinge – a Belgian military cemetery, now removed, 800m south of Lizerne. It contained the graves of thirteen British men who fell from December 1917 to March 1918.
Pilkem Road Cemetery, Boezinge – near Colne Valley Cemetery with Glimpse Farm and Fusilier Farm Road cemeteries. It contained twenty-seven British men, eighteen of them from the 1/5th

(Buchan and Formartin) Gordon Highlanders, who fell in July and August 1917.
St. Jan Churchyard – forty-four British men who fell in 1915 were buried in the churchyard.
Spree Farm Cemetery, Langemark – 800m south-east of St. Juliaan near Bridge House Cemetery. It contained fourteen British men and three New Zealanders who fell from August to October 1917.
Vanheule Farm Cemetery, Langemark – on the St. Juliaan – Ypres road just north of Seaforth Cemetery. It contained twenty-two British men and one New Zealander who fell from August to October 1917.
Yorkshire Cemetery, Zouave Villa, St. Jan – 700m west of here. It contained twenty-four British men, twenty-two of the 6th King's Own Yorkshire Light Infantry and two of the 6th East Yorkshires, who fell in August 1917.

UK – 4272	Aust – 54	NZ – 23	Can – 254
NF – 3	S Afr – 6	BWI – 1	India – 5
KUG – 12	Ger – 1	Chinese Labour Corps – 7	
Unnamed – 3267 (75% of whole)			

Special Memorials to thirty-seven British men and one Canadian known/believed to be buried among the unnamed.

Special Memorials to twenty-six British men and four New Zealanders buried in four cemeteries whose graves were destroyed by shell-fire.

Area – 17615 sq yds

LOCATION
New Irish farm Cemetery lies 300m north of the N38 northern by-pass about 1 km north of St. Jan, clearly signed and visible from the N38.

Journey Time – 15 mins

C.W.G.C. Reference – 5/21

HISTORY

The Communal Cemetery was used by the British from October 1914 to November 1917 and from September to November 1918. The Germans buried one man near the entrance when he died as their prisoner in April 1918.

INFORMATION

A New Zealand Chaplain is believed to be buried under the Cross of Sacrifice though the majority of the graves are in several Plots near the middle of the cemetery, with one grave described above, by the entrance.

The 4th Division established their headquarters in Nieppe in October 1914 having pushed the Germans back across the River Lys from the Mont des Flandres. A line then was established north from Armentieres to the edge of Ploegsteert Wood. Following the German attack on 21 October 1914, in which the 11th and 12th Brigades took German ground, the 4th Division extended their line north of Ploegsteert Wood.

John Laffin in *On the Western Front*, page 202, tells this story. A Canadian unit billeted in Nieppe in 1917 had a new commanding officer who was not used to the less than formal military behaviour of troops from the Dominions. At the end of a parade he gave the order 'All gentlemen fall out' rather than the more usual 'All officers fall out'. Naturally all the Canadian troops dismissed themselves and the Colonel learnt to never use that command again.

UK – 43	Aust – 6	NZ – 11	S Afr – 2

Area – 378 sq yds

LOCATION

Nieppe Communal Cemetery is situated on the northern edge of Nieppe village, 300m from the town square, and about 20km south of Ieper. It is on the eastern side of a road to Le Romarin, also signed for 'Cemetiere Bourg', that leads north from the large square in Nieppe.

Journey Time – 1 hr

C.W.G.C. Reference – 5/103

HISTORY

The churchyard was used for British burials at various times throughout the War.

INFORMATION

The church, destroyed in the War but later rebuilt, was used for many burials early in the War by the Canadians and the 5th Division. The British graves are on the left, or north, side of the church as you enter, next to the road, but three graves are set apart from the main Plot. There are also a number of World War II burials.

Gray and Argyle in *Chronicle of the First World War* tell us that on 22 November 1914, Lieutenants L. A. Strange and F. G. Small of No. 5 Squadron, Royal Flying Corps, forced down a German Albatross near this village and landed to take prisoners. They found the German officer observer beating the non-commissioned officer pilot for crashing the plane. Strange was one of the first pilots to mount a machine-gun on his plane and finished the War as a Colonel with the Distinguished Service Order, Military Cross and Distinguished Flying Cross.

On 11 April 1918 the 2nd Worcesters were east of the village but were forced back on 12 April by the German Spring Offensive. The 16th (Church Lads Brigade) King's Royal Rifle Corps came up in support but were wiped out in the battle here. Corporal McBride manned a succession of machine-guns for the three days of the battle holding up the German advance.

The Germans set up machine-gun posts at the crossroads on the edge of the village and behind the buildings on the south side of the square. The brewery and the Town Hall opposite the church housed the 2nd Worcesters who were having breakfast when the Germans attacked. At the end of the day the remaining sixty men of the Worcesters broke out of the rear of the Town Hall to escape from Nieuwkerke back to the British lines west of the village. Although forced to retreat the Worcesters had cost the enemy much in time and men. The village was recaptured by the 36th (Ulster) Division on 2 September 1918.

UK – 76   Aust – 10   NZ – 5   Can – 1
India – 1   Fr – 4   Unnamed – 1
WWII – 11 UK, 3 Bel + 1 Fr

LOCATION
Nieuwkerke Churchyard lies in the centre of the village on the edge of the large village square. Nieuwkerke is about 15 km south of Ieper.

Journey Time – 45 mins

C.W.G.C. Reference – 5/90

NINE ELMS BRITISH CEMETERY, POPERINGE   *No. 98*

HISTORY
This cemetery was created on 16 September 1917, as the result of the British Flanders Offensive in 1917, and used until September 1918.

INFORMATION
The Plots are numbered in the order that units were posted to the area which gives us a good idea of the men from all over the world involved in the fighting.

The first Plots contain the graves of those who died in the 3rd Australian and 44th Casualty Clearing Stations that had been moved here from Brandhoek and Lijssenthoek in September 1917. The later Plots are of those who died in the German Spring Offensive and the final breakout from the Salient in 1918.

There is a German Plot containing prisoners who died from September 1917 to March 1918. There was a group of ninety-five American soldiers but these have been removed, as have the French graves.

The space created has been used for the burial of twenty-two British men who fell in late May 1940. One of these is the grave of Company Sergeant-Major C. T. Baily, Oxford and Bucks Light Infantry, who was killed, aged 44, and possibly now lies among comrades with whom he may have fought twenty years before.

Also buried here are two men who were executed nearby by the British Army. Private John McFarlane of the 4th King's (98th Brigade, 33rd Division) was shot for desertion on 22 May 1918. Private Joseph Nisbet of the 1st Leicesters (71st Brigade, 6th Division) deserted while he was moving to the front-line and while he was under a suspended sentence of death for a previous desertion attempt. Nisbet was shot on 23 August 1918.

UK – 955   Aust – 149   NZ – 118   Can – 289
NF – 7   S Afr – 26   BWI – 2   Bermuda – 1
India – 1   Guernsey – 8   Ger – 37   WWII – 22

LOCATION
Nine Elms Cemetery can be found west of Ieper about 1 km west of the centre of Poperinge. It is about 300 m south of the Poperinge by-pass, on a small road leading to Hilhoek.

Journey Time – 35 mins

C.W.G.C. Reference – 5/39

HISTORY
This was begun at the end of July 1917 in a captured area of no man's land, and used until March 1918.

INFORMATION
The cemetery derived its name from a nearby farm building that was located in no man's land for much of the War before this cemetery was opened. There are forty-five men buried here from the 51st (Highland) Division who attacked through the position of this cemetery on the first day of the Third Battle of Ypres.

On 19 December 1915 the Germans tried to break the line that had been held for much of the previous five months by the 1/6th West Yorkshires (146th Brigade, 49th (West Riding) Division). So much gas was released in this, the first use of phosgene, that it left crystals on the ground, but the West Yorkshires all had gas masks so the line was held even though the attack caused 1,069 casualties, 120 of whom died.

On 19 April 1916, Germans from the 6th Division captured the trenches here but they were retaken by the 1st King's Shropshire Light Infantry (16th Brigade, 6th Division) on 21 April who found that they could only advance by lying on the mud and crawling ahead. They inflicted heavy casualties on the enemy but lost their commanding officer, eight officers and 163 men.

The 1/4th Duke of Wellington's (147th Brigade, 49th (West Riding) Division) were stationed here throughout the winter of 1916-17. After one forty-eight hour period an officer brought back only twenty-eight men, the rest being casualties. On 19 December 1916 the Duke's were ordered to withdraw from the front-line as the artillery were to fire on the nearby German lines (no man's land being very narrow at this point). As the Duke's withdrew the Germans launched a gas attack which decimated the Yorkshire battalion, many of whom are buried

here. A reserve battalion of the Brigade was called up and subsequently held the line.

The 29th Division, who had fought at Gallipoli and suffered so greatly on the Somme in 1916, were stationed here for the first day of the Flanders Offensive. Their artillery was used on 31 July 1917 to provide cover for the attack by the 51st (Scottish), 38th (Welsh) and 39th Divisions, and helped the attack by silencing the German blockhouses.

UK – 79   Area – 375 sq mts

LOCATION
No Man's Cot Cemetery lies north of Ieper in open fields about half way between Boezinge and St. Juliaan. It is reached most easily by taking the Pilkemsweg north from the N38 northern by-pass and following the C.W.G.C. signs. It is interesting to note the small stones marking the limit of C.W.G.C. land at the edge of the path from the road to the cemetery.

Journey Time – 20 mins

C.W.G.C. Reference – 5/13

OAK DUMP CEMETERY, VOORMEZELE   *No. 100*

HISTORY
This cemetery was used during the British Flanders Offensive in 1917.

INFORMATION
On 14 February 1915 the 2nd East Surreys (85th Brigade, 28th Division) rushed here to recapture some trenches just taken by the Germans at Triangular Wood which was just to the south of Oak Dump. The trenches on either side of the area to be

recaptured were still held by British troops. Therefore, the East Surreys were ordered to advance without firing their guns. Only two officers and twenty-five men attended roll-call that evening.

The British front-line at the start of the Battle of Messines was 150m east of Oak Dump and the German line 200m beyond. The Germans withdrew to the Chateau in the wood on 7 June holding up the 1/7th Londons and though the 1/6th (London Rifles) Londons arrived to help they also failed to move the enemy. It was not until the arrival of a tank, and another artillery bombardment that the Germans withdrew. The British then turned the cellar of the Chateau into an Advanced Dressing Station.

In March 1918 a sap (observation post) opposite the cemetery was destroyed during which seven men of 180th Siege Battery were killed. However, their bodies were not recovered and buried in this cemetery until 1927. Of the men buried here fifty-nine are of various battalions of the London Regiment reflecting their contribution nearby in June 1917. One grave was brought here after the Armistice.

It is possible to follow the road through the new golf course which is part of the redevelopment of the Chateau Bayernschloss, once used by the Germans as a headquarters, and now a country club. The canal and Pallingbeek Park in what was known as 'The Bluff' are to the left of the road. (See 1st D.C.L.I. Cemetery and Larch Wood Cemetery). On the corner of the next junction in front of the house is the Memorial to Freres Mahieu. The road from the chateau to St. Eloi, called the 'Dammstrasse', ran from the Memorial south-west to the St. Eloi – Comines road.

UK – 109   Aust – 2   Unnamed – 5

Special Memorials to two British graves destroyed by shell-fire.

Area – 1266 sq yds

LOCATION
Oak Dump Cemetery lies south of Ieper midway between St. Eloi and Hill 60 on the edge of the ridges here and clearly signed from the St. Eloi – Ieper road.

Journey Time – 20 mins

C.W.G.C. Reference – 5/115

OOSTAVERNE WOOD CEMETERY, WIJTSCHATE   *No. 101*

HISTORY
This cemetery was begun on 7 June 1917, after this area had been captured on the first day of the Battle of Messines, and remained in use until September 1917. It was greatly enlarged after the Armistice with the concentration of 1,000 graves from the surrounding battlefields and from German cemeteries that had been removed.

INFORMATION
The wood from which the cemetery gets its name was a large formal wood with avenues, walks and drives, but it was destroyed in the War and is now only a small copse.

The 'Oostaverne Line' was one of the main objectives on the first day of the Battle of Messines. It was a line of trenches and defences that ran from the Lys to the Ypres – Comines canal and passed just east of here. Part of the defences of that line, a pill-box, can still be seen next to the cemetery. The wood and the village were taken by the 19th (Western) and 11th (Northern) Divisions.

There were, in fact, two cemeteries created next

to each other here which now make up Plots I to III of this cemetery. An unknown number of Germans lie in Plot I. A German cemetery at the edge of the road to Wijtschate, which contained 1,100 graves concentrated there after the Armistice, was removed in the 1950's.

Opposite the cemetery is the Memorial to the 19th Division, also known as the 'Butterfly' Division. It marks the site of their advance on 7 June 1917.

Concentrated here:

Hoogemotte Farm German Cemetery, Wervik – on the Belgian side of the River Lys near Comines. It contained twelve British men who fell in April 1918.
Houthem-les-Ypres German Cemetery – on the west side of the village. It contained seventeen British men who fell in 1916 and 1917.
Inderster German Cemetery, Beselare – on the road from Beselare to Broodseinde, at a small crossroads 1.4 km north of Beselare. It was made by the German XXVII Reserve Corps and contained fifty-three British men who fell in October and November 1914.

Koekuit German Cemetery, Langemark – on the road to Houthulst north of Langemark German Cemetery. It contained eight British men who fell in October 1914.

Ten-Brielen Amerika German Cemetery – north of Comines. It contained 850 Germans with six British soldiers who fell in April 1917.

Three Houses German Cemetery (Hollebeke Cemetery No. 60) – near Hollebeke Chateau on the road to Kortewilde. Among the Germans three British men and two Canadians who fell in 1916 were buried.

Zwaanhoek German Cemetery, Beselare – in a hamlet 400 m north of Besalare. It was made by the German XXVII Reserve Corps and contained six British men who fell in October 1914.

UK – 923   Aust – 43   NZ – 19   Can – 133
Fr – 1   Ger – unknown no.
Unnamed – 783 (75% of total)

Special Memorial to one British soldier buried in Three House German Cemetery, Hollebeke whose grave has been lost.

Area – 5190 sq yds

LOCATION

Oostaverne Wood Cemetery is south of Ieper about 1.5 km south of St. Eloi on the road signed to Rijsel (Lille). It lies on the west side of the road next to a small crossroads that has the 19th Division Memorial on the south-east corner.

Journey Time – 20 mins

C.W.G.C. Reference – 5/69

OXFORD ROAD CEMETERY, IEPER   *No. 102*

HISTORY

Begun in August 1917 as the front-line moved east from here this burial ground remained in use until April 1918. After the Armistice, the cemetery was greatly enlarged with the concentration of graves from isolated positions east and south-east of Ypres.

INFORMATION

This is a deceptively large graveyard as it is in the shape of a 'Y', of which you can only see the stem from the road. The original cemetery, 134 graves in Plot I, is on the extreme left as you enter and contains the War Stone.

A second cemetery, Oxford Road No. 2, was begun next to No. 1 in October 1917 and used until April 1918. These were incorporated into one burial ground after the Armistice so that the 255 graves in No. 2 Cemetery now make up Plot V which is on the extreme right as you enter. The other Plots are made up of concentrated graves.

The Memorial to the 50th (Northumbrian) Division, unveiled in September 1927, is 100 m north-east of this cemetery. East of it, near the motorway, are a series of bunkers known as the Cambrai Redoubt which were attacked, and taken at heavy cost, on 31 July 1917.

The first Victoria Cross awarded to a non-commissioned officer of a Territorial unit in the Great War, was won just south-east of the cemetery by Lance-Sergeant (later Captain) Douglas Walter Belcher of the 1/5th (London Rifle Brigade) Londons on 13 May 1915.

V.C. – Acting Captain Clement Robertson, V.C..
3rd Queen's Royal West Surrey Regiment,
Special Reserve, attached Tank Corps.
From County Wicklow, Ireland.
Died – 4 October 1917. Age 28.
Won – 4 October 1917. This was the first
Victoria Cross for a member of the Tank
Corps. He guided his tanks into action on
foot knowing that it probably meant his
death and was killed as they reached their
objective.

UK – 398   Aust – 74   NZ – 37   Can – 74
NF – 9   Guernsey – 2   Unnamed – 254   Ger – 2

Special Memorials to three British men known/
believed to be buried among the unnamed.

Area – 4432 sq yds

LOCATION
Oxford Road Cemetery can be found north-east of
Ieper just east of the old road (N313) from the town,
through St. Jan, to St. Juliaan. It lies on the south
side of the road that used to run from St. Jan to
Passendale which has been blocked by the motorway. The cemetery is well signed from the N313.

Journey Time – 20 mins

C.W.G.C. Reference – 5/33

PACKHORSE FARM SHRINE CEMETERY, WULVERGEM   *No. 103*

HISTORY
This cemetery was only used from April to June
1915.

INFORMATION
Packhorse Farm was the name given by the British
Army in the War to the nearby buildings. A shrine
used to be just south of it at the point where the path
to the cemetery now reaches the road though the
shrine has been rebuilt nearer to the farm.

The 46th (North Midland) Division made two
cemeteries when they were stationed here in 1915.
One was at the farm, which has been removed to
Lindenhoek Chalet Cemetery, and this one at the
shrine.

As a result, fifty-six of the graves here are of men
of the 46th Division, of which, twenty-seven are of
the 1/5th Lincolns and twenty-seven of the 1/4th
Leicesters.

UK – 59 Area – 805 sq yds

LOCATION
Packhorse Farm Shrine Cemetery lies in fields south
of Ieper and about 1 km south-east of Kemmel, 50 m

east of a local road that runs south from Lindenhoek. It is reached most easily from the crossroads in the small hamlet of Lindenhoek turning
right at the fork 20 m from the Ieper – Nieuwkerke
road.

Journey Time – 40 mins

C.W.G.C. Reference – 5/81

HISTORY

This cemetery was created after the Armistice with the concentration of graves from the battlefields of Passendale.

INFORMATION

The entrance building which gives the feeling of a prison makes the cemetery unusual. More importantly Passendale has given its name to one of the most infamous military conflicts in history.

Passendale was to be an early objective in Haig's (q.v.) plan to break out of the Salient, reach the Belgian coast and win the War by the end of 1917. Though the plan had failed Haig pressed on to Passendale. It had taken 100 days to reach Passendale from the line held on 31 July 1917, another five to take the village, and only mounting pressure from Downing Street stopped the slaughter on the Passendale Ridge.

Each part of the advance has been given its own title in the battle nomenclature because the advance was so slow and costly. The overall campaign is dealt with elsewhere, particularly well in a book by Lyn Macdonald titled *They Called it Passchendaele*, but the battles here at Passendale took place in the worst of the weather when the army was almost drained of reserves. Hence, troops of the Dominions did much of the work in October and November 1917.

On 26 October 1917, in the valleys ranging from this cemetery north-west to Poelkappele, the 63rd (Royal Naval) Division attacked assisting the Canadian Corps who suffered 2,481 casualties in three days. In the marsh and bottomless mud of the valleys the 63rd Division attacked and suffered counter-attack with the 1st and 2nd Royal Marine Light Infantry, and the 'Anson' and 'Hood' battalions playing major roles in the often chaotic fighting. Though some strong points were taken and 400 m gained the 188th Brigade lost fourteen officers and more than 500 men in each battalion.

On 30 October the next stage of the attack began but as the British prepared to go 'over the top' the Germans began their morning bombardment early, decimating the 190th Brigade. A company of Artists Rifles (1/28th Londons) was wiped out while the 7th Royal Fusiliers, 4th Bedfordshires and 5th King's Shropshire Light Infantry also suffered greatly.

As a result a new tactic, that may seem obvious to us, was employed – a night attack. The innovation was used on the 3 November during which the 'Drake' and 'Hood' battalions of the 63rd Division took the ridge from here to Poelkapelle, suffering only light casualties.

Haig had decided that the Canadians should take Passendale because the Australians, New Zealanders and British had been badly depleted by the fighting of the previous four months. General Currie, commanding the Canadian Expeditionary Force argued against the attack predicting that it would cost 16,000 casualties to take the objectives – he was 350 out. The Jägers that held the village were some of Germany's best battalions and as the roads had become the only secure ground among the marshy valleys and bottomless mud, the Jägers could anticipate the line of attack. The Canadians advanced in phases from 26 October to 10 November. The village was finally cleared of Germans by 10 November and the offensive closed on 11 November 1917.

In the fighting nearby the following Victoria Crosses were won:

Lieutenant Hugh MacKenzie who silenced a pill-box and is commemorated on the Menin Gate.

Sergeant (later Major) George Harry Mullin, M.M., of Princess Patricia's Canadian Light Infantry, for the same action as Lieutenant MacKenzie.

Corporal (later Sergeant) Collin Barron of the 3rd Battalion, 1st Central Ontario (Toronto) Regiment, Canadian Expeditionary Force, who stopped two enemy artillery batteries on 6 November just north of this cemetery.

Major (later Major-General) George Randolph Pearkes of the 5th Canadian Mounted Rifle Battalion, Quebec Regiment, who seized two farmhouse strong points just south of this cemetery on 30 October.

Private James Peter Robertson who disposed of an enemy position in the village saving many lives in the process. He is buried in Tyne Cot Cemetery.

Passendale had seen fighting from the earliest days of the formation of the Salient. On 13 October 1914 the 7th Division, with the Household Cavalry of the 7th Cavalry Brigade who had been billeted in Passendale, advanced to Roeselare. The Life Guards and Royal Horse Guards (the Blues), of the Household Cavalry, whose compliment included various ranks of the nobility, met almost no opposition before returning to their billets.

They were then ordered to take Menen but the Germans had captured an officer carrying the British battle plans; hence, they knew everything that the British intended to do and had rushed troops to Menen. Therefore, the 7th Division and Belgian troops were forced to withdraw.

The cavalry occupied Passendale on 17 October handing it over to French Cavalry and Territorials on 18 October, but on 20 October 1914 the village fell to the Germans who held it until the end of 1917. The Germans over-ran the village during their Spring Offensive in 1918 but it was finally captured on 29 September 1918 by Belgian troops who have now erected a Monument to this event next to the cemetery.

There are several Memorials in and around

Passendale which can be visited. In the church there is a Memorial window to the 66th (2nd East Lancashire) Division in the north transept. On the wall of the Town Hall, at the north end of the town square opposite the church, are five Memorials. Two tablets commemorate World War II units but the other three are to the 4th Belgian Regiment of Carabiniers, the Belgian Grenadiers and a plaque from the Western Front Association.

Near the village the Canadian Memorial is at Crest Farm, clearly signed from the town square about 400 m west of the church. The view from the small park is worth the visit, particularly the sight of Passendale from the direction that the Canadian troops must have come in the last days of the battle. Such a short distance but at what cost.

On the Passendale – Broodseinde road south of the village you can see, and visit, in the fields to the right of the road the Memorial to the 85th Canadian Infantry Battalion (Nova Scotia Highlanders). There is a path to the Memorial from the road.

UK – 1019   Aust – 292   NZ – 126   Can – 646
NF – 1   S Afr – 3   Guernsey – 4
Unnamed – 1602 (Over 75% of total)

Special Memorials to four British men and three Canadians believed to be buried among the unnamed.

Area – 7279 sq mts

LOCATION
Passendale Cemetery is north-east of Ieper on the ridges about 2 km north-west of Passendale. It lies 800 m south-west of the Passendale – Westrozebeke road on a local road signed to St. Jan from a crossroads near a water tower.

Journey Time – 50 mins

C.W.G.C. Reference – 6/2

PERTH CEMETERY (CHINA WALL), ZILLEBEKE   *No. 105*

HISTORY
Begun by the French in November 1914, the British took over the burial ground in June 1917 in preparation for the Third Battle of Ypres and then used it as a front-line cemetery until October 1917. It was enlarged after the Armistice with the concentration of 2,500 graves from the surrounding battlefields.

INFORMATION
The 'Great Wall of China' was one of the main British communication trenches that ran just north of here to the front-line. The Perth part of the name is thought to come from the fact that the first British burials here were made by the 2nd Cameronians (23rd Brigade, 8th Division). For some time the cemetery was also known as Halfway House.

The original cemetery is now Plot I, but the French Plot, also enlarged after the Armistice, has been removed. Most of the Special Memorials, which are near the road to the right of the entrance, are grouped by cemeteries in which the graves were lost.

Perth Cemetery contains a large number of men who were executed during 1915 by the British Army. Private George E. Roe of the 2nd King's Own Yorkshire Light Infantry (13th Brigade, 5th Division) deserted after fighting at Hill 60 in April and May 1915. He was executed and buried near Huts Cemetery, Dikkebus on 10 June 1915 though his grave was moved here after the War. Private Thomas Harris of the 1st Royal West Kents (13th Brigade, 5th Division) deserted in August 1914 and was captured in Paris. He was shot on 21 June 1915. Private Thomas Docherty of the 2nd King's Own Scottish Borderers (13th Brigade, 5th Division) deserted at the same time as Private Roe and was executed on 16 July 1915.

Corporal Frederick Ives and Private Ernest Fellows were among the group of five men of the 3rd Worcesters (7th Brigade, 3rd Division) executed on the ramparts in Ypres on 26 July 1915. Their graves were moved here after the War while the other three Privates were moved to Aeroplane Cemetery. Ives is now buried four graves away from Second Lieutenant Birks, V.C., whose story is told below, –

strange how men who had met such different ends are honoured equally in death so close together.

Private Evan Fraser of the 2nd Royal Scots (8th Brigade, 3rd Division) was the first soldier to be executed while under a suspended sentence of death for a previous attempt to desert. He had absconded four times in 1915 and was therefore executed on 2 August 1915. His grave is now marked by a Special Memorial.

Private Louis R. Phillips of the 6th Somerset Light Infantry (43rd Brigade, 14th (Light) Division) was executed on the ramparts in Ypres on 19 August 1915 and his grave was concentrated here after the War.

V.C. – Second Lieutenant Frederick Birks, M.M., V.C..

> 6th Battalion (Victoria) Australian Imperial Force, 2nd Australian Brigade, 1st Australian Division.
> Born in Flintshire.
> Died – 21 September 1917. Age – 23.
> Won – 20 September 1917. With his Corporal he attacked a strong point until the Corporal was injured and then Birks went on alone capturing the position. He then attacked another German position with a small party capturing one officer and fifteen men, killing the rest, after which he organised parties to consolidate the position. Birks was killed by a shell when trying to dig out men buried by another German shell.

Concentrated here:

Beselare German Cemetery No. 1 (246 Reserve Infantry Regiment) – situated close to the church. It contained 500 Germans and two British graves.

Belgian Chateau Cemetery, Vlamertinge – in the grounds of a chateau. It contained twelve British men, eleven Canadians and one French soldier who fell from 1914 to 1917.

Broodseinde German Cemeteries, Zonnebeke – several German cemeteries around Broodseinde were concentrated into one containing 5,000 German graves after the Armistice but it, in turn, was removed in the 1950's. In addition to the Germans there were twenty-seven British graves mainly of men who fell in 1914.

Durham Cemetery, Zillebeke – at the north end of the village. It contained fifty-two British graves, thirty-nine from Territorial battalions of the Durham Light Infantry, buried between December 1915 and March 1916.

Garter Point Cemetery, Zonnebeke – north of Polygon Wood on the road from Zonnebeke to Westhoek. It contained eight British men, nineteen Australians, one New Zealander, one German and three men 'Known Unto God' buried from September 1917 to April 1918.

Gordon House Cemetery No. 2, Zillebeke – sited 400 m north of this cemetery. It contained thirty British men buried from 1915 to 1917.

Hans Kirchner German Cemetery, Poelkapelle – situated 1.5 km south-east of the village. It contained four British men who fell in October 1914.

Houthulst German Cemetery – at the east end of the village. Removed in the 1950's it contained 1,000 Germans and one Royal Flying Corps officer.

Keerselare West German Cemetery, Langemark – near Vancouver Corner Canadian Memorial. It contained twenty-nine British men who fell in October 1914.

Keerselarehoek German Cemetery, Passendale – 200 m north-east of Tyne Cot Cemetery. It contained twelve British men and two Canadians who fell in 1914 and 1915.

Langemark German Cemetery No. 7 (Toten Walchden) – near the present German cemetery. It contained the graves of four British soldiers.

Langemark German Cemetery No. 8 – next to the route of the old railway on the road to Houthulst and the present German cemetery. It contained twenty-seven British men who fell in October 1914.

L'Ebbe Farm Cemetery, Poperinge – 1 mile north-west of the town. It contained twenty-one British soldiers who fell in 1915 and 1918.

Manneken Farm German Cemetery No. 3, Zarren – in Houthulst Forest. It contained 700 Germans and thirteen British men who fell in 1917.

Nachtigall (or Rossignol or Vieux-Chien) German Cemetery, Geluveld – 400 m north of the Menen Road and 1.5 km east of Geluveld. It contained 1,130 Germans and sixty-nine British men who fell from September to October 1915.

Poelkapelle German Cemetery No. 2 – 1.5 km south-east of the village. It contained ninety British men and four Canadians who fell in 1914 and 1915.

Poelkapelle German Cemetery No. 3 – 800 m south of the village. It contained twenty-three British men and nineteen Canadians who fell in 1914 and 1915.

Ration Dump Burial Ground, Zillebeke – 300 m north of here. It contained twenty-eight British graves, mainly London Scottish (14th Londons) and Liverpool Scottish (10th King's), and one Canadian soldier.

Reutal German Cemetery, Beselare (Kriegerfriedhof der XXVII Reserve Corps) – at the south-east corner of Polygon Wood on the Reutal – Zwaanhoek road. Many Germans, three British men, two Canadians and one New Zealander who fell from 1914 to 1917 were buried here.

St. Joseph German Cemetery, Hooglede – it contained four British airmen who died in 1918.

St. Juliaan Communal Cemetery – it contained six men of the 14th Canadian Infantry Battalion who fell in April 1915.

Schrieboom German Cemetery – 800m east of the village. It contained thirty-four British men who fell in October 1914.

Transport Farm Annex, Zillebeke – opposite Railway Dugouts Burial Ground. It contained twenty-seven British graves, sixteen of the 1st Dorsets (15th Brigade, 5th Division), who fell from November 1914 to June 1915.

Trench Railway Cemetery, Zillebeke – near Woods Cemetery. It contained twenty-one British men who fell in 1915 and 1916.

Treurniet German Cemetery, Poelkapelle – on the road to Houthulst. It contained one Canadian soldier.

Wallemolen German Cemetery, Passendale – half way between Poelkapelle and Passendale south of Wallemolen hamlet. It contained twenty British men and fifteen Canadians who fell in 1915.

Weidendreft German Cemetery, Langemark – at the farm of this name. Used from October 1914 to August 1915 it contained ninety-eight British men men who fell in 1914.

Westrozebeke German Cemetery No. 2 – 400m north-east of village on the road to Hooglede. It contained one Royal Air Force officer killed in 1918.

UK – 2360   Aust – 134   NZ – 22   Can – 129
S Afr – 7   KUG – 3   Unnamed – 1368 (50% of total)

Special Memorials to twenty-six British men and one Canadian soldier known/believed to be buried among the unnamed.

Special Memorials to ninety-one British men, thirteen Australians, one New Zealander and three Canadians buried in other cemeteries whose graves were destroyed by shell-fire.

Area – 9656 sq yds

LOCATION
Perth Cemetery is found east of Ieper and lies on the east side of the road from Zillebeke to Hellfire Corner, 700m north of Zillebeke and 750m south of Hellfire Corner. I would recommend visiting this as part of a circuit through Hellfire Corner, Zillebeke and Shrapnel Corner.

Journey Time – 10 mins

C.W.G.C. Reference – 5/48

PLOEGSTEERT CHURCHYARD   *No. 106*

HISTORY
The churchyard was used for the burials of Allied forces from October 1914 to February 1915.

INFORMATION
There are six graves of men of the 1st Hampshires (11th Brigade, 4th Division) near the church on the south side of the churchyard. The other British soldier buried here is Second Lieutenant Richard John Lumley of the 11th (Prince Albert's Own) Hussars who was killed in action on 17 October 1914.

An apocryphal story is told of a soldier with very large feet. At roll-call one morning the Company Sergeant-Major called his name, but as he received no reply another man shouted "He's gone to Ploegsteert crossroads to turn round".

UK – 7   Can – 2

LOCATION
Ploegsteert Churchyard is at the south-west corner of the town square in Ploegsteert. This is on the main road south from Ieper to Armentieres about 15km south of Ieper.

Journey Time – 35 mins

C.W.G.C. Reference – None

HISTORY
This cemetery was used from 1914 to August 1917.

INFORMATION
The graveyard was created by enclosing several small regimental cemeteries that lay next to each other. These dated from 1914 and 1915 and are typical of regimental burial grounds of the period. The cemetery as a whole was used for a few graves in 1916 and then for many burials in July and August 1917.

Plot I   – 1st Somerset Light Infantry made in December 1914.

Plot II   – 1st Somerset Light Infantry made in December 1914.

Plot III – 1/5th Gloucesters, 8th Loyal North Lancashires and Canadians made in April – May and October – December 1915.

Plot IV – 8th Loyal North Lancashires, Canadians and the Buckinghamshire Battalion, Oxford and Bucks Light Infantry made in June – October 1915 and formerly known as Canadian Cemetery, Strand.

The wood was known to the troops as Plugstreet Wood. It is now a pleasant place in which to walk but you must keep to the paths, the land is private as signs make quite clear throughout the wood; all paths, other than the clearly marked route, are fenced off.

This was usually a quiet place in the War interrupted by periods of intense fighting. Soldiers have commented that in the quiet times nightingales could be heard singing in the wood as if there was no War. It was captured by British Cavalry in October 1914 but part of the wood fell to the Germans who were not cleared until 1917. On 20 December 1914 an attack was launched from the eastern edge of the wood near Le Gheer by the 11th Brigade of the 4th Division. The Germans were prepared for the attack because the Brigade had used telephones, into which the Germans had patched lines, to synchronize the time of the start of the attack. The result was that no ground was gained and 226 casualties suffered.

In early 1915 the 21st (Yeoman Rifles) King's Royal Rifle Corps (124th Brigade, 41st Division) arrived at the wood. They suffered their first casualty when an inexperienced officer paraded his platoon for inspection in an area that the Germans could see. The Germans captured the wood on 10-11 April 1918 with the British taking it back in September.

While the Germans were in the wood they turned it into a fortress and, though there are still bunkers in the wood, it is not possible to visit them today. During the time that the Germans held the wood in 1918 the British destroyed it by artillery bombardment.

A Y.M.C.A. hut in the wood was destroyed by shell-fire in early 1916. The only remains were some coins fused together by the heat.

UK – 117   Aust – 1   NZ – 18   Can – 28
KUG – 1   Area – 1359 sq yds

LOCATION
Ploegsteert Wood Cemetery lies in the heart of Ploegsteert Wood about 2 km north-east of Ploegsteert. A dirt track 50 m from Prowse Point Cemetery leads to the three cemeteries in Ploegsteert Wood. The path past Mud Corner is fairly easy to follow as it is fenced on either side. There are also C.W.G.C. signs from the Armentieres road and in the wood.

Journey Time – 35 mins + 15 mins walk

C.W.G.C. Reference – 5/97

POELKAPELLE BRITISH CEMETERY, POELKAPELLE   *No. 108*

HISTORY
Poelkapelle Cemetery was created after the Armistice with the concentration of graves from the battlefields.

INFORMATION
The formal layout marks this clearly as a concentration cemetery though most of the dead here fell during the Third Battle of Ypres. Notably it contains

the grave of the youngest soldier to die on the Salient, Private John Condon, 6322, 2nd Royal Irish Regiment (12th Brigade, 4th Division), who died on the 24 May 1915, aged 14. He was from Waterford and is buried on the far side of the cemetery from the entrance in Plot LVI, Row F. Of the graves here 6,231, or nearly 90%, are unnamed.

There were several burial grounds in the area, most of which have been removed, including, close by, Poelkapelle East German Cemetery made by the Germans, and Poelkapelle New German Cemetery made by the British.

Poelkapelle was the site of severe fighting during the Third Battle of Ypres. On 4 October 1917 the 48th (South Midland) Division took the west part of the village with the 11th (Northern) and 14th (Light) Divisions in support. On 9 October the 11th Division, who fought their way from house to house up the main street, took the rest of the village.

The 18th (Eastern) Division attacked to the east of the village on 14 October. The 8th East Surreys and 7th Buffs north of main road, with the 7th Royal West Kents south of the road, pushed out of the village towards Westrozebeke during which the Buffs were reduced to 100 men.

On 22 October the 10th Essex and 8th Norfolks attacked again reaching the area now occupied by Poelkapelle Cemetery, but this was the limit of the British advance. The village was retaken by the Germans in their advance during the spring of 1918 but was finally captured by the Belgians in September.

On route to Poelkapelle you may have passed through Vancouver Corner with the tall Canadian Monument at the Keerselare crossroads. The Canadians occupied this position at the start of the first gas attack by the Germans in April 1915 and, sometimes called 'Gas Attack Corner', it marked the eastern limit of the affected area. Close by the Totenmuhle, or 'Mill of the Dead', was used as a German observation post during the War, but as it was constantly under fire from the British, the men chosen for duty here had a short life span.

During the German gas attack at Vancouver Corner on 24 April 1915 Captain Edward Donald Bellew of the 7th Battalion, British Columbia Regiment, Canadian Expeditionary Force, continued to fight vigorously, with any weapon that came to hand, after his unit were all killed or wounded. He was eventually captured by the Germans who court-martialed him at Staden and sentenced him to death. As the officer in charge of the execution would not carry out the order, Bellew was reprieved and when liberated awarded the Victoria Cross.

On 19, 20 and 22 August 1917 twelve, seven and eighteen tanks respectively supported the infantry in taking the pill-boxes between St. Juliaan and Vancouver Corner. The success of the tanks was an encouraging event but an unusual success due to the deteriorating nature of the ground caused by the poor weather that summer, even so there were over 3,000 casualties among the infantry.

At the roundabout in Poelkapelle there is the Memorial to Georges Guynemer, the French air ace, who was killed in a 'dog-fight' over Poelkapelle on 11 September 1917. His body was not found though the Germans claimed that they had recovered it but that it was lost in a British artillery bombardment later that day. He was a member of the Escadrille des Cogognes and therefore, the flying stork, emblem of the squadron, surmounts the Monument. A tank that was disabled in the Battle of Poelkapelle in 1917 was still stuck in the mud and ruins of the village when the Guynemer Memorial was unveiled in July 1923.

The church in Poelkapelle was, like the rest of the village, destroyed in the War and rebuilt in the 1920's. The church bells, weighing over 16,000 lbs, are cast out of metal made from shell-cases collected by local inhabitants.

On the road to Westrozebeke is the Memorial to Lieutenant Dewinde on the right hand side of the road who was killed on the spot in the Belgian attack on Westrozebeke on 28 September 1918. To the right of the roundabout in Westrozebeke there is a Monument to the 1st, 2nd and 3rd Regiments of Belgian Carabiniers who took the village in September 1918.

Concentrated here:

Houthulst Forest New Military Cemetery – near the south of a forest on Houthulst – Poelkapelle road. It contained several French graves and twenty-three British men who fell in the winter of 1917-1918.
Keerselare French Cemetery, Langemark – 1 km west of the hamlet at Vancouver Corner. It contained two British, five Canadian and twenty-nine French men who were buried in 1915.
Pilkem Road German Cemetery, Langemark – next to the bridge over the Hannebeke. It contained thirteen British men and one Canadian buried by the Germans from 1914 to 1917.

Poelkapelle Communal Cemetery – one British soldier was buried here in 1915.
Poelkapelle German Cemetery No. 2 – 1 km south-east of the village. It contained ninety-six British and Canadian graves of men who fell from 1914 to 1915.
St. Jan Churchyard – it contained forty-four British men buried in 1915 but whose graves were destroyed in later fighting.
Staden French Military Cemetery – made by the 169th Infantry Regiment. It contained eighty French graves and one Royal Air Force officer.
Vijfwegen German Cemetery No. 1 – it contained three British men buried by the Germans.

UK – 6541	Aust – 117	NZ – 237	Can – 525
NF – 9	S Afr – 10		Jersey – 4
Unnamed – 6231	WWII – 1		

Special Memorials to eight British men and one Channel Islander known/believed to be buried among the unnamed.

Special Memorials to twenty-four British men and three Canadians buried by the Germans in other cemeteries but whose graves have been lost.

Area – 22692 sq yds

LOCATION
Poelkapelle Cemetery lies on the south side of the N313 Poelkapelle – Westrozebeke road, approximately 1 km from the village and 9 km north-east of Ieper.

Journey Time – 45 mins

C.W.G.C. Reference – 5/1

POLYGON WOOD CEMETERY, ZONNEBEKE   *No. 109*

HISTORY
The cemetery was created in August 1917 and used until the German advance in April 1918. It was used again in September 1918.

INFORMATION
This is an interesting small cemetery with an unusual entrance. Nearby there was a German cemetery, the Kriegerfriedhof des Reserve Infantry Regiment 248 am Polygonenwald, made in 1914-15 containing 347 German graves, but it has been removed.

On 12 November 1914 Brigadier-General Charles Fitzclarence, V.C., known to his men as G.O.C. (General Officer Commanding) Menin Road, was killed leading an attack by the 2nd Grenadier Guards and 1st Irish Guards on German trenches near Black Watch Corner. This is at the south-east corner of Polygon Wood where a bridge now crosses the motorway. He was at the time officially the commanding officer of the 1st Brigade which mustered 468 men and five officers out of a strength that should have been 4,000 men and 100 Officers. As his grave was lost Fitzclarence is commemorated on the Menin Gate.

The Battle of Polygon Wood, in which this area fell to the 5th Australian Division, was given the dates 26 September to 3rd October 1917. The British deployed fifteen tanks in the battle, when the wood was finally cleared of Germans and the line pushed to the east. On 26 September a major air battle took place over the wood in which ninety-four British and German aeroplanes fought for supremacy of the skies. This battle was repeated on the following day as the British lured the Germans into a trap downing approximately thirty German machines. The Memorial to the 5th Australian Division is in the wood at Buttes Cemetery.

On 4 October 1917 tanks of the 1st Tank Battalion attacked in an easterly direction from Black Watch Corner. The route markers which had been laid out were destroyed, therefore, the unit leader, Captain Clement Robertson, led his tanks into battle on foot. He was killed, and is buried in Oxford Road Cemetery, but gained the first Victoria Cross for a member of the Tank Corps.

The wood was evacuated during the Battles of the Lys in the spring of 1918 but was retaken by the 9th (Scottish) Division on 28 September 1918. It had been completely destroyed and it is thought that many bodies still lie undiscovered within its boundaries.

In the nearby Glencorse Wood a Memorial has been erected to Captain Ewen James Brodie of the 1st Cameron Highlanders who fell in the wood during the German attack on 11 November 1914. Glencorse Wood is on the north side of the road from the Menen Road to Black Watch Corner.

UK – 32	NZ – 57	Ger – 1
KUG – 11	Unnamed – 17	

Special Memorials to seventeen British men and thirteen New Zealanders known/believed to be buried among the unnamed.

Area – 2129 sq yds

LOCATION

Polygon Wood Cemetery is on the north-east edge of Polygon Wood which lies east of Ieper and north of the Menen Road and motorway. You can leave the Menen Road at the junction just east of the Bellewaerde Pleasure Park known in the War as Clapham Junction where a C.W.G.C. sign indicates to the left to the Princess Patricia's Canadian Light Infantry Monument.

Journey Time – 20 mins

C.W.G.C. Reference – 6/5

POND FARM CEMETERY, WULVERGEM   *No. 110*

HISTORY

This cemetery was begun during the Third Battle of Ypres in July 1917 by the 3rd Rifle Brigade and 8th Buffs. It remained in use until October 1917 and was then used again in April and September 1918.

INFORMATION

Wulvergem fell to the Germans in April 1918 but they had tried to take it before in April 1916 when they launched an unsuccessful gas attack east of the village. The village was retaken by the 30th Division on 2 September 1918.

The cemetery lies in the grounds of the farm from which it gets its name and 178 of the men buried here were from Irish Regiments.

UK – 293	Ger – 5	Unnamed – 4

Special Memorials to three British men of 1/7th Cheshires buried here in September 1918 but whose graves have been lost.

Area – 2539 sq yds

LOCATION

This used to be one of the most difficult cemeteries to find on the Salient. It is behind a farm and is well hidden from the road. I spent an hour trying to find the place before the new C.W.G.C. signs were put in place. It lies south of Ieper about 3 km south-east of Kemmel and 1 km north-west of Wulvergem.

Turn east from the Nieuwkerke road at the small crossroads in Lindenhoek on the slopes of the Kemmelberg and turn right downhill at the crossroads reached in 800 m. A path leads through the farmer's field and farm buildings past the pond to the cemetery. Please remember that this is private property.

Journey Time – 45 mins

C.W.G.C. Reference – 5/82

PONT d'ACHELLES MILITARY CEMETERY, NIEPPE   *No. 111*

HISTORY

Begun in June 1917, the cemetery remained in use until the German advance during the Battles of the Lys in April 1918, but was used again in September and October.

INFORMATION

The 1st Royal Newfoundland Regiment and 1/2nd Monmouths fought here on 11 April 1918 during the German advance as the British were pushed back along the road from Armentieres and Nieppe.

When the Germans occupied the area they used the cemetery giving it the name Papot Military Cemetery. Of the graves here thirty-three are men of the 10th East Yorkshires (92nd Brigade, 31st Division).

Also buried here is Private Ernest Worsley of the 2nd Middlesex (23rd Brigade, 8th Division). He deserted from his battalion while in the rear collecting rations for his unit which was in the front-line. He was arrested at Calais and executed near this cemetery on 22 October 1917.

UK – 173   Aust – 72   NZ – 48   Ger – 36
KUG – 7   Area – 1611 sq yds

LOCATION

Pont d'Achelles Cemetery is south of Ieper on the Franco-Belgian border, 150 m north of the Bailleul – Armentieres road (D933), from which it is well signed.

Journey Time – 55 mins

C.W.G.C. Reference – 5/100

PONT de NIEPPE COMMUNAL CEMETERY   *No. 112*

HISTORY

The cemetery was used from October 1914 until the German advance in March 1918 and again from September to November 1918.

INFORMATION

The British graves are to the right at the eastern end of the cemetery. There is also a large German cemetery at the west end of the graveyard which was made when they held the village in the summer of 1918 and after the War with the concentration of German graves from the area. It includes forty-six graves which were moved from the boundaries of the Communal Cemetery. There is also a French military cemetery next to the British Plots so that it almost seems as if the British and French dead face the German burials over a no man's land of civil graves.

During the Battles of the Lys in April 1918 the 18th (1st Tyneside Pioneers) Northumberland Fusiliers held the bridge from which the village gets its name when the Germans attacked on 7 April. From Armentieres to Ploegsteert five German Divisions advanced upon five British Brigades. The Fusiliers held the bridge for British troops to withdraw until 11 April before blowing it as the Germans began to cross.

The village was retaken by the 29th Division on 3rd September 1918. It had been taken by the 1st Hampshires on 16 October 1914 and the 6th Division had used Nieppe as their Divisional headquarters in late 1914.

UK – 122   Aust – 12   KUG – 1   Unnamed – 11

Area – 682 sq yds

LOCATION
Pont de Nieppe Cemetery lies south of Ieper within the village of Nieppe west of Armentieres. It can be found at the end of a road that leads north from the Bailleul – Armentieres road (D933) about 100 m east of the turn to the motorway from Nieppe. The turn to the cemetery has a German War Graves Commission sign on the corner but no C.W.G.C. sign.

Journey Time – 55 mins

C.W.G.C. Reference – 5/104

POPERINGE COMMUNAL CEMETERY   *No. 113*

HISTORY
The Communal Cemetery was used by the British from October 1914 to March 1915.

INFORMATION
The British graves are in several Plots, one against the wall by the main road, and the others in the eastern part of the graveyard. Each group of graves consists of burials of one month, eleven of October 1914, one of November 1914, nine of December 1914 and two of March 1915. There are also the graves of five workers of the I.W.G.C. who died between 1922 and 1951 though one has been removed to Ypres Reservoir Cemetery.

Poperinge was the main forward base in the area of the Salient. It was entered by the Germans on 4 October 1914 but when the French arrived on 15 October the Germans withdrew. The British 7th Division soon took over the town and it became a centre for hospitals, munition dumps and entertainment.

The baths in Poperinge in the War were in the Sugar Refinery which had been taken over as a delousing centre. Three huge vats contained increasingly cleaner degrees of water through which the men passed while their clothes were fumigated. Even so, the men were lousy again within days.

There are several interesting features in the town near the central square. The Town Hall at the east end of the Grote Markt or town square is in the Gothic style near St. Bertin's Church. At the west end is an old chapel, next to which is Gassthuistraat, known in the War as Rue de L'Hopital due, unsurprisingly, to the hospital on the street.

On Gassthuistraat is one of the most famous houses in Poperinge, if not the area of the Salient, Talbot House. In 1915, the Reverend Neville Talbot, 6th Division Chaplain, persuaded the Army to take over a house as a soldier's club, partly to provide an alternative to the less reputable establishments in the town. Talbot had his friend, Reverend Philip 'Tubby' Clayton, transferred to Poperinge to help him; they named the club Talbot House after Reverend Talbot's brother who was killed at Hooge in July 1915 and is buried in Sanctuary Wood Cemetery. The house provided a haven for soldiers as a club downstairs with a chapel in the attic which was open until the German Spring Offensive in 1918, and again afterwards.

The spirit of Talbot House spawned a Christian organisation, Toc H, which is artillery signalling code for Talbot House, formed by 'Tubby' Clayton, which expanded to become world-wide. In 1929, Lord Wakefield, who had brought the Spanbroekmolen Mine Crater – now the Pool of Peace – for the movement, (See Lone Tree Crater Cemetery) bought Talbot House for Toc H.

Opposite Talbot House was a popular shop which supplied souvenirs and material, such as methylated blocks of fuel for cookers and tobacco, that the soldiers considered essential for life in the trenches. Ironically the shops real trade was as an undertakers.

Also on Gassthuistraat was a place called 'Skindles' formerly run by Madame Beutin and her two daughters as an estaminet for officers. It was called the Cafe de la Commerce des Houblons but changed its name to Skindles at the suggestion of an officer from Maidenhead.

On Bertinstraat, next to the church, is the College Stanislas which was used as a hospital from 1915 to 1918 for civilian casualties caused by the bombing of Poperinge. The railway station on the road out of Poperinge to Ypres was the main target for the German guns as millions of troops passed through it on their way to the front.

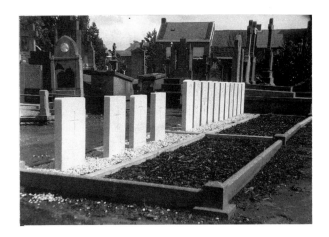

LOCATION
Poperinge Communal Cemetery, enclosed by a high red brick wall near the Old Military Cemetery, lies in Poperinge west of Ieper. It is found on the east side of the road from Reningelst to Poperinge about 700 m north of the by-pass.

Journey Time – 25 mins

C.W.G.C. Reference – None

POPERINGE OLD MILITARY CEMETERY   *No. 114*

HISTORY
The Old Military Cemetery was used from October 1914 until it was closed in May 1915 though a few burials were made after the War.

INFORMATION
This cemetery, enclosed by a high wall and set back from the road, is entered by a walled path and through a pavilion. I like this place as it feels like an English country garden.

The graves of 800 French and Belgian soldiers, as well as nearly 500 civilians, have been removed. Most of the civilians died during a flu epidemic.

A Chinese labourer was buried here in 1919. Coolie Wang Ch'un Ch'ih of the 107th Company, Chinese Labour Corps, had murdered a fellow Chinese labourer after the War. He was executed at Poperinge Town Hall on 8 May 1919. For further information about Poperinge please refer to the Communal Cemetery.

UK – 397   Can – 46   Chinese Labour Corps – 1
Unnamed – 22 UK and 2 Can   Ger – 2

Special Memorials to five British men and two Canadians known/believed to be buried here.

Area – 1860 sq yds

LOCATION
Poperinge Old Cemetery lies on the west side of the road from Reningelst to Poperinge, within the town of Poperinge, which is west of Ieper. It is about 700 m north of the by-pass, from which it is clearly signed, and 500 m north of the New Military Cemetery.

Journey Time – 25 mins

C.W.G.C. Reference – 5/41

POPERINGE NEW MILITARY CEMETERY   *No. 115*

HISTORY
The New Military Cemetery was opened in June 1915 as the Old Cemetery was closed when the space available was filled, and remained in use until the end of the War.

INFORMATION
For information about the town please refer to the Communal Cemetery. The New Cemetery is raised above the level of the road and has a good view of the spires over the town. There are a large number

of French graves here.

This cemetery holds an infamous record in that it contains the largest number of men to be executed by the British Army and buried in one place. This is because most disciplinary matters were dealt with when battalions were in camp away from the front-line and Poperinge was one of the most important centres for military camps in the British sector of the Western Front. Hence, there are seventeen men buried here who were shot in Poperinge for various crimes under the terms of the British Army Act. Six men who were executed are buried among the forty-five men in Plot II, Row F, possible the highest concentration of executed men anywhere on the Western Front.

Private James H. Wilson of the 4th Battalion, Canadian Expeditionary Force, deserted on 13 June 1916 during the Battle of Mount Sorrel. He was executed on 9 July 1916. Private Comte LaLiberte of the 3rd Battalion, Canadian Expeditionary Force, was executed for desertion on 4 August 1916.

Private John Bennett of the 1st Hampshires (11th Brigade, 4th Division) deserted during a German gas attack on 8 August 1916 only six weeks after experiencing the first day of the Battle of the Somme. He was executed for cowardice on 28 August 1916.

Private Albert Botfield of the 9th South Staffordshires (23rd Division Pioneers) deserted from a trenching detail near Contalmaison in the battlefield of the Somme on 21 September 1916. He was tried for cowardice, and executed on 18 October 1916, when his Division had been posted to the Salient.

Private Richard Stevenson of the 1/4th Loyal North Lancashires (164th Brigade, 55th (West Lancashire) Division) deserted at Fricourt on the Somme on 7 September 1916 but was captured four days later. He was tried, and executed for desertion on 25 October 1916, when his Division had been posted to Ypres. Private Bernard McGeehan of the 1/8th (Liverpool Irish) King's (also of the 164th Brigade) also deserted on the Somme in September 1916. He was executed on 2 November 1916.

Private Reginald T. Tite of the 13th (3rd South Downs) Royal Sussex (116th Brigade, 39th Division) was charged with cowardice during fighting near Thiepval on the Somme on 21 October 1916. He was tried on the Somme on 2 November but not executed until 25 November 1916 by which time his unit had moved north to Flanders. Tite's brother and two cousins who all served with the 13th Royal Sussex were also killed in the War.

Private William H. Simmonds of the 23rd (2nd Football) Middlesex (123rd Brigade, 41st Division) was another who had deserted on the Somme in 1916 but for whom justice was served once his Division had transferred to Belgium. He was executed on 1 December 1916.

Second Lieutenant Eric Sheffington Poole of the 11th West Yorkshires (69th Brigade, 23rd Division) was the first officer (one of three) to be executed in

the War. He deserted when his battalion took over trenches near Bailleul after he had been previously wounded by shrapnel. Poole was tried on 21 November and executed on 10 December 1916.

Private James Crampton of the 9th York and Lancasters (70th Brigade, 23rd Division) deserted in August 1916 while attached to the Royal Engineers. He was arrested in November and executed on 4 February 1917.

Private John W. Fryer of the 12th (Bermondsey) East Surreys (122nd Brigade, 41st Division) was executed on 14 June 1917 while under a suspended sentence of death for a previous offence. Private James S. Michael of the 10th Cameronians (46th Brigade, 15th (Scottish) Division) was executed for desertion on 24 August 1917.

Private Joseph Stedman of 117th Company, Machine Gun Corps, was the first member of the Corps to be executed when he was shot for desertion on 5 September 1917.

Sergeant John T. Wall was the sixth man of the 3rd Worcesters (7th Brigade, 25th Division) to be executed in the War. He had fought since 1914 but deserted on the Bellewaerde Ridge in August 1917. Wall was shot on 6 September 1917.

Private George Everill of the 1st North Staffordshires (72nd Brigade, 24th Division) had a poor record including several desertion attempts. He absconded for the last time as his battalion moved from Dikkebus to the front-line on 24 August 1917, but he was captured during the next day. He was shot on 14 September 1917.

Private Herbert Morris became the only man of the British West Indies Regiment to be executed on the Western Front when he was shot on 20 September 1917.

Private Frederick C. Gore of the 7th East Surreys (37th Brigade, 12th (Eastern) Division) had deserted twice and had also been charged with cowardice. He was the last soldier to be executed in Poperinge when he was shot on 16 October 1917.

UK – 596	Aust – 20	NZ – 3	Can – 55
BWI – 2	Chinese Labour Corps – 1		Fr – 275
Ger – 1	Area – 3716 sq yds		

LOCATION

Poperinge New Cemetery lies on the east side of the road from Reningelst to Poperinge, within the town of Poperinge, west of Ieper. It is just north of the by-pass from which it is clearly signed.

Journey Time – 25 mins

C.W.G.C. Reference – 5/41

POTIJZE BURIAL GROUND, IEPER   *No. 116*

HISTORY

The Burial ground was used from April to October 1918 when the cemeteries at the chateau came into the front-line during the German offensive.

INFORMATION

The 2nd and 14th Durham Light Infantry (both of the 18th Brigade, 6th Division) have 102 men buried here, the Guards Division have sixty-two, the 2nd Hampshires (88th Brigade, 29th Division) forty-six and the 1st West Yorkshires (18th Brigade, 6th Division) forty-three.

For information about Potijze Chateau and the fighting in the village, please refer to Potijze Chateau Grounds Cemetery.

UK – 580	Aust – 3	Can – 1	Ger – 2
Unnamed – 21	Area – 4420 sq mts		

LOCATION

Potijze Burial Grounds Cemetery can be found east of Ieper about 200 m north of the roundabout in Potijze which is at the junction of the Ieper – Zonnebeke and St. Jan – Zillebeke roads.

Journey Time – 10 mins

C.W.G.C. Reference – 5/34

POTIJZE CHATEAU GROUNDS CEMETERY, IEPER   *No. 117*

HISTORY

The Chateau Grounds Cemetery was used from May 1915 to September 1918 though Plot II was created after the Armistice.

INFORMATION

The Grounds Cemetery is separated from the Lawn Cemetery by a grass path and bank but as the two are enclosed by the same wall they are easy to confuse as being one graveyard. They are behind the relatively new houses and hence seem isolated, reached by a sheltered path from the road.

The chateau, one of several known to the Army as the 'White Chateau', was within the British lines for most of the War and had an Advanced Dressing Station in the grounds. The chateau came close to the front-lines during the Second Battle of Ypres in 1915, when it was the headquarters for the 27th Division, and came into the line in the summer of 1918. Due to the fighting and heavy shelling, which also damaged the three cemeteries in its grounds, very little remains of the chateau.

UK – 304	Aust – 23	NZ – 2	Can – 49
S Afr – 1	Fr – 1	Ger – 1	KUG – 85
Unnamed – 111			

Special Memorials to ten British men and ten Australians known/believed to be buried among the unnamed.

Area – 4003 sq mts (with the Lawn Cemetery)

The cemeteries here, east of Ieper, lie about 50 m north of the road from Potijze to Zonnebeke and 200 m east of the roundabout.

Journey Time – 10 mins

C.W.G.C. Reference – 5/34

POTIJZE CHATEAU LAWN CEMETERY, IEPER   *No. 118*

HISTORY
This cemetery was used from May to December 1915 and from July 1917 to October 1918.

INFORMATION
For information about this cemetery and fighting in this area please refer to the Chateau Grounds Cemetery.

UK – 191	Aust – 4	Can – 22
S Afr – 9	Ger – 3	Unnamed – 29

Special Memorial to one British man believed to be buried here among the unnamed.

Area – 4003 sq mts (with Grounds Cemetery)

LOCATION
Directions for this cemetery are exactly as for the Potijze Chateau Grounds Cemetery except that this is on the left as you enter the gate.

Journey Time – 10 mins

C.W.G.C. Reference – 5/34

POTIJZE CHATEAU WOOD CEMETERY, IEPER   *No. 119*

HISTORY
This cemetery was used from April 1915 to June 1917 and for three burials in 1918.

INFORMATION
For information about the fighting here and the chateau please refer to Potijze Chateau Grounds Cemetery.

Of the men buried here forty-six are of the 2nd Hampshires (88th Brigade, 29th Division) and nineteen of the 1st Royal Inniskilling Fusiliers (87th Brigade, 29th Division) who fell in the gas attack of August 1916 and lie buried close together.

UK – 145	Can – 6	Unnamed – 6

Area – 799 sq mts

LOCATION
Directions to this cemetery are exactly the same as for the Chateau Grounds and Chateau Lawn Cemeteries. However, as you enter them you will see a gate on the far side of the path that separates the two. A path from this gate leads to the Wood Cemetery 150 m away across the fields.

Journey Time – 10 mins

C.W.G.C. Reference – 5/34

HISTORY
This cemetery was begun in November 1914 by the 2nd Royal Dublin Fusiliers (19th Brigade, 4th Division) and 1st Royal Warwickshires (10th Brigade, 4th Division), and used until April 1918.

INFORMATION
The cemetery is the only one on the Salient to be named after a person. Major, later Brigadier-General, Charles Bertie Prowse, D.S.O., of the 1st Somerset Light Infantry fell on 1 July 1916 while commanding the 11th Infantry Brigade at Beaumont Hamel on the first day of the Battle of the Somme.

The cemetery, and the line along the eastern edge of the wood, mark the site of the stands by the 1st Hampshires and 1st Somerset Light Infantry in trying to hold St. Yvon in October 1914.

By the Cross of Sacrifice is a small pool which was part of the front line here. The track by the cemetery is now the only official access to the cemeteries in Ploegsteert Wood.

UK – 159	Aust – 13	NZ – 42	Can – 1
Ger – 12	Area – 4996 sq yds		

LOCATION
Prowse Point Cemetery lies at the northern edge of Ploegsteert Wood, south of Mesen and about 2 km north-east of Ploegsteert.

Journey Time – 35 mins

C.W.G.C. Reference – 5/94

RAILWAY CHATEAU CEMETERY, VLAMERTINGE *No. 121*

HISTORY
The graveyard was used from November 1914 until October 1916.

INFORMATION
The cemetery, with the chateau as a backdrop, is set back from the road next to a private house. It was also known as 'St. Augustine Street Cabaret' and 'L.4 Post'. One French grave has been removed.

UK – 105	Unnamed – 6	Area – 533 sq yds

LOCATION
Railway Chateau Cemetery lies in the western suburbs of Ieper about 300 m north of the N308 to Poperinge, from which it is clearly signed, and 200 m north of the railway.

Journey Time – 5 mins

C.W.G.C. Reference – 5/27

RAILWAY DUGOUTS BURIAL GROUND (TRANSPORT FARM) *No. 122*

HISTORY
This burial ground was used from April 1915 until 1918. It was enlarged after the Armistice with the concentration of about 400 graves.

INFORMATION
This is a deceptively large, but inviting, burial ground as much lies behind trees at the pond near the farm. It is an unplanned cemetery which reflects

the nature of its use in the War and the effect of the fighting. The entrance, with a large number of Special Memorials, is, I feel, particularly well designed.

The cemetery gets its two names from the farm and from the dug-outs that were in the embankments upon which the railway runs. Many of the burials date from 1916 and 1917 when there were Advanced Dressing Stations posted in the farm. A number of graves from the Third Battle of Ypres in late 1917 were destroyed by shell-fire before they could be properly marked.

To get here you may have passed through Shrapnel Corner at the junction of the Comines, Armentieres and Kemmel roads. It was the main route for men who were moving to the front-line as it was better sheltered than the more famous exit at Hellfire Corner.

You can see the entrance to Zillebeke Lake from here. Now a restaurant with a path around the lake the soldiers only knew it as a dangerous swamp surrounded by artillery positions.

In July 1915 the railway line to Hill 60 had been ruined so that troops had to transport all supplies manually. Lieutenant Ashford, and men of the 1/6th South Staffordshires, (137th Brigade, 46th (North Midland) Division) repaired the line here so that the 'Hill 60 Express' could run again.

V.C. – Temporary Second Lieutenant Frederick Youens, V.C..
13th Durham Light Infantry, 68th Brigade, 23rd Division.
From High Wycombe, Bucks.
Died – 9 July 1917.
Won – 7 July 1917. Lieutenant Youens was wounded while on patrol near Hill 60. He returned to the Field Ambulance for attention but as his wound was being dressed the Germans attacked, so he manned a machine-gun. As mortar bombs fell near him he threw them back at the Germans but one exploded in his hand and he subsequently died of wounds.

Concentrated here:

Valley Cottages Cemetery, Zillebeke – east of the

village on the road to Maple Copse Cemetery. It contained the graves of 111 British and Canadian soldiers. Many of the graves had been destroyed by shell-fire so that seventy-three are now represented by Special Memorials.

Transport Farm Annex – 100m south-east of here next to the road. The graves were removed to Perth Cemetery, but one officer whose grave was destroyed is commemorated here by a Special Memorial.

UK – 1629	Aust – 154	NZ – 3	Can – 594
BWI – 1	India – 4	KUG – 2	Ger – 3
Unnamed – 430			

Special Memorials to 258 men known/believed to be buried among the unnamed.

Special Memorials to thirty British men and forty-two Canadians buried in other cemeteries but whose graves were destroyed by shell-fire.

Area – 19584 sq yds

LOCATION
Railway Dugouts Cemetery lies south of Ieper on the west side of the road to Comines about 750m from Shrapnel Corner.

Journey Time – 10 mins

C.W.G.C. Reference – 5/47

RAMPARTS CEMETERY (LILLE GATE), IEPER   *No. 123*

HISTORY
The first burials on the ramparts surrounding Ypres were made by French troops in November 1914. The ramparts were used for burials by the British from February 1915 to April 1918 though many of the bodies have been concentrated in other cemeteries and only one section of graves now remains.

INFORMATION

The cemetery is particularly beautiful with its view of the moat surrounding Ypres and is the only Military Cemetery within the old walls of the town. The French graves have been removed.

The Lille Gate or Rijselpoort, which used to be known as the Messines Gate, is next to the cemetery. One of the main exits from Ypres for troops moving to the front, it was used more than the Menin Gate as this route was better sheltered from German guns. The main bastions of the Gate date from 1383 despite the damage in the War though the balcony over the road and the bridge over the moat are both post-war.

If you walk west along the ramparts, in the opposite direction from the Menin Gate and towards the railway station, you will come to the Lion Tower which dates from 1383. There are two islands in the moat which were created as part of the town's defences and further on there is a small deer park and machine-gun post. Finally you will reach the esplanade gardens and Old Powder Magazine, which has a pre- Seventeenth Century base upon which the rest was built in 1818. It was one of the few buildings to survive the German artillery bombardment in the War.

UK – 153   Aust – 11   NZ – 14
Can – 10   Unnamed – 5

LOCATION

To bring a coach here from the coach park or Cathedral involves such a tortuous route that it is not worth the effort. Walk from the Grote Markt which is no more than a ten minute walk on the road to Rijsel (Lille). The walk passes many interesting features that are outlined in the general information about Ieper at the start of this book. It is worth the walk.

Walk – 10 mins

C.W.G.C. Reference – 5/46

RATION FARM (LA PLUS DOUVE) ANNEXE, PLOEGSTEERT   *No. 124*

HISTORY

This cemetery was used from January 1915 until January 1918.

INFORMATION

This is not as attractive a cemetery as its nearby partner, La Plus Douve Cemetery, but you can get good views of the valley from here as well as Hill 63 and the Mesen Ridge. It is possible to imagine the cavalry charges in the valley during the early parts of the War and also the importance of holding the ridge.

For further information about the fighting here please refer to La Plus Douve Farm Cemetery.

UK – 185   Aust – 12   NZ – 4   Unnamed – 1
Ger – 1 Area – 1745 sq yds

LOCATION

Ration Farm Cemetery lies in the valley of the Douve about 8 km south of Ieper, south-west of Mesen and about 2 km south-east of Wulvergem. It is reached by means of a well signed farm track from the Mesen – Wulvergem road and you will find the cemetery on the north side of the farm. Please respect the farmer's privacy, you are on his land by his good graces.

Journey Time – 40 mins

C.W.G.C. Reference – 5/116

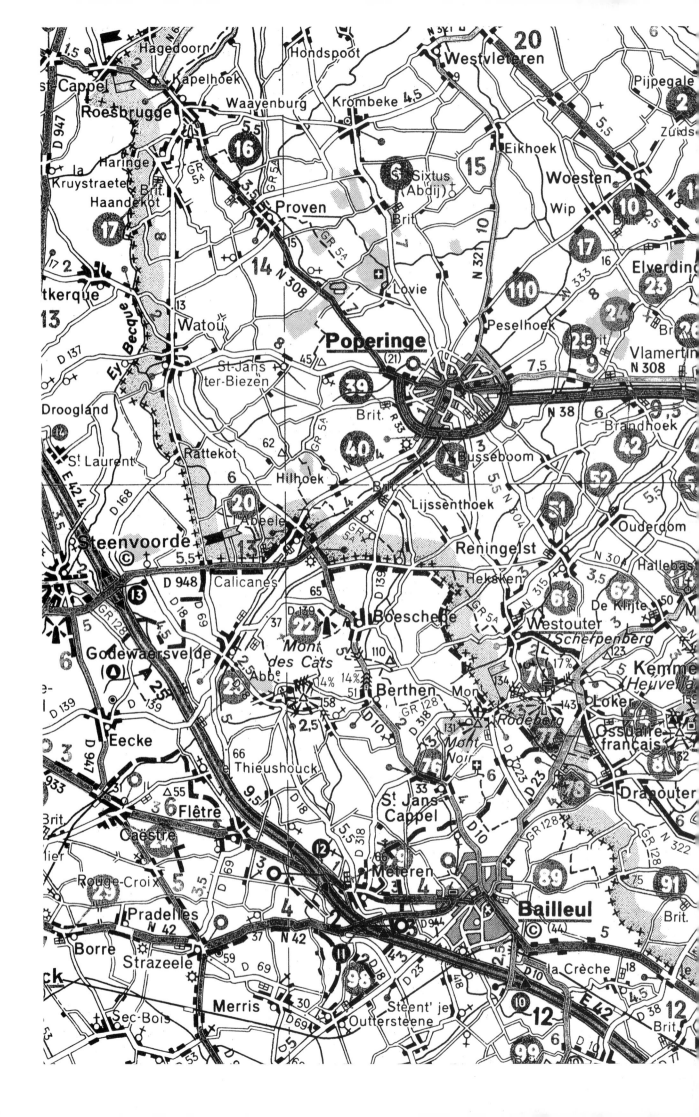

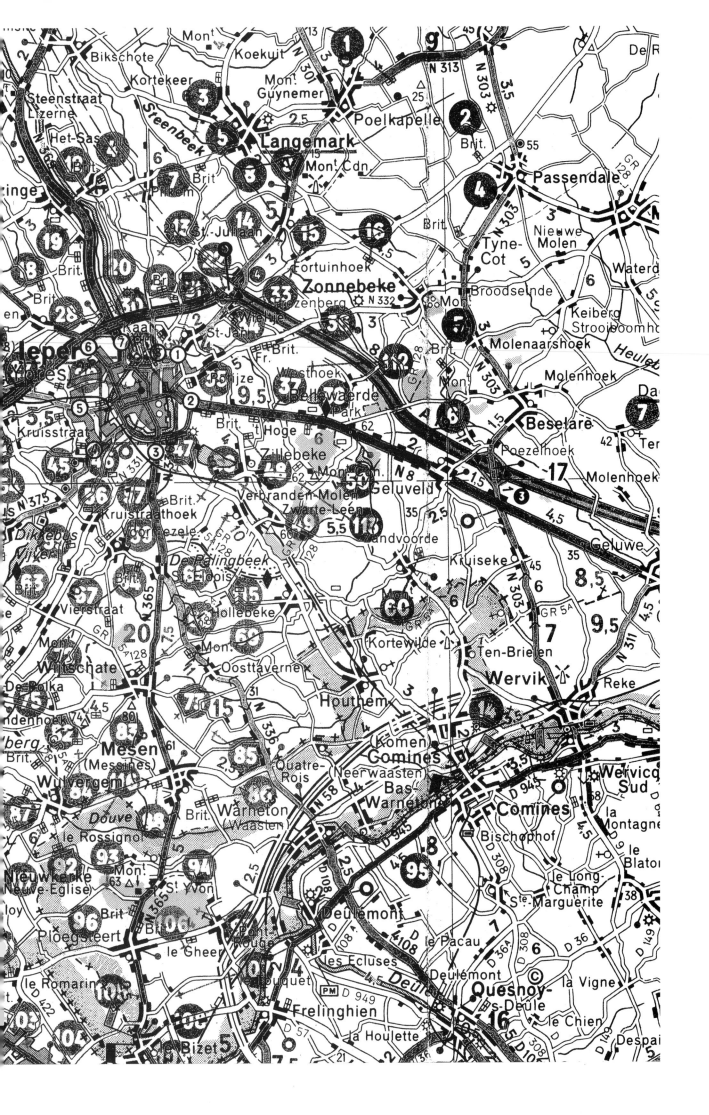

HISTORY

Begun in December 1914 by the 1st Dorsets (15th Brigade, 5th Division), the cemetery was used until April 1916 and for some burials in 1917 though it was enlarged after the War.

INFORMATION

R.E. Farm was the name given by the Army, its real name being the Ferme des Douze Bonniers. It was in Allied territory until the Germans captured it in their Spring Offensive of 1918.

In January 1915 the 1st Dorsets began a second cemetery here on the other side of the farm but it was hardly used. After the War the graves in it, twenty-three British and one Canadian, were concentrated into the No. 1 Cemetery, along with one isolated grave from the battlefield. The three French graves have been removed.

UK – 132   Can – 47   Unnamed – 11

Area – 1652 sq yds

LOCATION

R.E. Farm Cemetery lies south of Ieper about 1 km north of Wulvergem on the west side of the road from Wulvergem to Wijtschate. Only the entrance can be seen from the road, as the cemetery lies behind a farmhouse, set back from the road, and reached by a small path.

Journey Time – 45 mins

C.W.G.C. Reference – 5/84

HISTORY

The cemetery is the grave of twelve men buried from 1915 to 1917 during tunnelling operations beneath the Bellewaerde Spur.

INFORMATION

This is a fitting Memorial to these men who are buried in tunnels many feet below the surface. The Cross of Sacrifice stands high on the spur north of the Menen Road and can be seen from some distance away though there are no headstones in the small enclosure. The base of the Cross of Sacrifice bears an inscription:

"Beneath this spot lie the bodies of an officer, three N.C.O.'s and eight men of, or attached to, the 177th Tunnelling Company, R.E., who were killed in action underground during the defence of Ypres between November 1915 and August 1917."

and the names of the following:

Second Lieutenant C. G. Boothby, died 28 April 1916
Corporal R. Brindley, died 28 April 1916
Sapper M. Carter, died 13 June 1916

Sapper G. A. Chatt, died 14 December 1915
Sapper J. H. Cotterill, died 22 July 1917
Private T. E. Davis, died 25 February 1917
Corporal D. B. Evans, died 9 April 1917
Sapper S. Firth, died 9 March 1917
Private E. Poulton, died 25 April 1917
Private R. Roberts, died 9 April 1917
Sapper W. Spooner, died 28 April 1916
Corporal G. A. Woolley, died 22 July 1917

The Battle of Bellewaerde Ridge was fought on 24 and 25 May 1915 as part of the Second Battle of Ypres. The British responded with unsuccessful attacks on the ridge from June to September 1915 though it was not retaken until July 1917 during the British Flanders Offensive. The ridge was given up during the German advance in April 1918 and finally retaken by the 9th (Scottish) Division on 28 September 1918.

If you continue east rather than try to turn at the dirt track you will come to the Memorial to the Princess Patricia's Canadian Light Infantry on the south side of the road. During heavy fighting, where the Princess Patricia's Canadian Light Infantry Memorial now stands, a German attack on 8 May 1915 left the regiment exposed. They were subjected to a bombardment and gas attack during which they lost all their officers. Corporal Dove lost an arm and leg using a machine-gun to defend the line but the Canadians were still forced to withdraw as was most of the British line on this day. A Monument in the form of a simple circular stone seat surrounding a maple tree was erected in their honour. It bears the inscription:

"Here in May 1915
The originals of
Princess Patricia's Canadian Light Infantry
Commanded by the Founder
Major A. Hamilton-Gault, D.S.O.
Held firm and counted not the cost"

On 16 June 1915, battalions of the 3rd Division, the 2nd Royal Scots, 1st Royal Scots Fusiliers, 1st Wiltshires and 4th South Lancashires, attacked the spur upon which this grave stands. They were to take the German second line, after the 9th Brigade had captured the front-line here, and by 4.30 am, after ten minutes of bayonet combat, they had reached their objective. The commanding officer of the 1st Lincolns, Major Hugh Edward Boxer, D.S.O., then took a party of fifty men on a raid east of here, reaching the west end of the lake about 100 m away, before they were cut off. Major Boxer was wounded and sent most of his men back, he, however, never returned and was posthumously awarded the Distinguished Service Order. Despite a German counter-attack in the evening the 3rd Division had succeeded in pushing the Germans back to the Hooge Chateau grounds. The 9th Brigade took a small amount of ground but lost 143 officers and 3,417 men. The 1st Lincolns were to spend 248 days in the Salient during 1915 losing thirty officers and 1,046 men but no ground.

On 31 July 1917 the attack here by the 2nd Northamptonshires failed. During the attack Captain Colyer-Fergusson became isolated with six men but still took an enemy trench winning the Victoria Cross. He was later killed by a sniper and is buried in Menin Road South Cemetery. At the same time Lieutenant (temporary Brigadier-General and later a Major-General) Clifford Coffin, C.B., D.S.O. and Bar, of the Royal Engineers, won a Victoria Cross for his efforts in encouraging his men who were pinned down in shell-holes during an attack on Westhoek.

From 1–8 August 1917 the 8th South Lancashires were in action nearby pushing the line east from Westhoek towards Zonnebeke. In doing so they gained territory in which many of the wounded of 31 July still lay, hence, they rescued 150 men.

On the Cambridge Road leading to St. Charles are two Memorials on the right of the road 200 m past the turn to this cemetery. Next to the road is the Memorial Cross to Captain Henry Langton Skrine, 6th Somerset Light Infantry (43rd Brigade, 14th (Light) Division), who was killed and buried here on 25 September 1915. The monument is also the battalion Memorial. Close by is the Memorial to Captain Geoffrey Vaux Salvin Bowlby of the Royal Horse Guards who was killed in action on 13 May 1915. Both men are commemorated on the Menin Gate as their graves were destroyed in later fighting.

UK – 12 Area – 100 sq yds

LOCATION
R.E. Grave lies on a ridge about 500 m north of the Menen Road, east of Ieper. It is reached by taking the turn north, onto what the 'Tommies' knew as Cambridge Road, from the Menen Road 200 m east of Birr Crossroads Cemetery. The route from the Menen Road is clearly signed and although the roads are narrow they are passable. However, I would not advise anyone to try to take a car on the farm track that leads to the grave.

Journey Time – 10 mins

C.W.G.C. Reference – 5/112

RED FARM MILITARY CEMETERY, VLAMERTINGE   *No. 127*

HISTORY
The cemetery was only used during the German Spring Offensive in April and May 1918.

INFORMATION
This is one of the smallest cemeteries on the Salient and was begun as many of the other cemeteries in

the area of Vlamertinge had been filled. It was made near 'Red Farm' as a result of the number of men dying in the local Dressing Stations.

UK – 46   Unnamed – 17   Bel Civilians – 3

Area – 206 sq yds

LOCATION
Red Farm Cemetery lies west of Ieper just north of the old road to Poperinge (N308) 500 m west of the turn to the Brandhoek cemeteries.

Journey Time – 20 mins

C.W.G.C. Reference – 5/25

RENINGELST CHURCHYARD AND EXTENSION   *No. 128*

HISTORY
Begun in March 1915 the Churchyard and Extension were used until November 1915 when the New Military Cemetery was opened on the edge of the village.

INFORMATION
There are three headstones in the Churchyard in the far right corner (east) as you look from the road, close to the Extension. They are for two British graves and one Special Memorial to a British soldier whose grave was destroyed by shell-fire and lost.

The Extension is on the right side of the churchyard as you look from the road. It was used for burials from the local Field Ambulances in 1915 as well as two single burials later in the War. There are also two burials of men who fell during World War II.

UK – 55 (+ 2)   Aust – 1   WWII – 2

Special Memorial to one British soldier in the churchyard whose grave is lost.

Area – 834 sq mts

LOCATION
Reningelst Churchyard is in the centre of the village which is south-west of Ieper.

Journey Time – 30 mins

C.W.G.C. Reference – 5/51

RENINGELST NEW MILITARY CEMETERY, RENINGELST   *No. 129*

HISTORY
This cemetery was opened in November 1915, when it was considered that the Churchyard and Extension were not able to cope with the number of dead from the local Dressing Stations. It remained in use until September 1918.

INFORMATION
The wall of the cemetery seems higher on one side because of the slope, one effect of this is that the Cross of Sacrifice is considerably raised above the level of the cemetery.

The village never fell to the Germans and always

contained a number of Field Ambulances or Dressing Stations. Of the men who lie here 275 were from artillery units reflecting the nature of the activity in this area.

There are three men buried here who deserted while in action but for whom justice was administered when their battalions were in camp near Reningelst. Private Robert Loveless Barker of the 1/6th (London Rifles) Londons (140th Brigade, 47th (2nd London) Division) was charged with cowardice after his battalion was almost wiped out during the Battle of Flers on the Somme on 15 September 1916. He was executed on 4 November 1916 when his unit had been transferred to the Salient.

Private Frederick Loader of the 1/22nd (The Queen's) Londons (142nd Brigade, 47th (2nd London) Division) deserted when his battalion attacked 'The Bluff' on 7 June 1917 as part of the attack on the first day of the Battle of Messines. He was executed on 19 August 1917.

Private William Smith of the 3/5th Lancashire Fusiliers (197th Brigade, 66th (2nd East Lancashire) Division) deserted with two others in the quagmire between the Frezenberg Ridge and Poelkapelle on 4 October 1917. They surrendered three days later but Smith was the only one to be executed when he was shot on 14 November 1917.

Several reliable sources tell us of the following unhappy story. In a house on the L'Abeele road just north-west of this cemetery an event happened that serves as a good example of the danger to civilians remaining in the Salient during the War. Shrapnel fired at German aeroplanes from anti-aircraft guns in Ouderdom fell through the house. It killed a child sitting on its mother's knee, and sliced through her leg, the mother later died in a Casualty Clearing Station at Godewaersvelde.

UK – 452	Aust – 104	NZ – 2	Can – 230
S Afr – 1	Chinese Labour Corps – 7		Ger – 2
KUG – 1	UK Civilian – 1	Area – 4600 sq yds	

LOCATION
Reningelst Cemetery lies south-west of Ieper, about 200 m north-east of the church, on the road from Reningelst to Poperinge. It is on the left and though there is a C.W.G.C. sign you do not see it clearly until you are at the end of the houses. The path leads beside the houses to the cemetery although it seems as if you are walking into their back gardens.

Journey Time – 30 mins

C.W.G.C. Reference – 5/51

RIDGE WOOD MILITARY CEMETERY, VOORMEZELE *No. 130*

HISTORY
Begun as a regimental front-line cemetery in May 1915, it remained in use until July 1918 when the wood had come back into the front-line during the German Spring Offensive.

INFORMATION
Ridge Wood was the name given to a wood on the western edge of the ridge that runs parallel to the Ypres – Kemmel road. The cemetery is on the western edge of the wood.

The first burials were made by the 2nd Royal Irish Rifles (7th Brigade, 3rd Division). Units that made burials here, when they occupied the front-line, included the 1/9th Durham Light Infantry (151st Brigade, 50th (Northumbrian) Division), and 18th, 19th, 20th and 21st Canadian Infantry Battalions.

There were some French graves here but they have been removed.

On 8 May 1918 the British line ran north from Ridge Wood to Scottish Wood when the Germans attacked the 98th and 19th Brigades of the 33rd Division stationed here. The 2nd Argyll and Sutherland Highlanders fought heroically but were pushed back and away from the 1st Cameronians who had suffered heavy casualties. The action of Lieutenant Liddiard, Sergeant Goode and Corporal McKirdy of the Machine Gun Corps halted the German advance so that the 5/6th Cameronians could be used in a counter-attack to retake the wood.

UK – 260	Aust – 44	NZ – 3	Can – 292
Ger – 2	KUG – 20		Unnamed – 5

Special Memorials to two British men whose graves have been lost.

Area – 4460 sq yds

LOCATION
Ridge Wood Cemetery lies south of Ieper about 800 m west of the road to Kemmel. It is reached by turning west at the Elsenwalle Brasserie crossroads. The road to the cemetery is left and right at the next junction.

Journey Time – 10 mins

C.W.G.C. Reference – 5/55

RIFLE HOUSE CEMETERY, PLOEGSTEERT   *No. 131*

HISTORY
This cemetery was used from November 1914 until June 1916.

INFORMATION
The earliest burials here are of men of the 1st Rifle Brigade who died defending a strong point which was destroyed during the War. For more general information about the wood please refer to Ploegsteert Wood Cemetery.

UK – 229   Can – 1   Area – 1966 sq yds

LOCATION
Rifle House Cemetery lies in the heart of Ploegsteert Wood about 2 km north-east of Ploegsteert. A dirt track 50 m from Prowse Point Cemetery leads to the three cemeteries in Ploegsteert Wood of which this is the deepest into the wood. The path past Mud Corner is fairly easy to follow as it is fenced on either side and the walk is quite pleasant. There are also

C.W.G.C. signs from the Armentieres road and in the wood.

Journey Time – 35 mins + walk

C.W.G.C. Reference – 5/97

RUISSEAU FARM CEMETERY, LANGEMARK   *No. 132*

HISTORY
The cemetery was begun after the Guards Division had taken the farm on 8 October 1917 and it remained in use until November 1917.

INFORMATION
This small cemetery is on the edge of the farmyard. Please remember that this farmyard is private property and a home – you are allowed onto the farmer's property by his good grace.

The area around this cemetery saw severe fighting in 1917 with which I have dealt elsewhere. However, there was an important battle nearby in October 1914. The Germans used new mobilized troops to attack towards the canal and southwards to Ypres on 22 October. They pushed the line held by the 1st Infantry Brigade, and in particular the 1st Black Watch, to just west and north of this cemetery but it cost them 1,500 casualties.

These men of the I Corps under Sir Douglas Haig

(q.v.) had been thrown into action because of the French retreat from Houthulst Forest which meant that the Germans threatened to outflank the British 3rd Cavalry Division. Hence, I Corps took over the line from Zonnebeke to Bikschote until relieved by the French a few days later.

The 1st Northamptonshires were sent to assist in retaking the line from Ruisseau Farm to a crossroads on the Bikschote road known as the Kortekeer Cabaret. The battalion took most of the trenches but could not capture the position despite a valiant attack in which they lost five officers and over 100 men.

The 1st Loyal North Lancashires and 2nd King's Royal Rifle Corps were then sent in, reaching the Pilkem – Langemark road south-west of here, early on 23 October taking up positions on a line that ran parallel to that road south of this cemetery. The Loyal North Lancashires were under their third commanding officer of the War, Major Aubrey John Carter, D.S.O.; their first, Lieutenant-Colonel Walter Reginald Lloyd was killed on 14 September and their second, Lieutenant-Colonel Guy Cunninghame Knight, during the Battle of the Marne – Major Carter was to fall on 4 November 1914.

During 23 October the area north to the cabaret and to Langemark was taken by the 1st Loyal North Lancashires, 2nd King's Royal Rifle Corps, 2nd South Staffordshires, 1st Queen's and 1st Northamptonshires, but on 24 October it was decided that the trenches were too exposed and were to be abandoned.

UK – 82   Unnamed – 6   Area – 581 sq yds

LOCATION
Ruisseau Farm Cemetery lies about 2 km west of Langemark north-east of Ieper. It is 1 km north of the Langemark – Boezinge road and is reached from the crossroads, known as the Iron Cross, 400 m west of Cement House Cemetery.

Journey Time – 40 mins

C.W.G.C. Reference – 5/3

St. JULIEN DRESSING STATION (D.S.) CEMETERY, St. JULIAAN
No. 133

HISTORY
The Dressing Station Cemetery was opened in September 1917, after the village had been captured from the Germans during the Third Battle of Ypres, and it remained in use until the German Spring Offensive in March 1918. The cemetery was doubled in size after the Armistice with the concentration of graves from the surrounding battlefields.

INFORMATION
St. Juliaan, known during the War as St. Julien, saw much fighting in the War. It was an important objective in 1915 during the German offensive after the British had held it since autumn 1914. In Kitchener's Wood, north-west of the village, during one hour on the night of 22 April 1915, the 10th Canadian Infantry Battalion had three commanding officers as two, Lieutenant-Colonel Boyle and Major McLaren, were killed in the fighting in the wood. The third, Major Ormond, decided to retreat after consultation with the commanding officer of the 16th Canadian Battalion, Lieutenant-Colonel Leckie.

The 10th Brigade were rushed to the front-line here on 24 April to halt the German advance. Two Companies of the 3rd Canadian Infantry Battalion found themselves isolated between St.Juliaan and Kitchener's Wood, known locally as Bois des Cuisiniers, and now just an open field. When they were finally withdrawn the forty-three survivors were all wounded but had stemmed the German advance. Corporal Fisher of the 13th Canadian Infantry Battalion won the first Victoria Cross awarded to a Canadian in the War. He attacked the Germans alone with one machine-gun, and is commemorated on the Menin Gate as his body was never identified.

On 25 April the 10th Brigade were sent in to a new line in front of Kitchener's Wood. The Brigade counter-attacked to within 100 m of St. Juliaan Church, roughly the point of this cemetery, but they could advance no further and in some places were forced back a short distance. Many troops were buried by the Germans in the following weeks, for example, the 1st Royal Warwickshires suffered casualties of sixteen officers and over 500 men.

On 26 April the 149th (Northumberland) Brigade became the first complete Brigade of Territorials to go into action, earning much respect through their courageous advance. They attacked along the road from Wieltje to St. Juliaan past the present site of Seaforth Cemetery but achieved nothing as they had to retreat almost immediately. In this action they suffered casualties of forty-three officers, including their commanding officer, Brigadier-General J. P. Riddell, and 1,912 men.

The Germans used gas here on 2/3 May 1915 to force the British to retire. Hence, 10th Brigade were withdrawn having lost seventy-three officers and 2,346 men.

The village again saw action in 1917 when the 39th Division entered the village, which had been turned into one of the fortresses of the Langemark line, on the first day of the Third Battle of Ypres. The rain on 31 July was a problem so that the battalions who tried to take the village suffered heavy casualties and could not hold the village though it was taken on 3 August. In capturing the village, the 39th Division suffered casualties of 145 officers and 3,716 men.

St. Juliaan was given up to the Germans without a fight during the Battle of the Lys when the British Command had decided to "readjust the line in the Salient". It was taken back for the last time on 28 September 1918 by the Belgians.

Many of the graves in the cemetery were destroyed by shell-fire, British and German, in 1918. The original cemetery now makes up Plots I, III and part of Plot II. There was a German cemetery in the village but it has been removed.

| UK – 290 | Aust – 10 | NZ – 3 | Can – 15 |
| NF – 1 | S Afr – 3 | KUG – 96 | Unnamed – 180 |

Special Memorials to nine British men and two South Africans known to be buried among the unnamed.

Area – 2173 sq yds

LOCATION
St. Julien D.S. Cemetery lies to the north-east of Ieper on the western edge of the village. It is clearly signed from the N313 as you enter the village from the direction of Ieper.

Journey Time – 20 mins

C.W.G.C. Reference – 5/9

St. QUENTIN CABARET MILITARY CEMETERY, *No. 134*
WULVERGEM

HISTORY
The cemetery was opened in February 1915 and used by Divisions holding this sector until the German advance in spring 1918. Two burials were made in September 1918.

INFORMATION
This is a large cemetery with good views of the valley, Hill 63 and other cemeteries in the area. The cabaret was an inn on the south side of the village of Wulvergem that was sometimes used as a battalion headquarters. The cemetery was begun by the 46th (North Midland) Division. Of the graves here eighty are of men of the Royal Irish Rifles of the 36th (Ulster) Division.

| UK – 316 | Aust – 7 | NZ – 64 | Can – 68 |
| Ger – 5 | KUG – 5 | | Area – 5554 sq yds |

LOCATION
St. Quentin Cabaret Cemetery lies south of Ieper about 300 m south of Wulvergem and is reached via the turn opposite the church which leads into the river valley.

Journey Time – 50 mins

C.W.G.C. Reference – 5/92

HISTORY

A cemetery was begun here in May 1915 but was severely damaged during the Battle of Mount Sorrel in June 1916. The present cemetery which was, in effect, begun in 1916, remained in use until the end of the War and was greatly enlarged after the Armistice.

INFORMATION

Sanctuary Wood gained its name in November 1914 when it was used to screen troops behind the front-line. Men lost from their regiments during the First Battle of Ypres gathered in the wood under the command of General E. S. Bulfin of the 2nd Brigade who ordered that they could not be used without his permission; hence, the word went out that this was a 'Sanctuary Wood'.

On 21 February 1915 the wood came into the front-line as the Germans blew three mines here. The 16th (The Queen's) Lancers held the line, and although a Lieutenant and ten men who had been partially buried by the mines were captured, resolute defence by the battalion meant that the German attack failed.

The wood was in the centre of the Battle of Mount Sorrel in June 1916. On 2 June, when the line was held by the 3rd Canadian Division, the Germans launched a heavy bombardment upon the Canadians who had never before been in battle. The attack drove a hole 700 m deep and 3000 m wide in the line occupied by the British Second Army consisting of the three Divisions of the Canadian Corps and the British 20th (Light) Division. A German infantry attack followed which took much of Sanctuary Wood, Hill 62, Armagh Wood and Mount Sorrel inflicting many casualties.

The Canadian commander, General Sir Julian Byng, ordered an immediate counter-attack using four battalions. But the attack was poorly prepared and not executed until the morning of 3 June by which time the Germans had consolidated their gains. Hence, the counter-attack was a failure.

On 6 June the Germans captured more Allied trenches pushing the Canadians towards Ypres at which point Byng determined to retake the 'high ground', so careful planning and practice took place over the next week. The attack was launched at 1.30 am on 13 June, in poor weather, but despite hard fighting the Wurtembergers, who had attacked the week before, were forced back to their old trench line. This is regarded as the first planned and co-ordinated Canadian attack of the Great War and was a complete success.

During the War the road, Maple Avenue, or Canadalaan, from the Menen Road to Hill 62, did not exist. A copse known as Zouave Wood immediately south of here was named after the French Colonial troops who held the position until the British came in 1914. On the morning of 30 July 1915 the 126th Prussian Infantry Regiment used flame-throwers ('liquid fire') for the first time in war against the 8th Rifle Brigade (41st brigade, 14th (Light) Division) who had only arrived on the Western Front on 18 June. The Germans bayoneted the few survivors who had already been badly burned. That afternoon the 6th Duke of Cornwall's Light Infantry, (43rd Brigade, 14th Division) who had witnessed the German attack, retaliated on a front along the length of Maple Avenue. As the Duke of Cornwall's Light Infantry started from the low ground they suffered heavy casualties but took, and held, the enemy positions until relieved.

In 1917 the 18th Division attacked from here across the valley towards Hooge on the first day of the Third Battle of Ypres. The Division was meant to attack Glencorse and Polygon Woods but got lost and suffered heavy casualties. (See Hooge Cemetery) Even so, the Germans gave up all the territory in Sanctuary Wood that they had controlled since 1915.

The 56th (London) Division were in Sanctuary Wood preparing for an attack on Glencorse and Polygon Woods on 15 August 1917. The Division successfully took Glencorse Wood and some men even managed to get through the wood to see Polgon Wood a short distance away. However, they failed to achieve all of their objectives. The two woods are today seperated by the A19 motorway.

Sanctuary Wood was lost to the Germans in their Spring Offensive of 1918 but was retaken by the 9th (Scottish) Division on 28 September 1918.

Maple Avenue was laid after the War to Hill 62. Beyond the cemetery is a cafe and museum, run by Jacques Schier, at which there is a section of preserved trenches, part of the Vince Street – Jam Row complex, that are worth a visit. I have seen young pupils thigh deep in mud which has given them a good idea of what conditions were like for 'Tommies' in the front-line. The owner sells a wide range of souvenirs and refreshments, so this is a good place for a lunch break. Though there is a small charge for the museum I recommend it without reservation.

Beyond the museum, at the end of Maple Avenue, is the Memorial to the Canadian troops who died in this part of the Salient. It is on the highest point of Observatory Ridge and gives excellent views of the battlefields; for example, Mount Sorrel can be seen to the south, Maple Copse to the east, a very good view of Ypres to the west as well as a view to the east as far as the Zandvoorde-Geluveld ridge.

Just outside the cemetery is the Memorial to Second Lieutenant Thomas Kieth Hedley Rae of the 8th Rifle Brigade who was killed in Hooge Chateau grounds on 30 July 1915. His parents raised the monument at the spot where he was believed to have fallen but in 1978, Baron de Vinck, the chateau's owner, asked that the cross be moved as he could not maintain the area properly.

There were three British cemeteries in Sanctuary Wood before June 1916 but they were destroyed during the Battle of Mount Sorrel. The traces of the only one that could be identified after the battle have formed the basis for the cemetery we see now. Sanctuary Wood Cemetery contained 137 graves at the Armistice but eighty-eight were represented by Special Memorials as their position could not properly be identified.

The cemetery was enlarged between 1927 and 1932 as graves were brought from as far away as Nieuport on the coast though most were from the Salient. Some 60% of the graves are unnamed and many are identified as buried in the cemetery but location unknown. One that is identified is that of Lieutenant Gilbert Walter Lytleton Talbot, 7th Rifle Brigade (41st Brigade, 14th (Light) Division) after whom Talbot House in Poperinge was named. He was killed during the attack that had been launched in retaliation for the first use of flame throwers. (See Poperinge Communal Cemetery)

Concentrated here:

Beythem Communal Cemetery – it contained one British burial made in October 1918.
Deerlijk German Cemetery – four British burials were made here in October 1918 of whom two were brought to Sanctuary Wood and two taken to Dadizele.
Donegal Farm German Cemetery, Dranouter – on the road from Dranouter to Wulvergem 800 m east of the village. One British unnamed officer was buried there.
Eiskellar German Cemetery, Geluveld – on the Menen Road near Herentage Chateau. It contained one British unidentified soldier.
Flanders Field American Cemetery, Waregem – one British Royal Air Force officer was buried there.
Ingelmunster German Cemetery – it contained two British Royal Flying Corps men.

Kastelhoek German Cemetery (No. 61), Hollebeke – on the main road near village. It contained five British men who fell in January and February 1917.
Klien-Zillebeke German Cemetery, Zillebeke – just south of Hill 60, it contained three British unidentified men.
Kortekeer German Cemetery No. 12a, Langemark – north of the cabaret between Langemark and Bikschote. It contained three British graves of 1914.
Kruiseeke German Cemetery, Comines – on the main road near the village. Two British unnamed men were brought to Sanctuary Wood while the others were taken to Zantvoorde Military Cemetery.
L'Alouette German Cemetery, Nieuwkerke – between the village and Hill 63. It contained three British unnamed men.
Langemark German Cemetery No. 9 – on the road to Pilkem. It contained five British soldiers.
Menen Communal Cemetery – it contained one British grave dating from 1914.
Messines German Cemetery No. 2 – north east of the village. It contained seven British graves dating from from 1915.
Messines German Cemetery No. 3 – just east of the church. It contained one British man and one Canadian grave.
Motor Car Corner Cemetery German Extension, Ploegsteert – at the northern edge of the present Motor Car Corner Cemetery. It contained seven British unidentified men who fell in 1918.
Petit-Pont German Cemetery, Ploegsteert – near Hill 63. It contained two British unnamed officers of the Machine Gun Corps.
Rabschloss German Cemetery No. 64, Mesen – it contained one British unnamed burial.
Reutal German Cemetery, Beselare – ten British unnamed graves were moved here while the others were moved to Perth Cemetery.
Slijpskapelle Churchyard, Moorslede – two British graves and one Newfoundlander were moved to Sanctuary Wood while one British burial remained there.
Terdegem Churchyard – it contained four British men of the Royal Garrison Artillery and one Canadian grave.

Three Houses German Cemetery (Hollebeke Cemetery No. 60) – it contained one British unnamed soldier who was brought here while the others were taken to Oostaverne Wood Cemetery.

Thourout Germen Cemetery No. 2 – it contained two British men of the Royal Air Force who fell in September 1918.

UK – 1734 (1215 unnamed)	Aust – 88 (54 unnamed)
NZ – 18 (13 unnamed)	Can – 142 (69 unnamed)
NF – 3 (2 unnamed)	S Afr – 3
Ger – 1	Area – 8373 sq yds

Special Memorials to eighty-eight men whose graves were destroyed by shell-fire.

LOCATION
Sanctuary Wood Cemetery lies east of Ieper about 500 m south of the Menen Road and is reached by taking Maple Avenue, which is very clearly signed from the Menen Road. Use the Memorial at Hill 62 to turn.

Journey Time – 10 mins

C.W.G.C. Reference – 5/50

SEAFORTH CEMETERY, CHEDDAR VILLA, LANGEMARK   *No. 136*

HISTORY
This cemetery was created on the 25 and 26 April 1915.

INFORMATION
This is a fascinating and unique cemetery with very good views of the Salient.

The farm here was known in the War as Cheddar Villa, and this area saw heavy fighting during the German advance in 1915. Action was particularly severe on 25 and 26 April when this cemetery was created as the dead were buried in the front-line. The trenches were then held by the 2nd Seaforth Highlanders who have 101 men buried here.

On 25 April the 10th Brigade counter-attacked from the site of the Oxford Road Cemetery through the position of this cemetery and Buffs Road in the early morning. The Brigade included Second Lieutenant Bruce Bairnsfather of the 1st Royal Warwickshires who became famous for his cartoons and postcards of characters on the Western Front. The Brigade was exceptional in that it was one of the few Regular Army Brigades that was at full strength, but by the time it reached a position 1 km north of Cheddar Villa 2,000 men had fallen. The 1/7th Argyll and Sutherland Highlanders lost twelve officers and 425 men in this attack which took no ground.

On 8 May 1915, in another German attack at this point, the 2nd Northumberland Fusiliers held the line. In the evening a German unit appeared in the rear of the Fusiliers but the Northumbrians continued to fight so that when they finally withdrew only 116 men of the battalion were alive. (For other events in 1915 near this cemetery please refer to Buffs Road Cemetery) Eventually in 1915 the line was pushed back to the west to a line through Mousetrap Farm.

Near the cemetery is a bunker, the original Cheddar Villa, that is now used as a farm building. It was captured on the first day of the Third Battle of Ypres by the 39th Division and turned into a battalion headquarters by the 1/3rd Oxford and Bucks Light Infantry. On 7 August 1917 the Light Infantry began a Dressing Station here, but a shell found its way into the main entrance causing many casualties.

The name of the burial ground was changed from Cheddar Villa Cemetery in 1922. This was at the request of the commanding officer of the Seaforth Highlanders, in memory of the large number of Seaforths who were buried here but whose graves were destroyed by shelling in later fighting.

Row A, Grave 8 and Row B, Grave 1 are large graves with Special Memorial headstones placed against the walls of the cemetery as the original graves were destroyed by shell-fire and we do not know precisely where each man is buried. A plaque, at the far end of the cemetery from the road, commemorates twenty-three officers and men of the 2nd Seaforth Highlanders who fell here but whose graves are lost.

UK – 147   Can – 1   Unnamed – 21   C.W.G.C. Reference – 5/14

Special Memorials to nineteen British graves des-troyed by shell-fire.

Area – 1205 sq yds

LOCATION
Seaforth Cemetery is north-east of Ieper and lies on the north side of the N313 north-west of the junction with the motorway and the N38 northern by-pass.

Journey Time – 20 mins

SOLFERINO FARM CEMETERY, BRIELEN   *No. 137*

HISTORY
Although the French had a Dressing Station and camp here early in the War, the cemetery was not begun until October 1917 during the Third Battle of Ypres. It remained in use until August 1918.

INFORMATION
The south end of the cemetery dips to a pond and gives quite a good view. Solferino was the name given to the farm opposite by the French. Of the graves here 100 are men from artillery units, twenty-one are engineers and twenty-four are from Labour Battalions of the Royal Army Service Corps. This shows that this area was always well behind the front-lines.

To get here you may have passed the Reigersburg Chateau in northern Ypres near the crossroads of the N8 and N38 which was used during the War, first by the Royal Field Artillery, and then as an headquarters for various units.

Brielen was completely destroyed in the War, however, the nearby Chateau des Trois Tours was hardly touched. The chateau was the headquarters of the 1st Canadian Division in 1915 and after the War became the headquarters for the Ypres League and the Anglo-Belgian Union. The junction with the N8 was known as Dawson's Corner after the camp that was here in the War.

UK – 293   Can – 1   NF – 1   BWI – 1
Ger – 3   WWII – 5 UK (1 Unnamed)

Area – 1440 sq yds

LOCATION
Solferino Farm Cemetery lies about 4 km north-west of Ieper and 1 km north of Brielen. The cemetery is about 600 m east of the N8.

Journey Time – 15 mins

C.W.G.C. Reference – 5/18

SOMER FARM CEMETERY, WIJTSCHATE   *No. 138*

HISTORY
This cemetery was begun during the Battle of Messines in June 1917 after this area had been taken from the Germans at the start of the battle. It is named after the farm by which it stands, and remained in use until the German advance in March

1918. A number of burials were made in October 1918.

INFORMATION
On the night of 31 October to 1 November 1914 the 1/14th (London Scottish) Londons were filling a gap

in the line here. They, and the 6th (Carabiniers) Dragoon Guards, were defending Wijtschate when the Germans attacked. The rifles of the London Scots began to jam, so they suffered heavy casualties until their commanding officer issued the order to withdraw. He took the remnants of his battalion back to Wulvergem, through the village, which fell to the Germans during the night. The London Scottish, all civilian workers in London and members of the same club, had become the first complete Territorial battalion to fight in the War but there were only 150 of them left on the next day to tell the tale.

In 1917 the village fell to the British following the blowing of mines here on the first day of the Battle of Messines, 7 June 1917.

On 25 April 1918 the 1st East Yorkshires held the line here, defending Wijtschate as part of the 64th Brigade, when the Germans attacked with a substantial superiority of numbers. The East Yorkshires were forced back across the Mesen – St. Eloi road north of the village and into the woods. At the day's end the battalion numbered two officers and twenty-seven men.

UK – 64   Aust – 20

Special Memorials to three British men and two Australians whose graves in this cemetery are lost.

Area – 757 sq yds

LOCATION
Somer Farm Cemetery lies west of the St. Eloi – Mesen road, south of Ieper, on the west edge of Wijtschate. It is clearly signed from the main road, at a crossroads in Wijtschate.

Journey Time – 20 mins

C.W.G.C. Reference – 5/68

SPANBROEKMOLEN BRITISH CEMETERY, WIJTSCHATE
No. 139

HISTORY
The cemetery was used almost solely on the first day of the Battle of Messines, 7 June 1917.

INFORMATION
This cemetery stands in a valley about 100 m from the road with excellent views of the village and its position on the ridge. This gives us a good idea of the task facing the British to take the well defended village. For information about the British advance here in 1917 please refer to Lone Tree Cemetery.

The burial ground contains the graves of men of the 36th (Ulster) Division who advanced here on 7 June 1917. All except one man buried here are from that Division and all except one fell on 7 June, the other on 8 June. The cemetery was lost in later fighting and only rediscovered after the Armistice.

On 12 March 1915 an attack by the 1st Wiltshires and 3rd Worcesters (both of the 7th Brigade, 3rd Division) captured a section of German trenches for two hours before they were ordered to withdraw. The attack cost casualties of twenty officers and 400 men. During the action Lieutenant (later Brigadier) Cyril Gordon Martin, C.B.E., D.S.O., who led a unit of the 56th Company, Royal Engineers, won the Victoria Cross.

Near the turn from the Wijtschate – Kemmel road there are a number of craters, one of which is the Peckham Crater visited by King George V in July 1917. This indicates how safe this area was considered to have become in such a short time and how successful the British advance had been in the Battle of Messines.

UK – 58   KUG – 5

Special Memorials to six graves lost in later fighting.

Area – 364 sq yds

LOCATION
Spanbroekmolen Cemetery is south of Ieper, about 2km south-west of Wijtschate and 4km east of Kemmel. It is approximately 400m south of the Wijtschate – Kemmel road and 100m from a side road. There are C.W.G.C. signs from the main road and at the path to the cemetery which lies in the valley below the level of the road.

Journey Time – 30 mins

C.W.G.C. Reference – 5/83

SPOILBANK CEMETERY, ZILLEBEKE   *No. 140*

HISTORY
This cemetery was begun as the British arrived in this sector in February 1915. It was used until the German advance in March 1918 and enlarged after the Armistice.

INFORMATION
The cemetery lies next to the old canal from Ypres to Comines, with this section known to the British as the 'Kingsway'. It is possible to walk along its route into Ypres, or, alternatively, you can take the path opposite the cemetery through Pallingbeek Park. (See Larch Wood Cemetery)

Spoilbank was also known as Chester Farm Lower Cemetery or Gordon Terrace Cemetery. Many of the 2nd Suffolks who died on 'The Bluff' are buried here. For further information about 'The Bluff' please refer to 1st D.C.L.I. Cemetery.

UK – 426   Aust – 67   Can – 16   Unnamed – 125

Special Memorials to ten British men and one Australian known/believed to be buried among the unnamed.

Area – 4975 sq yds

LOCATION
Spoilbank Cemetery is located south of Ieper, west of the Comines road between Zillebeke and St. Eloi. The cemetery is on the right 1.5km from the Comines road.

Journey Time – 15 mins

C.W.G.C. Reference – 5/59

STRAND MILITARY CEMETERY, PLOEGSTEERT   *No. 141*

HISTORY
The cemetery was begun in October 1914 when two burials were made from a Dressing Station located at the end of a trench, known as the Strand, that led from the road into Ploegsteert Wood. The burial ground was used again from April to July 1917 but its main use was after the Armistice when over 750 graves were concentrated here from the surrounding battlefields.

INFORMATION
The British Army called this location Charing Cross, nearby was a trench called Broadway which ended at Dead Horse Corner, just north of Piccadilly Circus. The Strand was held by the Germans in the summer of 1918, when they made a few burials, though most of the men buried here in the War were from Australian units. Those who were concentrated here

were mainly from the area between Wijtschate and Armentieres.

Concentrated here:

Epinette Road Cemetery, Houplines – to the south of the village. It contained twenty-four British men who fell from November 1914 to September 1915.

La Basse-Ville German Cemetery, Warneton – between Ploegsteert Wood and Warneton. It contained sixty-eight British men and one South African who died as German prisoners from April to August 1918.

Le Bizet Convent Military Cemetery, Ploegsteert – near Motor Car Corner Cemetery. It contained eighty-eight British men and one Canadian who fell from October 1914 to October 1916.

Nachtegaal German Cemetery No. 1, Merkem – between Merkem and Houthulst. It contained the graves of two British Royal Flying Corps officers who fell in June 1917.

Ploegsteert Wood New Cemetery, Warneton – in the south-east corner of the wood near Le Gheer. It contained nineteen British soldiers who fell at Le Gheer in October 1914.

Prowse Point Lower Cemetery, Warneton – between Prowse Point and Mud Corner Cemeteries. It was made by the 1st Rifle Brigade and contained the graves of thirteen British soldiers who fell in 1915 and 1916.

Touquet-Berthe German Cemetery, Ploegsteert – between Ploegsteert and Lancashire Cottage Cemetery. It contained two British unidentified Royal Air Force officers who fell in July 1918.

Warneton Churchyard – it contained the grave of one British soldier buried by the Germans in December 1914.

UK – 725   Aust – 284   NZ – 87   Can – 26
S Afr – 1   Ger – 11   Unnamed – 356   WWII – 8 UK

Special Memorials to four Australians and one New Zealander known/believed to be buried among the unnamed.

Special Memorials to thirteen British men and one New Zealander whose graves in other cemeteries concentrated here have been lost in later fighting.

Area – 5456 sq yds

LOCATION
Strand Cemetery is south of Ieper on the east side of the Armentieres road about 700 m north of the square in Ploegsteert.

Journey Time – 35 mins

C.W.G.C. Reference – 5/96

SUFFOLK CEMETERY, VIERSTRAAT, KEMMEL   *No. 142*

HISTORY
This cemetery was used in March and April 1915 by the 2nd Suffolks (8th Brigade, 3rd Division). It was also used in November 1917 for one burial, and October 1918.

INFORMATION
The graveyard is a very small and secluded cemetery next to houses and surrounded by a high hedge, set back from the road and reached by a short path. Suffolk Cemetery was used by the 38th Labour Group, Royal Army Sevice Corps, in 1918 to bury twenty-eight men, most of the 1/4th (Hallamshire) and 1/5th York and Lancasters (both 148th Brigade, 49th (West Riding) Division) who had died in the German advance of April 1918 but whose bodies had only just been recovered. At this time it was called the Cheapside Cemetery after the road here.

Private William Scotton of the 4th Middlesex (8th Brigade, 3rd Division) was executed in Vierstraat and buried near this cemetery on 3 February 1915. He had deserted on 23 January 1915 and surrendered to the authorities on the next day. However, his grave was lost in the War, probably when the front-line ran nearby during the German Spring Offensive in 1918. He is now commemorated on the Menin Gate.

UK – 47   Unnamed – 8   Area – 459 sq yds

113

LOCATION

Suffolk Cemetery is located south of Ieper about 2 km north of Kemmel. It is approximately 300 m west of the Ieper – Kemmel road and reached from the crossroads at the two unmistakeable large warehouses in Vierstraat. At the west end of the warehouses is another C.W.G.C. sign leading to the cemetery on the west side of 'Cheapside'.

Journey Time – 15 mins

C.W.G.C. Reference – 5/114

TALANA FARM CEMETERY, BOEZINGE   *No. 143*

HISTORY

The cemetery was begun in April 1915 by French colonial troops (Zouaves) but only used by the British from June 1915 until March 1918.

INFORMATION

This cemetery is set in fields some distance from the road. There are few formal rows of graves, hence, the disorganised nature and many single graves make the graveyard unusual.

Talana Farm was one of several features nearby that were named after events in the South African Wars. The first British burials here were by the 1st Rifle Brigade and 1st Somerset Light Infantry (both 11th Brigade, 4th Division).

There are several burials of men of the 1st East Lancashires, also of the 11th Brigade, who fell in a raid on 6 July 1915 though there are also many graves of men from the 49th (West Riding) Division who attacked from the nearby front-line at the start of the Third Battle of Ypres. The area was then occupied by artillery units who buried their dead here. It is thought that there are graves in the cemetery that were destroyed in later fighting and have been lost. The graves of twenty-seven French and two American men have been removed.

UK – 529   Unnamed – 14

Special Memorials to ten British men whose graves have been lost.

Area – 4477 sq yds

LOCATION

Talana Farm Cemetery is north of Ieper in fields about 100 m west of the main road from Ieper to Diksmuide and 700 m south of Boezinge.

Journey Time – 10 mins

C.W.G.C. Reference – 5/19

TANCREZ FARM MILITARY CEMETERY,   *No. 144*
PLOEGSTEERT

HISTORY

Begun in December 1914, the cemetery remained in use until the German Spring Offensive of March 1918.

INFORMATION

This cemetery has an attractive entrance but the view is spoilt by the local factories. It was made next to a Dressing Station that was in the factory for

114

much of the War.

This cemetery marked the point that is considered to be the southern limit of the Ypres Salient during most of the War. It was captured by the Germans for short periods in 1914 and 1918 but was usually just behind the front-line that was about 500m east of this cemetery.

The Special Memorial is near the gate in the attractive and unusual entrance garden.

| UK – 306 | Aust – 19 | NZ – 3 |
| S Afr – 4 | Ger – 2 | Unnamed – 6 |

Special Memorial to one British soldier known to be buried here.

Area – 2239 sq yds

LOCATION
Tancrez Farm Cemetery is found south of Ieper about 4km south-east of Ploegsteert. 1.4km south of Ploegteert square you can find on the east side of the road, near a supermarket, a tree of C.W.G.C. signs.

The road to the left and then the tree-lined avenue to the right will take you past Motor Car Corner Cemetery to a junction at which you turn left to Tancrez Farm Cemetery.

Journey Time – 40 mins

C.W.G.C. Reference – 5/108

TORONTO AVENUE CEMETERY, PLOEGSTEERT   *No. 145*

HISTORY
This cemetery was used for the burial of seventy-eight Australians who fell during the Battle of Messines from 7 to 10 June 1917.

INFORMATION
A secluded cemetery on the edge of the Ploegsteert Wood, this is one of three that reflect the importance of the wood and how difficult it must have been to take it.

Those buried here all belonged to the 9th Australian Brigade, 3rd Australian Division, many from the 36th Infantry Battalion, Australian Imperial Force, who erected a Memorial here to their comrades. The 37th (Victoria) Australian Infantry Battalion also advanced here on 7 June 1917 successfully taking all their objectives. Captain Robert Cuthbert Grieve was awarded the Victoria Cross for capturing two enemy machine-gun emplacements during the action.

For further information about the fighting in Ploegsteert Wood please refer to Ploegsteert Wood Cemetery.

Aust – 78   Area – 366 sq yds

LOCATION
Toronto Avenue Cemetery lies in the heart of

Ploegsteert Wood about 2km north-east of Ploegsteert. A dirt track 50m from Prowse Point Cemetery leads to the three cemeteries in Ploegsteert Wood. The path past Mud Corner is fairly easy to follow as it is fenced on either side and Toronto Avenue Cemetery is clearly visible from the C.W.G.C. signs at a junction of paths in the wood. There are also C.W.G.C. signs from the Armentieres road and in the wood.

Journey Time – 35 mins + 15 mins walk

C.W.G.C. Reference – 5/94

HISTORY

This cemetery was begun by the 5th Dorsets in June 1917 after this part of no man's land had been captured during the Battle of Messines. The burial ground remained in use as a front-line cemetery until the German advance in April 1918.

INFORMATION

The cemetery is about 100 m from the road behind some houses and in a field that is often populated by cows, hence watch where you step! Some cemeteries are entered through gardens and some through farmer's fields, but this has both garden and field. Please remember to shut and secure the gates.

On 1 November 1914 the line north from here defending Wijtschate was held by 400 men of the Composite Household Cavalry from the 4th Cavalry Brigade when nine Battalions of Germans attacked them. Unsurprisingly the Household Cavalry were forced to retreat through the village. (See Wytschaete Military Cemetery) The cemetery fell to the Germans in April 1918 but was finally recaptured in September.

UK – 70	Aust – 20	Ger – 14

Area – 638 sq yds

LOCATION

Torroken Farm Cemetery is found south of Ieper, south-east of Wijtschate, about 300 m east of the road to Mesen. It is clearly signed from the main road and lies about 100 m from the side road, behind houses in the middle of fields.

Journey Time – 30 mins

C.W.G.C. Reference – 5/73

TRACK 'X' CEMETERY, St. JAN   *No. 147*

HISTORY

This cemetery was begun on the first day of the Third Battle of Ypres after the British had captured this area of no man's land. It remained in use until November 1917 and two further burials were made in May 1918.

INFORMATION

The road here, Admiral's Road, was named after a Captain of the 6th Division who used to ride up and down in 1915, when it was in the front-line of battle, to encourage the troops. He used an armoured car of the Royal Navy Division for his escapades.

On 27 April 1915 the Sirhind Brigade of the Lahore Division, Indian Army, attacked through here towards No Man's Cot and Minty Farms, the Ghurha battalions being followed by the 1st Highland Light Infantry and the 4th King's. The 1st Ghurkha Rifles reached the crossroads of Admiral's and Boundary roads 900 m north of here, before being pinned down in no man's land. By that time the battalion numbered only three officers and thirty

men out of a compliment of thirty-eight officers and 1,648 men. An order was made to create a Brigade out of the remaining 260 men of the 2nd Duke of Cornwall's Light Infantry, 280 men of the 1st York and Lancasters, 400 men of the 1/5th King's and 350 men of the 2nd Duke of Wellington's. The Brigade was to make a repeat of the attack that had decimated the Sirhind Brigade, but sense prevailed and the order was not carried out.

This part of no man's land was captured by the 39th and 48th (South Midland) Divisions on 31 July 1917. My grandfather's regiment in the 39th Division, found out on the first day of the Third battle of Ypres just how high the cost could be in such an attack. The regiment lost its commanding officer, seven officers and 150 men dead, and almost 400 wounded in the action out of 650 men who began the attack. The 1/1st Hertfordshires were wiped out in one day, a fate they were to suffer twice more in the War. Most of the men lost in the attack were just that, lost, and their names are now commemorated on the Menin Gate.

For further information about the fighting here please refer to Buffs Road, No Man's Cot and Seaforth Cemeteries.

UK – 126   Can – 5   Unnamed – 12

Area – 860 sq yds

LOCATION
Track 'X' Cemetery lies north-east of Ieper about 500 m north of the N38 northern by-pass. It is reached by turning from the N38, at the small crossroads just west of the end of the motorway, onto Admiral's Road, known today as the Mortel-weg. The cemetery is in fields 100 m east of the road.

Journey Time – 20 mins

C.W.G.C. Reference – 5/22

TROIS ARBRES CEMETERY, STEENWERCK   *No. 148*

HISTORY
The cemetery was used from July 1916 until the German advance in April 1918 during the Battles of the Lys, and again in October and November 1918 after the German withdrawal. It was greatly enlarged after the War with the concentration of graves from the surrounding battlefields.

INFORMATION
As the cemetery was begun next to the 2nd Australian Casualty Clearing Station here, 50% of the graves made in the original cemetery, Plot I, are of Australians.

There are four men buried in this cemetery who were executed for desertion during the War. Corporal George W. Latham of the 2nd Lancashire Fusiliers (12th Brigade, 4th Division) deserted in August 1914 and was not captured until Christmas. He was the second man to be executed in the Salient when he was shot on 22 January 1915 and his grave was moved here after the War.

Private Fortunat Auger of the 14th Battalion, Canadian Expeditionary Force, was the first Canadian executed in the War. He was put to death on 26 March 1916 for his third offense of desertion.

Private Peter Black of the 1/7th (Fife) Black Watch (153rd Brigade, 51st (Highland) Division) deserted in the summer of 1916 while under a suspended sentence of death. He was executed on 18 September 1916.

Private 'John King' of the 1st Canterbury Regiment, New Zealand Expeditionary Force, was an Australian serving under an assumed name. He deserted in May 1917 and was captured on 23 July. He was tried on 5 August and executed on 19 August 1917, this reflects the usual speed with which such matters were dealt.

Steenwerck, to the south-west, was in British hands for most of the War but it fell to the Germans during the Battles of the Lys on 10 April 1918. The hamlet of Trois Arbres fell on 11 April, after a defence by the 34th Division, but was retaken by the British in October 1918.

On the road to Steenwerck, and on the left immediately after the bridge over the motorway, there is Steenwerck German Military Cemetery. This is worth a visit while you are in this area.

Concentrated here:

Douanne Cemetery, Nieuwkerke – at the point where the road from Nieuwkerke reaches the Bailleul – Armentieres road. It contained four British and fifteen Canadian graves of men who fell from 1915-1916.

Fortrie Farm Cemetery, Nieuwkerke – 1 mile west of Le Romarin. It contained twenty-seven British soldiers who fell in November and December 1914.

Linen Factory Cemetery, Bac St. Maur – near Crois du Bac Military Cemetery, 2 miles south of Steenwerck. It contained twenty British men, one Indian grave and seven Germans, who were removed to Steenwerck German Military Cemetery.

UK – 954	Aust – 470	NZ – 214	Can – 20
NF – 1	S Afr – 1	Guernsey – 33	India – 1
Unnamed – 435			

Special Memorials to nine British soldiers and one Canadian known/believed to be buried here among the unnamed.

Area – 7099 sq yds

LOCATION
Trois Arbres Cemetery lies south of Ieper, in northern France, about 2 km south of the Bailleul – Armentieres road (D933). It is clearly signed from the D933 and lies on the west side of the road to Steenwerck about 200 m south of the railway crossing.

Journey Time – 50 mins

C.W.G.C. Reference – 5/102

TUILERIES BRITISH CEMETERY, ZILLEBEKE   *No. 149*

HISTORY
This cemetery was used in the early months of 1915.

INFORMATION
Some of the earliest British burials in the Salient were made here when 106 British soldiers were buried next to some Frenchmen. However, the cemetery was then destroyed by heavy shelling and, as a result, most of the graves were lost. Just twenty-six could be found and marked though only ten bodies could be individually identified. The other sixteen remain unnamed, and some eighty graves were lost.

Three French soldiers who were known to have been buried here but whose graves could not be found are commemorated by a French Cross near the entrance.

The effect of all this is that the cemetery has a lot of open space, with many of the headstones around the walls, creating an unusual cemetery.

UK – 26	Unnamed – 16	KUG – 11

Special Memorials to sixty-nine British men and three French soldiers known to be buried here but whose graves were destroyed by shell-fire.

Area – 2243 sq yds

LOCATION
Tuileries Cemetery is east of Ieper on the west side of the road from Zillebeke to Hellfire Corner, about 500 m north of Zillebeke church. It is set back from the road behind the houses and is reached by a short path.

Journey Time – 10 mins

C.W.G.C. Reference – 5/48

HISTORY

This cemetery was opened two days after the German line here had been captured during the Battle of Broodseinde. It was next to an Advanced Dressing Station established in a captured pill-box and used until the German Spring Offensive in March 1918 though it was greatly enlarged after the Armistice with the concentration of 11,500 graves.

INFORMATION

This is a breath-taking cemetery, on a hill, at the highest point of the Salient. The position of the Cross of Sacrifice on a pill-box with the backdrop of the Memorial is stunning and stands out against the ridge from a very great distance. In fact, it is sometimes best seen for the first time from across the valleys towards Langemark.

The Memorial at the east end of the cemetery is one of four on the Salient built to commemorate the men of Britain and the Dominions whose bodies were lost and have no known grave. The Menin Gate records the names of all who fell, and were lost, in the War from the Dominions (except New Zealand who have several Monuments in Flanders) and Britain up to 15 August 1917. The Tyne Cot Memorial bears the names of all soldiers who were lost in Flanders, 33,707 British, 1,179 New Zealanders and one Newfoundlander, from 15 August 1917 to the end of the War. The Monument is a semi-circular wall with three apses of which the central one is a Memorial to the men of New Zealand who fell in October 1917.

The area here was mainly the site of action in late 1917 during the Third Battle of Ypres as the front was pushed towards Passendale. This location was a strong point in the German line captured by the 2nd Australian Division on 4 October 1917. Several pill-boxes remain preserved within the cemetery. The 34th Battalion of the Australian Imperial Force reached the blockhouses here before being stopped. Captain Clarence Smith Jeffries, aged 23, led the attack on the blockhouse that now forms the base of the Cross of Sacrifice capturing four machine-guns and thirty-five prisoners. He then continued with a Sergeant and ten men to the pill-box in the south-east corner of the cemetery, in front of which he was killed and is now buried. For his courage and example he was posthumously awarded the Victoria Cross.

The blockhouse now used as the base for the Cross of Sacrifice, was the Advanced Dressing Station here in 1917 and 1918 around which the original cemetery grew. The 11th Canadian Field Ambulance had three squads of eight men working in each pill-box as it took six men to carry one stretcher in the mud. You can make out that original burial ground as the irregular graves between the Cross and the terrace. The graves were made by the 50th (Northumrian) Division, who named the cemetery 'Tyne Cot' or 'Tyne Cottage', and 33rd Division.

If you stand at the Cross of Sacrifice and look back towards the entrance, scan the area beyond and you will see the ground fought over on 4 October 1917, known as the Abraham Heights. The obelisk that you can see in the distance is a Memorial to the New Zealand Division who fought with the Australian Divisions in the Battle of Broodseinde.

A friend, Richard Pearson, has told me the story of his great-uncle, Second Lieutenant Herbert Milnes, who was killed on the Abraham Heights on 4 October 1917. His tale serves as a good example of the attitude of the men who fought in the War. Milnes had been forced to leave England for health reasons in 1905 becoming a lecturer at Auckland University. His family had made considerable financial sacrifices to find the money to be able to send him to New Zealand to escape the English winters, but at the outbreak of the War Milnes had joined up. It is ironic that "love of his country of birth and his hatred of injustice and oppression of the weak" brought him back to Europe into the worst conditions that man can imagine. He was killed by an explosion whilst sitting in a shell-hole and buried first in Otto Farm Cemetery, Zonnebeke before he was re-buried here. It is said of him that as Principal of his college, devoting himself to his students, he inspired in them great enthusiasm and laid a broad foundation for their professional life. In the hour of his former Country's need he gave up his work to enlist as Lieutenant of 'A' Company, 3rd Auckland Regiment. He was a worthy exponent of the college motto 'Totis Viribus'.

One casualty of the Battle of Broodseinde was Sergeant Lewis McGee of the 40th Battalion, Australian Imperial Force, who led a platoon that had been stopped by a blockhouse and was suffering heavy casualties. He rushed past with a revolver and managed to capture the pill-box with most of its

occupants. He was killed a few days later but was awarded the Victoria Cross posthumously and is buried here.

Although the Germans attempted to retake this vital position they failed. Tyne Cot was consolidated by the A.N.Z.A.C.'s in one of the most important successes of the War because the Germans no longer held the heights around Ypres.

The Memorial to the 7th Division, one of the first to be erected on the Salient, in commemoration of their action here on the ridge in 1914 and 1917, is to the south of the roundabout at Broodseinde through which you may have passed to reach the cemetery from Zonnebeke. The hill from Zonnebeke to Broodseinde was known as 'Devil's Hill'. A number of German and British cemeteries were made by the Germans on either side of the road during the War but they have been removed.

Please refer to Dochy Farm and Passendale Cemeteries for further information about events in this area. There are six men either buried in the Cemetery or commemorated on the Memorial who have been awarded the Victoria Cross.

Captain Clarence Smith Jeffries, V.C..
  34th Battalion (New South Wales), 9th Australian
  Brigade, 3rd Australian Division, Australian
  Imperial Force.
  Won – 12 October 1917, at Passendale.
  Died – 12 October 1917. Aged 23.
Sergeant Lewis McGee, V.C..
  40th Battalion (Tasmania), 10th Australian
  Brigade, 3rd Australian Division, Australian
  Imperial Force.
  Won – 4 October 1917, at Ypres.
  Died – 13 October 1917.
Private James Peter Robertson, V.C..
  27th Battalion, 2nd Manitoba (Winnipeg), 6th
  Canadian Brigade, 2nd Canadian Division,
  Canadian Expeditionary Force.
  Won – 6 November 1917, at Passendale.
  Died – 6 November 1917. Aged 35.

Memorial –

Temporary Lieutenant-Colonel Philip Eric Bent,
  D.S.O., V.C..
  9th Leicestershire Regiment, 110th Brigade, 21st
  Division.
  Won – 1 October 1917, at Polygon Wood.
  Died – 1 October 1917.
Corporal W. Clamp, V.C..
  6th Yorkshire Regiment (Alexandra, Princess of
  Wales's Own), 32nd Brigade, 11th (Northern)
  Division.
  Won – 9 October 1917, at Poelkapelle.
  Died – 9 October 1917.
Lance-Corporal Ernest Seaman, M.M., V.C..
  2nd Royal Inniskilling Fusiliers, 109th Brigade,
  36th (Ulster) Division.
  Won – 29 September 1918, at Terhaud.
  Died – 29 September 1918.

Concentrated here:

Iberian South Cemetery and Iberian Trench Cemetery, Langemark – 1000 m south-east of Bridge House Cemetery and 1000 m west of Dochy Farm Cemetery at a farm known to the Army as Iberian Farm. They contained thirty British men who fell in August and September 1917 and March 1918.
Kink Corner Cemetery, Zonnebeke – at the Potsdam Redoubt. It contained fourteen British men, nine Canadians and nine Australians who fell from September to November 1917.
Levi Cottage Cemetery, Zonnebeke – near the road to Langemark. It contained ten British men, eight Canadians and three Australians who fell from September to November 1917.
Oostnieuwkerke German Cemetery – it contained two British men.
Staden German Cemetery – just south-west of the village. It contained fourteen British men and ten Canadians who fell from 1915 to 1917.
Vladslo-Praatbos German Military Cemetery, Diksmuide – the present German cemetery contained six officers of the Royal Flying Corps and Royal Air Force who fell in 1917 and 1918.

Waterloo Farm Cemetery, Passendale – on the road to Passendale 500m north-east of Gravenstafel Memorial. It contained seven British men, ten Canadians and two New Zealanders who fell in 1917 and 1918.

Zonnebeke British Cemetery No. 2 – on the road to Broodseinde known as Devil's Hill. It contained thirty-eight British men buried by the Germans in one of four cemeteries they made for British soldiers who fell here. Of those, eighteen were of the 2nd Buffs, twenty of the 3rd Royal Fusiliers and all fell in April 1915.

UK – 8961	Aust – 1368	NZ – 520	Can – 1011
NF – 14	S Afr – 90	BWI – 2	Guernsey – 6
Ger – 4		Unnamed – 8366 (70% of total)	

Special Memorials to thirty-eight British, twenty-seven Canadian, fifteen Australian soldiers and a New Zealander believed/known to be buried among the unnamed.

Special Memorials to sixteen British and four Canadian men buried in other cemeteries but whose graves have been lost.

Area – 35,103 sq mts

LOCATION

Tyne Cot Cemetery is north-east of Ieper about 3 km south-west of Passendale. It lies approximately 300 m from the Beselare – Passendale road (N303). Once on the side road you want the third right turn to reach the cemetery entrance, the other right turns are narrow roads to Passendale and though one is by the back of the cemetery there is no real access.

Journey Time – 45 mins

C.W.G.C. Reference – 6/4

UNDERHILL FARM CEMETERY, PLOEGSTEERT   *No. 151*

HISTORY
This cemetery was opened in June 1917 during the Battle of Messines and remained in use until January 1918.

INFORMATION
The cemetery lies in the shadow of Hill 63, one of the most prominent features of the southern part of the Salient. Hill 63 was also known as Rossignol Heights upon which are the remains of the Chateau de la Hutte. It was defended by the 19th (Queen Alexandra's Own Royal) Hussars and 1st Dorsets in 1914, and in 1918 by the 25th Division. The burial ground was used in September 1918 when it was known as the 'Military Cemetery at the Foot of Nightingale Hill'.

UK – 102	Aust – 47	NZ – 39	Can – 1	KUG – 1

Special Memorials to two British men and three Australians whose graves here were destroyed in later fighting and lost.

Area – 2021 sq yds

LOCATION
Underhill Farm Cemetery is found south of Ieper, 1 km west of the Armentieres road, and about 2 km north-west of Ploegsteert. The turn from the N365 is at the foot of Hill 63 though the C.W.G.C. sign is only visible from the Ploegsteert direction.

Journey Time – 35 mins

C.W.G.C. Reference – 5/93

HISTORY

The cemetery was begun by the French in 1914. A small number of British men were buried here in 1914, but the graveyard did not became an official British cemetery until 1915. It was then used until June 1917 when, as the available space had been filled, the New Military Cemetery was opened to the south of the village.

INFORMATION

The burial ground lies above the level of the road, and a notable feature is the way men of the same unit are buried together. Many of the 55th (West Lancashire) Division are buried here as the battalions in that Division made every effort to get their dead from the front-line to this cemetery for burial.

Also buried here are two men who were executed during the War by the British Army. Driver Alexander Lamb of 21st Battery, 2nd Brigade, Royal Field Artillery deserted on 19 October 1914 and was not captured until 19 June 1915. An unusually long time passed before his trial but he was executed in the village soon after that on 2 October 1915.

Private Albert Rickman of the 1st Royal Dublin Fusiliers (86th Brigade, 29th Division) deserted on 2 July 1916 after taking part in the first day of the Battle of the Somme during which the British suffered 59,000 casualties. Rickman was caught on 20 July 1916 but not tried until September when his battalion had moved to the Salient. He was shot nearby on 15 September 1916.

The village, at the limit of the range of German guns, was destroyed by artillery during the War, so that only the church tower was left by 1918. Vlamertinge was held by the Germans briefly from 7 to 10 October 1914, after that it became an important Allied centre for hospitals, camps and munition dumps.

The gates to the cemetery were donated by Lord Redesdale in memorial of his son, Major, the Honourable Clement Bertram Ogilvy Mitford, D.S.O., of the 10th (Prince of Wales's) Hussars, who lies in this cemetery. There are four graves of men who fell in World War II though the French graves have been removed.

V.C. – Captain Francis Octavius Grenfell, V.C..
9th (Queen's Royal) Lancers, 2nd Cavalry Brigade, Cavalry Division.
Died – 24 May 1915.
Won – 24 August 1914. At Audregnies for saving the guns of the 119th Battery, Royal Field Artillery near Doubon and for bravery against infantry on the same day.

UK – 1113	Aust – 4	Can – 52	NF – 2
S Afr – 2	India – 1	Ger – 3	KUG – 1
WWII – 4	Area – 6875 sq yds		

LOCATION

Vlamertinge Military Cemetery is west of Ieper in the village of Vlamertinge. The cemetery is on the right of a side road 50 m north of Vlamertinge church and the N308.

Journey Time – 15 mins

C.W.G.C. Reference – 5/111

VLAMERTINGE NEW MILITARY CEMETERY,   *No. 153*
VLAMERTINGE

HISTORY

This cemetery was opened on 1 June 1917 in preparation for the Flanders Offensive as the Military Cemetery in Vlamertinge had been filled. It remained in use until the end of the War though most of the burials were made by the end of 1917.

INFORMATION

The cemetery is set back from the road behind a group of houses. When I visited the New Military Cemetery for the first time I had to persuade myself that I was not entering private property. Trust your instincts and you will see the cemetery once you are behind the houses.

Among those buried here is Private Edward Delargy of the 1/8th Royal Scots (51st (Highland) Division Pioneers). He had deserted in February 1917 and was arrested in Arras in August. He was tried when his unit had moved to the Salient and executed in Vlamertinge on 6 September 1917.

For most of the War the village was at the limit of the German artillery. The cemetery is on two levels with the Cross of Sacrifice, War Stone and pavilion raised above the level of the graves. Of the men here, 884 were from artillery units, reflecting the distance from the front-line and the activity in this area, and one was a member of the Y.M.C.A.. Apart from the entrance the most notable feature is the grave of a recipient of the Victoria Cross.

V.C. – Acting Company Sergeant-Major John
     Skinner, D.C.M., V.C..
     1st King's Own Scottish Borderers, 87th
     Brigade, 29th Division.
     From Pollokshields, Scotland.
     Died – 17 March 1918.
     Won – John Skinner won his Victoria
     Cross on 16 August 1917 during the Third
     Battle of Ypres. As his regiment was
     advancing it came under fire from three
     blockhouses near Langemark. Skinner and
     his commanding officer, Captain Currie,
     crawled forward and silenced three
     machine-guns and two trench mortars.
     Then Skinner continued to the
     blockhouses as Currie put up covering fire,
     bombing two of them into surrender, and
     capturing sixty prisoners, so that Captain
     Currie could order the company forward
     in a successful, but costly, attack. Skinner
     received his Victoria Cross from King
     George V and took fourteen days leave,
     but when he tried to return to his battalion
     he was posted to the reserve in Edinburgh.
     Risking a Court Martial, Skinner used his
     travel warrant to get back to his unit. He
     had a bet with Quarter-Master Sergeant-
     Major Victor Ross as to which of them
     would be wounded for the ninth time first.
     Skinner won the bet, though he did not
     live to collect the money, because he was
     shot between the eyes on 17 March 1918,
     while trying to rescue a comrade.

Ironically, records show that in his seventeen year military career since he had joined the Army in 1900 at the age of 16, Skinner had already been wounded nine times, three in the Boer War and six times from 1914 to 1917. At his funeral on 19 March six holders of the Victoria Cross of the 29th Division, (a Division often used to do the toughest fighting and hence, more than usually endowed with live recipients of the Victoria Cross), carried his coffin in a ceremony unique in military history. He was probably the only soldier to be carried to his resting place on the Western Front upon a gun carriage drawn by a team of horses and with full military honours.

| UK – 1609 | Aust – 44 | NZ – 1 | Can – 155 |
| S Afr – 3 | | Guernsey – 1 | Ger – 7 |

LOCATION
Vlamertinge New Military Cemetery lies on the southern edge of Vlamertinge west of Ieper. It is 500 m south of the dual carriageway Ieper – Poperinge road behind the housing on the east side of the Vlamertinge – Reningelst road. A C.W.G.C. sign indicates the path from the road.

Journey Time – 15 mins

C.W.G.C. Reference – 5/43

VOORMEZELE ENCLOSURES Nos. 1 AND 2,   *No. 154*
VOORMEZELE

HISTORY
This cemetery was used from March 1915 until April 1918, when the village fell to the Germans, and again after the German withdrawal.

INFORMATION
The enclosures were originally regimental burial grounds typical of those made early in the War. No.'s 1 and 2 are now treated as one cemetery and

bounded by the same wall but it is possible to distinguish between the two.

Enclosure No. 1 is the larger and further from the road. It was begun in March 1915 by the 28th Division and remained in use until the end of the War, though it was used by the Germans when they held the village in the summer of 1918.

Enclosure No. 2 was used from March 1915 to April 1917. Enclosure No. 4, formerly sited a short distance to the south and concentrated here after the Armistice, was used by the French in December 1914 and by the 4th Rifle Brigade (80th Brigade, 27th Division) from January to November 1915. It contained forty-two British men and two Germans brought here while the graves of thirty-three French soldiers were moved elsewhere.

The village was in British hands for most of the War though it fell to the Germans on 26 and 27 April. It was over-run by the U.S. 30th Division on 31 August 1918.

In the churchyard, 200m east of this cemetery, there is a Special Memorial to one British officer who was buried there but whose grave was destroyed by shell-fire. He is:
Lieutenant Edwin Winwood Robinson.
'D' Squadron, 5th (Royal Irish) Lancers.
Killed in action on 25 October 1914.

UK – 502	Aust – 17	NZ – 2
Can – 53	Ger – 5	Unnamed – 43

Special Memorials to fourteen British men and one German soldier whose graves here were destroyed by shell-fire.

Special Memorials to two British men buried in Enclosure No. 4 whose graves were destroyed and lost.

Area – 3162 sq yds

LOCATION
The Voormezele Enclosures are in the village south-west of Ieper. They are on the south side of the road into the village 700m east of the large crossroads on the N375.

Journey Time – 10 mins

C.W.G.C. Reference – 5/56

VOORMEZELE ENCLOSURE No. 3, VOORMEZELE   *No. 155*

HISTORY
This cemetery was begun by the Princess Patricia's Canadian Light Infantry in February 1915 when the Canadians were part of the 27th Division, and remained in use until April 1918. The graveyard was used again in October 1918 and after the Armistice for the concentration of over 1,200 graves.

INFORMATION
This is now the largest of the three Enclosures that remain in Voormezele though its position on the edge of the village next to modern housing creates a strange atmosphere. The concentrated graves include many of the 15th (Carabiniers) Hampshires who captured this village in September 1918. Several French graves were removed after the Armistice.

Concentrated here:

Eikhof Farm Cemetery, Voormezele – south of Oak Dump Cemetery and east of St. Eloi. It contained nineteen British men who fell in June 1917.

Elsenwalle Chateau Cemetery, Voormezele – in the grounds of the chateau north of the Brasserie Cemetery. It contained thirty British men, mainly of the 1st Wiltshires and Honourable Artillery Company (both 7th Brigade, 3rd Division), who fell from February to June 1915.

Haringhebeek Cemetery, Kemmel – 600m east of La Laiterie Cemetery on the bank of the stream. It contained thirteen British soldiers who fell on 7 June 1917.

Pheasant Wood Cemetery, Voormezele – on the 'Dammstrasse' and south-east of St. Eloi. It contained thirteen British men who fell in July and August 1917.
Vijverhoek Brasserie Cemetery, Vlamertinge – at the northern edge of Dikkebus lake near the main road. It contained sixteen British men, one Canadian and one New Zealander who fell in April, May and October 1918.

UK – 1481	Aust – 8	NZ – 2	Can – 100
S Afr – 1	KUG – 1		Unnamed – 612

Special Memorials to twelve British men and three Australians known/believed to be buried here among the unnamed.

Special Memorials to five British men buried in Pheasant Wood Cemetery whose graves have been destroyed in later fighting and lost.

Area – 5772 sq mts

LOCATION
Directions are the same as those for the No. 1 & 2 Enclosures but No. 3 is on the north side of the road into Voormezele 50 m west of the others.

Journey Time – 10 mins

C.W.G.C. Reference – 5/56

WATOU CHURCHYARD   *No. 156*

HISTORY
This churchyard was used occasionally from April 1915 until April 1918.

INFORMATION
The graves are on the northern side of the church in two small Plots. Watou was always well behind the front-line and was, therefore, used as a centre for camps. Many theatrical shows were performed in the village for soldiers in reserve.

UK – 11   Can – 1

LOCATION
Watou Churchyard is in the centre of the village that can be found west of Ieper and about 8 km west of Poperinge.

Journey Time – 35 mins

C.W.G.C. Reference – None

WELSH CEMETERY (CAESAR'S NOSE), BOEZINGE   *No. 157*

HISTORY
This cemetery was begun during the Third Battle of Ypres in July 1917 and remained in use until November 1917.

INFORMATION
Located some distance from the road in the middle

of fields, this is an isolated little cemetery positioned on the German front-line of 31 July 1917 at a point known as Caesar's Nose. Though many of the burials are of the 38th (Welsh) Division, many other units and areas are also represented in the cemetery.

On 26 April 1915, the Lahore Division of the Indian Army, pushed the Germans back from Colne

Valley to the north and east of here as far as No Man's Cot. All the battalions of the Lahore Division suffered heavy casualties. Serving in the Division were the 1st Manchesters, who by the end of the attack found most companies were being commanded by Sergeants. The attack cost 1,943 men, the 47th Sikhs numbered two officers and ninety-two men, the 40th Pathans had lost thirty officers and 300 men.

The 1st Welsh Guards of the 38th Division attacked through here on 29 July 1917. The Division also took a large area from the Germans on 31 July 1917. During the attack Sergeant Robert James Bye gained the Victoria Cross by capturing two pill-boxes and accounting for seventy of the enemy.

The Memorial to the Welsh Division is close by at Goumier farm. See Minty Farm Cemetery for directions.

UK – 68   Unnamed – 6   Area – 395 sq mts

LOCATION
Welsh Cemetery lies in fields about 3 km north of Ieper and about 2 km south-east of Boezinge. It is reached most easily via Boezinge and the French Memorial on the Boezinge – Langemark road. Turn south past the entrance to Dragoon Camp Cemetery and then left at the crossroads reaching the path to the cemetery on the south side of the road in 400 m.

Journey Time – 25 mins + 5 mins walk

C.W.G.C. Reference – 5/12

WESTHOF FARM CEMETERY, NIEUWKERKE   *No. 158*

HISTORY
The cemetery was begun in May 1917 and remained in use until the German advance during the Battles of the Lys in April 1918.

INFORMATION
This is an isolated little graveyard on the edge of the ridge, partly above the level of the road. The entrance is up a flight of steps but the effect of the slope is that some of the cemetery is at road level.

The cemetery was named after the farm, on the road here known as Waterloo Road, that served as Divisional headquarters for the New Zealand Division in May and June 1917. There are forty-five graves of men from artillery units. The Germans used the cemetery briefly in the summer of 1918.

A soldier buried here was executed for desertion nearby, on 31 October 1917, when his unit had been withdrawn from the front-line. Rifleman Thomas Donovan of the 16th (Church Lads Brigade) King's Royal Rifle Corps (100th Brigade, 33rd Division) already had a poor service record when he absconded for the fourth time on 22 August. He was captured on 1 September 1917 but not tried until 17 October.

UK – 69   Aust – 43   NZ – 12
Can – 1   Ger – 5

Special Memorials to four British men and two New Zealanders whose graves here were destroyed by shell-fire.

Area – 536 sq mts

LOCATION
Westhof Farm Cemetery is south of Ieper and about 2 km south-west of Nieuwkerke. It is reached from the road south of Nieuwkerke by turning west at a junction, with a C.W.G.C. sign on the corner, in the hamlet of Le Maloy. The cemetery is on the south side of the road and is hidden by a house.

Journey Time – 50 mins

C.W.G.C. Reference – 5/91

HISTORY

This cemetery was begun in October 1917 and used until the German advance in April 1918 when this village came close to the front-line. The graveyard was used again from August to October 1918 and was enlarged after the Armistice with the concentration of graves from the surrounding battlefields.

INFORMATION

The cemetery is entered by means of a few steps that could cause some problems for the disabled and stands among the new housing on the northern edge of the village. Westouter is a pretty village with a green, sports area, church and several good cafe-bars. It lies on the edge of the Monts des Flandres, and it is clear to see how they dominated the battlefield.

The cemetery was used by the French when they were defending the Monts des Flandres from April to August 1918 but their seventy-two graves have been removed. Approximately fifty British graves were concentrated here in their stead.

On route to Westouter it is possible to drive onto the Scherpenberg. Turn from the N375 approximately 1 km south of De Klijte as the road reaches a crest. This is onto a very small road that rises rapidly onto the Scherpenberg, there are hardly any passing places and it is illegal to stop. However, there are some excellent views of the battlefields below the Scherpenberg as you can see to the Kemmelberg and beyond. Dug-outs still exist in the hill that were used in the War particularly during the German advance in 1918 when they were halted here by the French with limited help from British units.

Two cemeteries have been concentrated in Westoutre Military Cemetery. They are the Bikschote German Cemetery also known as 'Friedhof XI' and the Kemmel French Cemetery No. 2 which was near the No. 1 Cemetery that we can still visit today.

V.C. – Acting Captain Eric Stuart Dougall, M.C., V.C..
'A' Battery, 88th Royal Field Artillery, 19th (Western) Division.
From Tunbridge Wells.
Died – 14 April 1918.

Won – 10 April 1918. When the infantry had been pushed back to the line of artillery on the Kemmelberg, Captain Dougall, unable to withdraw his guns, took command and formed a new infantry line just in front of the guns. He inspired and encouraged the troops, who held the German advance for twelve hours, but was ordered to withdraw at night when out of ammunition. Captain Dougall was killed four days later while directing the fire of his Battery. His grave was destroyed in later fighting and is marked by a Special Memorial.

UK – 157	NZ – 3	Can – 3
Chinese Labour Corps – 3		KUG – 2
WWII – 4 UK and 1Fr	Unnamed – 52	

Special Memorials to five British men known/believed to be buried among the unnamed.

Area – 1614 sq yds

LOCATION

Westoutre Military Cemetery lies about 200 m north of the village green in Westouter which is south of Ieper. The cemetery is on the east side of the Westouter – Reningelst road.

Journey Time – 35 mins

C.W.G.C. Reference – 5/61

WESTOUTRE CHURCHYARD AND EXTENSION,   *No. 160*
WESTOUTER

HISTORY

The Churchyard and its Extension were used occasionally from November 1914 to September 1918.

INFORMATION

The two parts of this burial ground are almost indistinguishable, the only difference being that the two Plots are separated by a few yards. The Churchyard, containing twelve British graves and four Canadians, makes up Plot I and the Extension is Plot II.

After the First Battle of Ypres the 3rd Division came to camps in the village. Divisional headquarters was at Mont Noir Chateau with the day-time command post on the eastern slope of the Scherpenberg.

| UK – 77 | Aust – 1 | NZ – 1 |
| Can – 19 | Ger – 1 | Unnamed – 1 |

Area – 533 sq yds

LOCATION
Westouter church is found in the centre of the village which is south of Ieper.

Journey Time – 35 mins

C.W.G.C. Reference – 5/61

WHITE HOUSE CEMETERY, St. JAN   *No. 161*

HISTORY
Begun in March 1915 by units holding the front-line nearby, the cemetery remained in use until April 1918 with over 700 graves concentrated here after the Armistice.

INFORMATION
Among those buried here there are four men who were executed during the War and whose graves were concentrated here after the Armistice. Private Herbert H. Chase of the 2nd Lancashire Fusiliers (12th Brigade, 4th Division) absconded during a German gas attack at Mousetrap Farm near Buffs Road Cemetery on 23 May 1915. This was his second offence of desertion. Chase was executed for cowardice at St. Sixtus Monastery, near Dozinghem Cemetery north of Poperinge, and buried nearby on 12 June 1915 while his unit where in camp near to Proven.

Private William J. Turpie of the 2nd East Surreys (85th Brigade, 28th Division) deserted while his battalion was moving from Vlamertinge to the front-line near Zonnebeke on 16 April 1915. He was one of the few deserters to reach England but was arrested two days after his arrival. Turpie was executed and buried near Dikkebus on 1 July 1915.

Privates Alfred E. Eveleigh and Robert W. Gawler, both of the 1st Buffs (16th Brigade, 6th Division), had each previously deserted. They were executed together at Burgomaster Farm, south-west of Poperinge, and buried nearby on 24 February 1916.

V.C. – Private Robert Morrow, V.C..
    1st Royal Irish Fusiliers (Princess Victoria's), 10th Brigade, 4th Division.
    From Dungannon, County Tyrone.
    Died – 26 April 1915. Age 24.
    Won – 12 April 1915. For rescuing comrades from his Regiment (known as the Faugh-a-Ballaghs) who were injured in no man's land south of Mesen when under heavy fire and without a Commander.

Concentrated here:

Basseville Farm German Cemetery, Zandvoorde – situated on the Zandvoorde – Zillebeke road at the foot of Zandvoorde hill. It contained five British men killed in November 1914.

Bavaria House Cemetery, Verlorenhoek – at the Advanced Dressing Station on the Zonnebeke road just east of the hamlet. It contained seventeen British men, four Australians, three New Zealanders, four Canadians and one man of the British West Indies Regiment, who fell from September to November 1917.

Bedford House Enclosure No. 1 – situated on the Ypres – St. Eloi road about 1 km south of the town. It contained fourteen British men who fell in 1915 and 1917.

Cottage Garden Cemetery, St. Jan – in the village close to the church. It contained forty-four British men and one Canadian who fell in 1914 and 1915.

Green Hunter Cemetery, Vlamertinge – close to the Den Groenen Jäger Cabaret estaminet at a crossroads on the Vlamertinge – Voormezele road. It contained twenty British men who fell in 1915 and 1918.

Hengebarte Cemetery, Dikkebus – 1 mile north of the village. It contained ten Royal Air Force men and fifteen Australians who fell from 1915 to 1917.

North Bank Cemetery, Voormezele – also known as the Lankhof, this cemetery was situated about 400 m south of Bedford House near the canal. It contained eleven Canadians killed in April and May 1916 but the cemetery was completely destroyed.

Wilde Wood Cemetery, Zonnebeke – north of the railway. It contained seventeen British men who fell from July to September 1917.

UK – 974	Aust – 40	NZ – 25	Can – 73
S Afr – 5	Bermuda – 1		BWI – 1
WWII – 9 (8 UK and 1 Bel)		Unnamed – 325	

Special Memorials to fifteen British men and one Canadian known to be buried here.

Special Memorials to twelve British men, eleven Canadians and five Australians buried elsewhere but whose graves were destroyed by shell-fire.

Area – 4902 sq mts

LOCATION
White House Cemetery is in the northern suburbs of Ieper on the north side of the road to St. Jan, called the Brugseweg or N313, about 1 km west of St. Jan.

Journey Time – 10 mins

C.W.G.C. Reference – 5/31

WIELTJE FARM CEMETERY, St. JAN   *No. 162*

HISTORY
This cemetery was used throughout the War, with the exception of the period of the German offensive in 1918.

INFORMATION
The cemetery is set back from the road in fields that were just behind British front-lines for much of the War. The farm from which it gets its name was destroyed in the War and never rebuilt.

Prowse Farm used to be about 300 m south of Wieltje Farm Cemetery. It was named after Major Charles Bertie Prowse, D.S.O., who led the 1st Somerset Light Infantry into action here during the German offensive in 1915 before being promoted to Brigadier-General in command of the 11th Brigade. Prowse Point Cemetery next to Ploegsteert Wood is the only cemetery on the Salient to be named after an individual.

UK – 113	NZ – 1	Can – 1
Ger – 1	Unnamed – 10	

Special Memorials to eighteen British men whose graves were destroyed in later fighting and have been lost.

Area – 480 sq mts

LOCATION
Wieltje Farm Cemetery lies in fields about 2 km north-east of Ieper between the N38 northern by-pass and the old road to St. Juliaan, the Brugseweg (N313). It is reached by a path from the N313 that is clearly marked by a C.W.G.C. sign.

Journey Time – 20 mins

C.W.G.C. Reference – 5/33

HISTORY

The cemetery was begun in April 1915 and remained in use until September 1917.

INFORMATION

This is the nearest to the road of the three cemeteries here associated with 'The Bluff'. Therefore, it is the most accessible of the group.

This was begun by the 1st Dorsets (15th Brigade, 5th Division) and 1st East Surreys (14th Brigade, 5th Division) next to a wood in an area known as 'The Ravine'. Many of the graves are of men of the 2nd, 3rd and 10th Canadian Infantry Battalions or the London Regiment. The number of burials in Plot I, Row B is unknown but is thought to be six.

For further information about the fighting at 'The Bluff' please refer to 1st D.C.L.I. Cemetery.

UK – 212   Aust – 3   Can – 111   KUG – 32

Area – 3181 sq mts

LOCATION

Woods Cemetery is about 5 km south of Ieper lying in fields halfway between the Comines and Warne-ton roads south-west of Zillebeke near Hill 60. There is a turn from the Comines road to several cemeteries about 200 m south of the turn to Zillebeke. Near Chester Farm Cemetery is a left turn, at C.W.G.C. signs, on to a narrow road leading to the three cemeteries on 'The Bluff' that you can see in the fields to the south of the road.

Journey Time – 20 mins

C.W.G.C. Reference – 5/65

HISTORY

The churchyard was used from November 1914 to April 1915.

INFORMATION

By February 1915 only two houses were still standing in the village. The church was destroyed in the War and later rebuilt being completed in 1925 but a large number of the graves were lost.

The village was close to the front-line in 1914. Bandsman (later Sergeant) Thomas Edward Rendle of the 1st Duke of Cornwall's Light Infantry earned the Victoria Cross in trenches near here on 20 November 1914 for rescuing some men injured in the fighting.

Corporal George H. Povey of the 1st Cheshires (15th Brigade, 5th Division) fled from the front-line near Wulvergem on 28 January 1915 accompanied by four Privates. The Privates were imprisoned for their desertion and Corporal Povey was executed on 11 February 1915 having been found guilty of leaving his post. After the War his grave could not be identified and he is now commemorated on the Menin Gate.

The Germans launched an unsuccessful gas attack here on 30 April 1916 when the line nearby was held by the 2nd Leinsters (73rd Brigade, 24th Division). Wulvergem fell to the Germans on 14 April 1918 during the Battles of the Lys but was retaken by the 30th Division on 2 September.

UK – 33   Unnamed – 1   KUG – 5

Special Memorials to twenty-three men whose graves were destroyed by shell-fire.

LOCATION
Wulvergem Churchyard is in the centre of the village which is about 8 km south of Ieper and can be reached either through Mesen or Kemmel.

Journey Time – 45 mins

C.W.G.C. Reference – None

WULVERGEM – LINDENHOEK ROAD MILITARY CEMETERY

No. 165

HISTORY
The cemetery was begun in December 1914 and remained in use until June 1917. It was used again from September to October 1918 and was enlarged after the Armistice with the concentration of graves from the surrounding battlefields.

INFORMATION
The burial ground begun by the 5th Division next to the Dressing Station here was first known as Wulvergem Dressing Station Cemetery. By the time of the Armistice it contained 162 graves that now form Plot I, the other graves, in Plots II to V, were concentrated here after the War. Many of the men brought here were killed during the German Spring Offensive at Kemmel and during the break-out from the Salient. There are Special Memorials to five British soldiers buried in Frenchman's Farm Cemetery and two British service-men buried in Cornwall Cemetery whose graves have been destroyed by shell-fire.

Concentrated here:

Auckland Cemetery, Mesen – just east of the village on the road to Mesen and on the north bank of the Douve. It contained twelve New Zealanders who fell on the first day of the Battle of Messines, 7 June 1917.
Cornwall Cemetery, Mesen – 140 m west of Auckland

Cemetery. It contained twenty-one British men, twenty of the 1st Duke of Cornwall's Light Infantry (14th Brigade, 5th Division) who fell from December 1914 to January 1915.
Frenchman's Farm, Wulvergem – 1 mile north of the village. It contained twenty-nine British men in several groups of graves, and one French 'Poilu', removed elsewhere, who fell in 1914 to 1915.
Nieuwkerke North Cemetery – situated in the river valley on the road to Lindenhoek. It contained twenty British men, sixteen of the 1st Royal Irish Fusiliers (108th Brigade, 36th (Ulster) Division) who fell on 2 and 3 September 1918.
Nieuwkerke Railway Halt Cemetery – on the south side of the village. It contained fourteen British men, seven of the 1/9th (Queen Victoria's Rifles) Londons (13th Brigade, 5th Division) who fell on 5 January 1915.

UK – 835	Aust – 35	NZ – 69
Can – 54	S Afr – 9	Unnamed – 353

Special Memorials to two British men known/believed to be buried among the unnamed.

Special Memorials to seven British men buried in cemeteries concentrated here but whose graves were destroyed by shell-fire and lost.

Area – 4017 sq mts

LOCATION

Wulvergem – Lindenhoek Road Cemetery can be found about 700 m west of Wulvergem and 8 km south of Ieper. It is on the south side of the road from Wulvergem to the N331 Nieuwkerke – Kemmel road.

Journey Time – 45 mins

C.W.G.C. Reference – 5/87

WYTSCHAETE MILITARY CEMETERY, WIJTSCHATE *No. 166*

HISTORY

This cemetery was made after the Armistice with the concentration of graves from other cemeteries and isolated positions on the battlefield around Wijtschate.

INFORMATION

The village was held by the French and British at the start of the War until the Germans attacked on 1 November 1914 and captured Wijtschate. This was despite a valiant defence by several Allied regiments to the east of the village.

On 2 November 1914 troops from the reserve grouped to the west of this cemetery attacked with the aim of driving the Germans from Wijtschate. This force included the 12th (Prince of Wales's Royal) Lancers, 800 men of the 1st Lincolns, 350 men of the 1st Northumberland Fusiliers from Kemmel, the 3rd (King's Own) Hussars, 20th Hussars and a detachment of the French 32nd Division. In the early light of day the Lincolns and Fusiliers attacked from here aiding the 1/14th (London Scottish) Londons in pushing the enemy across the Mesen Road south of the village and reaching the area of Torroken Farm Cemetery. While the Germans were thus occupied the 12th Lancers and 20th Hussars attacked them north of the village almost clearing it by 10.00 am. However, German troops over-ran Wijtschate again and remained in the village until 1917.

The village was captured comparatively easily by the 16th (Irish) Division on the first day of the Battle of Messines, 7 June 1917. Wijtschate fell to the Germans during their Spring Offensive in 1918 on 16 April but was finally retaken on 28 September 1918.

Next to the cemetery can be found the Memorial to the 16th (Irish) Division. There are Special Memorials to four British men buried at Rossignol Estaminet, three British men buried at R.E. (Beaver) Farm and two British men buried at Rest And Be Thankful Cemeteries whose graves were destroyed by shell-fire and lost.

Concentrated here:

Rest and Be Thankful Farm, Kemmel – 1 mile north of the village. It contained twenty-three British men, including thirteen of the 2nd Suffolks (8th Brigade, 3rd Division) who fell in 1915.

R.E. (Beaver) Farm, Kemmel – near the village on the road to Godezonne Farm Cemetery. It contained eighteen British men and four Canadian Royal Engineers who fell from 1915 to 1917.

Cemetery Near Rossignol Estaminet, Kemmel – 300m north of the Kemmel crossroads on main road. It contained eighteen British men, eleven of 1st Wiltshires (7th Brigade, 3rd Division), who fell from January to April 1915.
Gordon Cemetery, Kemmel – between the American Monument and La Laiterie Cemetery. It contained nineteen British soldiers, including fifteen from the Gordon Highlanders, who fell from January to May 1915.
Somer Farm No. 2 Cemetery – next to the present Somer Farm Cemetery. It contained thirteen British men buried by the IX Corps in June 1917.

UK – 486	Aust – 31	NZ – 7	Can – 19
S Afr – 11	KUG – 423	Ger – 1	Unnamed – 673

Special Memorials to sixteen British men known/believed to be buried here among the unnamed.

Special Memorials to nine British men buried in other cemeteries concentrated here whose graves were destroyed in fighting and have been lost.

Area – 3907 sq yds

LOCATION
Wijtschate Cemetery lies on the western edge of the village, south of Ieper, on the north side of the road to Kemmel. It is 300m from the town square.

Journey Time – 25 mins

C.W.G.C. Reference – 5/72

YPRES RESERVOIR CEMETERY, IEPER   *No. 167*

HISTORY
Opened in October 1915 the cemetery remained in use until after the Armistice when it was doubled in size with the concentration of 1500 graves.

INFORMATION
The cemetery is on the south side of the Maarschalk Plumerlaan, named after Field Marshal, Viscount Plumer (q.v.), architect of the successful Battle of Messines. This cemetery provides an excellent view of the spires of the town.

There were three cemeteries made in this area, two of which were concentrated here in the third known during the War as the 'Cemetery North of the Prison' and then 'Ypres Reservoir North Cemetery' before it gained its present name.

There are Special Memorials to two British men buried at the Infantry Barracks, and eight British men buried in Ypres Reservoir Middle, Cemeteries whose graves had been destroyed by shell-fire. There are also graves of officers and men of the 6th Duke of Cornwall's Light Infantry (43rd Brigade, 14th (Light) Division) who were killed in the vaults of the Cathedral when it was shelled on 12 August 1915. The survivors were rescued by men of the 11th King's (14th (Light) Division Pioneers) but the dead were not recovered until after the War.

Among those buried here there are three men who were executed in Ypres Prison for desertion during the War. Private Thomas Lionel Moles of the 54th (2nd Central Ontario) Battalion, Canadian Expeditionary Force, originated from Somerset and had previously served in the British Army. He was executed on 22 October 1917 after deserting on 4 October.

Private Ernest Lawrence of the 2nd Devonshires (23rd Brigade, 8th Division) deserted on 5 May 1917

and reached Rouen in France before his capture. He deserted again on 8 May, was recaptured, escaped and, in August, captured once more. Lawrence was executed on 22 November 1917.

Private Charles F. McColl of the 1/4th East Yorkshires (150th Brigade, 50th (Northumbrian) Division) served well from 1914 until wounded in 1916. He deserted on 28 October 1917 near Houthulst Forest and was executed on 28 December 1917.

V.C. – Lieutenant (later Brigadier-General) Francis Aylmer Maxwell, C.S.I., D.S.O. and Bar, V.C.
Indian Staff Corps, attached Robert's Light Horse.
Commanding, 27th Brigade, 9th (Scottish) Division.
Died – 21 September 1917. Age 46.
Won – at Korn Spruit on 31 March 1900 saving the guns of the Royal Horse Artillery during the South African Wars.

133

Concentrated here:

Ypres Reservoir South Cemetery – situated between the prison and the reservoir. It was also called 'Broadley's Cemetery' and 'Prison Cemetery No. 1'. The cemetery contained eighteen British men buried between October 1914 and October 1915.

Ypres Reservoir Middle Cemetery – just north of the 'South' cemetery. It was also called 'Prison Cemetery No. 2' and 'Middle Prison Cemetery'. The graveyard contained 107 British men, forty-one of the 6th King's Own Yorkshire Light Infantry (43rd Brigade, 14th (Light) Division), and one Belgian who were buried in August and September 1915.

Infantry Barracks Cemetery – also known as 'The Esplanade'. It contained fourteen British men, ten of the 6th Siege Battery, Royal Garrison Artillery, buried from April 1915 to July 1916.

UK – 2248	Aust – 142	NZ – 28	Can – 151
NF – 4	S Afr – 12	BWI – 6	Guernsey – 2
India – 1	Ger – 1	KUG – 7	Unnamed – 1035

Special Memorials to two British men known/ believed to be buried among the unnamed.

Special Memorials to ten British men buried in cemeteries concentrated here whose graves were destroyed by shell-fire.

Area – 14261 sq yds

LOCATION

Ypres Reservoir Cemetery is in the north of the town not far from the Grote Markt. The easiest route by car is via the Elverdingsesstraat past the C.W.G.C. office and then onto the Veurne road. The turn to the cemetery is clearly marked from the Veurne road with a C.W.G.C. sign on the corner. There are a number of shorter routes through the town to the cemetery but it is extremely easy to get lost. However, it is worth trying to walk through the back streets of Ieper to the cemetery as a good way to take in the atmosphere of the town.

Journey Time – 5 mins

C.W.G.C. Reference – 5/29

YPRES TOWN CEMETERY, IEPER   *No. 168*

HISTORY
This burial ground was used by the British Army from October 1914 until February 1915 and again in 1918.

INFORMATION
The Town Cemetery is a large graveyard that is still in use and there are British burials in many locations. There is a small group in the south corner against the Menen Road but the largest group is to the left of the main path.

The British section is interesting in the way that the chaotic nature of a communal graveyard has had the same effect on the usually organised layout of a C.W.G.C. cemetery. There are a large number of I.W.G.C. burials and also a Belgian Military Cemetery.

One of the most notable graves is that of Prince Maurice Victor Donald of Battenberg, K.C.V.O., grandson of Queen Victoria and a Lieutenant with the 1st King's Royal Rifle Corps when he was killed in action at the Broodseinde Ridge, on 27 October 1914. His cousins fought on the German side and his nephew was known to us as Earl Mountbatten.

UK – 142	India – 1	IWGC – 49

LOCATION

Access to Ypres Town Cemetery is very much like that to the Lille Gate Cemetery. It is far easier to walk than it is to bring a vehicle. Walk to the Menin Gate from the Grote Markt and continue up the hill. The Town Cemetery is behind high walls on the right of the Rose-lare and Zonnebeke road 200 m beyond the traffic lights.

Journey Time – 10 mins (Walk – 5 mins)

C.W.G.C. Reference – 5/32

HISTORY

Begun a few days after the first British burial in the Town Cemetery in October 1914, the Extension remained in use until February 1915. It was used again in 1918, after the Armistice for the concentration of widely scattered graves, and also in World War II.

INFORMATION

This is much smaller than the main burial ground and is separated from it by a wall and hedge. It is set back from the road behind houses.

One notable grave is that of Lord Charles Sackville Pelham Worsley, Bt, son of the Earl of Yarborough and a Lieutenant in the Royal Horse Guards when he was killed while taking part in the defence of Zandvoorde on 30 October 1914, aged 22. His body was buried by the Germans but transferred here by the British. The Memorial to the Household Cavalry at Zandvoorde stands on the spot where his body was found.

There were forty-three World War II burials made in the Extension when Ypres fell after heavy fighting in 1940. The Allied Commanders had tried to make their stand at Ypres, as had been done in World War I. But Hitler's army was stronger than the Kaiser's had been, and the British and French were weaker, so the attempt failed.

Concentrated here:

Dragoon Camp, Ypres – 300m south of Potijze. It contained twenty-four British men, including twenty of the 11th Argyll and Sutherland Highlanders, who fell in June and July 1917.
La Premiere Borne, Ypres – on the south side of the Menen Road near this cemetery. It contained twenty British graves.
Ypres Benedictine Convent Grounds – it contained ten British men buried from July to September 1915. Four were moved here and six to the Reservoir Cemetery.

UK – 462	Aust – 13	Can – 15	S Afr – 1
India – 1	Ger – 2	Unnamed – 137	
WWII – 42 UK and 1 Canadian			

Special Memorials to sixteen British men believed to be buried here among the unnamed.

LOCATION

Directions are as for the Town Cemetery but the Extension is at the west end of the Communal area and has its own entrance from the road.

Journey Time – 5 mins

C.W.G.C. Reference – 5/32

HISTORY

The cemetery was created after the Armistice with the concentration of graves from the surrounding battlefields.

INFORMATION

You can see the importance of holding the high ground and the ridges towards the north and west from here. On the morning of 26 October 1914 the trenches of the 1st South Staffordshires and 2nd Borders, in the fields that you can see between Kruiseeke and Zandvoorde, were destroyed by shell-fire. The Borders were overwhelmed and the Germans outflanked the 2nd Scots Guards and 1st Grenadier Guards so that when Lord Dalrymple of the Scots eventually surrendered it was with only five surviving men.

On 29 October 1914 the ridge running north from here towards the Menen Road was thinly held by the 2nd Royal Scots Fusiliers and 1st Royal Welsh Fusiliers who had been in action since 19 October. Throughout the day the Germans attacked believing the line to be strongly defended, but a combination of valiant defence and German incompetence – shells landing in the midst of their own machine-gun sections – meant that the line held until the evening when the surviving officers decided it was time to fall back from a position that was now almost surrounded. Only 120 wounded men reached the new British line closer to Ypres, and of the Welsh

Fusiliers only eighty-six returned.

On the 30 October 350 men of the 1st and 2nd Life Guards held the front-line on the slopes of Zandvoorde hill. In the German attack that took place a squadron of each regiment became isolated as the message to withdraw had not reached Captain Lord Hugh Williams Grosvenor commanding his squadron of the 1st Life Guards. Hence, his men gave up no wounded and no prisoners, every man falling at his post. Lord Grosvenor was related by marriage to Haig (q.v.), commanding I Corps, who heard of the loss of Zandvoorde while at his headquarters a few miles away.

The British bodies were buried by the Germans. That of Lord Worsley (q.v.) was buried by Leutnant von Neubert of the 1st Bavarian Jäger Regiment who made a map of the exact site of the burial and sent it via the War Office in Berlin to Worsley's home. After the War Worsley's body was recovered and buried in Ypres Town Cemetery Extension.

Lord Worsley should not have been in the line at all as his regiment, the Royal Horse Guards (the Blues), had been relieved by the Life Guards. Lord Worsley and a machine-gun section had remained behind. The situation was made worse for these cavalrymen because they were dismounted, an undignified position for the premiere cavalry troops of the British Empire.

The line from Zandvoorde to Geluveld, held by the 1st Queen's, 2nd King's Royal Rifle Corps, 1st Loyal North Lancashires and 1st Royal Welsh Fusiliers, was attacked by thirteen German battalions on 31 October 1914 who followed a heavy bombardment with an attack which broke through between the Queen's and King's Royal Rifle Corps. The Queen's lost their commanding officer so another officer was sent to headquarters for orders, but when he returned and searched for his battalion he could not find them. They had lost 624 out of 850 men. As the line was forced back, the 1st Loyal North Lancashires, who were ordered to cover the retreat, lost 400 men.

The battle continued for two weeks but even the German Kaiser, Wilhelm II, had come to realise that Ypres would not fall easily, as on 2 November he withdrew from his forward headquarters at Kortrijk having become frustrated at the inability to head his victorious army through Ypres as he had demanded on 31 October.

The cemetery contains the bodies of many men who fell in this area in 1914 but because of the nature of the fighting, and the fact that they were buried by Germans, the identity of the soldier buried in each grave was lost. Hence, most of the graves concentrated into this cemetery after the War are unnamed.

The churchyard in the village contains four men of the 10th (Prince of Wales's Own Royal) Hussars, who fell on 26 October 1914, buried on the north side of the church. Also in the village is the Memorial to the Household Brigade, 200 m from the town square on the road to Comines, set back from the road and reached by a small path from the road. Unveiled by Earl Haig (q.v.) in May 1924, it stands on the spot that Lord Worsley's body was found in 1914.

V.C. – Lieutenant (posthumously Captain) James Aaron Otho Brooke, V.C..
2nd Gordon Highlanders, 20th Brigade, 7th Division.
From Countesswells, Aberdeenshire.
Died – 29 October 1914. Age 30.
Won – 29 October 1914. He led the attacks on Geluveld under heavy fire, recapturing lost trenches, and prevented the enemy from breaking the line when no reserves were available. He was killed later in the day.

V.C. – Acting Sergeant Louis McGuffie, V.C..
1/5th King's Own Scottish Borderers, 103rd Brigade, 34th Division.
From Wigtown, Wigtownshire.
Died – 4 October 1918. Age – 24.
Won – 28 September 1918. Under heavy fire between St. Eloi and Wijtschate, during the advance on Piccadilly Farm, he single-handedly captured enemy dug-outs taking many prisoners and saving many men.

Concentrated here:

Kruiseeke German Cemetery, Comines – at the north end of the village. It contained 138 British men most of whom fell in October and November 1914.
Wervik German Cemetery – on the north side of the road to Comines. It contained two British men and one Canadian.

UK – 1525   Aust – 2   Can – 22   India – 1
Unnamed – 1135 (70% of total)

Special Memorial to a British soldier known/believed to be buried among the unnamed.

Special Memorials to thirty-two British men buried in German cemeteries but whose graves are lost.

Area – 5700 sq yds

LOCATION
Zantvoorde Cemetery lies on the eastern edge of the village on the north side of the road to Kruiseeke. This is about 6 km south-east of Ieper and is reached most easily via Geluveld. An interesting return route to Ieper is via Zillebeke, which brings you by the south side of Shrewsbury Forest across the battlefield of 1914 on an uncomfortable cobbled road that the 'Tommies' must have experienced. You should pass Battle Wood and just to the east of Hill 60 (See Larch Wood Cemetery) before descending into Zillebeke.

Journey Time – 30 mins

C.W.G.C. Reference – 5/60

ZILLEBEKE CHURCHYARD *No. 171*

HISTORY
The churchyard was mainly used in 1914 but a few burials were made later in the War.

INFORMATION
Some of the earliest burials in the Salient were made in this churchyard, including fourteen from the Foot Guards or Household Cavalry. There are some unusual headstones that seem to be made by families and not the C.W.G.C.. One of my favourite tombstones is that of Lieutenant-Colonel Gordon Chesney Wilson, M.V.O., of the Royal Horse Guards, killed in action on 6 November 1914. Carved upon the stone are the words "Life is a city of crooked streets, death is the market place where all men meet".

A number of French graves have been removed. In the church there is a stained glass window installed as a Memorial to Second Lieutenant Harold Avenal Blight St. George of the 1st Life Guards who was killed in action on 15 November 1915.

Zillebeke was in the front-line for much of the War and its buildings were destroyed by the fighting. The village is at the east end of Zillebeke lake, which was created in the Medieval period to provide fish for Ypres. The lake can be reached by a path from opposite the church to the eastern point of the lake, known as Hellblast Corner.

This became the scene of heavy fighting when, in October 1914, the Irish Guards held the village. From 1914 the positions around the lake were taken over by artillery. The 10th Siege Battery, Royal Garrison Artillery, were stationed here and lost over twenty men in two weeks.

From the beginning of 1915 the Cavalry Corps held the village until the 18th (Eastern) Division relieved them in July. On 28 March 1915 a raid on trenches east of the village captured a German officer who warned of the gas attack that we now know as the start of the Second Battle of Ypres. However, his story seemed so improbable that it was ignored at the time. Zillebeke fell to the Germans in April 1918 but was retaken in September.

UK – 22   Can – 10

Special Memorials to two British men whose graves here have been destroyed by shell-fire.

Area – 889 sq yds

LOCATION
Zillebeke Churchyard is in the centre of the village which is east of Ieper and reached through either Shrapnel or Hellfire Corners.

Journey Time – 10 mins

C.W.G.C. Reference – None

INFORMATION

I include Zuidschote Churchyard as an introduction to the large number of World War I Memorials in the area. The only link of the church to the Great War are the graves of five French 'Poilu' buried next to the seventy-six British World War II graves, who are mostly men from the Suffolks and Royal Berkshires. Zuidschote was in the French and Belgian sector of the front which begins at Boezinge and, therefore, the Memorials are to French and Belgian units or individuals. However, the journey through this northern section of the Salient gives a new perspective on the battles at Ypres.

I will deal with each Memorial in turn giving directions from the junction, at Lizerne, north of Boezinge, on the N369 road to Diksmuide where you turn left to Zuidschote. It is possible to visit all of these Memorials in one morning.

CHURCHYARD – this is on the road to Reninge about 600 m west of the N369.

BELGIAN CARABINIERS, 1915 – just north of the Lizerne crossroads west of the N369. The Memorial is a plaque 2 m above the ground between the windows on the wall of the house which is next to a brick tower.

CROSS OF RECONCILIATION TO THE FIRST VICTIMS OF GAS, 1915 – a tall narrow cross made of aluminium on the north side of the N369 just north-east of the turn for Zuidschote. It is a French Memorial which replaced the original one erected in memory of those, especially the 418th French Infantry Regiment, killed and affected by the gas attack in April 1915. The first Cross was destroyed in 1942 by the German Trophy Company who did not like the reference on the inscription calling Germans 'barbarians'. The present Memorial was designed by Paul Tourneau and inaugurated in 1961 on the base of the original.

This section of line was held by the 87th and 45th (Algerian) Divisions in 1915 when it was lost in the first gas attack. The Canadians filled much of the breach in the line caused by the French retreat though the French retook this position on 15 May 1915 finding many Germans dead and dying on the battlefield.

BELGIAN GRENADIERS, 1915 – 400 m west of the N369 on the side road by the Cross of Reconcilliation. The monument, an obelisk, is also the monument to the enthronement of King Leopold III in 1934.

3rd/23rd BELGIAN INFANTRY, 1915 – this small monument is 100 m beyond the Cross of Reconcilia-

tion on the road to Diksmuide, on the right just before the hotel and bridge over the canal.

GEBROEDERS VAN RAEMDONCK (d. 26-3-17), 6th/24th BELGIAN INFANTRY – next to the footpath on the north-east bank of the Ypres – Ijzer canal about 300 m north of the N369.

The next group of Memorials are near Merkem. Continue on the N369 for 3 km to a left turn to Merkem.

3rd BELGIAN DIVISION, 1918 – this is on the left of the main N369 200 m before the turn to Merkem. It takes the form of a plaque on a stone and marks the area from which this Division advanced in the final breakout from the Salient in 1918.

9th BELGIAN INFANTRY, 1918
11th BELGIAN INFANTRY, APRIL 1918
13th BELGIAN INFANTRY, 1918
The Memorial plaques to these three regiments that fought in the defence of Merkem during the German Spring Offensive, can be found on the ground floor wall between the windows at the south-east corner of Merkem Town Hall.

19th BELGIAN INFANTRY, APRIL 1918 – beyond the Town Hall as the road bears right before the church. The Memorial is an obelisk, situated in front of the wood on the left hand side of the road, to a regiment that was also involved in the defence of Merkem in 1918.

1st ZOUAVES, 1914 – north-west of Merkem next to the canal bridge is a cafe at Driegrachten. The Memorial to the Zouaves who fell in 1914 but have no known grave is on the wall of the cafe. There is a demarcation stone 100 m beyond as the Germans just crossed the canal here in 1918 during their

Spring Offensive. The Belgians also fought here when an attack was repulsed on 5 April 1915.

ADJ. ARMAND VAN EECKE (d. 9-9-18), 3rd BELGIAN INFANTRY – situated on the west side of the N369 500m beyond the crossroads with the Houthulst road. This small Memorial is surrounded by a hedge between houses opposite a field and is very easy to miss.

ADJ. TAYMANS (d. 18-11-17), 19th BELGIAN INFANTRY – just before the crossroads described above, there is a small right turn next to the cement/stone store and shop. In 300m on this very poor road there is a farm on the left and the monument is in the farmyard.

HOUTHULST FOREST BELGIAN MILITARY CEMETERY *No. 173*

INFORMATION

This is a large Belgian Military Cemetery of which there are few on the Salient, peaceful, beautiful and well worth a visit.

The forest fell to the Germans on 21 October 1914 and remained in their hands, during which time they installed artillery capable of shelling Ypres, until the Flanders Offensive in 1917. The forest was one of the key routes to the North Sea ports, and as a result, there was heavy fighting here. Even so, the forest and village were not recaptured until 28 September 1918 when the Belgians took this area during the breakout from the Salient.

Although it is possible to walk in the forest there are areas fenced off to the public that you must not try to enter. They are used by the Belgian Army Disposal Service who deal with the unexploded munitions that appear from the mud of the Salient every year. It is estimated that in an average year the Disposal unit will have to remove 15,000 unexploded shells, including gas shells, that they detonate twice a day during the summer. Some men have lost their lives clearing the mess left by earlier armies, for example, on 7 May 1986, four men were killed in one accident.

There are a number of Italian and French graves here and three Memorials in the forest and village. These are to the 1st, 7th and 13th Belgian Artillery, 1914-1918; 3rd/23rd Belgian Infantry for their actions here on 28 September 1918; and the 4th/24th Belgian Artillery, 1914-1918.

In the village churchyard seven British men who fell in World War II are buried. There are three soldiers from May 1940 and four airmen of 1941.

Bel – 1704   Fr – 146   Italian – 81

LOCATION

Houthulst Forest Belgian Cemetery is about 15 km north-east of Ieper on the east side of the road from Poelkapelle to Houthulst (N301).

Journey Time – 1 hr

C.W.G.C. Reference – None

MONT KEMMEL (OSSUARY), KEMMEL   *No. 174*

HISTORY

The Ossuary was created after the Armistice with the concentration of unidentified graves from the battlefields.

INFORMATION

Situated on the edge of the Kemmelberg the Ossuary overlooks an area in which many French soldiers died in 1914 and 1918 particularly in defending the Mount. There are over 5,000 unknown 'Poilu' buried beneath the obelisk as well as a small number of identified men whose names are inscribed on a plaque.

On route you may pass the Cafe Belvedere as you climb to the summit of the Mount. The tower was used by Sir Douglas Haig (q.v.) and other commanding officers as a vantage point over the Salient. It was rebuilt on the site of the original cafe which was destroyed in 1918 when the French were pushed off the Kemmelberg by the Germans on 25 April. The Mount remained in enemy hands until 31 August when the U.S. 27th Division assisted by the British

34th Division retook the hill.

On the summit of the Kemmelberg (159 m) a site has been chosen for a Memorial to the French who died in Belgium during the Great War, especially those who fell defending the Mount in 1918. Unveiled in 1932 by Marshal Petain, who had masterminded the defence of Verdun in 1916 and went on to be the Leader of Vichy France in World War II, for which he was sentenced to death, the column is 18 m high with a winged victory on the front. It used to have a 'Poilu's' helmet carved on top but it was not replaced after being struck by lightning.

Fr – 5294   KUG – 5237   Area – 2050 sq mts

LOCATION
The Kemmelberg is about 8 km south of Ieper, 1 km south of Kemmel, and is clearly signed from the centre of the village. The climb is very steep, on a cobbled road passing the Cafe Belvedere, to the summit. At this point the road bears right and downhill for 100 m to the Ossuary but I recommend parking at the Monument and walking the short distance to the Ossuary.

Journey Time – 35 mins

C.W.G.C. Reference – None

St. CHARLES – POTIJZE FRENCH MILITARY CEMETERY, IEPER   *No. 175*

HISTORY
Although the burial ground was begun during the War most of the graves in this cemetery were concentrated here after the Armistice.

INFORMATION
It is almost impossible to miss this large cemetery though it is screened by trees as you approach it from Ypres. Sculptures within the cemetery are of a Crucifix and Mourning Mother and a Memorial to the 17th Infantry Regiment. There are 3,547 graves of which 2,983 are in individual graves, the other 'Poilu' are unidentified or are buried in a mass grave. Poilu literally means the hairy ones, and has become the nickname for the common French soldier.

The men concentrated here came from many cemeteries including those at L'Abeele, Dikkebus, Geluveld, Hooge, Kemmel, Langemark, Loker, Passendale, Ploegsteert, Poelkapelle, Poperinge, St. Juliaan, Voormezele, Westouter, Wijtschate, Ypres, Zandvoorde, Zillebeke and Zonnebeke.

French – 3547   KUG – 609   Area – 29,900 sq mts

LOCATION
Potijze French Cemetery lies on the south side of the Zonnebeke road, east of Ieper, and about 900 m east of Potijze.

Journey Time – 15 mins

C.W.G.C. Reference – None

LANGEMARK GERMAN MILITARY CEMETERY   *No. 176*

HISTORY
The cemetery was created after the Armistice when bodies were concentrated here in the 1920's and again in the 1950's.

INFORMATION
German soldiers have said of Ypres that it was "The worst of the hell of Verdun plus the horror of the Somme".

At the end of the War 670 German War Cemeteries existed in West Flanders. Between the Wars the German War Graves Service, which was part of the Foreign Office, undertook to care for the 128 German War Cemeteries which remained in existence after many had been concentrated following the Armistice.

In 1954, a War Cemeteries Agreement between Belgium and the new state of West Germany superseded the agreement of 1925. The Volksbund, from that point, took responsibility for the extension and maintenance of the four cemeteries in West Flanders which remained after 1954-6 when the other 120 German Cemeteries were concentrated. The identified remains were buried in single graves while the unknown were placed in a mass grave here where single graves are so close together that up to forty men are marked on each gravestone.

The final concentrations were made in 1970-2 and were carried out according to the plans of the chief architect, Robert Tischler, who had prepared the cemeteries at Langemark and Roselare. The Volksbund today cares for the cemeteries and provides much the same service as the C.W.G.C. for those who wish to find the graves of relatives who fell in the Great War.

Langemark Cemetery is entered through a building made of red stone brought from the Vosges. Inside the building there are two Chapels of Remembrance, one contains a map of German War Cemeteries in Belgium, the other contains, carved on oak tablets, the name of the known dead who lay in the cemetery before the concentration of 1954-6.

Through the entrance the first thing you see is the mass grave, the Kameradengrab, which contains the remains of 24,917 German soldiers, surrounded by a series of bronze blocks bearing the 16,940 names of men known to be in the grave. Beyond the Kameradengrab can be seen a set of four bronze mourning soldiers, the work of Professor Emile Krieger, that cast an eerie shadow across the graves.

The cemetery is in two distinct sections. You enter the Alter Friedhof, planted with oaks and, as such, always cool; I have known many people comment on

the temperature difference at all times of the year. Within this part of the cemetery 10,143 men are buried, 3,836 of whom are unnamed.

To the right from the entrance building, at the north end of the cemetery, is the more open and brighter Einbettungs Friedhof Nord in which lie 9,475 men. It includes three bunkers and a series of tank traps that formed part of the Langemark line. Upon the tank traps are Memorials to many of the German units who fought on the Salient including:

46th Reserve Division
51st Reserve Division
52nd Reserve Division
2nd Westfalian Pioneer Battalion (Koln)
24th Pioneer Battalion
15th Reserve Jäger Battalion (Potsdam)
18th Reserve Jäger Battalion
52nd Reserve Infantry Regiment (Brandenburgisches)
201st to 206th Reserve Infantry Regiments
238th Reserve Infantry Regiment (Karlsruhe)
43rd and 44th Reserve Field Artillery Regiments
Kyffhauserverband der Vereine Deutscherstudenten
Deutsche Werschaft
Deutsche Christliche Studenten Vereinigung DC5V

One of the main German attacks upon the village, on 23 October 1914, was by students from Hiedelberg and Munich who went into battle singing and linking arms. Many of them now lie in this cemetery as the Germans lost 2,000 casualties against the British 2nd Division. The students formed Reserve Corps, No.'s XXII to XXVII, in which 75% of the men were under military age, and most of the officers were cadets or from the retired list. They had received less than six weeks training when they were thrown into the battle, so the German Command was severely criticized for the use of volunteers such as these in War. (From *1914* by Lyn Macdonald, page 365) Haig's (q.v.) first involvement in the War was here, on the same day, as commander of the I Corps. Though the village fell briefly to the Germans, it was retaken by the French on 4 December 1914.

The village was over-run again by the Germans during their gas attack in 1915. This was despite the fact that the British knew the attack was coming because on 14 April 1915 a prisoner from the 234th Reserve Regiment, XXVI Corps, who had been taken near Langemark, revealed the German plans.

The cylinders used for the German gas attack were stored just north of the present cemetery in 1915. On 24 April the German line was 100m north of the cemetery facing French Zouaves, colonial troops, 100m south of the cemetery when the gas was released from the point where the Houthulst road crosses the St. Jansbeek. Four thousand containers released 168 tons of chlorine gas in ten minutes. Please refer to the information given under other relevant cemeteries for further details of the effects of the attack.

Langemark was not retaken until the Flanders Offensive in 1917 when it was captured at great cost by the 20th (Light) Division. On 4 October 1917 an attack was launched from here against Hill 19 and Eagle Trench which was north of the village, across the road to Poelkapelle, and part of a huge German defensive line attacked by the British in the next stage of the Third Battle of Ypres. The 2nd Seaforth Highlanders, 3/10th Middlesex and 1st Royal Warwickshires succeeded in taking the hill so that the 2nd East Lancashires and 1st Royal Dublin Fusiliers could form a new line east of Langemark during the night.

The village was over-run again in the German Spring Offensive in 1918 before being finally retaken by the Belgians on 28 September 1918.

Just north of the cemetery are two small Memorials. They are on the road running next to the St. Jansbeek which is north of the cemetery. The Memorial to the 34th Division Royal Artillery and Royal Engineers is on the right in front of a bunker used as an Advanced Dressing Station in September 1918. It was also used as an headquarters for the 34th Division Artillery, 152nd and 160th Brigade Field Artillery and the Divisional Ammunition Column. When the stream had to be crossed in 1917 it took the Artillery and Engineers eight to ten hours to get an 18 pounder artillery piece across.

The other Memorial, to Adjutant Andre Malliavin and Brigadier Emilien Girault of the French 2nd African Hunters who both fell on 9 October 1917, is in a field on the other side of the stream.

Ger – 44535   Unnamed – 11813   Area – 3200 sq yds

DIRECTIONS
Langemark German Cemetery lies on the northern edge of Langemark about 5km north-east of Ieper. It is on the west side of the road from Langemark to Madonna and Houthulst and is clearly marked from the centre of the village.

Journey Time – 40 mins (+ 5 mins to Memorials)

C.W.G.C. Reference – None

MISCELLANEOUS CEMETERIES

There are a number of cemeteries in the northern part of the Salient that you might find of interest but which do not warrant a great deal of detail within the pages of this book. They are either French or Belgian cemeteries or communal churchyards that contain British burials dating from World War II. I have chosen a line approximately parallel to Houthulst as the northern limit for cemeteries and Memorials to be included in this book, all the following are within that boundary and can be reached from the Veurne road (N8).

WOESTEN CHURCHYARD (No. 177) – this is in the centre of the village on the east side of the N8 and town square. There are 282 French graves in the north-east corner dating from 1914-1918, and on the south side there are nine World War II British graves made in May 1940.

WESTVLETEREN CHURCHYARD (No. 178) – the church is in the village about 14km north-west of Ypres, on the south side of the N321 2km west of the N8. There are 189 French World War I graves at the eastern end of the church.

WESTVLETEREN BELGIAN MILITARY CEME-TERY (No. 179) – as to the churchyard in the village, and then follow the road round by the church towards Poperinge and in 100 m you will see, if you look carefully, a small road on the left at which is a small blue and white sign bearing the words 'Militaire Begraafplaats'. The cemetery is at the end of a dead-end lane 100 m from the road next to the car park. There are 1,100 graves here that have been concentrated from the surrounding battle-fields.

OOSTVLETEREN CHURCHYARD (No. 180) – in the centre of the village 14 km north-west of Ypres, the church is 400 m east of the N8 on the road to Reninge. There are thirty-nine French graves dating from 1914 – 1918 in the north-west corner with seventeen British World War II graves, ten men who fell in May 1940 and seven airmen who died on 11 May 1944. The airmen must have all been in one aeroplane that crashed as there are a Pilot, Flight Engineer, Navigator, Air Bomber, Wireless Operator/Gunner and two Air Gunners.

NOORDSCHOTE CHURCHYARD (No. 181) – the church is in the village centre on the left hand side of the road from Reninge. There are fourteen British World War II graves on the north side of the church

POLLINKHOVE CHURCHYARD (No. 182) – the church is in the centre of the village which is about 18 km north-west of Ypres. There are eight British World War II graves in the north-east part of the church.

HOOGSTADE CHURCHYARD (No. 183) – the church is set back from the N8, in the village 20 km north-west of Ypres, behind houses on the right. There are twelve British World War II graves dating from May 1940 in the northern corner of the churchyard.

The three German cemeteries into which all the others were concentrated (with the one at Lange-mark) in the 1950's are not within the strict limits of the Salient but are within a relatively near distance and I will deal with them here.

HOOGLEDE GERMAN MILITARY CEMETERY (No. 184) – created after the Armistice for 8,247 burials, Hooglede literally took my breath away the first time I saw it. As you park outside you cannot see the cemetery because it is hidden behind a hedge, but as you reach the narrow entrance the cemetery stretches away up the hill to the massive pavilions.

The narrow entrance is a wrought iron grill which leads to a small tiled square from which you get an outstanding view across the cemetery planted with a blaze of heather. There are groups of trees on both sides which lead to the Hall of Remembrance at the top of the hill.

The Hall was built before World War II by the German War Graves Service who used the stone material from the German Pavilions at the World's Fair in Paris in 1937. An elaborate cast iron grating forms the entrance to the memorial room at the west end of the hall in the middle of which is a stone desk made of rock from the Dolerites.

The cemetery is on the south-eastern outskirts of the village, which is about 20 km north-east of Ypres. A German War Graves Commission sign is on the corner of the road to this cemetery from near the church in the village.

MENEN-WALD GERMAN MILITARY CEME-TERY, MENEN (No. 185) – created after the Armistice, the biggest German Cemetery in Flan-ders, with 47,864 burials, is near the Franco-Belgian frontier on the north-eastern edge of Menen. You enter through a small entrance building onto a flagged path leading to the octagonal Chapel of Remembrance shaded by high trees. The interior of the chapel consists of a high room supported by arches, and the walls are decorated partially with mosaics, illustrating bible stories. There are two elaborate shrines containing the books of remembr-ance.

The cemetery lies on the north-east edge of the town which is about 20 km east of Ypres. Once through Menen and on the road to Wevelgem and Kortrijk the cemetery is signed from the N8 and relatively easy to find just north of the railway.

VLADSLO-PRAATBOS GERMAN MILITARY CEMETERY, DIKSMUIDE (No. 186) – this cemetery was created within the wood during the War but most of the burials were concentrated here after the Armistice making a total of 25,644. After passing through the entrance building, which contains a room with the books of remembrance, you can see the sculpted figures of the 'Mourning Parents' at the far end of the cemetery. These were created by Kathe Kollwitz who erected the figures, bearing the facial features of her family, in memory of her son, Peter, who fell in Flanders in October 1914 and is now buried in front of the group. In 1932 the finished figures made of Belgian granite were unveiled in the presence of Kollwitz and her husband.

In Diksmuide, you can find the Diksmuide Peace Tower on the road to Veurne next to the bridge on the west bank of the River Ijzer. It is a Memorial tower to the Free Flemish and all patriots of the Flemish nation. There is a crypt, a museum which explains some of the battles in the area, and other exhibits including an art collection. A lift takes you to the top from where you can get an excellent view. The inscription is made up of the letters V.V.K.-A.V.V. interlinked in the form of a cross which stands for 'Vlanders Voor Kristus – Alles Voor Vlanders' or 'Flanders for Christ – All for Flanders'.

The cemetery is approximately 30 km north of Ypres and about 6 km north-east of Diksmuide. It is 500 m north of the Beerst – Tourhout road (N363) and is reached from a crossroads with a turn south to Vladslo and north, with a German Commission sign on the corner, to Leke.

COMMONWEALTH WAR GRAVES COMMISSION

During the first months of the War in 1914 the dead were buried by their comrades, or by local inhabitants, in communal cemeteries, and burial returns were made by chaplains or serving officers. The Royal Engineers were involved in fighting so they could not perform the task as they had done during the South African Wars.

General Fowke, Engineering Adviser to the British Expeditionary Force, was happy to hand over the task of marking and registration of graves to Fabian Ware. Ware had volunteered his ambulance unit for the job at the end of October 1914 before Lord Kitchener, Minister of War, sanctioned the development. The unit was officially appointed by Sir John French (q.v.), Commander-in-Chief, in February 1915 and was given the title of Graves Registration Commission. It was technically still a civilian group, manned by the Red Cross but became a military unit in October 1915 with Army officers in charge.

The Commission's task was the systematic marking and registration of all graves in France and Flanders. To achieve this the British zone of warfare was divided into seven areas in which all known graves were located with an appropriate religious marker, and photographs taken of every grave. Late in 1915 the French Government donated land for cemeteries to Britain and the Dominions. At the same time the British Government set up a national committee to make provision for the care of all graves in France and Flanders.

The committee, called the Commission of Graves Registration and Enquiries, headed by the Prince of Wales, was to arrange for the care of the graves, acquire land and provide a service for the relatives of the dead. It set up units in each sector to care for thirty-three cemeteries and 49,413 graves then identified. In May 1916 the Commission suggested that identity disks should be made of metal and that each man have two to replace the leather disks used previously.

Usually up to 1916 the dead were buried where they fell or in scattered graves in the rear. However, it became normal for trenches to be pre-dug before battles in preparation for the dead, a system that eased the job of identification and continued until the end of the War.

The Commission received a Royal Charter on 21 May 1917 and its membership represented all the countries of the Empire and Dominions who were taking part in the War and had dead buried on the battlefields. In 1919 the Commission announced that, despite many families wanting the remains of the dead to be repatriated, the bodies would remain where they fell and would not be returned to Britain. The main reason for this was the expense, though the care lavished on the cemeteries over the century has outstripped the cost of removal to Britain, and the effect has been a much more emotive memorial to the fallen of the Great War.

The Imperial (now Commonwealth) War Graves Commission took over from the Empire War Office in 1921. The cost of its work is shared by those countries who have dead in Commission Cemeteries and in proportion to the number of dead from each country.

The main objective of the Commission at the end of the War, in caring for what French (q.v.) lamented as the 'Silent Army' of the dead, was to commemorate each individual equally. Thus, all men received the same tribute in the form of a headstone or as a line on a Memorial such as the Menin Gate. Each headstone is 2ft 8ins in height and 1ft 3ins wide, upon which is carved the badge of the regiment or unit, rank, name, date of death and age with an appropriate religious symbol. At the foot of the stone relatives were allowed to have a small inscription at their own expense. Exceptions to this design are for the few men who were awarded the Victoria Cross or the headstones that bear an inscription such as 'Known (or Believed) to be buried in this Cemetery' when the exact place of burial is lost. For bodies that could not be identified the headstone bears the simple words, chosen by Rudyard Kipling, 'Known unto God'.

Each cemetery has a character of its own though a number of features, particularly the Cross of Sacrifice set upon an octagonal base and bearing a crusaders sword of bronze, are common to all. The larger cemeteries also have the War Stone, a plinth that looks like an altar and bears the words 'Their Name Liveth for Evermore', chosen by Rudyard Kipling, from the Book of Ecclesiastes. Most headstones are set in rows or narrow borders planted with a variety of flowers and shrubs.

The developmental work of the Commission was completed in 1938 with the unveiling of the Australian National Memorial in France. The area of the front had been divided into squares, each searched six times for bodies, between 1921 and 1928 nearly 30,000 corpses, of which only 25% could be identified, were re-buried. Even today when remains are still being found and interred in the War Cemeteries, there are still over 500,000 missing on the Western Front.

The work of the Commission is protected by international agreements. It is a shame that the registers of each cemetery cannot be equally well protected. A record for each cemetery is held at the offices of the Commission in Ypres and at Beaurains, France, but there used to be a relevant copy stored in most cemeteries. Found in small repositories usually near the entrance, too many have been removed for the Commission to afford constantly replacing them. My finding three registers to be missing in one day is part of the inspiration for this book.

I cannot thank the officers of the Commission enough for their help in compiling this book. Their advice, information and immense efforts over the years has eased my work and research on innumerable occasions. I would like to especially mention the staff of the office in Ypres, and in particular Mr R. Strachan, who have shown a great deal of patience at some of my more unusual requests.

Address – Commonwealth War Graves Commission
Elverdingsestraat 82,
B 8900 Ieper,
Belgium.

Tel: 057 20 01 18

The Cross of Sacrifice at Hop Store Cemetery, Vlamertinge.

YPRES SALIENT

THE START OF THE SALIENT

The Salient began life as part of the first, and short-lived stage of the War, the War of Movement, that culminated in the 'Race to the Sea'. The Germans who had seen their meticulous, and seemingly invincible, Schlieffen Plan, fail because of the resilience of the Belgians, the unexpected arrival of the British Expeditionary Force, and to some extent the indecisiveness of their own leaders, had decided that it was now vital to take the Channel Ports as a means of defeating the Allies.

During this early period from 3 October 1914, and before the arrival of the British 7th Division, the only troops at Ypres were the Yeomanry of the Queen's Own Oxfordshire Hussars who were the first Territorials in Flanders. They were present because of the intervention of Winston Churchill, then First Lord of the Admiralty, who had ordered in September, that when the Royal Marines were sent to hold the northern sector, particularly Dunkirk, a unit of cavalry must go with them. Although there were no cavalry units to spare from the fighting Churchill knew of a Yeomanry regiment that could do the job. These just happened to be Yeomanry with whom his family had a long relationship and within which some of his family were serving – a quick way for them to get to the War. Hence, for some time the Hussars were the only troops between the German Army and the Channel Ports.

The Germans managed to enter Ypres and a few local villages before being forced back to the ridges around Ypres by the arrival of the British 7th Division. French (q.v.), Commander-in-Chief of the B.E.F., hurled his forces at the Germans in an heroic action forming a line from La Bassee to just north of Ypres. Then from mid-October to mid-November the struggle raged to take Ypres which became known as the First Battle of Ypres.

FIRST BATTLE OF YPRES

Battle of Messines	12 October – 2 November
Battle of Armentieres	13 October – 2 November
Battles of Ypres, 1914	19 October – 22 November
Battle of Langemark	21 October – 24 October
Battle of Geluveld	29 October – 31 October
Battle of Nonne Boschen	11 November

The two sides that faced each other in this daily series of battles were unevenly matched as the B.E.F. was outnumbered, poorly equipped and poorly positioned. The battles of late 1914 saw a change in the nature of warfare from mobile infantry, with some use of cavalry charges, to full scale trench warfare where defence was the best form of attrition. Although the Belgians had dug three lines of trenches at Liege before the War, trench warfare was not at first the usual form of fighting. Fortunately for the B.E.F. and the Allies

the defenders at Ypres in 1914 were the forces of the 'Entente'.

Possibly the most important action of the First Battle of Ypres was at Geluveld. From 29-31 October the Germans attacked the British battalions trying valiantly to hold the village and the line north and south of the Menen Road. Even so, the line broke temporarily and it seemed as if the road to Ypres was open.

On 31 October, north of the Menen Road, the 1st Scots Guards, 2nd Welsh Regiment and 1st South Wales Borderers were fighting in Geluveld chateau grounds, and though the Welsh had only eighteen working rifles the line to Polygon Wood was just holding. General Fitzclarence, V.C., commanding the 1st Brigade, called for reinforcements so three companies of the 2nd Worcesters were sent from Polygon Wood. The 357 men of the Worcesters charged with the Scots Guards and South Wales Borderers, taking the Germans by surprise to save the day and halt the Kaiser's march on Ypres.

The Germans tried again on 11 November as the Prussian Guard were ordered to break through and take Ypres. They broke the first line but were stopped by men of 16th, 22nd and 51st Batteries, Royal Field Artillery and the 5th Field Company, Royal Engineers – cooks, drivers and the like. The guns and rifle fire seemed like a strong new line to the Prussians amongst whom the shells caused havoc, so they fell back into Nonne Boschen (Nun's Wood). The 2nd Oxford and Bucks Light Infantry then counter-attacked south through the wood driving the Prussian Guard before them either into Glencorse Wood, where they were attacked by the 1st Cameron Highlanders, or east towards Polygon Wood where the 5th Field Company awaited them.

During the night battalions of the Territorials were rushed up to the front-line to fill the gaps. They were proud to claim Nonne Boschen as their first battle honour of the War, though the fight was really over by the time of their arrival. Even so, they were greatly welcomed by the remnants of the B.E.F..

The German Kaiser also seemed to realise that the first attempt to capture Ypres had failed. He had ordered his strongest and most famous regiments to take Ypres and break the British Army on 11 November. Over 17,500 Germans in twelve Divisions had attacked on a nine mile front against less than 8,000 British and failed to overcome them.

During the First Battle of Ypres the original B.E.F. had been destroyed, for example, General Capper, commanding the 7th Division, once described himself as a divisional commanding officer without a command; his Division had lost 732 officers and 9,493 men in eighteen days since it had come to the front. In the 100 days from 4 August to the end of the First Battle of Ypres the British Army had lost more officers than it had in all the wars involving British troops during the previous 100 years. British casualties in 1914 numbered 90,000, or 90% of original size of the B.E.F., of which 30% lay in the soil of Belgium. German casualties in the same period were 134,315. Average battalion size was one officer and thirty men out of forty officers and 1,000 men, and of the eighty-four British battalions at Ypres on 1 November 1914, eighteen had less than 100 men, thirty-one less than 200 men, twenty-six less than 300 men and only nine had greater than 300 men.

By the end of the First Battle of Ypres many British regiments had almost ceased to exist, but the German Army and the ambitions of its leaders, who could not believe that such a 'thin line' had held at Ypres, had been severely blunted. The town itself was to die during subsequent actions but in 1914 a cause had been born. The 'Contemptible Little Army', as the German Kaiser, Wilhelm II, had called the B.E.F. in his Order of the Day on 19 August 1914, was no more, and those who could call themselves 'Old Contemptibles' had much of which to be proud.

SECOND BATTLE OF YPRES

Battles of Ypres, 1915	22 April – 25 May
Battle of Gravenstafel	22 April – 23 April
Battle of St. Juliaan	24 April – 4 May
Battle of Frezenberg	8 May – 13 May
Battle of Bellewaerde	24 May – 25 May

The British were glad to use the quiet of the winter to recuperate, though some may find the word 'quiet' a strange choice. For example, in December 1914 the 3rd Division suffered casualties of thirty-three officers and 717 men. The defence of Ypres in 1914 had established a political significance for the town that greatly outweighed its strategic and military importance. However, the British Army, always officially titled the B.E.F., had held it once and were determined to continue to hold Ypres.

The fighting in 1915 again saw the British strategically in the poorer position. The Germans introduced a new element to war, gas, used, for the first time, on 22 April 1915, in the north of the Salient against French troops. There was a time when Ypres was open to the Germans, but the actions of Canadian troops in closing and holding the line in the north-east of the Salient is well known. Less well known is the contribution of British troops, notably the 'Geddes Detachment'.

In the attack on 24 April 1915 Frezenberg was defended by 122nd Heavy Battery, 37th Howitzer Battery, a section of the 6th Battery of the Canadian Field Artillery and a Company of the 8th Middlesex. These were soon supplemented by sections from the 356th and 367th Batteries of the 28th Division Royal Field Artillery. This then was the complete extent of the British defences from Zonnebeke to Potijze but these Batteries temporarily halted the German attack.

Another German advance was attempted again at Frezenberg on 8 May. A new British line had been formed but the defenders had been greatly depleted in numbers over the previous weeks. The 1/3rd Monmouths numbered four officers and 130 men; the 2nd King's Own four officers and ninety-four men; the 1st King's Own Yorkshire Light Infantry five officers and 201 men. From 23 April to 8 May the 83rd Brigade had lost 128 officers and 4,379 men. It is thought that the Brigade's defence at Frezenberg, in holding the Germans and ignoring orders to retire, was probably the turning point in British fortunes during the Second Battle of Ypres.

The Germans then spent the next month trying to defeat the defenders of Ypres. Action took place mostly in the north and east of the Salient, and although the line contracted substantially during the month, the town did not fall. However, it was during this battle that the civilians were evacuated from Ypres as a result of what the Germans called a 'hate shoot' on the town on 24 April. In holding Ypres the British suffered 60,000 casualties. The 10th Brigade lost seventy-three officers and 2,346 men, almost ceasing to exist; the 149th Brigade forty-two officers and 1,192 men, or 75 % of their total. German losses were 34,933. These were shocking figures at the time though small by the scale of what was to follow.

During 1916 the main action was elsewhere on the Somme and at Verdun. Even so there were some battles at Ypres, notably that of Mount Sorrel.

As a result of the disasters of 1916 General Haig, Commander-in-Chief since 1915, and the Chief of the Imperial General Staff, Robertson, needed a new plan leading to a victory. Douglas Haig had become Commander-in-Chief of the British Army on 18 December 1915 and was later made an Earl and Field Marshal. He had begun the War as commander of the I Corps and achieved some notable victories though these are mostly masked by the horrors of trench warfare and his policy of attrition. Haig decided to capture the ridges around Ypres and push through to the Belgian coast, hence, stopping the U-Boat threat to the British convoys. Although this plan met with opposition from the Prime Minister, David Lloyd George, Haig gained enough support for the plan to be implemented. Even so, Haig decided on a preliminary event in the South of the Salient before implementing the main event in the north.

THIRD BATTLE OF YPRES

Battle of Messines	7 June – 14 June

The preliminary action in the south, known as the Battle of Messines, had the aim of taking the Mesen – Wijtschate Ridge on 7 June 1917. Extremely thorough preparation was undertaken involving the development of a cohesive plan, extensive training and the placing of massive mines under the German lines. The objective was the Oostaverne Line occupied by General Sixt von Armin's Fourth Army and General Otto von Below's Sixth Army.

The German position, in a small salient south of Ypres, relied mainly on the physical advantages of holding the ridge. The British ranged round it on a nine mile front from the north at Hill 60 to south of Wijtschate 100,000 troops in the 41st, 47th (2nd London), 23rd, 36th (Ulster), 16th (Irish) and 19th (Western) Divisions with the II A.N.Z.A.C. Corps of the 3rd Australian Division, New Zealand Division and British 25th Division in the extreme south near Mesen.

After an artillery bombardment using 3,258,000 (144,000 tons) shells from 2,250 guns, nineteen mines were blown at 3.10am on 7 June, using 933,200lbs of ammonal, destroying the German front-line in the largest single explosion up to that date. The mines were the idea of J. Norton-Griffiths M.P. who developed the initial plan in May 1915 though it was not accepted until 1916. By the end of 1916, fifteen mines were in place and by 7 June 1917 another six were ready, though one had been discovered, one damaged and two abandoned. They were set at Hill 60 and under the nearby hill called 'The Caterpiller' by the 1st Australian Tunnelling Company, St. Eloi by the 1st Canadian Tunnelling Company, Hollandscheschuur Farm, Petit Bois, Maedelstede Farm and Peckham by the 250th Tunnelling Company, Spanbroekmolen, Kruistraat and Ontario Farm by the 171st Tunnelling Company, Trench 127 and Factory Farm by the 3rd Canadian Tunnelling Company.

The attack was a complete success. Most enemy positions were over-run with ease, some battalions lost as few as ten men, though the 47th Division encountered stiff resistance at St. Eloi on the Dammstrasse and there was heavy fighting at Ravine Wood, Battle Wood and Hill 60. Allied casualties were light, vindicating the careful planning and caution of Plumer (q.v.), and some 6,400 German prisoners were taken.

Battles of Ypres, 1917	31 July	– 10 November
Battle of Pilkem Ridge	31 July	– 2 August
Battle of Langemark	16 August	– 18 August
Battle of the Menin Road	20 September	– 25 September
Battle of Polygon Wood	26 September	– 3 October
Battle of Broodseinde	4 October	
Battle of Poelkapelle	9 October	
Battle of Passendale I	12 October	
Battle of Passendale II	26 October	– 10 November

Six weeks later, after a bombardment from 16 to 31 July using 4.3 million shells from 3,091 guns, including 100,000 rounds of gas shells, the Third Battle of Ypres began. The basic plan was an attack by General Gough's relatively new, and untested, Fifth Army consisting of ten Divisions, east of Ypres on a seven mile front, with the French on its left, and five Divisions of Plumer's (q.v.) Second Army on the right, with seventeen Divisions in reserve. Sir Hubert de la Poer Gough, known as 'Goughie', was in command of the 3rd Cavalry Division when the War started. On 26 May 1915, at the age of 45, he became the youngest Army Commander when he took over the Fifth Army, but was recalled to England after the German attack on the Somme in 1918. The Battle of Pilkem Ridge did not have the preparation and planning of Messines, also the German defences, deploying fifteen front-line Divisions, were significantly better developed than in the south.

The battle opened, in rain, on 31 July at 3.50am, at the beginning of what was to become one of the wettest August to November periods on record. The first day saw most objectives taken, Pilkem fell to the 38th (Welsh) Division, the Steenbeek to the 51st (Highland) Division, Frezenberg to the 15th (Scottish) Division and Pomern Castle to the 55th (West Lancashire) Division, though at great cost, notably for the 8th and 30th Divisions on the Menen Road at Hooge, before the rain halted any effective further action. On the first day of the attack 15,000 casualties were incurred (31,850 by 2 August), twelve Victoria Crosses were won, and twelve villages captured in a penetration of 2 to 3km.

This pattern, of heavy casualties suffered in taking increasingly limited objectives, was repeated through the late summer and autumn. The offensive developed in three phases – 31 July to 2 August by Gough's (q.v.) Fifth Army; 20 September, 26 September and 4 October by Plumer's (q.v.) Second Army; and 26 October to 11 November by the Canadian Corps. These battles were some of the clearest examples of the advantage in the Great War of defence. Why did Haig persist when his original plan had failed ? Did he believe in ultimate success ? Was there any real alternative to such infantry attacks ? Was he forced to continue because he had to show some success – the taking of Passendale – for such cost ? Certainly when 270,000 casualties were incurred in the advance something had to be seen to be achieved.

Passendale was captured in early November by the Canadians with the British 63rd (Royal Naval) Division and Territorials in support. The Germans had been pushed off a small part of the ridge around Ypres but at a considerable sacrifice. As a Sergeant from Scotland wrote in a letter home "Ypres; well may they call it Ypres", for this had a sad meaning at his home in Argyllshire as Ypres is Gaelic for 'sacrifice'. That the British Army did not suffer a mutiny like the French can only tell us much about the British character.

FOURTH BATTLE OF YPRES

Battles of the Lys	9 April – 29 April
Battle of Estaires	9 April – 11 April
Battle of Messines, 1918	10 April – 11 April
Battle of Hazebrouck	12 April – 15 April
Battle of Bailleul	13 April – 15 April

Battle of Kemmel I	17 April – 19 April
Battle of Bethune	18 April
Battle of Kemmel II	25 April – 26 April
Battle of Scherpenberg	29 April

This battle was Germany's 'Great Gamble', a spring offensive to win the War using troops released from the Russian Front before the 'Doughboys' arrived from the U.S.A.. Having started on the Somme in March, the offensive came to the Salient in April 1918, along the valley of the Lys when the Allied front-line was pushed back to the outskirts of Ypres accentuating the Salient. The Germans used forty-nine Divisions in the attack against troops who had previously been involved in the battles on the Somme and had been transferred north to recuperate.

In early April the Germans pushed the line that was south of Ypres from a position east of Armentieres and Ploegsteert Wood back to the Monts des Flandres and west of Bailleul. The Battle of the Scherpenberg began at 5.40am as thirteen German Divisions attacked on a ten mile front. The British commanders, Plumer (q.v.) and Haig (q.v.), contemplated withdrawing to a new line at St. Omer abandoning Ypres but on 30 April the German Commander, General Ludendorff, halted Operation Georgette, as the Battles of the Lys were then known to the German High Command. He planned a number of diversionary attacks to the south to draw the French troops away from Ypres before recommencing the attack.

All the ground taken by the British at such great cost only six months before was given up in a 'planned withdrawal' to shorten the line and concentrate troop dispositions to turn the tide. Fresh troops, French support and some desperate last ditch stands such as those by the 12th Royal Scots, 6th King's Own Scottish Borderers, 26th Brigade and advances by the 39th Division (Composite) Brigade played an important part in holding the Germans.

But the most important element of the failure was that the British naval blockade was finally having an effect on Germany and their 'Gamble' failed through lack of resources. This was fortunate for the Allies because only forty-eight British Divisions were considered to be prepared for battle.

THE FINAL BREAKOUT

Battle of Ypres, 1918	28 September – 2 October
Battle of Kortrijk	14 October – 19 October

The final breakout from the Salient came in September 1918 using the same plan as that used in 1917, a series of staged advances. But the Germans did not have the strength of 1917 to face the Allied Flanders Army Group, under King Albert of Belgium, composed of thirteen Belgian, ten British and six French Divisions. Therefore, the advance and breakout was completed in two stages. The first, on a twenty-three mile front, saw the edge of the Salient reached.

The attack began on 28 September 1918. By midday Geluveld, the Wijtschate – Mesen Ridge and Zandvoorde had been taken, and in the afternoon Beselare fell to the 11th and 12th Royal Scots. By 30 September 1918 the Menen – Roeselare road had been crossed. However, although the British Second Army had advanced up to six miles, casualties numbered 4,500 Belgian and 4,695 British, and lines of communication were being stretched due to the unexpectedly speedy advance, so a period of consolidation was undertaken.

As a result, key objectives such as the towns of Roeselare and Menen were not taken, though 11,000 prisoners, 300 artillery pieces and 600 machine-guns had been captured.

Finally the British troops pushed on in the Battle of Kortrijk, unwilling to wait for a French and Belgian breakthrough to their north. The British Second Army of sixteen Divisions, supported by the Royal Air Force who dropped over forty tons of bombs, and a Franco-Belgian force began the attack at 5.30am against the German Fourth Army composed of sixteen Divisions. An eighteen mile advance took 12,000 prisoners and 550 artillery pieces, and with the fall of Ledegem the Salient was decreed to have been broken. By the day of the Armistice the British Army was fifty-one miles from the Salient.

FIRST YPRES (OCTOBER – NOVEMBER 1914)

1st CAVALRY DIVISION (Regular) : Major-General H. de B. de Lisle

    Battle of Messines 12 Oct – 2 Nov (Cavalry Corps)

1st Cavalry Brigade : Brigadier-General C. J. Briggs
2nd (Queen's Bays) Dragoon Guards   5th (Princess Charlotte of Wales's) Dragoon Guards
11th (Prince Albert's Own) Hussars

2nd Cavalry Brigade : Brigadier-General R. L. Mullens
4th (Royal Irish) Dragoon Guards   9th (Queen's Royal) Lancers
18th (Queen Mary's Own) Hussars
 1st Queen's Own Oxfordshire Hussars

2nd CAVALRY DIVISION (Regular) : Major-General H. de la P. Gough

    Battle of Messines 12 Oct – 2 Nov (Cavalry Corps)
    Battle of Armentieres 13 – 17 Oct (Cavalry Corps)
    Battle of Geluveld 30 – 31 Oct (I Corps)

3rd Cavalry Brigade : Brigadier-General J. Vaughan
4th (Queen's Own) Hussars   5th (Royal Irish) Lancers
16th (The Queen's) Lancers

4th Cavalry Brigade : Brigadier-General Hon. C. E. Bingham
6th (Carabiniers) Dragoon Guards   3rd (King's Own) Hussars
Composite Battalion of the Household Cavalry

5th Cavalry Brigade : Brigadier-General Sir P. W. Chetwode, Bt
2nd Dragoons (Royal Scots Greys)   12th (Prince of Wales's Royal) Lancers
20th Hussars

3rd CAVALRY DIVISION (Regular) : Major-General Hon. J. H. G. Byng

    Battle of Langemark 21 – 24 Oct (IV Corps)
    Battle of Geluveld 29 – 31 Oct (I Corps)
    Battle of Nonne Boschen 11 Nov (I Corps)

6th Cavalry Brigade : Brigadier-General E. Makins to 7 Nov (Sick)
                 Lieutenant-Colonel O. B. B. Smith-Bingham to 9 Nov
                 Brigadier-General D. G. M. Campbell
1st (Royal) Dragoons   3rd (Prince of Wales's) Dragoon Guards (from 4 Nov)
10th (Prince of Wales's Own Royal) Hussars

7th Cavalry Brigade : Brigadier-General C. T. Kavanagh
1st Life Guards   2nd Life Guards
Royal Horse Guards (the Blues)

1st DIVISION (Regular) : Major-General S. H. Lomax to 31 Oct (wounded)
                 Major-General H. J. S. Landon

    Battle of Langemark 21 – 24 Oct (I Corps)
    Battle of Geluveld 29 – 31 Oct (I Corps)
    Battle of Nonne Boschen 11 Nov (I Corps)

1st (Guards) Brigade : Brigadier-General C. Fitzclarence, V.C.
1st Coldstream Guards   1st Black Watch
1st Scots Guards   1st Cameron Highlanders
1/14th (London Scottish) Londons

2nd Brigade : Brigadier-General E. S. Bulfin to 1 Nov (wounded)
            Colonel C. Cunliffe-Owen
2nd Royal Sussex   1st Northhamptons
1st Loyal North Lancashires   2nd King's Royal Rifle Corps

3rd Brigade : Brigadier-General H. J. S. Landon to 31 Oct
          Colonel A. C. Lovett
1st Queen's (to 9 Nov)   1st South Wales Borderers
1st Gloucesters   2nd Welsh
2nd Royal Munster Fusiliers (from 9 Nov)

2nd DIVISION (Regular) : Major-General C. C. Monro

    Battle of Langemark 21 – 24 Oct (I Corps)
    Battle of Geluveld 29 – 31 Oct (I Corps)
    Battle of Nonne Boschen 11 Nov (I Corps)

4th (Guards) Brigade : Brigadier-General F. R. Earl of Cavan
2nd Grenadier Guards
1st Irish Guards

2nd Coldstream Guards
3rd Coldstream Guards

5th Brigade : Colonel C. B. Westmacott
2nd Worcesters
2nd Oxford & Bucks Light Infantry

2nd Highland Light Infantry
2nd Connaught Rangers

6th Brigade : Brigadier-General R. Fanshawe
1st King's
2nd South Staffordshires

1st Royal Berkshires
1st King's Royal Rifle Corps

3rd DIVISION (Regular) : Major-General F. D. V. Wing

  Battle of Messines 31 Oct – 2 Nov (Cavalry Corps)
  Battle of Nonne Boschen 11 Nov (I Corps)

7th Brigade : Brigadier-General F. W. N. McCraken
3rd Worcesters
2nd South Lancashires

1st Wiltshires
2nd Royal Irish Rifles

8th Brigade : Brigadier-General W. H. Bowes
2nd Royal Scots
2nd Suffolks

4th Middlesex
1st Gordon Highlanders

9th Brigade : Brigadier-General F. C. Shaw
1st Northumberland Fusiliers
4th Royal Fusiliers

1st Lincolns
1st Royal Scots Fusiliers

4th DIVISION (Regular) : Major-General H. F. M. Wilson

  Battle of Armentieres 13 Oct – 2 Nov (III Corps)
  Battle of Messines 21 – 31 Oct (2nd Essex on 21 Oct, 2nd Royal Inniskilling Fusiliers on 30-31 Oct)

10th Brigade : Brigadier-General J. A. L. Haldane
1st Royal Warwickshires
2nd Seaforth Highlanders

1st Royal Irish Fusiliers
2nd Royal Dublin Fusiliers

11th Brigade : Brigadier-General A. G. Hunter-Weston
1st Somerset Light Infantry
1st East Lancashires

1st Hampshires
1st Rifle Brigade

12th Brigade : Brigadier-General F. G. Anley
1st King's Own
2nd Lancashire Fusiliers

2nd Royal Inniskilling Fusiliers
2nd Essex

5th DIVISION (Regular) : Major-General T. L. N. Morland

  Battle of Messines 31 Oct – 2 Nov (2nd King's Own Scottish Borderers & 2nd King's Own Yorkshire Light Infantry in
    Cavalry Corps)
  Battle of Armentieres 1 – 2 Nov (1st Dorsets in III Corps)
  Battle of Nonne Boschen 11 Nov (2nd King's Own Scottish Borderers, 2nd Duke of Wellington's, 1st Bedfordshires &
    1st Cheshires in III Corps)

13th Brigade : Colonel A. Martyn to 7 Nov (Wounded)
            Lieutenant-Colonel W. M. Withycombe
2nd King's Own Scottish Borderers
1st Royal West Kents

2nd Duke of Wellington's
2nd King's Own Yorkshire Light Infantry

14th Brigade : Brigadier-General F. S. Maude
1st Devonshires
1st East Surreys

2nd Duke of Cornwall's Light Infantry
2nd Manchesters

15th Brigade : Brigadier-General Count Gleichen
1st Norfolks
1st Bedfordshires

1st Cheshires
1st Dorsets

6th DIVISION (Regular) : Major-General J. L. Keir

  Battle of Armentieres 13 Oct – 2 Nov (III Corps)

16th Brigade : Brigadier-General E. C. Ingouville-Williams
1st Buffs
1st Leicesters

1st King's Shropshire Light Infantry
2nd York & Lancasters

17th Brigade : Brigadier-General W. R. B. Doran
1st Royal Fusiliers
1st North Staffordshires

2nd Leinsters
3rd Rifle Brigade

18th Brigade : Brigadier-General W. N. Congreve, V.C.
1st West Yorkshires
1st East Yorkshires

2nd Sherwood Foresters
2nd Durham Light Infantry

19th Brigade : Brigadier-General Hon. F. Gordon
2nd Royal Welsh Fusiliers
1st Cameronians

1st Middlesex
2nd Argyll & Sutherland Highlanders

7th DIVISION (Regular) : Major-General T. Capper

    Battle of Langemark 21 – 24 Oct (IV Corps)
    Battle of Geluveld 29 – 31 Oct (I Corps)

20th Brigade : Brigadier-General H. Ruggle-Brise
1st Grenadier Guards
2nd Scots Guards

2nd Border
2nd Gordon Highlanders

21st Brigade : Brigadier-General H. E. Watts
2nd Bedfordshires
2nd Yorkshires

2nd Royal Scots Fusiliers
2nd Wiltshires

22nd Brigade : Brigadier-General S. T. B. Lawford
2nd Queen's
2nd Royal Warwickshires

1st Royal Welsh Fusiliers
1st South Staffordshires

SECOND BATTLE OF YPRES (APRIL – MAY 1915)

1ST CAVALRY DIVISION (Regular) : Major-General H. de B. de Lisle

    Battle of Frezenberg Ridge 9 – 13 May (Cavalry Corps, Second Army)
    Battle of Bellewaerde Ridge 24 May (Cavalry Corps, Second Army)

1st Cavalry Brigade : Lieutenant-Colonel T. T. Pitman to 15 May
                  Brigadier-General E. Makins
2nd (Queen's Bays) Dragoon Guards
5th (Princess Charlotte of Wales's) Dragoon Guards

11th (Prince Albert's Own) Hussars

2nd Cavalry Brigade : Brigadier-General R. L. Mullens
4th (Royal Irish) Dragoon Guards
9th (Queen's Royal) Lancers

18th (Queen Mary's Own) Hussars

9th Cavalry Brigade : Brigadier-General W. H. Greenly
15th (The King's) Hussars

19th (Queen Alexandra's Own Royal) Hussars

2ND CAVALRY DIVISION (Regular) : Major-General C. T. Kavanagh

    Battle of St Juliaan 26 Apr – 3 May (Plumer's Force, Second Army)
    Battle of Bellewaerde Ridge 24 – 25 May (V Corps, Second Army)

3rd Cavalry Brigade : Brigadier-General J. Vaughan
4th (Queen's Own) Hussars
5th (Royal Irish) Lancers

16th (The Queen's) Lancers

4th Cavalry Brigade : Brigadier-General Hon. C. E. Bingham
Household Cavalry
6th (Carabiniers) Dragoon Guards

3rd (King's Own) Hussars

5th Cavalry Brigade : Brigadier-General Sir P. W. Chetwode, Bt
2nd Dragoons (Royal Scots Greys)
12th (Prince of Wales's Royal) Lancers

20th Hussars

3RD CAVALRY DIVISION (Regular) : Major-General C. J. Briggs

    Battle of Frezenberg Ridge 11 – 13 May (Cavalry Corps, Second Army)

6th Cavalry Brigade: Brigadier-General D. G. M. Campbell
3rd (Prince of Wales's) Dragoon Guards
1st (Royal) Dragoons

1st North Somerset Yeomanry

7th Cavalry Brigade : Brigadier-General A. A. Kennedy
1st Life Guards
2nd Life Guards

1st Leicester Yeomanry

8th Cavalry Brigade : Brigadier-General C. B. Bulkeley-Johnson
Royal Horse Guards (the Blues)
10th (Prince of Wales's Own Royal) Hussars

1st Essex Yeomanry

4TH DIVISION (Regular) : Major-General H. F. M. Wilson

    Battle of St Juliaan 25 Apr – 4 May (V Corps, Second Army)
    Battle of Frezenberg Ridge 8 – 13 May (V Corps, Second Army)
    Battle of Bellewaerde Ridge 24 – 25 May (V Corps, Second Army)

10th Brigade : Brigadier-General C. P. A. Hull

1st Royal Warwickshires	1st Royal Irish Fusiliers
2nd Seaforth Highlanders	2nd Royal Dublin Fusiliers
1/7th Argyll & Sutherland Highlanders	

11th Brigade : Brigadier-General J. A. Hasler, killed in action 27 April
               Lieutenant-Colonel F. R. Hicks to 29 April
               Brigadier-General C. B. Prowse, D.S.O.

1st Somerset Light Infantry	1st Hampshires
1st East Lancashires	1st Rifle Brigade
1/5th (London Rifle Brigade) Londons	

12th Brigade : Brigadier-General F. G. Anley

1st King's Own	2nd Royal Irish
2nd Lancashire Fusiliers	2nd Essex
1/5th South Lancashires	1/2nd Monmouths

5TH DIVISION (Regular) : Major-General T. L. N. Morland

    Battles of Ypres 23 Apr – 1 May (V Corps, Second Army)
    Battle of Gravenstafel Ridge 23 April (13th Brigade only)
    Battle of St Juliaan 24 April – 1 May (13th Brigade only)

13th Brigade : Brigadier-General R. Wanless O'Gowan

2nd King's Own Scottish Borderers	1st Royal West Kents
2nd Duke of Wellington's	2nd King's Own Yorkshire Light Infantry
1/9th (Queen Victoria's Rifles) Londons	

14th Brigade : Brigadier-General G. H. Thesiger

1st Devonshires	1st Duke of Cornwall's Light Infantry
1st East Surreys	2nd Manchesters
1/5th (Earl of Chester's) Cheshires	

15th Brigade : Brigadier-General E. Northey

1st Norfolks	1st Cheshires
1st Bedfordshires	1st Dorsets
1/6th (Liverpool Rifles) King's	

27th DIVISION (Regular) : Major-General T. Snow

    Battle of Gravenstafel Ridge 22 – 23 April (V Corps, Second Army)
    Battle of St Juliaan 24 April – 4 May (V Corps, Second Army)
    Battle of Frezenberg Ridge 8 – 13 May (V Corps, Second Army)
    Battle of Bellewaerde Ridge 24 -25 May (V Corps, Second Army)

80th Brigade: Brigadier-General W. E. B. Smith

2nd King's Shropshire Light Infantry	3rd King's Royal Rifle Corps
4th Rifle Brigade	4th King's Royal Rifle Corps
Princess Patricia's Canadian Light Infantry	

81st Brigade : Brigadier-General H. L. Croker

1st Royal Scots	2nd Gloucesters
1/9th (Highlanders) Royal Scots	1st Argyll & Sutherland Highlanders
2nd Cameron Highlanders	1/9th (Dumbartonshire) Argyll & Sutherland Highlanders

82nd Brigade : Brigadier-General J. R. Longley

1st Royal Irish	2nd Royal Inniskilling Fusiliers
2nd Duke of Cornwall's Light Infantry	1st Leinsters
1/1st Cambridgeshires	

28th DIVISION (Regular) : Major-General E. S. Bulfin

    Battle of Gravenstafel Ridge 22 – 23 April (V Corps, Second Army)
    Battle of St Juliaan 24 Apr – 4 May (II Corps, Second Army)
    Battle of Frezenberg Ridge 8 – 13 May (II Corps, Second Army)
    Battle of Bellewaerde Ridge 24 -25 May (II Corps, Second Army)

83rd Brigade : Brigadier-General R. C. Boyle to 13 May (sick)
               Lieutenant-Colonel T. O. Marden
               Brigadier-General H. S. L. Ravenshaw

2nd King's Own	1st King's Own Yorkshire Light Infantry
1/5th King's Own	1st York & Lancasters
2nd East Yorkshires	1/3rd Monmouths

84th Brigade : Brigadier-General L. J. Bols

2nd Northumberland Fusiliers	2nd Cheshires
1/1st Monmouths	1st Suffolks
1/12th (Rangers) Londons (to 20 May)	1st Welsh

85th Brigade : Brigadier-General A. J. Chapman to 18 May
              Brigadier-General C. E. Pereira

2nd Buffs	2nd East Surreys
3rd Royal Fusiliers	3rd Middlesex
1/8th Middlesex	

50th (NORTHUMBRIAN) DIVISION (T.F.) : Major-General Sir W. F. L. Lindsay

Battle of St Juliaan 24 Apr – 3 May (V Corps until 28 April then Plumer's Force, Second Army)
Battle of Frezenberg Ridge 11 – 13 May (V Corps, Second Army)
Battle of Bellewaerde Ridge 24 – 25 May (149th Brigade only)

149th (Northumberland) Brigade : Brigadier-General J. F. Riddell, killed in action, 26 Apr
                    Lieutenant-Colonel A. J. Forster, 26 Apr
                    Lieutenant-Colonel A. H. Coles to 27 Apr
                    Brigadier-General G. P. T. Feilding

1/4th Northumberland Fusiliers	1/5th Northumberland Fusiliers
1/6th Northumberland Fusiliers	1/7th Northumberland Fusiliers

150th (York & Durham) Brigade : Brigadier-General J. E. Bush

1/4th East Yorkshires	1/4th Yorkshires
1/5th Durham Light Infantry	1/5th Yorkshires

151st (Durham Light Infantry) Brigade : Brigadier-General H. Martin

1/6th Durham Light Infantry	1/7th Durham Light Infantry
1/8th Durham Light Infantry	1/9th Durham Light Infantry

THIRD BATTLES OF YPRES (JUNE – NOVEMBER 1917)

GUARDS DIVISION (Regular) : Major-General G. P. T. Feilding

Battle of Pilkem Ridge 31 July – 2 Aug (XIV Corps, Fifth Army)
Battle of Poelkapelle 9 Oct (XIV Corps, Fifth Army)
First Battle of Passendale 12 Oct (XIV Corps, Fifth Army)

1st Guards Brigade : Brigadier-General G. D. Jeffreys to 22 September
                  Brigadier-General C. R. Champion de Crespigny

2nd Grenadier Guards	2nd Coldstream Guards
1st Irish Guards	3rd Coldstream Guards

2nd Guards Brigade : Brigadier-General J. Ponsonby to 22 August
                  Brigadier-General B. N. Sergison-Brooke

3rd Grenadier Guards	1st Coldstream Guards
1st Scots Guards	2nd Irish Guards

3rd Guards Brigade : Brigadier-General Lord H. C. Seymour

1st Grenadier Guards	2nd Scots Guards
4th Grenadier Guards	1st Welsh Guards

Pioneers : 4th Coldstrean Guards

1st DIVISION (Regular) : Major-General E. P. Strickland

Second Battle of Passendale 5 – 10 Nov (II Corps, Second Army)

1st Brigade : Brigadier-General C. J. C. Grant

1st Black Watch	1st Cameron Highlanders
10th Gloucesters	8th Royal Berkshires

2nd Brigade : Brigadier-General G. C. Kemp

2nd Royal Sussex	1st Loyal North Lancashires
1st Northamptons	2nd King's Royal Rifle Corps

3rd Brigade : Brigadier-General R. C. A. McCalmont

1st South Wales Borderers	1st Gloucesters
2nd Welsh	2nd Royal Munster Fusiliers

Pioneers : 6th Welsh

3rd DIVISION (Regular) : Major-General C. J. Deverell

Battle of the Menin Road 22 – 25 Sept (V Corps, Fifth Army)
Battle of Polygon Wood 26 – 30 Sept (V Corps, Fifth Army to 28 Sept then II A.N.Z.A.C. Corps, Second Army)

8th Brigade : Brigadier-General H. G. Holmes
2nd Royal Scots
8th East Yorkshires

1st Royal Scots Fusiliers
7th King's Shropshire Light Infantry

9th Brigade : Brigadier-General H. C. Potter
1st Northumberland Fusiliers
13th King's

4th Royal Fusiliers
12th West Yorkshires

76th Brigade : Brigadier-General C. L. Porter
2nd Suffolks
8th King's Own

1st Gordon Highlanders
10th Royal Welsh Fusiliers

Pioneers : 20th (British Empire League) King's Royal Rifle Corps

4th DIVISION (Regular) : Major-General T. G. Matheson

Battle of Polygon Wood 28 Sept – 3 Oct (XIV Corps, Fifth Army)
Battle of Broodseinde 4 Oct (XIV Corps, Fifth Army)
Battle of Poelkapelle 9 Oct (XIV Corps, Fifth Army)
Second Battle of Passendale 12 Oct (XIV Corps, Fifth Army)

10th Brigade : Brigadier-General A. G. Pritchard
Household Battalion
2nd Seaforth Highlanders

1st Royal Warwickshires
3/10th Middlesex

11th Brigade : Brigadier-General R. A. Berners
1st Somerset Light Infantry
1st Manchesters

1st East Lancashires
1st Rifle Brigade

12th Brigade : Brigadier-General A. Carton de Wiart, V.C.
1st King's Own
2nd Duke of Wellington's

2nd Lancashire Fusiliers
2nd Essex

Pioneers : 21st (Wool Textile Pioneers) West Yorkshires

5th DIVISION (Regular) : Major-General R. B. Stephens

Battle of Polygon Wood 1 – 3 Oct (X Corps, Second Army)
Battle of Broodseinde 4 Oct (X Corps, Second Army)
Battle of Poekapelle 9 Oct (X Corps, Second Army)
Second Battle of Passendale 26 Oct – 10 Nov (X Corps, Second Army)

13th Brigade : Brigadier-General L. O. W. Jones
2nd King's Own Scottish Borderers
14th (1st Birmingham Pals) Royal Warwickshires

1st Royal West Kents
15th (2nd Birmingham Pals) Royal Warwickshires

15th Brigade : Brigadier-General M. N. Turner
1st Norfolks
1st Cheshires

1st Bedfordshires
16th (3rd Birmingham Pals) Royal Warwickshires

95th Brigade : Brigadier-General Lord E. C. Gordon-Lennox
1st Devonshires
1st Duke of Cornwall's Light Infantry

1st East Surreys
12th (Bristol Pals) Gloucesters

Pioneers : 1/6th (Renfrewshire) Argyll & Sutherland Highlanders

7th DIVISION (Regular) : Major-General T. Capper

Battle of Polygon Wood 1 – 3 Oct (X Corps, Second Army)
Battle of Broodseinde 4 Oct (X Corps, Second Army)
Battle of Poelkapelle 9 Oct (X Corps, Second Army)
Second Battle of Passendale 26 – 29 Oct (X Corps, Second Army)

20th Brigade : Brigadier-General H. C. R. Green
2nd Border
2nd Gordon Highlanders

8th Devonshires
9th Devonshires

22nd Brigade : Brigadier-General J. Steele
2nd Royal Warwickshires
20th (5th Manchester Pals) Manchesters

1st Royal Welsh Fusiliers
2/1st Honourable Artillery Company

91st Brigade : Brigadier-General R. T. Pelly
2nd Queen's
1st South Staffordshires

21st (6th Manchester Pals) Manchesters
22nd (7th Manchester Pals) Manchesters

Pioneers : 24th (Oldham Pals) Manchesters

8th DIVISION (Regular) : Major-General W. C. G. Heneker

Battle of Pilkem Ridge 31 July – 1 Aug (II Corps, Fifth Army)
Battle of Langemark 16 – 18 Aug (II Corps, Fifth Army)

23rd Brigade : Brigadier-General G. W. St. G. Grogan, V.C.
2nd Devonshires
2nd Cameronians

2nd West Yorkshires
2nd Middlesex

24th Brigade : Brigadier-General H. W. Cobham
1st Worcesters
1st Sherwood Foresters

2nd East Lancashires
2nd Northamptons

25th Brigade : Brigadier-General C. Coffin, V.C.
2nd Lincolns
1st Royal Irish Rifles

2nd Royal Berkshires
2nd Rifle Brigade

Pioneers : 22nd (3rd County of Durham Pals) Durham Light Infantry

9th (SCOTTISH) DIVISION (N.A.) : Major-General H. T. Lukin

Battle of the Menin Road 20 – 23 Sept (V Corps, Fifth Army)
First Battle of Passendale 12 Oct (XVIII Corps, Fifth Army)

26th Brigade : Brigadier-General J. Kennedy
8th Black Watch
5th Cameron Highlanders

7th Seaforth Highlanders
10th Argyll & Sutherland Highlanders

27th Brigade : Brigadier-General F. A. Maxwell, V.C., killed in action 21 Sept
        Lieutenant-Colonel H. D. N. McLean to 23 Sept
        Brigadier-General W. D. Croft
11th Royal Scots
12th Royal Scots

6th King's Own Scottish Borderers
9th Cameronians

South African Brigade : Brigadier-General F. S. Dawson
1st South African Infantry
2nd South African Infantry

3rd South African Infantry
4th South African Infantry

Pioneers : 9th Seaforth Highlanders

11th (NORTHERN) DIVISION (N.A.) : Major-General H. R. Davies

Battle of Messines 9 – 14 June (IX Corps, Second Army)
Battle of Langemark 16 – 18 Aug (XVIII Corps, Fifth Army)
Battle of Polygon Wood 26 Sept – 3 Oct (XVIII Corps, Fifth Army)
Battle of Broodseinde 4 Oct (XVIII Corps, Fifth Army)
Battle of Poelkapelle 9 Oct (XVIII Corps, Fifth Army)

32nd Brigade : Brigadier-General T. H. F. Price
9th West Yorkshires
8th Duke of Wellington's

6th Yorkshires
6th York & Lancasters

33rd Brigade : Brigadier-General A. C. Daly to 15 Sept
        Brigadier-General F. G. Spring
6th Lincolns
7th South Staffordshires

6th Border
9th Sherwood Foresters

34th Brigade : Brigadier-General S. H. Pedley to 22 Aug
        Brigadier-General B. G. Clay
8th Northumberland Fusiliers
5th Dorsets

9th Lancashire Fusiliers
11th Manchesters

Pioneers : 6th East Yorkshires

14th (LIGHT) DIVISION (N.A.) : Major-General V. A. Couper

Battle of Langemark 18 Aug (II Corps, Fifth Army)
First Battle of Passendale 12 Oct (X Corps, Second Army)

41st Brigade : Brigadier-General P. C. B. Skinner
7th King's Royal Rifle Corps
8th King's Royal Rifle Corps

7th Rifle Brigade
8th Rifle Brigade

42nd Brigade : Brigadier-General G. N. B. Forster
5th Oxford & Bucks Light Infantry
9th King's Royal Rifle Corps

5th King's Shropshire Light Infantry
9th Rifle Brigade

43rd Brigade : Brigadier-General P. R. Wood to 1 Sept
        Brigadier-General R. S. Tempest
6th Somerset Light Infantry
6th King's Own Yorkshire Light Infantry

6th Duke of Cornwall's Light Infantry
10th Durham Light Infantry

Pioneers : 11th King's

15th (SCOTTISH) DIVISION (N.A.) : Maj-Gen H. F. Thuillier

Battle of Pilkem Ridge 31 July – 2 Aug (XIX Corps, Fifth Army)
Battle of Langemark 17 – 18 Aug (46th Brigade only)

44th Brigade : Brigadier-General F. J. Marshall
9th Black Watch
8/10th Gordon Highlanders

8th Seaforth Highlanders
7th Cameron Highlanders

45th Brigade : Brigadier-General W. H. L. Allgood
13th Royal Scots
6th Cameron Highlanders

6/7th Royal Scots Fusiliers
11th Argyll & Sutherland Highlanders

46th Brigade : Lieutenant-Colonel K. J. Buchanan to 2 Aug
               Brigadier-General D. R. Sladen
7/8th King's Own Scottish Borderers
10/11th Highland Light Infantry

10th Cameronians
12th Highland Light Infantry

Pioneers : 9th Gordon Highlanders

16th (IRISH) DIVISION (N.A.) : Major-General W. B. Hickie

    Battle of Messines 7 – 9 June (IX Corps, Second Army)
    Battle of Pilkem Ridge 31 July – 2 Aug (Reserve, XIX Corps, Fifth Army)
    Battle of Langemark 16 – 18 Aug (XIX Corps, Fifth Army)

47th Brigade : Brigadier-General G. E. Pereira
6th Royal Irish
7th Leinsters

6th Connaught Rangers
1st Royal Munster Fusiliers

48th Brigade : Brigadier-General F. W. Ramsey
7th Royal Irish Rifles
8th Royal Dublin Fusiliers
10th Royal Dublin Fusiliers

2nd Royal Dublin Fusiliers
9th Royal Dublin Fusiliers

49th Brigade : Brigadier-General P. Leveson-Gower
2nd Royal Irish
7/8th Royal Irish Fusiliers

7th Royal Inniskilling Fusiliers
8th Royal Inniskilling Fusiliers

Pioneers : 11th Hampshires

17th (NORTHERN) DIVISION (N.A.) : Major-General P. R. Robertson

    First Battle of Passendale 12 Oct (XIV Corps, Fifth Army)
    Second Battle of Passendale 8 – 10 Nov (XIX Corps, Fifth Army)

50th Brigade : Brigadier-General C. Yatman
10th West Yorkshires
7th Yorkshires

7th East Yorkshires
6th Dorsets

51st Brigade : Brigadier-General C. E. Bond to 14 Oct (sick)
               Lieutenant-Colonel F. E. Metcalfe
7th Lincolns
7th (Westmorland & Cumberland Yeomanry) Border

8th South Staffordshires
10th Sherwood Foresters

52nd Brigade : Brigadier-General A. J. F. Eden
9th (Northumberland Hussars Yeomanry)
  Northumberland Fusiliers
12th (Duke of Lancaster's Own Yeomanry) Manchesters

10th Lancashire Fusiliers
9th Duke of Wellington's
3/4th Royal West Kents

Pioneers : 7th York & Lancasters

18th (EASTERN) DIVISION (N.A.) : Major-General R. P. Lee

    Battle of Pilkem Ridge 31 July (II Corps, Fifth Army)
    Battle of Langemark 16 – 17 Aug (53rd Brigade with 56th Division)
    First Battle of Passendale 12 Oct (XVIII Corps, Fifth Army)
    Second Battle of Passendale 5 – 10 Nov (XIX Corps, Fifth Army)

53rd Brigade : Brigadier-General H. W. Higginson
8th Norfolks
10th Essex

8th Suffolks
6th Royal Berkshires

54th Brigade : Brigadier-General C. Cunliffe-Owen to 22 Oct
               Brigadier-General L. W. de V. Sadleir-Jackson
11th Royal Fusiliers
6th Northamptons

7th Bedfordshires
12th Middlesex

55th Brigade : Brigadier-General B. D. Price
7th Queen's
8th East Surreys

7th Buffs
7th Royal West Kents

Pioneers : 8th Royal Sussex

19th (WESTERN) DIVISION (N.A.) : Major-General C. D. Shute

    Battle of Messines 7 – 14 June (IX Corps, Second Army)
    Battle of the Menin Road 20 – 25 Sept (IX Corps, Second Army)
    Battle of Polygon Wood 26 Sept – 3 Oct (IX Corps, Second Army)
    Battle of Broodseinde 4 Oct (IX Corps, Second Army)
    First Battle of Passendale 12 Oct (IX Corps, Second Army)
    Second Battle of Passendale 26 Oct – 10 Nov (IX Corps, Second Army)

56th Brigade : Brigadier-General E. Craig-Brown to 5 Sept
             Lieutenant-Colonel T. Fitzjohn to 6 Sept
             Lieutenant-Colonel C. R. P. Winser on 6 Sept
             Brigadier-General F. G. Willan

7th King's Own   7th East Lancashires
7th South Lancashires   7th Loyal North Lancashires

57th Brigade : Brigadier-General T. A. Cubitt
10th Royal Warwickshires   8th Gloucesters
10th Worcesters   8th North Staffordshires

58th Brigade : Brigadier-General A. E. Glasgow
9th Cheshires   9th Royal Welsh Fusiliers
9th Welsh   6th Wiltshires (Wilts Yeomanry from 3 Sept)
             Pioneers : 5th South Wales Borderers

20th (LIGHT) DIVISION (N.A.) : Major-General W. Douglas-Smith

    Battle of Langemark 16 – 18 Aug (XIV Corps, Fifth Army)
    Battle of the Menin Road 20 – 25 Sept (XIV Corps, Fifth Army)
    Battle of Polygon Wood 26 – 28 Sept (XIV Corps, Fifth Army)

59th Brigade : Brig-Gen R. C. Browne-Clayton to 26 Aug
             Brigadier-General H. H. G. Hyslop
10th King's Royal Rifle Corps   10th Rifle Brigade
11th King's Royal Rifle Corps   11th Rifle Brigade

60th Brigade : Brigadier-General Hon. L. J. P. Butler
6th Oxford & Bucks Light Infantry   6th King's Shropshire Light Infantry
12th King's Royal Rifle Corps   12th Rifle Brigade

61st Brigade : Brigadier-General W. E. Banbury
12th King's   7th Somerset Light Infantry
7th Duke of Cornwall's Light Infantry   7th King's Own Yorkshire Light Infantry
             Pioneers : 11th Durham Light Infantry

21st DIVISION (N.A.) : Major-General D. G. M. Campbell

    Battle of Polygon Wood 29 Sept – 3 Oct (X Corps, Second Army)
    Battle of Broodseinde 4 Oct (X Corps, Second Army)
    Second Battle of Passendale 26 Oct – 10 Nov (X Corps, Second Army)

62nd Brigade : Brigadier-General C. G. Rawling, killed in action 28 Oct
             Captain G. M. Sharpe to 1 Nov
             Brigadier-General G. H. Gater
12th Northumberland Fusiliers   1st Lincolns
13th Northumberland Fusiliers   10th Yorkshires
3/4th Queen's

64th Brigade : Brigadier-General H. R. Headlam
1st East Yorkshires   9th King's Own Yorkshire Light Infantry
15th Durham Light Infantry   10th King's Own Yorkshire Light Infantry

110th Brigade : Brigadier-General Lord Leach
6th Leicesters   8th Leicesters
7th Leicesters   9th Leicesters
             Pioneers : 14th Northumberland Fusiliers

23rd DIVISION (N.A.) : Major-General J. M. Babington

    Battle of Messines 7 – 14 June (X Corps, Second Army)
    Battle of the Menin Road 20 – 24 Sept (X Corps, Second Army)
    Battle of Polygon Wood 28 Sept – 2 Oct (X Corps, Second Army)
    First Battle of Passendale 12 Oct (X Corps, Second Army)

68th Brigade : Brigadier-General G. N. Colvile to 27 Sept
             Lieutenant-Colonel M. G. H. Barker
10th Northumberland Fusiliers   12th Durham Light Infantry
11th Northumberland Fusiliers   13th Durham Light Infantry

69th Brigade : Brigadier-General T. S. Lambert
11th West Yorkshires   8th Yorkshires
10th Duke of Wellington's   9th Yorkshires

70th Brigade : Brigadier-General H. Gordon
11th Sherwood Foresters   8th York & Lancasters
8th Kings Own Yorkshire Light Infantry 9th York & Lancasters
             Pioneers : 9th South Staffordshires

24th DIVISION (N.A.) : Major-General L. J. Bols

Battle of Messines 7 – 14 June (X Corps, Second Army)
Battle Pilkem Ridge 31 July – 2 Aug (II Corps, Fifth Army)
Battle of Langemark 16 – 18 Aug (II Corps, Fifth Army)

17th Brigade : Brigadier-General P. V. P. Stone
8th Buffs   1st Royal Fusiliers
3rd Rifle Brigade   12th Royal Fusiliers

72nd Brigade : Brigadier-General W. F. Sweny
8th Queen's   9th East Surreys
8th Royal West Kents   1st North Staffordshires

73rd Brigade : Brigadier-General W. J. Dugan
9th Royal Sussex   7th Northamptons
13th Middlesex   2nd Leinsters
                    Pioneers : 12th Sherwood Foresters

25th DIVISION (N.A.) : Major-General E. G. T. Bainbridge

Battle of Messines 7 – 14 June (II A.N.Z.A.C. Corps, Second Army)
Battle of Pilkem Ridge 31 July – 2 Aug (II Corps, Fifth Army)

7th Brigade : Brigadier-General C. C. Onslow
10th Cheshires   3rd Worcesters
8th Loyal North Lancashires   1st Wiltshires

74th Brigade : Brigadier-General H. K. Bethell
11th Lancashire Fusiliers   13th Cheshires
9th Loyal North Lancashires   2nd Royal Irish Rifles

75th Brigade : Brigadier-General H. B. D. Baird
11th Cheshires   8th Border
2nd South Lancashires   8th South Lancashires
                    Pioneers : 6th South Wales Borderers

29th DIVISION (Regular) : Major-General H. de B. de Lisle

Battle of Langemark 16 – 18 Aug (XIV Corps, Fifth Army)
Battle of Broodseinde 4 Oct (XIV Corps, Fifth Army)
Battle of Poelkapelle 9 Oct (XIV Corps, Fifth Army)

86th Brigade : Lieutenant-Colonel H. Nelson to 24 Aug
              Brigadier-General G. R. H. Cheape
2nd Royal Fusiliers   1st Lancashire Fusiliers
16th (Public Schools) Middlesex   1st Royal Dublin Fusiliers
Royal Guernsey Light Infantry (from 2 Oct)

87th Brigade : Brigadier-General C. H. Lucas
2nd South Wales Borderers   1st King's Own Scottish Borderers
1st Royal Inniskilling Fusiliers   1st Border

88th Brigade : Brigadier-General D. E. Cayley to 1 Oct
              Brigadier-General H. Nelson
4th Worcesters   2nd Hampshires
1st Essex   1st Royal Newfoundlanders
                    Pioneers : 1/2nd Monmouths

30th DIVISION (N.A.) : Major-General W. de L. Williams

Battle of Pilkem Ridge 31 July – 2 Aug (II Corps, Fifth Army)

21st Brigade : Brigadier-General G. D. Goodman
18th (2nd Liverpool Pals) King's   2nd Yorkshires
2nd Wiltshires   19th (4th Manchester Pals) Manchesters

89th Brigade : Brigadier-General W. W. Norman
17th (1st Liverpool Pals) King's   20th (4th Liverpool Pals) King's
19th (3rd Liverpool Pals) King's   2nd Bedfordshires

90th Brigade : Brigadier-General J. H. Lloyd
2nd Royal Scots Fusiliers   16th (1st Manchester Pals) Manchesters
17th (2nd Manchester Pals) Manchesters   18th (3rd (Clerks & Warehousemen) Manchester Pals)
                                          Manchesters
                Pioneers : 11th (St. Helens Pals) South Lancashires

33rd DIVISION (N.A.) : Major-General P. R. Wood

Battle of the Menin Road 24 – 25 Sept (X Corps, Second Army)
Battle of Polygon Wood 26 – 27 Sept (X Corps, Second Army)

19th Brigade : Brigadier-General C. R. G. Mayne
20th (3rd Public Schools) Royal Fusiliers
1st Cameronians

2nd Royal Welsh Fusiliers
5/6th Cameronians

98th Brigade : Brigadier-General J. D. Heriot-Maitland
4th King's
1st Middlesex

1/4th Suffolks
2nd Argyll & Sutherland Highlanders

100th Brigade : Brigadier-General A. W. F. Baird
1st Queen's
16th (Church Lads Brigade) King's Royal Rifle Corps

2nd Worcesters
1/9th (Glasgow Highland) Highland Light Infantry

Pioneers : 18th (1st Public Works) Middlesex

34th DIVISION (N.A.) : Major-General C. L. Nicholson

Battles of Ypres 13 – 23 Oct (XIV Corps, Fifth Army)

101st Brigade : Brigadier-General R. C. Gore
15th (1st City of Edinburgh) Royal Scots
16th (2nd City of Edinburgh) Royal Scots

10th (Grimsby Chums) Lincolns
11th (Cambridge) Suffolks

102nd Brigade : Brigadier-General N. A. Thomson
20th (1st Tyneside Scots) Northumberland Fusiliers
21st (2nd Tyneside Scots) Northumberland Fusiliers

22nd (3rd Tyneside Scots) Northumberland Fusiliers
23rd (4th Tyneside Scots) Northumberland Fusiliers

103rd Brigade : Brigadier-General H. E. Trevor to 21 Oct (gassed)
Lieutenant-Colonel E. M. Moulton-Barrett
24th (1st Tyneside Irish) Northumberland Fusiliers
25th (2nd Tyneside Irish) Northumberland Fusiliers

26th (3rd Tyneside Irish) Northumberland Fusiliers
27th (4th Tyneside Irish) Northumberland Fusiliers

Pioneers : 18th (1st Tyneside Pioneers) Northumberland Fusiliers

---

35th DIVISION (N.A.) : Major-General G. Franks

Second Battle of Passendale 26 Oct – 4 Nov (XIV Corps, Fifth Army to 30 Oct then XIX Corps, Fifth Army)

104th Brigade : Brigadier-General J. W. Sandilands
17th (1st South-East Lancashire Pals) Lancashire Fusiliers
18th (2nd South-East Lancashire Pals) Lancashire Fusiliers

20th (4th Salford Pals) Lancashire Fusiliers
23rd (8th Manchester Pals) Manchesters

105th Brigade : Brigadier-General A. H. Marindin
15th (1st Birkenhead Pals) Cheshires
16th (2nd Birkenhead Pals) Cheshires

14th (West of England) Gloucesters
15th (Nottingham Pals) Sherwood Foresters

106th Brigade : Brigadier-General J. H. W. Pollard
17th (Earl of Roseberry) Royal Scots
17th (2nd Leeds Pals) West Yorkshires

18th (4th Glasgow Pals) Highland Light Infantry
19th (2nd County of Durham Pals) Durham Light Infantry

Pioneers : 19th (2nd Tyneside Pioneers) Northumberland Fusiliers

---

36th (ULSTER) DIVISION (N.A.) : Major-General O. S. W. Nugent

Battle of Messines 7 – 9 June (IX Corps, Second Army)
Battle of Langemark 16 – 17 Aug (XIX Corps, Fifth Army)

107th Brigade : Brigadier-General W. M. Withycombe
8th (East Belfast Volunteers) Royal Irish Rifles
9th (West Belfast Volunteers) Royal Irish Rifles

10th (South Belfast Volunteers) Royal Irish Rifles
15th (North Belfast Volunteers) Royal Irish Rifles

108th Brigade : Brigadier-General C. R. J. Griffith
11th (South Antrim Volunteers) Royal Irish Rifles
12th (Central Antrim Volunteers) Royal Irish Rifles

13th (1st County Down Volunteers) Royal Irish Rifles
9th (County Armagh, Monaghan & Cavan) Royal Irish Fusiliers

109th Brigade : Brigadier-General A. Ricardo
9th (County Tyrone Volunteers) Royal Inniskilling Fusiliers
14th (Belfast Young Citizens) Royal Irish Rifles

10th (County Derry Volunteers) Royal Inniskilling Fusiliers
11th (Donegal & Fermanagh Vols) Royal Inniskilling Fusiliers

Pioneers : 16th (2nd County Down Volunteers) Royal Irish Rifles

---

37th DIVISION (N.A.) : Major-General H. Bruce-Williams

Battle of Pilkem Ridge 31 July – 2 Aug (IX Corps, Second Army)
Battle of the Menin Road 22 – 25 Sept (112th Brigade with 39th Division, 22–23 Sept and 19th Division 23–25 Sept)
Battle of Polygon Wood 27 Sept – 3 Oct (IX Corps, Second Army)
Battle of Broodseinde 4 Oct (IX Corps, Second Army)
Battle of Poelkapelle 9 Oct (IX Corps, Second Army)
First Battle of Passendale 12 Oct (IX Corps, Second Army)

63rd Brigade : Brigadier-General E. L. Challenor
8th Lincolns
4th Middlesex

8th Somerset Light Infantry
10th York & Lancasters

111th Brigade : Brigadier-General C. W. Compton
10th (Stock Exchange) Royal Fusiliers
13th Royal Fusiliers

13th King's Royal Rifle Corps
12th Rifle Brigade

112th Brigade : Brigadier-General R. C. Maclachlan, killed in action 11 Aug
　　　　　　Lieutenant-Colonel R. C. Chester-Master to 16 Aug
　　　　　　Brigadier-General A. E. Irvine
11th Royal Warwickshires
8th East Lancashires

6th Bedfordshires
10th Loyal North Lancashires

Pioneers : 9th North Staffordshires

38th (WELSH) DIVISION (N.A.) : Major-General C. G. Blackader

Battle of Pilkem Ridge 31 July – 2 Aug (XIV Corps, Fifth Army)

113th Brigade : Brigadier-General L. A. E. Price-Davies, V.C.
13th (1st North Wales Pals) Royal Welsh Fusiliers
14th (Caernarvon & Anglesey Pals) Royal Welsh Fusiliers

15th (1st London Welsh) Royal Welsh Fusiliers
16th Royal Welsh Fusiliers

114th Brigade : Brigadier-General T. O. Marden
10th (1st Rhondda Pals) Welsh
13th (2nd Rhondda Pals) Welsh

14th (Swansea Pals) Welsh
15th (Carmarthenshire Pals) Welsh

115th Brigade : Brigadier-General G. Gwyn-Thomas
17th (2nd North Wales Pals) Royal Welsh Fusiliers
16th (Cardiff City Pals) Welsh

10th (1st Gwent – Colliers & Ironworkers – Pals) South Wales Borderers
11th (2nd Gwent Pals) South Wales Borderers

Pioneers : 19th (Glamorgan Pioneers) Welsh

39th DIVISION (N.A.) : Major-General G. J. Cuthbert to 20 Aug
Major-General E. Feetham

Battle of Pilkem Ridge 31 July – 2 Aug (XVIII Corps, Fifth Army)
Battle of Langemark 16 – 18 Aug (X Corps, Second Army)
Battle of the Menin Road 20 – 25 Sept (X Corps, Second Army)
Battle of Polygon Wood 26 – 27 Sept (X Corps, Second Army)
Second Battle of Passendale 29 Oct – 10 Nov (X Corps, Second Army)

116 Brigade : Brigadier-General M. L. Hornby
11th (1st South Downs) Royal Sussex
12th (2nd South Downs) Royal Sussex

13th (3rd South Downs) Royal Sussex
14th (1st Portsmouth Pals) Hampshires

117th Brigade : Brigadier-General G. A. Armytage
16th (Chatsworth Rifles) Sherwood Foresters
17th (Welbeck Rangers) Sherwood Foresters

17th (British Empire League) King's Royal Rifle Corps
16th (St. Pancras) Rifle Brigade

118th Brigade : Brigadier-General E. H. C. P. Bellingham
1/6th Cheshires
1/1st Cambridgeshires

4/5th Black Watch
1/1st Hertfordshires

Pioneers : 13th (Forest of Dean) Gloucesters

41st DIVISION (N.A.) : Major-General S. T. B. Lawford

Battle of Messines 7 – 14 June (X Corps, Second Army)
Battle of Pilkem Ridge 31 July – 2 Aug (X Corps, Second Army)
Battle of the Menin Road 20 – 22 Sept (X Corps, Second Army)

122nd Brigade : Brigadier-General F. W. Towsey
12th (Bermondsey) East Surreys
11th (Lewisham) Royal West Kents

15th (2nd Portsmouth Pals) Hampshires
18th (Arts & Craftsmen) King's Royal Rifle Corps

123rd Brigade : Brigadier-General C. W. E. Gordon, killed in action 24 July
　　　　　　Brigadier-General W. F. Clemson to 3 Aug
　　　　　　Brigadier-General E. Pearce-Serocold
11th (Lambeth) Queen's
23rd (2nd Football) Middlesex

10th (Kent County) Royal West Kents
20th (Wearside) Durham Light Infantry

124th Brigade : Brigadier-General W. F. Clemson to 24 July
　　　　　　Lieutenant-Colonel W. C. Clark to 2 Aug
　　　　　　Brigadier-General W. F. Clemson
10th (Battersea) Queen's
21st (Yeoman Rifles) King's Royal Rifle Corps

26th (Bankers) Royal Fusiliers
32nd (East Ham) Royal Fusiliers

Pioneers : 19th (2nd Public Works) Middlesex

47th (2nd LONDON) DIVISION (T.F.) : Major-General Sir G. F. Gorringe

Battle of Pilkem Ridge 31 July – 2 Aug (In Reserve, X Corps, Second Army)

140th (4th London) Brigade : Brigadier-General H. B. P. L. Kennedy
1/6th (London Rifles) Londons
1/7th Londons

1/8th (Post Office Rifles) Londons
1/15th (Civil Service Rifles) Londons

141st (5th London) Brigade : Brigadier-General R. McDouall
1/17th (Poplar & Stepney) Londons
1/18th (London Irish Rifles) Londons

1/19th (St. Pancras) Londons
1/20th (Blackheath & Woolwich) Londons

142nd (6th London) Brigade : Brigadier-General V. T. Bailey
1/21st (Surrey Rifles) Londons
1/22nd (The Queen's) Londons

1/23rd Londons
1/24th (The Queen's) Londons

Pioneers : 4th Royal Welsh Fusiliers

48th (SOUTH MIDLAND) DIVISION (T.F.) : Major-General R. Fanshawe

Battle of Langemark 16 – 18 Aug (XVIII Corps, Fifth Army)
Battle of Polygon Wood 28 Sept – 3 Oct (XVIII Corps, Fifth Army)
Battle of Broodseinde 4 Oct (XVIII Corps, Fifth Army)
Battle of Poelkapelle 9 Oct (XVIII Corps, Fifth Army)

143rd (Warwickshire) Brigade : Brigadier-General G. C. Sladen
1/5th Royal Warwickshires
1/6th Royal Warwickshires

1/7th Royal Warwickshires
1/8th Royal Warwickshires

144th (Gloucester & Worcester) Brigade : Brigadier-General H. R. Done
1/4th (City of Bristol) Gloucesters
1/6th Gloucesters

1/7th Worcesters
1/8th Worcesters

145th (South Midland) Brigade : Brigadier-General D. M. Watt
1/5th Gloucesters
1/4th Royal Berkshires

1/4th Oxford & Bucks Light Infantry
1/1st (Bucks) Oxford & Bucks Light Infantry

Pioneers : 1/5th (Cinque Ports) Royal Sussex

49th (WEST RIDING) DIVISION (T.F.) : Major-General E. M. Perceval

Battle of Poelkapelle 9 Oct (II A.N.Z.A.C. Corps, Second Army)

146th (1st West Riding) Brigade : Brigadier-General M. D. Goring-Jones
1/5th West Yorkshires
1/6th West Yorkshires

1/7th (Leeds Rifles) West Yorkshires
1/8th (Leeds Rifles) West Yorkshires

147th (2nd West Riding) Brigade : Brigadier-General C. G. Lewes
1/4th Duke of Wellington's
1/5th Duke of Wellington's

1/6th Duke of Wellington's
1/7th Duke of Wellington's

148th (3rd West Riding) Brigade : Brigadier-General R. L. Adlercron
1/4th King's Own Yorkshire Light Infantry
1/5th King's Own Yorkshire Light Infantry

1/4th (Hallamshire) York & Lancasters
1/5th York & Lancasters

Pioneers : 19th (3rd Salford Pals) Lancashire Fusiliers

50th (NORTHUMBRIAN) DIVISION (T.F.) : Major-General P. S. Wilkinson

Second Battle of Passendale 26 Oct – 9 Nov (XIV Corps to 29 Oct XIX Corps, Fifth Army)

149th (Northumberland) Brigade : Brigadier-General E. P. A. Riddell
1/4th Northumberland Fusiliers
1/5th Northumberland Fusiliers

1/6th Northumberland Fusiliers
1/7th Northumberland Fusiliers

150th (York & Durham) Brigade : Brigadier-General B. G. Price
1/4th East Yorkshires
1/5th Durham Light Infantry

1/4th Yorkshires
1/5th Yorkshires

151st (Durham Light Infantry) Brigade : Brigadier-General C. T. Martin
1/5th (West Cumberland) Border
1/6th Durham Light Infantry

1/8th Durham Light Infantry
1/9th Durham Light Infantry

Pioneers : 1/7th Durham Light Infantry

51st (HIGHLAND) DIVISION (T.F.) : Major-General G. M. Harper

Battle of Pilkem Ridge 31 July – 2 Aug (XVIII Corps, Fifth Army)
Battle of the Menin Road 20 – 24 Sept (XVIII Corps, Fifth Army)

152nd (1st Highland) Brigade : Brigadier-General H. P. Burn
1/5th (Sutherland & Caithness) Seaforth Highlanders
1/6th (Morayshire) Seaforth Highlanders

1/6th (Banff & Donside) Gordon Highlanders
1/8th (Argyllshire) Argyll & Sutherland Highlanders

153rd (2nd Highland) Brigade : Lieutenant-Colonel H. G. Hyslop to 2 Aug
Brigadier-General A. T. Beckwith
1/6th (Perthshire) Black Watch
1/7th (Fife) Black Watch

1/5th (Buchan & Formartin) Gordon Highlanders
1/7th (Deeside Highland) Gordon Highlanders

154th (3rd Highland) Brigade : Brigadier-General J. G. H. Hamilton
1/9th (Highlanders) Royal Scots
1/4th Gordon Highlanders

1/4th (Ross-shire) Seaforth Highlanders
1/7th Argyll & Sutherland Highlanders

Pioneers : 1/8th Royal Scots

55th (WEST LANCASHIRE) DIVISION (T.F.) : Major-General H. S. Jeudwine

Battle of Pilkem Ridge 31 July – 2 Aug (XIX Corps, Fifth Army)
Battle of the Menin Road 20 – 23 Sept (V Corps, Fifth Army)

164th (North Lancashire) Brigade : Brigadier-General C. I. Stockwell
1/4th King's Own	1/8th (Liverpool Irish) King's
2/5th Lancashire Fusiliers	1/4th Loyal North Lancashires

165th (Liverpool) Brigade : Brigadier-General L. B. Boyd-Moss
1/5th King's	1/7th King's
1/6th (Liverpool Rifles) King's	1/9th King's

166th (South Lancashire) Brigade : Brigadier-General F. G. Lewis
1/5th King's Own	1/10th (Liverpool Scottish) King's
1/5th South Lancashires	1/5th Loyal North Lancashires

Pioneers : 1/4th South Lancashires

57th (2nd WEST LANCASHIRE) DIVISION (T.F.) : Major-General R. W. R. Barnes

Second Battle of Passendale 26 Oct – 7 Nov (XIV Corps to 29 Oct XIX Corps, Fifth Army)

170th (2nd/1st North Lancashire) Brigade : Brigadier-General F. G. Guggisberg
2/5th King's Own	2/4th Loyal North Lancashires
2/5th Loyal North Lancashires	4/5th Loyal North Lancashires

171st (2nd/1st Liverpool) Brigade : Brigadier-General H. N. Bray
2/5th King's	2/7th King's
2/6th King's	2/8th King's

172nd (2nd/1st South Lancashire) Brigade : Brigadier-General G. C. B. Paynter
2/9th King's	2/4th South Lancashires
2/10th King's	2/5th South Lancashires

**58th (2/1st LONDON) DIVISION (T.F.) : Major-General H. D. Fanshawe to 6 Oct
Major-General A. B. E. Cator**

Battle of the Menin Road 20 – 25 Sept (XVIII Corps, Fifth Army)
Battle of Polygon Wood 26 – 27 Sept (XVIII Corps, Fifth Army)
Second Battle of Passendale 26 Oct – 10 Nov (XVIII Corps, Fifth Army to 2 Nov then II Corps, Second Army)

173rd (3rd/1st London) Brigade : Lieutenant-Colonel W. R. H. Dann to 3 Oct
Brigadier-General R. B. Worgan
2/1st Londons	2/3rd Londons
2/2nd Londons	2/4th Londons

174th (2nd/2nd London) Brigade : Brigadier-General C. G. Higgins
2/5th Londons	2/7th Londons
2/6th Londons	2/8th Londons

175th (2nd/3rd London) Brigade : Brigadier-General H. C. Jackson
2/9th Londons	2/11th Londons
2/10th Londons	2/12th Londons

59th (2nd NORTH MIDLAND) DIVISION (T.F.) : Major-General C. F. Romer

Battle of the Menin Road 23 – 25 Sept (V Corps, Fifth Army)
Battle of Polygon Wood 26 – 30 Sept (V Corps, Fifth Army to 28 Sept then II A.N.Z.A.C. Corps, Second Army)

176th (2nd/1st Staffordshire) Brigade : Brigadier-General T. G. Cope
2/5th South Staffordshires	2/5th North Staffordshires
2/6th South Staffordshires	2/6th North Staffordshires

177th (2nd/1st Lincoln & Leicester) Brigade : Brigadier-General C. H. L. James
2/4th Lincolns	2/4th Leicesters
2/5th Lincolns	2/5th Leicesters

178th (2nd/1st Nottinghamshire & Derbyshire) Brigade : Brigadier-General T. W. Stansfeld
2/5th Sherwood Foresters	2/7th Sherwood Foresters
2/6th Sherwood Foresters	2/8th Sherwood Foresters

61st (2nd SOUTH MIDLAND) DIVISION (T.F.) : Major-General C. J. MacKenzie

Battle of Langemark 18 Aug (XIX Corps, Fifth Army)

182nd (2nd/1st Warwickshire) Brigade : Brigadier-General Hon. C. J. Sackville-West
2/5th Royal Warwickshires	2/7th Royal Warwickshires
2/6th Royal Warwickshires	2/8th Royal Warwickshires

183rd (2nd/1st Gloucester & Worcester) Brigade : Brigadier-General A. H. Spooner
2/4th Gloucesters	2/7th Worcesters
2/6th Gloucesters	2/8th Worcesters

184th (2nd/1st South Midland) Brigade : Brigadier-General Hon. R. White
2/5th Gloucesters   2/4th Oxford & Bucks Light Infantry
2/4th Royal Berkshires   2/1st Buckinghamshire (Oxford & Bucks Light Infantry)

63rd (ROYAL NAVAL) DIVISION (T.F.) : Brigadier-General C. E. Lawrie

   Second Battle of Passendale 26 Oct – 5 Nov (XVIII Corps, Fifth Army)

188th (1st Royal Naval) Brigade : Brigadier-General R. E. S. Prentice
Howe   1st Royal Marines Light Infantry
Anson   2nd Royal Marines Light Infantry

189th (2nd Royal Naval) Brigade : Brigadier-General L. F. Philips
Drake   Hawke
Nelson   Hood

190th (Royal Marine) Brigade : Brigadier-General A. R. H. Hutchinson
7th Royal Fusiliers   4th Bedfordshires
10th Royal Dublin Fusiliers   1/28th (Artist Rifles) Londons
                                                1/4th King's Shropshire Light Infantry
              Pioneers : 14th (Severn Valley Pioneers) Worcesters

66th (2nd EAST LANCASHIRE) DIVISION (T.F.) : Major-General Hon. H. A. Lawrence

   Battle of Poelkapelle 9 Oct (II A.N.Z.A.C. Corps, Second Army)

197th (2nd/1st Lancashire Fusiliers) Brigade : Brigadier-General O. C. Borrett
3/5th Lancashire Fusiliers   2/7th Lancashire Fusiliers
2/6th Lancashire Fusiliers   2/8th Lancashire Fusiliers

198th (2nd/1st East Lancashire) Brigade : Brigadier-General A. J. Hunter
2/4th East Lancashires   2/9th Manchesters
2/5th East Lancashires   2/10th Manchesters
199th (2nd/1st Manchester) Brigade : Brigadier-General J. O. Travers
2/5th Manchesters   2/7th Manchesters
2/6th Manchesters   2/8th Manchesters
         Pioneers : 10th (Cornwall Pioneers) Duke of Cornwall's Light Infantry

BATTLES OF THE LYS (FOURTH YPRES APRIL 1918)

2nd CAVALRY DIVISION (Regular) : Brigadier-General T. T. Pitman

   Battle of Hazebrouck 14 – 15 April (Cavalry Corps, Second Army)

3rd Cavalry Brigade : Brigadier-General J. A. Bell-Smyth
4th (Queen's Own) Hussars   5th (Royal Irish) Lancers
16th (The Queen's) Lancers

4th Cavalry Brigade : Brigadier-General C. H. Rankin
6th (Carabiniers) Dragoon Guards   3rd (King's Own) Hussars
1st Queen's Own Oxfordshire Hussars

5th Cavalry Brigade : Brigadier-General N. W. Haig
2nd Dragoons (Royal Scots Greys)   12th (Prince of Wales's Royal) Lancers
20th Hussars

1st DIVISION (Regular) : Major-General E. P. Strickland

   Battle of Estaires 9 – 11 Apr (I Corps, First Army)
   Battle of Hazebrouck 15 Apr (3rd Brigade with 55th Division, XI Corps, First Army)
   Battle of Bethune 18-19 Apr (I Corps, First Army)

1st Brigade : Brigadier-General W. B. Thornton
1st Black Watch   1st Loyal North Lancashires
1st Cameron Highlanders

2nd Brigade : Brigadier-General G. C. Kelly
2nd Royal Sussex   1st Northamptons
2nd King's Royal Rifle Corps

3rd Brigade : Brigadier-General H. H. S. Morant
1st South Wales Borderers   1st Gloucesters
2nd Welsh
                        Pioneers : 6th Welsh

3rd DIVISION (Regular) : Major-General C. J. Deverell

    Battle of Estaires 9 – 11 Apr (I Corps, First Army)
    Battle of Hazebrouck 12 – 15 Apr (I Corps, First Army)
    Battle of Bethune 18 Apr (I Corps, First Army)

8th Brigade : Brigadier-General L. A. E. Price-Davies, V.C., to 12 Apr
                Brigadier-General B. D. Fisher

2nd Royal Scots	7th King's Shropshire Light Infantry
1st Royal Scots Fusiliers	

9th Brigade : Brigadier-General H. C. Potter

1st Northumberland Fusiliers	4th Royal Fusiliers
13th King's	

76th Brigade : Brigadier-General C. L. Porter

2nd Suffolks	1st Gordon Highlanders
8th King's Own	

            Pioneers : 20th (British Empire League) King's Royal Rifle Corps

4th DIVISION (Regular) : Major-General T. G. Matheson

    Battle of Hazebrouck 13 – 15 Apr (I Corps, First Army)
    Battle of Bethune 18 Apr (I Corps, First Army)

10th Brigade : Brigadier-General H. W. Green to 16 Apr
               Brigadier-General J. Greene

1st Royal Warwickshires	2nd Duke of Wellington's
2nd Seaforth Highlanders	

11th Brigade : Brigadier-General T. S. H. Wade

1st Somerset Light Infantry	1st Hampshires
1st Rifle Brigade	

12th Brigade : Brigadier-General E. A. Fagan

1st King's Own	2nd Lancashire Fusiliers
2nd Essex	

            Pioneers : 21st (Wool Textile Pioneers) West Yorkshires

5th DIVISION (Regular) : Major-General R. B. Stephens

    Battle of Hazebrouck 12 – 15 Apr (XI Corps, First Army)

13th Brigade : Brigadier-General L. O. W. Jones

2nd King's Own Scottish Borderers	14th (1st Birmingham Pals) Royal Warwickshires
1st Royal West Kents	15th (2nd Birmingham Pals) Royal Warwickshires

15th Brigade : Brigadier-General R. D. F. Oldman

1st Norfolks	1st Bedfordshires
1st Cheshires	16th (3rd Birmingham Pals) Royal Warwickshires

95th Brigade : Brigadier-General Lord E. C. Gordon-Lennox

1st Devonshires	1st East Surreys
1st Duke of Cornwall's Light Infantry	12th (Bristol Pals) Gloucesters

            Pioneers : 1/6th (Renfrewshire) Argyll & Sutherland Highlanders

6th DIVISION (Regular) : Major-General T. O. Marden

    Battle of Bailleul 13 – 15 Apr (71st Brigade with 49th Division, IX Corps, Second Army)
    First Battle of Kemmel 17 – 19 Apr (71st Brigade with 49th Division)
    Second Battle of Kemmel 25 – 26 Apr (XXII Corps, Second Army)
    Battle of Scherpenberg 29 Apr (XXII Corps, Second Army)

16th Brigade : Brigadier-General H. A. Walker

1st Buffs	1st King's Shropshire Light Infantry
2nd York & Lancasters	

18th Brigade : Brigadier-General G. S. G. Craufurd

1st West Yorkshires	2nd Durham Light Infantry
11th Essex	

71st Brigade : Brigadier-General P. W. Brown

1st Leicesters	2nd Sherwood Foresters
9th Norfolks	

            Pioneers : 11th (City of Leicester Pals) Leicesters

9th (SCOTTISH) DIVISION (N.A.) : Major-General H. H. Tudor

    Battle of Messines 10 – 11 Apr (IX Corps, Second Army)
    Battle of Bailleul 13 – 15 Apr (XXII Corps, Second Army)
    First Battle of Kemmel 17 – 19 Apr (XXII Corps, Second Army)
    Second Battle of Kemmel 25 – 26 Apr (XXII Corps, Second Army)
    Battle of Scherpenberg 29 Apr (South African Brigade with 49th Division)

26th Brigade : Brigadier-General J. Kennedy
8th Black Watch   7th Seaforth Highlanders
5th Cameron Highlanders

27th Brigade : Brigadier-General W. D. Croft
11th Royal Scots   6th King's Own Scottish Borderers
12th Royal Scots

South African Brigade : Brigadier-General W. E. C. Tanner
1st South African Infantry   4th South African Infantry
2nd South African Infantry   2nd Royal Scots Fusiliers (from 26 April)
                                               9th Cameronians (from 23 April)
                    Pioneers : 9th Seaforth Highlanders

19th (WESTERN) DIVISION (N.A.) : Major-General G. D. Jeffreys

    Battle of Messines 10 – 11 Apr (IX Corps, Second Army)
    Battle of Bailleul 13 – 15 Apr (IX Corps, Second Army)
    First Battle of Kemmel 17 – 18 Apr (IX Corps, Second Army)

56th Brigade : Brigadier-General R. M. Meath
9th Cheshires   1/4th King's Shropshire Light Infantry
8th North Staffordshires

57th Brigade : Brigadier-General T. A. Cubitt
10th Royal Warwickshires   8th Gloucesters
10th Worcesters

58th Brigade : Brigadier-General A. E. Glasgow
9th Royal Welsh Fusiliers   9th Welsh
6th (Wiltshire Yeomanry) Wiltshires
                    Pioneers : 5th South Wales Borderers

21st DIVISION (N.A.) : Major-General D. G. M. Campbell

    Battle of Messines 10 – 11 Apr (62nd Brigade with 9th Division, IX Corps, Second Army)
    Battle of Bailleul 13 – 15 Apr (62nd Brigade with 9th Division)
    First Battle of Kemmel 17 – 19 Apr (XXII Corps, Second Army)
    Second Battle of Kemmel 25 – 26 Apr (XXII Corps, Second Army)
    Battle of Scherpenberg 29 Apr (XXII Corps, Second Army)

62nd Brigade : Brigadier-General G. H. Gates
1st Lincolns   12/13th Northumberland Fusiliers
2nd Lincolns

64th Brigade : Brigadier-General H. R. Headlam
1st East Yorkshires   1st King's Own Yorkshire Light Infantry
15th Durham Light Infantry

110th Brigade : Brigadier-General H. R. Cumming
6th Leicesters   8th Leicesters
7th Leicesters
                    Pioneers : 14th Northumberland Fusiliers

Served with 21st Division :

    39th Composite Brigade, from 10 April to 1 May
    146th Brigade, 49th (West Riding) Division, from 10 to 19 April
    21st Brigade, 30th Division, from 20 April to 2 May
    89th Brigade, 30th Division, from 25 April to 2 May
    58th Brigade, 19th (Western) Division, from 28 to 30 April

25th DIVISION (N.A.) : Major-General E. G. T. Bainbridge

    Battle of Estaires 9 – 11 Apr (74th Brigade only, XV Corps, First Army)
    Battle of Messines 10 – 11 Apr (less 74th Brigade, IX Corps, Second Army)
    Battle of Bailleul 13 – 15 Apr (IX Corps, Second Army)
    First Battle of Kemmel 17 – 19 Apr (IX Corps, Second Army)
    Second Battle of Kemmel 25 -26 Apr (XXII Corps, Second Army)
    Battle of Scherpenberg 29 Apr (XXII Corps, Second Army)

7th Brigade : Brigadier-General C. J. Griffin
10th Cheshires   4th South Staffordshires
1st Wiltshires

74th Brigade : Brigadier-General H. M. Craigie-Halkett
11th Lancashire Fusiliers   3rd Worcesters
9th Loyal North Lancashires

75th Brigade : Brigadier-General C. C. Hannay
11th Cheshires   8th Border
2nd South Lancashires

Pioneers : 6th South Wales Borderers

29th DIVISION (Regular) : Major-General D. E. Cayley

Battle of Estaires 10 – 11 Apr (less 88th Brigade, XV Corps, First Army)
Battle of Messines 10 – 11 Apr (88th Brigade with 25th Division on 10 April and 34th Division on 11 April, IX Corps, Second Army)
Battle of Hazebrouck 12 – 13 Apr (less 88th Brigade, XV Corps, Second Army)
Battle of Bailleul 13 – 14 Apr (88th Brigade with 34th Division, IX Corps, Second Army)

86th Brigade : Brigadier-General G. R. H. Cheape
2nd Royal Fusiliers   1st Lancashire Fusiliers
Royal Guernsey Light Infantry

87th Brigade : Brigadier-General G. H. N. Jackson
2nd South Wales Borderers   1st King's Own Scottish Borderers
1st Border

88th Brigade : Brigadier-General B. C. Freyberg, V.C.
4th Worcesters   2nd Hampshires
1st Royal Newfoundlanders

Pioneers : 1/2nd Monmouths

30th DIVISION (N.A.) : Major-General W. de L. Williams

First Battle of Kemmel 17 – 19 Apr (89th Brigade only, IX Corps, Second Army)
Second Battle of Kemmel 25 – 26 Apr (89th & 21st (Composite) Brigades, XXII Corps, Second Army)
Battle of Scherpenberg 29 Apr (89th & 21st (Composite) Brigades, XXII Corps, Second Army)

21st (Composite) Brigade (with 21st Division from 19 Apr) : Brigadier-General G. D. Goodman
2nd Bedfordshires   2nd Wiltshires (2 Companies)
16th (1st Manchester Pals) Manchesters   2nd Yorkshires
17th (2nd Manchester Pals) Manchesters (2 Companies)

89th Brigade : Brigadier-General R. A. M. Currie
17th (1st Liverpool Pals) King's   19th (3rd Liverpool Pals) King's
18th (Lancashire Hussars) King's

Pioneers : 11th (St. Helens Pioneers) South Lancashires

31st DIVISION (N.A.) : Major-General R. J. Bridgford

Battle of Estaires 11 Apr (XV Corps, First Army)
Battle of Hazebrouck 12 – 14 Apr (XV Corps, Second Army)

4th (Guards) Brigade : Brigadier-General Hon. L. J. P. Butler
4th Grenadier Guards   3rd Coldstream Guards
2nd Irish Guards

92nd Brigade : Brigadier-General O. de L. Williams
10th (Hull Commercials) East Yorkshires   11th (Accrington Pals) East Lancashires
11th (Hull Tradesmen) East Yorkshires

93rd Brigade : Brigadier-General S. C. Taylor
15th (1st Leeds Pals) West Yorkshires   13th (1st Barnsley Pals) York & Lancasters
18th (1st County of Durham Pals) Durham Light Infantry

Pioneers : 12th (Halifax (Miners) Pals) King's Own Yorkshire Light Infantry

33rd DIVISION (N.A.) : Major-General R. J. Pinney

Battle of Messines 11 Apr (100th Brigade in Reserve to 25th Division, IX Corps, Second Army)
Battle of Hazebrouck 12 – 15 Apr (IX Corps, Second Army)
Battle of Bailleul 13 – 15 Apr (100th Brigade only with 25th Division)
First Battle of Kemmel 17 – 19 Apr (IX Corps, Second Army)

19th Brigade : Brigadier-General C. R. G. Mayne
1st Queen's   1st Cameronians
5/6th Cameronians

98th Brigade : Brigadier-General J. D. Heriot-Maitland
4th King's   1st Middlesex
2nd Argyll & Sutherland Highlanders

100th Brigade : Brigadier-General A. W. F. Baird
2nd Worcesters   16th (Church Lads Brigade) King's Royal Rifle Group
1/9th (Glasgow Highland) Highland Light Infantry

Pioneers : 18th (1st Public Works) Middlesex

34th DIVISION (N.A.) : Major-General C. L. Nicholson

Battle of Estaires 9 – 11 Apr (XV Corps, First Army)
Battle of Bailleul 12 – 15 Apr (IX Corps, First Army)
First Battle of Kemmel 17 – 19 Apr (IX Corps, First Army)

101st Brigade : Brigadier-General R. C. Gore, killed in action 14 Apr
                Lieutenant-Colonel A. Stephenson

15th (1st City of Edinburgh) Royal Scots	11th (Cambridge) Suffolk
16th (2nd City of Edinburgh) Royal Scots	

102nd Brigade : Brigadier-General N. A. Thomson

22nd (3rd Tyneside Scots) Northumberland Fusiliers	25th (2nd Tyneside Irish) Northumberland Fusiliers
23rd (4th Tyneside Scots) Northumberland Fusiliers	

103rd Brigade : Brigadier-General J. G. Chaplin

10th (Grimsby Chums) Lincolns	9th (Northumberland Hussars) Northumberland Fusiliers
1st East Lancashires	

Pioneers : 18th (1st Tyneside Pioneers) Northumberland Fusiliers

36th (ULSTER) DIVISION (N.A.) : Major-General O. S. W. Nugent

Battle of Messines 10 – 11 Apr (108th Brigade only with 19th Division, IX Corps, Second Army)
Battle of Bailleul 13 – 15 Apr (108th Brigade only with 19th Division)
First Battle of Kemmel 17 – 18 Apr (108th Brigade only with 19th Division)

108th Brigade : Brigadier-General C. R. J. Griffith

12th (Central Antrim Volunteers) Royal Irish Rifles	1st Royal Irish Fusiliers
9th (North Irish Horse) Royal Irish Fusiliers	

39th DIVISION (N.A.) : Major-General C. A. Blacklock

First Battle of Kemmel 17 – 19 Apr (39th Division Composite Brigade, XXII Corps, Second Army)
Second Battle of Kemmel 25 – 26 Apr (39th Division Composite Brigade)
Battle of Scherpenberg 29 Apr (39th Division Composite Brigade)

39th Division Composite Brigade : Major-General C. A. Blacklock
No. 1 Btn – 11th (1st South Down) Royal Sussex & 1/1st Hertfordshires
No. 2 Btn – 13th (Forest of Dean Pals) Gloucesters & 13th (3rd South Down) Royal Sussex
No. 3 Btn – 117th Brigade – 16th (Chatsworth Rifles) Sherwood Foresters, 17th (British Empire League) King's Royal Rifle
             Corps, 16th (St. Pancras) Rifle Brigade
No. 4 Btn – 118th Brigade – 1/6th Cheshires, 4/5th Black Watch, 1/1st Cambridgeshires

40th DIVISION (N.A.) : Major-General J. Ponsonby

Battle of Estaires 9 – 11 Apr (XV Corps, First Army)
Battle of Hazebrouck 12 – 13 Apr (XV Corps, Second Army)

119th Brigade : Brigadier-General F. P. Crozier

13th (Wandsworth) East Surreys	18th (2nd Glamorgan Pals) Welsh
21st (Islington) Middlesex	

120th Brigade : Brigadier-General C. J. Hobkirk

10/11th Highland Light Infantry	2nd Royal Scots Fusiliers
14th Argyll & Sutherland Highlanders	14th Highland Light Infantry

121st Brigade : Brigadier-General J. Campbell

12th (East Anglian) Suffolks	13th Yorkshires
20th (Shoreditch) Middlesex	

Pioneers : 12th (Tee-side Pioneers) Yorkshires

41st DIVISION (N.A.) : Major-General S. T. B. Lawford

Battles of the Lys 9 – 29 Apr (VIII Corps to 13 Apr then II Corps, Second Army)

122nd Brigade : Brigadier-General F. W. Towsey

12th (Bermondsey) East Surreys	15th King's Royal Rifle Corps
15th (Carabiniers) Hampshires	

123rd Brigade : Brigadier-General E. Pearce-Serocold

11th (Lambeth) Queen's	10th (Kent County) Royal West Kents
23rd (2nd Football) Middlesex	

124th Brigade : Brigadier-General W. F. Clemson

10th (Battersea) Queen's	26th (Bankers) Royal Fusiliers
20th (Wearside) Durham Light Infantry	

Pioneers : 19th (2nd Public Works) Middlesex

49th (WEST RIDING) DIVISION (T.F.) : Major-General N. J. G. Cameron

Battle of Estaires 10 – 11 Apr (147th Brigade only, XV Corps, First Army)
Battle of Messines 10 – 11 Apr (148th Brigade only, IX Corps, Second Army)
Battle of Bailleul 13 – 15 Apr (IX Corps, Second Army)
First Battle of Kemmel 17 – 19 Apr (IX Corps, Second Army; 146th Brigade with XXII Corps)
Second Battle of Kemmel 25 – 26 Apr (XXII Corps, Second Army)
Battle of Scherpenberg 29 Apr (XXII Corps, Second Army)

146th (1st West Riding) Brigade : Brigadier-General G. A. P. Rennie
1/5th West Yorkshires   1/7th (Leeds Rifles) West Yorkshires
1/6th West Yorkshires

147th (2nd West Riding) Brigade : Brigadier-General C. G. Lewes
1/4th Duke of Wellington's   1/6th Duke of Wellington's
1/7th Duke of Wellington's

148th (3rd West Riding) Brigade : Brigadier-General L. F. Green-Wilkinson
1/4th (Hallamshire) York & Lancasters   1/4th King's Own Yorkshire Light Infantry
1/5th York & Lancasters

Pioneers : 19th (3rd Salford Pals) Lancashire Fusiliers

50th (NORTHUMBRIAN) DIVISION (T.F.) : Major-General H. C. Jackson

Battle of Estaires 9 – 11 Apr (XV Corps, First Army)
Battle of Hazebrouck 12 Apr (XV Corps, First Army)

149th (Northumberland) Brigade : Brigadier-General E. P. A. Riddell
1/4th Northumberland Fusiliers   1/6th Northumberland Fusiliers
1/5th Northumberland Fusiliers

150th (York & Durham) Brigade : Brigadier-General H. C. Rees
1/4th Yorkshires   1/4th East Yorkshires
1/5th Yorkshires

151st (Durham Light Infantry) Brigade : Brigadier-General H. Martin
1/5th Durham Light Infantry   1/6th Durham Light Infantry
1/8th Durham Light Infantry

Pioneers : 1/7th Durham Light Infantry

51st (HIGHLAND) DIVISION (T.F.) : Major-General G. T. C. Carter-Campbell

Battle of Estaires 9 – 11 Apr (XI Corps, First Army)
Battle of Hazebrouck 12 – 15 Apr (XI Corps, First Army)

152nd (1st Highland) Brigade : Brigadier-General J. K. Dick-Cunyngham to 12 Apr (captured)
     Major A. A. Duff to 15 Apr
     Lieutenant-Colonel J. M. Scott
1/5th (Sutherland & Caithness) Seaforth Highlanders   1/6th (Banff & Donside) Gordon Highlanders
1/6th (Morayshire) Seaforth Highlanders

153rd (2nd Highland) Brigade : Brigadier-General A. T. Beckwith to 11 Apr (wounded)
     Lieutenant-Colonel L. M. Dyson to 13 Apr
     Major W. H. Newson on 13 Apr
     Lieutenant-Colonel J. M. Scott to 15 Apr
     Brigadier-General W. Green
1/6th (Perthshire) Black Watch   1/7th (Deeside Highland) Gordon Highlanders
1/7th (Fife) Black Watch

154th (3rd Highland) Brigade : Brigadier-General K. G. Buchanan
1/4th (Ross Highland) Seaforth Highlanders   1/4th Gordon Highlanders
1/7th Argyll & Sutherland Highlanders

Pioneers : 1/8th Royal Scots

55th (WEST LANCASHIRE) DIVISION (T.F.) : Major-General H. S. Jeudwine

Battle of Estaires 9 – 11 Apr (XI Corps, First Army)
Battle of Hazebrouck 12 – 15 Apr (I Corps, First Army)

164th (North Lancashire) Brigade : Brigadier-General C. I. Stockwell
1/4th King's Own   2/5th Lancashire Fusiliers
1/4th Loyal North Lancashires

165th (Liverpool) Brigade : Brigadier-General L. B. Boyd-Moss
1/5th King's   1/7th King's
1/6th (Leeds Rifles) King's

166th (South Lancashire) Brigade : Brigadier-General R. J. Kentish
1/5th King's Own   1/10th (Liverpool Scottish) King's
1/5th South Lancashires

Pioneers : 1/4th South Lancashires

59th (2nd NORTH MIDLAND) DIVISION (T.F.) : Major-General C. F. Romer

Battle of Bailleul 14 – 15 Apr (IX Corps, Second Army)
First Battle of Kemmel 17 – 18 Apr (IX Corps, Second Army)

176th (2nd/1st Staffordshire) Brigade : Brigadier-General T. G. Cope
5th North Staffordshires   2/6th South Staffordshires
2/6th North Staffordshires

177th (2nd/1st Lincoln & Leicester) Brigade : Brigadier-General C. H. L. James
4th Lincolns   2/4th Leicesters
2/5th Lincolns

178th (2nd/1st Nottinghamshire & Derbyshire) Brigade : Brigadier-General T. W. Stansfeld
2/5th Sherwood Foresters   7th Sherwood Foresters
2/6th Sherwood Foresters

Pioneers : 6/7th Royal Scots Fusiliers

61st (2nd SOUTH MIDLAND) DIVISION (T.F.) : Major-General C. J. MacKenzie

Battle of Estaires 11 Apr (XI Corps, First Army)
Battle of Hazebrouck 12 – 15 Apr (XI Corps, First Army)
Battle of Bethune 18 Apr (XI Corps, First Army)

182nd (2nd/1st Warwickshire) Brigade : Brigadier-General W. K. Evans
2/6th Royal Warwickshires   2/8th Royal Warwickshires
2/7th Royal Warwickshires

183rd (2nd/1st Gloucester & Worcester) Brigade : Brigadier-General A. H. Spooner
1/9th (Highlanders) Royal Scots   1/5th (Buchan & Formartin) Gordon Highlanders
1/8th (Argyllshire) Argyll & Sutherland Highlanders

184th (2nd/1st South Midland) Brigade : Brigadier-General A. W. Pagan
2/5th Gloucesters   2/4th Oxford & Bucks Light Infantry
2/4th Royal Berkshires

Pioneers : 1/5th Duke of Cornwall's Light Infantry

THE FINAL ADVANCE IN FLANDERS (SEPTEMBER – OCTOBER 1918)

9th (SCOTTISH) DIVISION (N.A.) : Major-General H.H.Tudor

Battle of Ypres 28 Sept – 2 Oct (II Corps, Second Army)
Battle of Kortrijk 14 – 19 Oct (II Corps, Second Army)

26th Brigade : Brigadier-General Hon. A. G. A. Hore-Ruthven, V.C.
8th Black Watch   5th Cameron Highlanders
7th Seaforth Highlanders

27th Brigade : Brigadier-General W. D. Croft
11th Royal Scots   6th King's Own Scottish Borderers
12th Royal Scots

28th Brigade : Brigadier-General J. L. Jack
2nd Royal Scots Fusiliers   1st Royal Newfoundlanders
9th Cameronians

Pioneers : 9th Seaforth Highlanders

14th (LIGHT) DIVISION (N.A.) : Major-General P. C. B. Skinner

Battle of Ypres 28 Sept – 2 Oct (XIX Corps, Second Army)
Battle of Kortrijk 14 – 19 Oct (XV Corps, Second Army)

41st Brigade : Brigadier-General W. F. Sweny
18th York & Lancasters   33rd (Rifle Brigade) Londons
29th Durham Light Infantry

42nd Brigade : Brigadier-General H. T. Dobbin
6th (Wiltshire Yeomanry) Wiltshires   16th (1st Manchester Pals) Manchesters
14th Argyll & Sutherland Highlanders

43rd Brigade : Brigadier-General G. E. Pereira
12th (East Anglian) Suffolks   10th Highland Light Infantry
20th (Shoreditch) Middlesex

Pioneers : 15th Loyal North Lancashires

29th DIVISION (Reg) : Major-General D. E. Cayley

    Battle of Ypres 28 Sept – 2 Oct (II Corps, Second Army)
    Battle of Kortrijk 14 – 19 Oct (II Corps, Second Army)

86th Brigade : Brigadier-General G. R. H. Cheape
2nd Royal Fusiliers   1st Royal Dublin Fusiliers
1st Lancashire Fusiliers

87th Brigade : Brigadier-General G. H. N. Jackson
1st South Wales Borderers   1st Border
1st King's Own Scottish Borderers

88th Brigade : Brigadier-General B. C. Freyberg, V.C.
4th Worcesters   2nd Leinsters
2nd Hampshires
                           Pioneers : 1/2nd Monmouths

30th DIVISION (N.A.) : Major-General W. de L. Williams

    Battle of Ypres 28 Sept – 2 Oct (X Corps, Second Army)
    Battle of Kortrijk 14 – 19 Oct (X Corps, Second Army)

21st Brigade : Brigadier-General G. D. Goodman
7th (South Irish Horse) Royal Irish   2/23rd Londons
1/6th Cheshires

89th Brigade : Brigadier-General R. A. M. Currie
2nd South Lancashires   2/17th Londons
7/8th Royal Inniskilling Fusiliers

90th Brigade : Brigadier-General G. A. Stevens
2/14th Londons   2/16th Londons
2/15th Londons
                     Pioneers : 6th South Wales Borderers

31st DIVISION (N.A.) : Major-General J. Campbell

    Battle of Ypres 28 Sept – 2 Oct (XV Corps, Second Army)

92nd Brigade : Brigadier-General O. de L. Williams
10th (Hull Commercials) East Yorkshires   11th (Accrington Pals) East Lancashires
11th (Hull Tradesmen) East Yorkshires

93rd Brigade : Brigadier-General S. C. Taylor
15th (1st Leeds Pals) West Yorkshires   18th (1st County of Durham Pals) Durham Light Infantry
13th (1st Barnsley Pals) York & Lancasters

94th (Yeomanry) Brigade : Brigadier-General A. Symons
12th (Norfolk Yeomanry) Norfolks   24th (Denbigh Yeomanry) Royal Welsh Fusiliers
12th (Ayr & Lanark Yeomanry) Royal Scots Fusiliers
            Pioneers : 12th (Halifax (Miners) Pals) King's Own Yorkshire Light Infantry

34th DIVISION (N.A.) : Major-General C. L. Nicholson

    Battle of Ypres 28 – 29 Sept (X Corps, Second Army)
    Battle of Kortrijk 14 – 19 Oct (X Corps, Second Army)

101st Brigade : Brigadier-General W. J. Woodcock
2/4th Queen's   2nd Loyal North Lancashires
1/4th Royal Sussex

102nd Brigade : Brigadier-General E. Hilliam
1/4th Cheshires   1/1st Herefordshires
1/7th Cheshires

103rd Brigade : Brigadier-General R. I. Rawson
1/5th King's Own Scottish Borderers   1/8th Cameronians
1/5th Argyll & Sutherland Highlanders
               Pioneers : 2/4th Somerset Light Infantry

35th DIVISION (N.A.) : Major-General A. H. Marindin

    Battle of Ypres 28 Sept – 2 Oct (XIX Corps, Second Army)
    Battle of Kortrijk 14 – 19 Oct (XIX Corps, Second Army)

104th Brigade : Brigadier-General J. W. Sandilands
17th (1st South East Lancashire Pals) Lancashire Fusiliers   19th (2nd County of Durham Pals) Durham Light Infantry
18th (2nd South East Lancashire Pals) Lancashire Fusiliers

105th Brigade : Brigadier-General A. J. Turner
15th (1st Birkenhead Pals) Cheshires   4th North Staffordshires
15th (Nottingham Pals) Sherwood Foresters

106th Brigade : Brigadier-General J. H. W. Pollard
17th (Earl of Roseberry) Royal Scots   12th Highland Light Infantry
18th (Glasgow Yeomanry) Highland Light Infantry
Pioneers : 19th (2nd Tyneside Pioneers) Northumberland Fusiliers

36th (ULSTER) DIVISION (N.A.) : Major-General C. Coffin, V.C.

    Battle of Ypres 28 Sept – 2 Oct (II Corps, Second Army)
    Battle of Kortrijk 14 – 19 Oct (II Corps, Second Army)

107th Brigade : Brigadier-General H. J. Brock
1st Royal Irish Rifles   15th (North Belfast Volunteers) Royal Irish Rifles
2nd Royal Irish Rifles

108th Brigade : Brigadier-General E. Vaughan
12th (Central Antrim Volunteers) Royal Irish Rifles   9th (North Irish Horse) Royal Irish Fusiliers
1st Royal Irish Fusiliers

109th Brigade : Brigadier-General W. F. Hessey
1st Royal Inniskilling Fusiliers   9th (County Tyrone Volunteers) Royal Inniskilling
2nd Royal Inniskilling Fusiliers   Fusiliers
Pioneers : 16th (2nd County Down Volunteers) Royal Irish Rifles

40th DIVISION (N.A.) : Major-General Sir W. E. Peyton

    Battle of Ypres 28 Sept – 2 Oct (XV Corps, Second Army)

119th Brigade : Brigadier-General F. P. Crozier
13th Royal Inniskilling Fusiliers   12th North Staffordshires
13th East Lancashires

120th Brigade : Brigadier-General C. J. Hobkirk
10th King's Own Scottish Borderers   11th Cameron Highlanders
15th King's Own Yorkshire Light Infantry

121st Brigade : Brigadier-General G. C. Stubbs
8th Royal Irish   23rd Cheshires
23rd Lancashire Fusiliers
Pioneers : 17th Worcesters

41st DIVISION (N.A.) : Major-General S. T. B. Lawford

    Battle of Ypres 28 Sept – 2 Oct (XIX Corps, Second Army)
    Battle of Kortrijk 14 – 19 Oct (XIX Corps, Second Army)

122nd Brigade : Brigadier-General S. V. P. Weston
12th (Bermondsey) East Surreys   15th King's Royal Rifle Corps
15th (Carabiniers) Hampshires

123rd Brigade : Brigadier-General M. Kemp-Welch
11th (Lambeth) Queen's   23rd (2nd Football) Middlesex
11th (Lewisham) Royal West Kents

124th Brigade : Brigadier-General R. L. Adlercron
10th (Battersea) Queen's   20th (Wearside) Durham Light Infantry
26th (Bankers) Royal Fusiliers
Pioneers : 19th (2nd Public Works) Middlesex

CEMETERY DEAD

	Cemetery	UK	Aust	NZ	Can	NF	SAfr	RGLI	BWI	India	Chinese	Fr	Bel	Ger	Others	Unnamed	KUG	WWII	TOTAL
1	Abeele Aerodrome	104					1												104
2	Aeroplane	825	204	17	47	1	1									637	1		1096
3	Artillery Wood	1243	5	2	30		1									506	5		1286
4	Bailleul Communal	586			21					4		1	2	8		10			622
5	Bailleul Extension	3411	396	252	290	1	1	1	1	4	31	2		111		181	1		4502
6	Bard Cottage	1615			9	6	2		3					4					1639
7	Bedford House	3951	201	30	335		17	3	6	20				2	1	2511	501		5067
8	Belgian Battery Corner	430	123	8	7					2							9		579
9	(Royal) Berkshire	295	51	45	3														394
10	Bertenacre	108			2														110
11	Bethleem Farm East	1	42													8			43
12	Bethleem Farm West	24	114	26												2			164
13	Birr Crossroads	625	140	12	15	1	1		1							336	11		806
14	Blauwepoort Farm	83															7		90
15	Bleuet Farm	437			1	1	3							1				9	452
16	Boezinge Churchyard	1																	1
17	Brandhoek	601	4		63									2	2				672
18	Brandhoek New	514	11		6									28					559
19	Brandhoek No. 3	849	46	18	46		5		1		1								966
20	Bridge House	45														4			45
21	Buffs Road	265	13		10		1									86			289
22	Bus House	190	10	1	2				1							12			204
23	Buttes	1317	564	167	50											1673	30		2128
24	Cabin Hill	42	25												0				67
25	Calvaire	218																	218
26	Canada Farm	879			5	4			19										907
27	Cement House	3415	19	10	57	14	1	5				1		1		2336	1	22	3546
28	Chester Farm	306	21		87									4					418
29	Colne Valley	47																	47
30	Croonaert Chapel	74									1					7			75
31	Derry House No. 2	126	37																163
32	Dickebusch Old	41			3									1				10	55
33	Dickebusch New	528	11		84														623
34	Dickebusch Extension	520	24		2	1								1			1		548
35	Divisional	188		65	26														281
36	Divisional Col. Post	579	102	5	73	2	1							1		512	1		763

No.	Name	UK	Aust	NZ	Can	NF	SAfr	RGLI	BWI	India	Chinese	Fr	Bel	Ger	Others	Unnamed	KUG	WWII	TOTAL
37	Dochy Farm	523	305	98	91	1	17									958	412		1437
38	Dozinghem	3021	6	14	61	19	15		34		3			65			1	73	3312
39	Dragoon Camp	66														6			66
40	Dranoutre Church	79														2			79
41	Dranoutre Military	421	17	1	19									1			3		462
42	Duhallow A.D.S.	1442	13	6	26	12	3		2	2		2	1	54				1	1564
43	Elsenwalle Brass.	106			41				2							5			149
44	Essex Farm	1088			9									5		19	83		1185
45	Ferme Olivier	407												3		3			410
46	1st D.C.L.I.	99														15			99
47	Godewaersvelde	985	65	2	5		2			3				19		19			1081
48	Godezonne Farm	74	1		1		3												79
49	Grootebeek	97		1			1			7					1	1	2		109
50	Gunners' Farm	163	2	1			9							4					179
51	Gwalia	444	2	5			1		14		4			3					473
52	Hagle Dump	397	26		14									2		142			439
53	Haringhe	732	2	11	1	5	7		4		4	1		39	1		5	5	817
54	Hedge Row	94			2												2		98
55	Hooge Crater	5182	513	121	105				2							3580			5923
56	Hop Store	247			1														248
57	Hospital Farm	115										1				4			116
58	Huts	815	243	19	5		4		1	1				6			6		1100
59	Hyde Park Corner	81	1		1									4		4			87
60	Irish House	103	13											4		40			120
61	Kandahar Farm	211	186	33	6									3			7		446
62	Kemmel Chateau	1030	24	1	80													22	1157
63	Kemmel Churchyard	23														3			23
64	Kemmel No. 1 French	277	12	3	3									253		259	1		549
65	Klien Vierstraat	777	8	7	8		1		1		1								803
66	La Belle Alliance	60														10			60
67	La Brique No. 1	90														4			90
68	La Brique No. 2	788	18	9	23		7									387	2		847
69	La Clytte	813	12	3	51		6		7							190			892
70	La Creche	3																	3
71	La Laiterie	468	7		197	1											78		751
72	Lancashire Cottage	229	23		2											5			254
73	La Plus Douve	101	86	61	88									9					345
74	Larch Wood	614	35		86				1							321	33		769
75	Ledegem	65														14			65

#		UK	Aust	NZ	Can	NF	SAfr	RGLI	BWI	India	Chinese	Fr	Bel	Ger	Others	Unnamed	KUG	WWII	TOTAL
76	Le Touquet Railway	71																	71
77	Lijssenthoek	7350	1131	291	1053	5	29		21	2	32	658		223	4	21	3		10802
78	Lindenhoek Chalet	282	10	8	15									2		67			317
79	Locre Churchyard	184			31											2			215
80	Locre Hospice	238	2	1	1				1					2		12			245
81	Locre No. 10	55												150		14			205
82	London Rifle Brigade	263	38	34										18		1			353
83	Lone Tree	82															6		88
84	Maple Copse	114			142											52			256
85	Maple Leaf	80	4	43	39		1							9					176
86	Mendinghem	2272	15	12	28	3	33		26		8			51					2448
88	Menin Road South	1051	263	52	145				3					1		121	65		1580
89	Messines Ridge	986	332	115	1		56									954	1		1491
90	Meteren	583	104	22	5	1	31			15		65				181		6	832
91	Minty Farm	188												1					189
92	Mont Noir	146	1			2						84				15	2		233
93	Motor Car Corner	36	9	84										1			2		132
94	Mud Corner	1	31	53															85
95	New Irish Farm	4272	54	23	254	3	6		1	5	7			1		3267	12		4638
96	Nieppe Communal	43	6	11			2												62
97	Nieuwkerke Church	76	10	5	1					1		4						15	112
98	Nine Elms	955	149	118	289	7	26	8	2	1				37	1			22	1615
99	No Man's Cot	79																	79
100	Oak Dump	109	2													5			111
101	Oostaverne Wood	923	43	19	133							1		25		783			1144
102	Oxford Road	398	74	37	74	9		2						2		254			596
103	Packhorse Farm	59																	59
104	Passendale New	1019	292	126	646	1	3	4								1602			2091
105	Perth (China Wall)	2360	134	22	129		7									1368	3		2655
106	Ploegsteert Church	7			2														9
107	Ploegsteert Wood	117	1	18	28												1		165
108	Peolkapelle	6541	117	237	525	9	10								4	6231		1	7444
109	Polygon Wood	32		57										1		17	11		101
110	Pond Farm	293												5		4			298
111	Pont d'Achelles	173	72	48										36			7		336
112	Pont de Nieppe	122	12													11	1		135
113	Poperinge Communal	23													5	1			28
114	Poperinge Old	397			46						1			2		24			446
115	Poperinge New	596	20	3	55				2		1	275		1					953

No.		UK	Aust	NZ	Can	NF	SAfr	RGLI	BWI	India	Chinese	Fr	Bel	Ger	Others Unnamed	KUG	WWII	TOTAL
116	Potijze Burial Ground	580	3		1									2	21			586
117	Potijze Grounds	304	23	2	49							1		1	111	85		466
118	Potijze Lawn	191	4		22		9							3	29			229
119	Potijze Wood	145			6										6			151
120	Prowse Point	159	13	42	1									12				227
121	Railway Chateau	105													6			105
122	Railway Dugouts	1629	154	3	594				1	4				3	430	2		2390
123	Ramparts	153	11	14	10										5			188
124	Ration Farm	185	12	4										1	1			202
125	R.E. Farm	132			47										11			179
126	R.E. Grave	12																12
127	Red Farm	46											3		17			49
128	Reningelst Church	57	1														2	60
129	Reningelst Military	453	104	2	230		1				7			2		1		800
130	Ridge Wood	260	44	3	292									2	5	20		621
131	Rifle House	229			1													230
132	Ruisseau Farm	82													6			82
133	St. Julien	290	10	3	15	1	3								180	96		418
134	St. Quentin Cabaret	316	7	64	68									5		5		465
135	Sanctuary Wood	1734	88	18	142	3	3							1	1353			1989
136	Seaforth	147			1										21			148
137	Solferino Farm	293		3	1	1			1					3			5	304
138	Somer Farm	64	20															84
139	Spanbroekmolen	53														5		58
140	Spoilbank	426	67		16										125			509
141	Strand	725	284	87	26		1							11	356		8	1142
142	Suffolk	47													8			47
143	Talana Farm	529													14			529
144	Tancrez Farm	306	19	3			4							2	6			334
145	Toronto Avenue		78															78
146	Torreken Farm	70	20											14				104
147	Track 'X'	126			5										12			131
148	Trois Arbres	954	470	214	20	1	1	33		1					435			1694
149	Tuileries	26													16	11		37
150	Tyne Cot	8961	1368	520	1011	14	90	6	2					4	8366			11976
151	Underhill Farm	102	47	39	1	2	2									1	190	384
152	Vlamertinge	1113	4	52		2	2			1				3		1	4	1182
153	Vlamertinge New	1609	44	1	155		3	1						7				1820
154	Voormezele Nos 1 & 2	502	17	2	53									5	43			579

		UK	Aust	NZ	Can	NF	SAfr	RGLI	BWI	India	Chinese	Fr	Bel	Ger	Others	Unnamed	KUG	WWII	TOTAL
155	Voormezele No. 3	1481	8	2	100		1									612	1		1593
156	Watou Churchyard	11			1														12
157	Welsh (Caesar's Nose)	68														6			68
158	Westhof Farm	69	43	12	1									5					130
159	Westoutre Military	157		3	3						3					52	2	5	173
160	Westoutre Church	77	1	1	19									1		1			99
161	White House	974	40	25	73		5		1					1		325		9	1128
162	Wieltje Farm	113		1	1									1		10			116
163	Woods	212	3		111												32		358
164	Wulvergem Church	33														1	5		38
165	W'gem-L'hoek Rd.	835	35	69	54		9									353			1002
166	Wytschaete	486	31	7	19		11							1		673	423		978
167	Ypres Reservoir	2248	142	28	151	4	12	2	6	1				1		1035	7		2602
168	Ypres Town	142								1	1				49				192
169	Ypres Extension	462	13		15		1			1				2		137		43	537
170	Zantvoorde	1525	2		22					1						1135			1550
171	Zillebeke	22			10														32
172	Zuidschote Church											5						76	81
173	Houthulst Belgian											146	1704		81				1931
174	Mont Kemmel French											5294				5237			5294
175	St. Charles French											3547				54			3547
176	Langemark German													44535		11813			44535
177	Woesten Church											282						9	291
178	Westvleteren Church											189							189
179	Westvleteren Belgian												1132						1132
180	Oostvleteren Church											39						17	56
181	Noordschote Church																	14	14
182	Pollinkhove Church																	8	8
183	Hoogstade Church																	12	12
184	Hooglede German													8247					8247
185	Menen-Wald German													47864					47864
186	Vladslo German													25644					25644
	TOTAL	111419	9939	3662	9231	135	471	65	167	77	104	10598	2842	127588	152	62825	2008	402	278858

VICTORIA CROSS HOLDERS BURIED IN CEMETERIES OR COMMEMORATED ON MEMORIALS INCLUDED IN THIS BOOK

Ackroyd, H., M.C., temporary Captain, R.A.M.C. attached 6th Royal Berkshire Regiment (Princess Charlotte of Wales's). Killed in action 11 August 1917, buried in Birr Crossroads Cemetery.

Barratt, T., Private, 7th South Staffordshire Regiment. Killed in action 27 July 1917, buried in Essex Farm Cemetery.

Bent, P. E., D.S.O., temporary Lieutenant-Colonel, 9th Leicestershire Regiment. Killed in action 1 October 1917, commemorated on Tyne Cot Memorial.

Birks, F, M.M., Second Lieutenant, 6th Battalion (Victoria), Australian Imperial Force. Killed in action 21 September 1917, buried in Perth Cemetery (China Wall).

Brooke, J. A. O., Lieutenant (posthumously Captain), 2nd Gordon Highlanders. Killed in action 29 October 1914, buried in Zantvoorde British Cemetery.

Bugden, P. J., Private, 31st Battalion (Queensland and Victoria), Australian Imperial Force. Killed in action 28 September 1917, buried in Hooge Crater Cemetery.

Chavasse, N. G., M.C., D.S.O., V.C. and Bar, Captain, R.A.M.C. attached 1/10th (Liverpool Scottish) King's (Liverpool Regiment). Died of wounds 4 August 1917, buried in Brandhoek New Military Cemetery.

Clamp, W., Corporal, 6th Yorkshire Regiment (Alexandra, Princess of Wales's Own). Killed in action 9 October 1917, commemorated on Tyne Cot Memorial.

Colyer - Fergusson, T. R., Second Lieutenant (acting Captain), 2nd Northamptonshire Regiment. Killed in action 31 July 1917, buried in Menin Road South Military Cemetery.

Davies, J. L., Corporal, 13th (1st North Wales Pals) Royal Welsh Fusiliers. Killed in action 31 July 1917, buried in Canada Farm Cemetery.

Dougall, E. S., M.C., acting Captain, 88th Brigade, Royal Field Artillery. Killed in action 14 April 1918, buried in Westoutre Military Cemetery.

Drake, A. G., Corporal, 8th Rifle Brigade (The Prince Consort's Own). Killed in action 23 November 1915, buried in La Brique Military Cemetery No. 2.

Best-Dunkley, B, Captain (temporary Lieutenant-Colonel), commanding 2/5th Lancashire Fusiliers. Died of wounds 5 August 1917, buried in Mendinghem Cemetery.

Fisher, F., Lance-Corporal, 13th Battalion, Quebec Regiment (Royal Highlanders of Canada), Canadian Expeditionary Force. Killed in action 24 April 1915, commemorated on Menin Gate Memorial.

Fitzclarence, C., Captain (later Brigadier-General), commanding 1st Brigade, 1st Division, late of the Royal Fusiliers and Irish Guards. Killed in action 12 November 1914, commemorated on Menin Gate Memorial.

Grenfell, F. O., Captain, 9th (Queen's Royal) Lancers. Killed in action 24 May 1915, buried in Vlamertinge Military Cemetery.

Hackett, W., Sapper, 254th Tunnelling Company, Corps of Royal Engineers. Killed in action 27 June 1916, commemorated on Ploegsteert Memorial.

Hall, F. W., Company Sergeant-Major, 8th Battalion (Manitoba Regiment), Canadian Expeditionary Force. Killed in action 25 April 1915, commemorated on Menin Gate Memorial.

Hallowes, R. P., M.C., temporary Second Lieutenant, 4th Middlesex (The Duke of Cambridge's Own). Killed in action 30 September 1915, buried in Bedford House Cemetery.

Hewitt, D. G. W., Second Lieutenant, 2nd Hampshire Regiment attached 14th (1st Portsmouth Pals) Hampshire Regiment. Killed in action 31 July 1917, commemorated on Menin Gate Memorial.

Jeffries, C. S., Captain, 34th Battalion (New South Wales), Australian Imperial Force. Killed in action 12 October 1917, buried in Tyne Cot Cemetery.

Johnston, W. H., Captain (later Major), 59th Field Company, Corps of Royal Engineers. Killed in action 8 June 1915, commemorated on Ploegsteert Memorial.

Lynn, J., D.C.M., Order of St. George, 4th Class (Russia), Private, 2nd Lancashire Fusiliers. Died of wounds 2 May 1915, buried in Grootebeek British Cemetery.

McGee, L., Sergeant, 40th Battalion (Tasmania), Australian Imperial Force. Killed in action 13 October 1917, buried in Tyne Cot Cemetery.

McGuffie, L., acting Sergeant, 1/5th King's Own Scottish Borderers. Killed in action 4 October 1918, buried in Zantvoorde Military Cemetery.

McKenzie, H., D.C.M., Lieutenant, 7th Company, Canadian Machine Gun Corps, Canadian Expeditionary Force. Killed in action 30 October 1917, commemorated on Menin Gate Memorial.

Mackenzie, J., Private, 2nd Scots Guards. Killed in action 19 December 1914, commemorated on Ploegsteert Memorial.

Maxwell, F. A., C.S.I., D.S.O. and Bar, G.O., Lieutenant (later Brigadier-General), Indian Staff Corps, attached Robert's Light Horse, commanding 27th Brigade, 9th (Scottish) Division. Killed in action 21 September 1917, buried in Ypres Reservoir Cemetery.

Morrow, R., Private, 1st Royal Irish Fusiliers (Princess Victoria's). Killed in action 26 April 1915, buried in White House Cemetery.

Mottershead, T., D.C.M., Sergeant, Royal Flying Corps. Died of wounds, 12 January 1917.

Pryce, T. T., M.C. and Bar, acting Captain, 4th Grenadier Guards, Special Reserve. Killed in action 13 April 1918, commemorated on Ploegsteert Memorial.

Robertson, C., acting Captain, 3rd The Queen's (Royal West Surrey Regiment), Special Reserve, attached Tank Corps. Killed in action 4 October 1917, buried in Oxford Road Cemetery.

Robertson, J. P., Private, 27th Battalion, 2nd Manitoba (Winnipeg) Regiment, Canadian Expeditionary Force. Killed in action 6 November 1917, buried in Tyne Cot Cemetery.

Seaman, E., M.M., Lance-Corporal, 2nd Royal Inniskilling Fusiliers. Killed in action 29 September 1918, commemorated on Tyne Cot Memorial.

Skinner, J., D.C.M., acting Company Sergeant-Major, 1st King's Own Scottish Borderers. Killed in action 17 March 1918, buried in Vlamertinge New British Military Cemetery.

Tubb, F. H., Lieutenant (later Major), 7th Battalion (Victoria), Australian Imperial Force. Killed in action 20 September 1917, buried in Lijssenthoek Military Cemetery.

Vallentin, J. F., Captain, 1st South Staffordshire Regiment. Killed in action 7 November 1917, commemorated on Menin Gate Memorial.

Warner, E., Private, 1st Bedfordshire Regiment. Killed in action 2 May 1915, commemorated on Menin Gate Memorial.

Woodroffe, S. C., Second Lieutenant, 8th Rifle Brigade (The Prince Consort's Own) attached 2nd Rifle Brigade. Killed in action 30 July 1915, commemorated on Menin Gate Memorial.

Youens, F., temporary Second Lieutenant, 13th Durham Light Infantry. Died of Wounds on 9 July 1917, buried in Railway Dugouts Cemetery.

The spires of Ypres from Ypres Reservoir Cemetery.

BIBLIOGRAPHY

REFERENCE

The Order of Battle of Divisions, Parts 1, 2A, 2B, 3A & 3B Major A. F. Becke (H.M.S.O.)

Official History of the Great War in France and Belgium Brig-Gen. James E. Edmunds (H.M.S.O.)

Commonwealth War Graves Commission Registers

Officers Died in the Great War 1914 – 1919 (J. B. Hayward and Son)

Soldiers Died in the Great War 1914 – 1919 (J. B. Hayward and Son)

FURTHER READING

My Bit, A Lancashire Fusilier at War 1914 – 1918 George Ashurst (Crowood Press)

The Battle Book of Ypres A reference to Military Operations in the Ypres Salient 1914-18 Beatrix Brice (Spa Books)

The Imperial War Museum Book of the First World War Malcolm Brown (Sidgwick and Jackson Ltd.)

An Illustrated Companion to the First World War Anthony Bruce (Michael Joseph)

Wipers: The First Battle of Ypres T. Carew (Hamish Hamilton)

Ypres 1914 – 1918, A Study in History Around Us Les Coate (Tressell)

Armegeddon Road, A V.C.'s Diary 1914-1916, Billy Congreve, V.C. (William Kimber & Co)

Before Endeavours Fade, A Guide to the Battlefields of the First World War Rose Coombs, M.B.E. (After the Battle Publications)

Machine Gunner 1914-1918, Personal Experiences of the Machine Gun Corps edited by C. E. Crutchley (Bailey Brothers and Swinfen Ltd.)

Death of an Army: The First Battle of Ypres A. Farrar-Hockley (Barker)

Flanders Then and Now John Giles (After the Battle Publications)

Ypres, 1917: a personal account N. Gladden (Kimber)

Chronical of the First World War, Volumes 1 and 2 Randal Gray and Christopher Argyle (Facts on File Ltd.)

Stand To! A Diary of the Trenches 1915-1918 Captain F. C. Hitchcock, M.C. (Gliddon Books)

British Regiments 1914-1918 Brig-Gen. E. A. James, O.B.E. (Samson Books)

On the Western Front, Soldiers' Stories from France and Flanders John Laffin (Alan Sutton)

The Soldier's War 1914-18 Peter H. Liddle (Blandford Press)

1914 Lyn Macdonald (Michael Joseph)

1914 – 1918: Voices and Images of the Great War Lyn Macdonald (Penguin)

Roses of No Man's Land Lyn Macdonald (Michael Joseph)

They Called it Passchendaele Lyn Macdonald (Michael Joseph)

Gas! The Battle for Ypres 1915 James L. McWilliams and R. James Steel (Vanwell)

Poor Bloody Infantry, A Subaltern on the Western Front 1916 – 1917 Bernard Martin (John Murray)

The Immortal Salient: an historical record and complete guide for pilgrims to Ypres Sir William Pulteney and Beatrix Brice (Ypres League)

Shot at Dawn, Executions in World War One by Authority of the British Army Act Julian Putkowski and Julian Sykes (Wharncliffe Publishing Ltd.)

World War One, The Western Front Peter Simkins (Colour Library Books)

The Old Contemtibles Keith Simpson (George Allen and Unwin)

The Fields of Death, Battle Scenes of the First World War Peter Slowe and Richard Woods (Robert Hale)

Het Verwoeste Gewest (The Devastated Region) Herman Stynen (Marc Van de Wiele)

History of World War One A. J. P. Taylor (Macdonald & Co.)

Passchendaele: The Story Behind the Tragic Victory of 1917 P. Warner (Sidgwick and Jackson Ltd.)

Honour Satisfied, A Dorset Rifleman at War 1916-1918 Second Lieutenant Frank Warren (Crowood Press)

Death's Men, Soldiers of the Great War Denis Winter (Penguin)

The Experience of World War One J. M. Winter (Macmillan)

Ypres and the battles of Ypres: An Illustrated History and Guide Michelin Tyre Co., Ltd.

ADDITIONAL SOURCES

Stand To! The Journal of the Western Front Association War

Diaries of the Hertfordshire and Royal Warwickshire Regiments

County Record Offices – Bedfordshire
        Hampshire
        Hertfordshire
        Leicestershire
        Warwickshire

The Army Records Centre, Hayes, Middlesex.

The National Army Museum.

The Imperial War Museum.

The Regimental Museum of the Royal Corps of Transport.

The Rifle Brigade (Royal Green Jackets) Museum.

The Hertfordshire Yeomanry and Artillery Museum.

The Army Museums Ogilby Trust.

The families of Herbert Milnes, Ernest Sinfield, Harold Sinfield, Archibald Sinfield, Sidney Sinfield and W. T. Rabey.

ACKNOWLEDGMENTS

Commonwealth War Graves Commission, Ieper Office

Mrs. Alma Brunt

Cloth Hall Museum, Ieper

Jacques Schier, Sanctuary Wood (Hill 62) Trench Museum, Belgium

Ieper Tourist Office

Richard Pearson

The Staff of the Paybody Ward, Coventry Hospital

Michelin

Kosmos Hotel, Rodeberg, Belgium

MILITARY INDEX

A.N.Z.A.C. II Corps, 149
Armentieres (1914), Battle of, 12, 147
Aubers Ridge (1915), Battle of, 12
Australian Imperial Force,
  Divisions
    1st, 62, 72, 85; 2nd, 119; 3rd, 13, 14, 61, 115,
      120, 149; 5th, 23, 45, 89
  Brigades
    2nd, 62, 85; 8th, 45; 9th, 115, 120; 10th, 120
  Battalions
    6th Btn, 85; 7th Btn, 62; 31st Btn, 45; 34th Btn,
      119, 120; 36th Btn, 115; 37th Btn, 115;
      40th Btn, 119, 120; 47th Btn, 29
Australian Tunnelling Company, 1st, 58, 149
Casualty Clearing Stations
  1st, 7; 2nd, 117; 3rd, 18, 78

Bailleul, Battle of, 7, 149
Belgian Army
  1st Groupe Regiment d'Artillerie Provisoire, 11
Bellewaerde Ridge, Battle of, 100, 148
Bethune, Battle of, 150
British Army:
  Armies
    British Expeditionary Force (B.E.F.), 3, 4, 145,
      147, 148
    Second, 4, 107, 149
    Fifth, 33, 149
    Eight (World War Two), 72
    Allied Flanders Army Group, 150
  Corps
    I, 104, 105, 136, 148
    II, 33
    III, 72
    V, 4
    VI, 33
    VIII, 33
    IX, 133
    XIV, 33
    Cavalry, 74, 137
    Tank, 82, 89
  Divisions
    Guards, 6, 7, 25, 38, 95, 104
    1st, 44, 69, 89
    2nd, 32, 44, 141
    3rd, 6, 8, 10, 15, 22, 30, 39, 40, 44, 45, 49, 63,
      66, 84, 85, 101, 103, 111, 113, 124, 128,
      132, 133, 148
    4th, 7, 12, 22, 38, 41, 53, 65, 72, 77, 86, 87, 88,
      94, 97, 114, 117, 128
    5th, 12, 57, 58, 69, 77, 84, 86, 100, 130, 131
    6th, 5, 12, 44, 53, 78, 79, 91, 92, 95, 116, 128
    7th, 12, 32, 44, 61, 69, 83, 92, 120, 136, 147
    8th, 11, 45, 54, 67, 70, 84, 91, 133, 149
    9th (Scottish), 41, 45, 60, 68, 72, 89, 100, 107, 133
    11th (Northern), 28, 37, 53, 80, 88, 120
    12th (Eastern), 94
    14th (Light), 14, 39, 49, 69, 71, 85, 88, 101, 107,
      133, 134

15th (Scottish), 5, 94, 149
16th (Irish), 5, 49, 51, 64, 66, 132, 149
17th (Northern), 10, 39, 70
18th (Eastern), 15, 17, 45, 88, 107, 137
19th (Western), 28, 63, 64, 80, 127, 149
20th (Light), 53, 68, 107, 142
21st, 63, 120
23rd, 54, 94, 98, 149
24th, 22, 35, 70, 94, 130
25th, 8, 48, 63, 71, 94, 121, 149
27th, 21, 95, 124
28th, 79, 124, 128, 148
29th, 7, 26, 38, 45, 60, 70, 79, 91, 95, 96, 122, 123
30th, 45, 50, 64, 90, 130, 149
31st, 7, 12, 72, 91
32nd, 35, 57
33rd, 30, 72, 78, 103, 119, 126
34th, 7, 33, 71, 74, 117, 136, 140, 142
35th, 26, 60
36th (Ulster), 13, 60, 64, 65, 66, 71, 74, 77, 106,
  120, 131, 149
37th, 35
38th (Welsh), 9, 25, 34, 37, 38, 73, 76, 79, 125,
  126, 149
39th, 69, 75, 79, 94, 106, 109, 116, 150
41st, 33, 61, 87, 94, 149
46th (North Midland), 57, 58, 82, 98, 106
47th (2nd London), 10, 58, 103, 149
48th (South Midlands), 31, 48, 57, 68, 88, 116
49th (West Riding), 9, 27, 33, 35, 37, 38, 42, 48,
  63, 79, 113, 114
50th (Northumbrian), 10, 55, 81, 103, 119, 133
51st (Highland), 37, 73, 76, 79, 117, 123, 149
55th (West Lancashire), 5, 19, 68, 94, 122, 149
56th (London), 107
58th (2/1st London), 17, 31
59th (2nd North Midland), 7, 20
63rd (Royal Naval), 83, 116, 149
66th (2nd East Lancashire), 84, 103
1st Cavalry, 122
3rd Cavalry, 105, 149
Brigades
1st, 69, 89, 104; 2nd, 107, 122; 4th (Guards), 7,
  12, 57; 7th, 6, 15, 30, 84, 94, 103, 111,
  124, 133; 8th, 10, 40, 44, 85, 113, 132;
  9th, 8, 63, 101; 10th, 72, 97, 105, 106,
  109, 128, 148; 11th, 32, 38, 77, 86, 87, 94,
  97, 114, 129; 12th, 12, 41, 77, 88, 117,
  128; 13th, 58, 84, 131; 14th, 58, 130, 131;
  15th, 58, 69, 86, 100, 130; 16th, 79, 128;
  17th, 5, 12, 44; 18th, 45, 95; 19th, 7, 97,
  103; 20th, 12, 61, 136; 22nd, 12, 32, 60,
  69; 23rd, 67, 84, 91, 133; 24th, 70; 25th,
  54; 26th, 150; 27th, 68, 133; 32nd, 120;
  33rd, 37, 53; 37th, 94; 41st, 69, 107, 108;
  43rd, 85, 101, 107, 133, 134; 46th, 94;
  47th, 51; 50th, 10; 51st, 70; 52nd, 39;
  53rd, 15, 45; 55th, 17; 57th, 63; 58th, 64;
  59th, 53, 68; 60th, 25; 61st, 25; 64th, 111;

68th, 98; 69th, 94; 70th, 54, 94; 71st, 78;
72nd, 22, 35, 70, 94; 73rd, 130; 74th, 48;
75th, 8; 76th, 39, 66; 80th, 21, 124; 82nd,
21; 83rd, 148; 84th, 20; 85th, 32, 79, 128;
86th, 122; 87th, 38, 96, 123; 88th, 95, 96,
127; 89th, 50, 64; 90th, 45, 50; 92nd, 91;
96th, 35; 98th, 98, 103; 100th, 126;
103rd, 136; 105th, 26; 108th, 131; 109th,
120; 110th, 120; 112th, 35; 113th, 25;
114th, 38; 116th, 69, 94; 122nd, 94;
123rd, 94; 124th, 61, 87; 137th, 98;
138th, 57; 140th, 103; 142nd, 103; 143rd,
68; 145th, 48; 146th, 79; 147th, 7, 42, 79;
148th, 35, 42, 48, 113; 149th, 10, 55, 106,
148; 150th, 133; 151st, 103; 152nd, 142;
153rd, 117; 160th, 142; 164th, 68, 94;
166th, 19; 174th, 17; 188th, 83; 190th, 83;
197th, 103; 1st Cavalry, 5; 2nd Cavalry,
122; 4th Cavalry, 116; 6th Cavalry, 5; 7th
Cavalry, 5, 83; 8th Cavalry, 5
Battalions
  Anson Battalion, 83
  Argyll and Sutherland Highlanders, 2nd Btn,
    103; 1/7th Btn, 109; 1/9th Btn, 21; 11th
    Btn, 32, 135
  Bedfordshires, 1st Btn, 58; 4th Btn, 83
  Black Watch, 1st Btn, 17, 104; 1/7th Btn, 117;
    9th Btn, 32
  Borders, 1st Btn, 7; 2nd Btn, 61, 135
  British West Indies Regiment, 94, 129
  Buffs, 1st Btn, 128; 2nd Btn, 32, 121; 6th Btn,
    24; 7th Btn, 88; 8th Btn, 90
  Cameron Highlanders, 1st Btn, 89, 147; 6th
    Btn, 32
  Cameronians, 1st Btn, 103; 2nd Btn, 84; 5/6th
    Btn, 103; 10th Btn, 94
  Cheshires, 1st Btn, 58, 130; 2nd Btn, 20; 1/7th
    Btn, 90; 11th Btn, 8
  Connaught Rangers, 6th Btn, 51
  Devonshires, 1st Btn, 6, 58; 2nd Btn, 133
  Dorsetshires, 1st Btn, 57, 58, 86, 100, 121, 130;
    5th Btn, 116
  Drake Battalion, 83
  Duke of Cornwall's Light Infantry, 1st Btn, 6,
    26, 38, 130, 131; 2nd Btn, 32, 147; 6th
    Btn, 107, 133
  Duke of Wellington's, 27, 31; 2nd Btn, 58, 116;
    1/4th Btn, 79
  Durham Light Infantry, 85; 2nd Btn, 45, 95;
    1/9th Btn, 103; 12th Btn, 58; 13th Btn,
    98; 14th Btn, 95
  East Lancashires, 1st Btn, 56, 114; 2nd Btn, 142
  East Surreys, 1st Btn, 58, 130; 2nd Btn, 10, 79,
    128; 7th Btn, 94; 8th Btn, 17, 88; 9th
    Btn, 70; 12th Btn, 94
  East Yorkshires, 1st Btn, 111; 2nd Btn, 27;
    1/4th Btn, 133; 6th Btn, 76; 7th Btn, 10;
    8th Btn, 22; 10th Btn, 91
  Essex, 2nd Btn, 12, 24; 9th Btn, 24, 41; 10th
    Btn, 88
  Essex Yeomanry, 5

Foot Guards, 17, 137
'Geddes Detachment', 148
Gloucestershires, 1st Btn, 45, 66; 2nd Btn, 45;
  1/5th Btn, 76, 87
Gordon Highlanders, 1st Btn, 39, 44, 49; 2nd
  Btn, 136; 1/4th Btn, 37; 1/5th Btn, 76;
  1/6th Btn, 73; 8/10th Btn, 32
Grenadier Guards, 1st Btn, 63, 135; 2nd Btn,
  57, 89; 4th Btn, 12
Guards Machine Gun Regiment, 17
Hampshires, 1st Btn, 38, 56, 86, 91, 94, 97; 2nd
  Btn, 69, 95, 96; 14th Btn, 69; 15th Btn,
  124
Hertfordshires, 1/1st Btn, 116
Highland Light Infantry, 1st Btn, 116; 2nd Btn,
  22; 12th Btn, 32
Honourable Artillery Company, 15, 124
Hood Battalion, 83
Irish Guards, 1st Btn, 57, 69, 89, 137
King's, 4th Btn, 78, 116; 1/5th Btn, 116; 1/6th
  Btn, 58; 1/8th Btn, 94; 1/10th Btn, 19, 49,
  86; 11th Btn, 133
King's Own, 2nd Btn, 23, 148; 5th Btn, 32; 8th
  Btn, 39
King's Own Scottish Borderers, 1st Btn, 26,
  123; 2nd Btn, 58, 71, 84; 1/5th Btn, 22,
  136; 6th Btn, 150; 7/8th Btn, 32
King's Own Yorkshire Light Infantry, 1st Btn,
  23, 148; 2nd Btn, 58, 71, 84; 1/4th Btn,
  42; 6th Btn, 76, 134; 7th Btn, 25
King's Royal Rifle Corps, 27, 45; 1st Btn, 134;
  2nd Btn, 105, 136; 3rd Btn, 21; 4th Btn,
  21; 10th Btn, 53, 68; 11th Btn, 53; 12th
  Btn, 25; 16th Btn, 77, 126; 21st Btn, 87
King's Shropshire Light Infantry, 1st Btn, 79;
  2nd Btn, 21, 32; 5th Btn, 83
Lancashire Fusiliers, 2nd Btn, 20, 21, 41, 60,
  117, 128; 9th Btn, 42; 10th Btn, 39; 11th
  Btn, 41; 2/5th Btn, 68; 3/5th Btn, 103
Leicesters, 1st Btn, 78; 1/4th Btn, 58, 82; 1/5th
  Btn, 57; 9th Btn, 120
Leinsters, 1st Btn, 15, 21; 2nd Btn, 12, 44, 53,
  60, 130
Lincolns, 1st Btn, 49, 63, 101, 132; 1/5th Btn, 82
London Regiment, 130; 1/5th, 65, 81; 1/6th Btn,
  58, 79, 103; 1/7th Btn, 79; 1/9th Btn, 58,
  131; 1/12th Btn, 20; 1/14th Btn, 21, 71,
  86, 110, 111, 132; 1/16th Btn, 29; 1/22nd
  Btn, 103; 1/28th Btn, 83; 2/6th Btn, 17;
  2/14th Btn, 28, 64; 2/16th Btn, 64
Loyal North Lancashires, 35; 1st Btn, 105, 136;
  1/4th Btn, 94; 8th Btn, 87; 9th Btn, 41
Manchesters, 1st Btn, 126; 2nd Btn, 26, 39
Middlesex Regiment, 26; 2nd Btn, 91; 3rd Btn,
  32; 4th Btn, 10, 40, 44, 113; 8th Btn, 148;
  11th Btn, 25; 23rd Btn, 94; 3/10th Btn, 142
Monmouthshires, 1/1st Btn, 20; 1/2nd Btn, 24,
  91; 1/3rd Btn, 23, 38, 148
Norfolk Regiment, 16; 1st Btn, 58; 8th Btn, 88
Northamptonshires, 1st Btn, 105; 2nd Btn, 70,
  101

North Staffordshires, 1st Btn, 5, 22, 94; 8th Btn, 63; 9th Btn, 66

Northumberland Fusiliers, 1st Btn, 22, 132; 2nd Btn, 109; 1/5th Btn, 55; 1/6th Btn, 10; 18th Btn, 91

Oxfordshire and Buckinghamshire Light Infantry, 78; 1st Btn, 57; 2nd Btn, 147; 1/3rd Btn, 109; Bucks Battalion, 87

Queen's, 1st Btn, 105, 135; 2nd Btn, 66; 3rd Btn, 82; 7th Btn, 17; 10th Btn, 13; 11th Btn, 24, 41

Rifle Brigade, 27, 37; 1st Btn, 60, 104, 113, 114; 2nd Btn, 69; 3rd Btn, 90; 4th Btn, 21, 32; 7th Btn, 108; 8th Btn, 54, 69, 107; 10th Btn, 25; 11th Btn, 25; 12th Btn, 25

Royal Berkshires, 138; 1/4th Btn, 48; 6th Btn, 15, 45

Royal Dublin Fusiliers, 1st Btn, 122, 142; 2nd Btn, 21, 97

Royal Fusiliers, 69; 1st Btn, 76; 3rd Btn, 121; 4th Btn, 8, 22, 124; 7th Btn, 83; 9th Btn, 24; 26th Btn, 61

Royal Inniskilling Fusiliers, 1st Btn, 96; 2nd Btn, 14, 57, 71, 120

Royal Irish, 2nd Btn, 88; 6th Btn, 64

Royal Irish Fusiliers, 1st Btn, 53, 76, 128, 131

Royal Irish Rifles, 65, 106; 2nd Btn, 48, 103; 8th Btn, 66; 11th Btn, 49

Royal Marines, 147

Royal Marines Light Infantry, 1st Btn, 83; 2nd Btn, 83

Royal Scots, 2nd Btn, 40, 49, 85, 101; 1/8th Btn, 123; 1/9th Btn, 32, 37; 11th Btn, 150; 12th Btn, 60, 68, 150; 13th Btn, 32

Royal Scots Fusiliers, 1st Btn, 63, 101; 2nd Btn, 50, 135; 6th Btn, 56; 6/7th Btn, 32

Royal Sussex, 1st Btn, 57; 2nd Btn, 17; 11th Btn, 20; 12th Btn, 20; 13th Btn, 20, 94

Royal Warwickshires, 1st Btn, 72, 97, 105, 109, 142; 2nd Btn, 12, 22; 1/5th Btn, 68; 10th Btn, 23, 48; 11th Btn, 35

Royal Welsh Fusiliers, 34; 1st Btn, 60, 135, 136; 9th Btn, 64; 10th Btn, 66; 13th Btn, 25, 34

Royal West Kents, 1st Btn, 58, 84; 7th Btn, 88; 10th Btn, 24, 41

Scots Guards, 1st Btn, 147; 2nd Btn, 12, 63, 135

Seaforth Highlanders, 109; 2nd Btn, 72, 109, 142

Sherwood Foresters, 50; 15th Btn, 26; 16th Btn, 19

Somerset Light Infantry, 69; 1st Btn, 87, 97, 114, 129; 6th Btn, 85, 101

South Lancashires, 2nd Btn, 8, 64; 4th Btn, 101; 8th Btn, 101

South Staffordshires, 1st Btn, 66, 69, 135; 2nd Btn, 105; 1/6th Btn, 98; 7th Btn, 37, 53; 8th Btn, 70; 9th Btn, 94

South Wales Borderers, 1st Btn, 45, 147

Suffolks, 138; 1st Btn, 20; 2nd Btn, 39, 112, 113, 132; 7th Btn, 24, 41; 8th Btn, 45

Welsh Guards, 1st Btn, 126

Welsh Regiment, 2nd Btn, 147; 13th Btn, 38

West Yorkshires, 1st Btn, 95; 2nd Btn, 67; 1/6th Btn, 79; 11th Btn, 58, 94; 12th Btn, 22

Wiltshires, 1st Btn, 28, 30, 101, 111, 124, 133; 2nd Btn, 22

Worcesters, 2nd Btn, 22, 45, 77, 147; 3rd Btn, 6, 84, 94, 111; 1/7th Btn, 24; 1/8th Btn, 24

York and Lancasters, 1st Btn, 27, 32, 116; 1/4th Btn, 35, 42, 113; 1/5th Btn, 48, 113; 7th Btn, 39; 8th Btn, 54; 9th Btn, 94

Yorkshires, 6th Btn, 120

Cavalry
Dragoon Guards, 2nd, 5, 71; 4th, 71; 5th, 4, 14, 71; 6th, 111

Household Cavalry, 83, 116, 136

Hussars, 3rd, 132; 10th, 5, 60, 71, 122, 136; 11th, 71, 86; 19th, 121; 20th, 132

Lancers, 5th, 124; 9th, 23, 71, 123; 12th, 132; 16th, 107

Life Guards, 1st, 57, 83, 136, 137; 2nd, 57, 136

Northumberland Hussars, 22

Queen's Own Oxfordshire Hussars, 147

Royal Horse Guards (the Blues), 5, 57, 83, 101, 135, 136, 137

Machine Gun Corps, 103, 108
33rd Battalion, 72; 19th Company, 30; 46th Company, 32; 117th Company, 94; 248th Company, 30

Royal Air Force, 4, 59, 86, 89, 108, 109, 113, 120, 129, 150

Royal Army Medical Corps, 5, 15, 19, 45
Casualty Clearing Stations
2nd, 7; 3rd, 7; 4th, 33; 8th, 7; 11th, 7, 35, 39; 12th, 68; 32nd, 18; 36th, 35, 43; 37th, 39; 41st, 39; 44th, 18, 35, 78; 46th (1/1st Wessex), 67, 68; 47th, 33; 53rd, 7; 61st, 33, 68; 62nd, 43; 63rd, 43; 64th, 68

Field Ambulances
9th, 38; 11th, 38; 16th, 38; 62nd, 38; 129th, 38; 130th, 38

Territorial Nursing Force, 39

Royal Army Service Corps, 42, 64, 110
34th Division Ammunition Column, 142; 13th Company, 35; 38th Labour Group, 113; 197th Company, 69

Royal Artillery, 25, 38, 47
34th Division, 142; 2nd City of Edinburgh Brigade, 30; 180th Seige Battery, 80; 122nd Heavy Battery, 148; 37th Howitzer Battery, 148

Royal Engineers, 12, 42, 46, 49, 58, 94, 101, 145
34th Division, 142; 5th Field Company, 147; 56th Field Company, 111; 59th Field Company, 12, 58; 79th Field Company, 45; 83rd Field Company, 25; 520th Field Company, 58; 171st Tunnelling Company, 58, 65, 149; 175th Tunnelling Company, 44, 58; 177th Tunnelling Company, 100; 250th Tunnelling Company, 149; Monmouth, 58

Royal Field Artillery, 34, 110
  5th Division, 62; 2nd Brigade, 122; 50th
     Brigade, 60; 88th Brigade, 127; 110th
     Brigade, 39; 152nd Brigade, 142; 160th
     Brigade, 142; 280th Brigade, 45; 16th
     Battery, 147; 21st Battery, 122; 22nd
     Battery, 147; 51st Battery, 147; 84th
     Battery, 63; 119th Battery, 122; 356th
     Battery, 148; 367th Battery, 148
  Royal Garrison Artillery, 108
    6th Seige Battery, 134; 10th Seige Battery,
     137
  Royal Horse Artillery, 133
    J Battery, 23
  Royal Flying Corps, 5, 8, 32, 59, 77, 85, 108,
    113, 120
    5 Squadron, 77; 6 Squadron, 32; 20
     Squadron, 8
Broodseinde, Battle of, 32, 149

Canadian Expeditionary Force, 69, 83
  Canadian Corps, 107, 149
  Divisions
    1st, 27, 69, 110; 2nd, 120; 3rd, 69
  Brigades
    2nd, 69; 3rd, 69, 107; 6th, 120; 7th, 69
  Battalions
    2nd Btn, 130; 3rd Btn, 94, 105, 130; 4th Btn, 94;
     8th Btn, 69; 10th Btn, 105; 13th Btn, 69,
     105; 14th Btn, 86, 117; 16th Btn, 105;
     18th Btn, 103; 19th Btn, 103; 20th Btn,
     103; 21st Btn, 103; 24th Btn, 55; 25th
     Btn, 55; 26th Btn, 55; 27th Btn, 120; 54th
     Btn, 132; Princess Patricia's Canadian
     Light Infantry, 21, 100, 101, 124; Royal
     Newfoundland Regiment, 1st, 60, 91; 7th
     Company, Canadian Machine Corps, 69
  Canadian Field Artillery,
    6th Battery, 148
  Canadian Flying Corps, 59
  Canadian Royal Engineers, 132
    1st Tunnelling Company, 149; 3rd Tunnelling
     Company, 58, 149
  Royal Canadian Medical Corps, 36
    1st Casualty Clearing Station, 7; 3rd Field
     Ambulance, 67; 11th Field Ambulance,
     119
Chinese Labour Corps, 9
  107th Company, 93

Estaires (1916), Battle of, 12
Estaires (1918), Battle of, 149

Flanders Offensive, 17, 20, 21, 25, 31, 33, 38, 43, 44,
    68, 78, 79, 100, 122, 139, 142
Flers, Battle of, 103
French Army
  Divisions
    32nd, 132; 45th (Algerian), 138; 87th, 138
  Battalions
    26th Dragoons, 74; 88th Infantry, 74; 169th

    Infantry, 89; 418th Infantry, 138;
    Chasseurs Alpins, 16; Chasseurs
    d'Afrique, 2nd, 142; Escadrille des
    Cogognes, 88; Casualty Clearing Station
    (Hopital d'Evacuation), 15th, 61
Frezenberg, Battle of, 148
Fromelles (1915), Battle of, 12

Geluveld, Battle of, 147
German Army
  Armies
    Fourth, 149
    Sixth, 149
  Corps
    Guards Cavalry, 57
    IV Cavalry, 3
    XXII Reserve, 141
    XXIII Reserve, 141
    XXIV Reserve, 141
    XXV Reserve, 141
    XXVI Reserve, 141
    XXVII Reserve, 80, 86, 141
  Divisions
    6th, 79; 26th, 71; 39th, 58; 3rd Cavalry, 3
  Battalions
    Prussian Guards, 147; 1st Bavarian Jager, 136;
     126th Prussian Infantry, 107; 234th
     Reserve Infantry, 141; 246th Reserve
     Infantry, 85; Wurtemburg Regiment,
     107; Trophy Company (World War
     Two), 138
Gravenstafel, Battle of, 148

Hazebrouck (1918), Battle of, 12, 149

Indian Army 14, 20, 125, 133
  Divisions
    Lahore, 20, 116, 125, 126
  Brigades
    Sirhind, 20, 116
  Battalions
    Ghurkha Rifles, 1st, 116; Pathans, 40th, 126;
     Rifles, 57th (Wilde's), 14, 71; Robert's
     Light Horse, 133; Sikhs, 47th, 126

Kemmel, First Battle of, 150
Kemmel, Second Battle of, 150
Kortrijk, Battle of 150

Langemark (1914), Battle of, 147
Langemark (1917), Battle of, 68, 69, 149
Loos (1915), Battle of, 12
Lys, Battles of the (Fourth Battle of Ypres), 5, 13,
    40, 42, 55, 61, 72, 89, 91, 106, 117, 126,
    130, 149

Marne (1914), Battle of the, 21, 105
Menin Road, Battle of the, 30, 149
Messines (1914), Battle of, 147
Messines (1917), Battle of, 4, 6, 13, 14, 21, 22, 23,
    25, 28, 30, 36, 39, 42, 49, 56, 58, 63, 65,

71, 74, 75, 79, 80, 103, 110, 111, 115, 116, 121, 131, 132, 133, 148, 149

Messines (1918), Battle of, 149

Mount Sorrel, Battle of, 45, 66, 94, 107, 148

New Zealand Expeditionary Force (N.Z.E.F.), 48, 117
New Zealand Division, 71, 75, 119, 126, 149
4th Brigade, 32
Auckland Regiment, 3rd, 119
Canterbury Regiment, 1st, 117
Otago Regiment, 1st, 48

Nonne Boschen, Battle of, 147

Operation Georgette, 150

Outersteene Ridge (1918), Battle of, 12

Passendale, First Battle of, 17, 149

Passendale, Second Battle of, 149

Pilkem Ridge, Battle of the, 149

Poelkapelle, Battle of, 17, 88, 149

Polygon Wood, Battle of, 20, 89, 149

St. George, Cross of the Order of (Russia), 21, 24

St. Juliaan, Battle of, 148

Scherpenberg (1918), Battle of, 12, 150

Schlieffen Plan, 147

Somme, Battle of the, 8, 38, 65, 94, 97, 122

South African Brigade, 50, 71

South African Composite Battalion, 72

U.S.A. (American Expeditionary Force)
27th Division, 55, 139
30th Division, 55, 124
Casualty Clearing Station, 68

Victoria Cross, 8, 10, 12, 15, 18, 19, 21, 22, 25, 26, 32, 36, 37, 41, 45, 54, 56, 58, 60, 66, 68, 69, 73, 81, 82, 83, 84, 85, 88, 89, 101, 105, 111, 115, 119, 120, 122, 123, 126, 127, 128, 130, 133, 136, 145, 147, 149

Ypres, First Battle of, 15, 23, 44, 71, 107, 128, 147, 148

Ypres, Second Battle of, 3, 32, 53, 95, 100, 137, 142, 148

Ypres, Third Battle of, 5, 6, 9, 17, 18, 19, 23, 25, 27, 31, 32, 34, 35, 37, 39, 42, 43, 47, 67, 73, 75, 79, 84, 87, 90, 98, 105, 106, 107, 109, 110, 114, 116, 119, 123, 125, 142, 149

Ypres, Fourth Battle of (Battles of the Lys), 149, 150

Ypres (1918), Battle of, 150

PEOPLE AND PLACES INDEX

Abeele Aerodrome Military Cemetery, 5
Abraham Heights, 32, 119
Ackroyd, Capt. H., 15, 45
Admiral's Cemetery, 76
Admiral's Corner, 20
Admiral's Road, 20, 73, 76, 116, 117
Aeroplane Cemetery, 5, 10, 84
Ainley, Pte. G., 42
Albert of Belgium, King, 4, 71, 150
America Crossroads German Cemetery, 59
American Memorials
   30th and 27th Division, York Road, 55, 133
Anglo-Belgian Union, 110
Armagh Wood, 66, 107
Armentieres, 13, 22, 29, 48, 55, 65, 75, 77, 86, 87,
      91, 98, 104, 113, 115, 117, 118, 121, 150
Armin, General Sixt von, 149
Artillery Wood Cemetery, 6, 17, 26
Ashford, Lt., 98
Asylum Cemetery, 10
Auckland Cemetery, 131
Auger, Pte. F., 117
Australian Memorials
   5th Division, 23, 89
   1st Tunnelling Company, 58
   National Memorial, France, 145

Baker, Pte. W., 61
Baker, Professor H. B., 7
Bailleul, 5, 7, 8, 13, 40, 55, 73, 74, 91, 92, 94, 117,
      118, 150
   Communal Cemetery, 7, 8
   Communal Cemetery Extension, 7, 8
Baily, C.S.M. C. T., 78
Bairnsfather, Lt. B., 109
Bard Cottage Cemetery, 9
Bard's Causeway, 9
Barker, Pte. R. L., 103
Barrett, Pte. T., 37
Barron, Cpl. C., 83
Basseville Farm German Cemetery, 128
Bass Wood Cemeteries No.'s 1 & 2, 45
Bas-Warneton Communal Cemetery, 61
Battenburg, Prince of, 134
Battle Wood, 137, 149
Bavaria House Cemetery, 129
Beaty-Pownall, Lt-Col. G. E., 61
Bedford House Cemetery, 6, 10, 11, 21, 129
Belcher, L/Sgt. D. W., 81
Belgian Army Disposal Service, 139
Belgian Battery Corner Cemetery, 11, 12
Belgian Chateau Cemetery, 85
Belgian Memorials,
   3rd Division, Merkem, 138
   1st Regiment of Carabiniers, Westrozebeke, 88
   2nd Regiment of Carabiniers, Westrozebeke, 88
   3rd Regiment of Carabiniers, Westrozebeke, 88
   4th Regiment of Carabiniers, Passendale, 84
   Carabiniers (1915), Lizerne, 138

Grenadiers, Passendale, 84
Grenadiers, Lizerne, 138
1st Artillery, Houthulst, 139
7th Artillery, Houthulst, 139
13th Artillery, Houthulst, 139
4th/24th Artillery, Houthulst, 139
3rd/23rd Infantry, Steenstraat, 138, 139
6th/24th Infantry, Steenstraat, 138
9th Infantry (1918), Merkem, 138
11th Infantry (1918), Merkem, 138
13th Infantry (1918), Merkem, 138
19th Infantry (1918), Merkem, 138, 139
Langemark, 26
Passendale, 83
Ypres, 4
(See Ypres)
Bellew, Capt. E. D., 88
Bellewaerde Farm, 44
Bellewaerde Pleasure Park, 23, 45, 90
Bellewaerde Ridge Military Cemetery, 16
Bell Farm Cemetery, 71
Bellow, General Otto von, 149
Bennett, Pte. J., 94
Bent, Lt-Col. P. E., 120
Bent, Drummer S. J., 56
Berkshire Corner Cemetery Extension (Royal), 12,
   13
Bertenacre Military Cemetery, 13
Berthen Churchyard, 72
Beselare, 80, 108, 121, 150
   German Cemetery No. 1, 85
Best-Dunkley, Lt-Col. B., 68
Bethleem Farm East Cemetery, 13, 14, 15
Bethleem Farm West Cemetery, 14, 15
Beythem Communal Cemetery, 108
Bikschote, 7, 105, 108
   German Cemetery, 127
Birks, 2nd Lt. F., 84, 85
Birr Crossroads, 15
Birr Crossroads Cemetery, 15, 16, 45, 101
Birr Crossroads Cemetery No. 2, 16
Birrell Anthony, Lt. H. A., Memorial to 20
Black, Pte. P., 117
Black Watch Corner, 89
Blakemore, Pte. D. J., 63
Blauwepoortebeek Cemetery, 71
Blauwepoort Farm Cemetery, 16
Bleuet Farm Cemetery, 17
Blomfield, Sir Reginald, 4, 68
Bluff, The, 26, 38, 39, 44, 59, 80, 103, 112, 130
Boeschepe Churchyard, 5
Boezinge, 6, 7, 9, 17, 26, 27, 32, 34, 36, 38, 53, 76,
     79, 114, 126, 138
   Chateau Grounds Cemetery, 6
   Churchyard, 17, 18
   French Cemetery No. 2, 10
Boothby, 2nd Lt. C. G., 100
Botfield, Pte. A., 94
Bousbecques East German Cemetery, 71

Bowlby, Memorial to Capt. G. V. S.
Boxer, Mjr. H. E., 101
Boyle, Lt-Col., 105
Bradshaw, H. C., 12
Brandhoek, 8, 11, 12, 18, 33, 78, 102
    Military Cemetery, 18, 19
    New Military Cemetery, 18, 19
    New Military Cemetery No. 3, 19
Bridge House Cemetery, 20, 76, 120
Brielen, 35, 110
    Churchyard, 20
    Military Cemetery, 42
Brindley, Cpl. R., 100
Brissein House Cemetery, 7
Bristol Castle Military Cemetery, 71
British Memorials,
    7th Division, 120
    14th (Light) Division, 58
    16th (Irish) Division, 132
    18th (Eastern) Division, 45
    19th (Western) Division, 80
    20th (Light) Division, 26
    25th Division, 8
    34th Division, 74
    34th Division (Royal Artillery and Royal
        Engineers), 142
    38th (Welsh) Division, 73, 126
    49th (West Riding) Division, 37
    50th (Northumbrian) Division, 81
    66th (2nd East Lancashire) Division, 84
    Gloucestershire Regiment, 45
    Household Cavalry, 135, 136
    King's Royal Rifle Corps, 45
    1/9th Londons (Queen Victoria's Rifles), 58
    1/14th Londons (London Scottish), 71
    1/1st Monmouthshires, 20
    1st South Wales Borderers, 45
    2nd Worcesters, 45
    Menin Gate Memorial to the Missing, 3, 4, 66, 68,
        69, 70, 89, 99, 101, 105, 113, 116, 119, 130,
        134, 145
    Ploegsteert Memorial to the Missing, 12, 48
    Tyne Cot Memorial to the Missing, 68, 69, 119,
        120
    Western Front Association Plaque, 84
    (See Ypres)
Britton, Pte. C., 68
Broadley's Cemetery, 134
Broadrick, Pte. F., 35
Broadway Trench, 112
Brodie, Memorial to Capt. E. J., 89
Broodseinde, 84, 85, 119, 120, 121
    German Cemeteries, 85
    Ridge, 134
Brooke, Lt. J. A. O., 136
Browne, Pte. A., 12
Bruges General Cemetery, 59
Buffs Road, 20, 53, 75, 109
Buffs Road Cemetery, 20, 21, 41, 109, 117, 128
Bugden, Pte. P. J., 45
Bulfin, Gen. E. S., 107

Burgomaster Farm, 128
Bus House, 22
Bus House Cemetery, 21, 22
Buttes New British Cemetery, 22, 23, 68, 71, 89
Bye, Sgt. R. J., 126
Byers, Pte. J., 63
Byng, Sir Julian, 107

Cabin Hill Cemetery, 23, 24
Cafe Belvedere, 139
Calvaire (Essex) Military Cemetery, 24, 41
Cambrai Redoubt, 81
Cambridge Road, 15, 101
Canada Farm Cemetery, 25
Canadian Cemetery, 87
Canadian Memorials
    D/21 Battery, Canadian Field Artillery, 32
    85th Infantry Battalion (Nova Scotia
        Highlanders), 84
    Crest Farm, 84
    Gas Attack/Vancouver Corner, 32, 85, 88
    Hill 62, 107, 109
    Princess Patricia's Canadian Light Infantry, 23,
        90, 100
Canopus Trench Cemetery, 76
Capper, Gen. T., 147
Captain's Farm Cemetery, 7
Carmichael, Sgt. J., 66
Carter, Mjr. A. J., 105
Carter, Spr. M., 100
Caterpillar, The, 57, 149
Caesar's Nose, 125
Cement House Cemetery, 25, 26, 38, 68, 76, 105
Cemetery near Rossignol Estaminet, 133
Cemetery North of the Prison, 133
Cemetiere de Calvaire de Bertenacre, 13
Centre de Lork Youth Hostel, 62
Chase, Pte. H. H., 128
Chateau
    Bayernschloss, 79, 80
    de la Hutte, 121
    des Trois Tours, 110
    Elsenwalle, 36, 124
    Elverdinge, 38
    Geluveld, 147
    Herentage, 45, 46, 108
    Hollebeke, 81
    Hooge, 44, 45
    La Lovie, 33
    Mont Noir, 128
    Potijze, 5, 95, 96
    Reigersburg, 110
    Rosendal, 10
    White, 15, 95
Chatt, Spr. G. A., 100
Chavasse, Capt. N. G., 19
Chavasse, C., 19
Cheddar Villa, 109
Cheapside, 40, 113, 114
Cheapside Cemetery, 113
Chester Farm Cemetery, 28, 29, 39, 44, 130

Chester Farm Lower Cemetery, 112
Chicken, Lt., 7
Churchill, Lt-Col. W. S., 56, 147
Ch'un Ch'ich, Collie Wang, 93
Clamp, Cpl. W., 120
Clapham Junction, 23, 45, 90
Clay, Lt-Col. B. G., 45
Clayton, Reverend P. 'Tubby', 92
Close-Brooks, Lt. Arthur Close, 39
Coffin, Lt. C., 101
Collins, Pte. G. E., 63
Colne Valley, 27, 126
    Cemetery, 27, 76
Colyer-Fergusson, Capt. T. R., 77, 101
Comedy Farm Cemetery, 76
Comines, 16, 27, 39, 44, 57, 59, 80, 81, 98, 108, 112,
    130, 136
    Communal Cemetery, 61
Commission of Graves Registration and Enquiries,
    145
Commonwealth War Graves Commission, 8, 12, 13,
    14, 16, 20, 22, 23, 24, 25, 29, 31, 34, 35, 39,
    40, 41, 42, 44, 47, 51, 53, 59, 61, 62, 64, 73,
    75, 79, 87, 90, 92, 103, 104, 112, 114, 115,
    121, 123, 126, 129, 130, 134, 137, 141, 145,
    146
Condon, Pte. J., 88
Coney Street Trench, 31, 53
Cooper, Sgt. E., 25
Cornwall Cemetery, 131
Cottage Garden Cemetery, 129
Cotterill, Spr. J. H., 100
Crampton, Pte. J., 94
Crois du Bac Military Cemetery, 118
Croonaert Chapel Cemetery, 28
Crossroads Cemetery, 76
Currie, Capt., 123
Currie, Gen., 83

Dadizele, 60, 108
    Communal Cemetery, 60
    New British Cemetery, 60
Damstrasse, 22, 80, 125, 149
Davies, Cpl. J. L., 25
Davis, Pte. T. E., 100
Dawson's Corner, 35, 110
Deerlijk Churchyard, 31
Deerlijk German Cemetery, 108
De Klijte, 54, 55, 127
    Church, 30, 54
Delargy, Pte. E., 123
Demarcation Stones, 15, 52, 138
Den Groenen Jager Cabaret, 129
Derry House Cemetery No. 1, 28
Derry House Cemetery No. 2, 28, 29
Devil's Hill, 10, 120
De Voorstraat German Cemetery (No. 49), 59
De Voorstraat German Cemetery (No. 50), 31
Dewinde, Memorial to Lt., 88
Dien Doel, 22
Dikkebus, 29, 30, 31, 34, 41, 47, 48, 84, 94, 128, 140

Church, 29, 30
    Dickebusch Old Military Cemetery, 29, 30
    Dickebusch New Military Cemetery, 29, 30
    Dickebusch New Military Cemetery Extension,
        29, 30
    Lake, 48, 125
Diksmuide, 18, 114, 138, 144
    Peace Tower, 144
Dirty Bucket Camp, 42
Divisional Cemetery, 31
Divisional Collecting Post Cemetery, 31
Docherty, Pte. T., 84
Dochy Farm New British Cemetery, 32, 33, 120
Donegal Farm German Cemetery, 108
Donovan, Rfmn. T., 126
Dossett, Pte. W., 42
Douanne Cemetery, 117
Dougall, Capt. E. S., 127
Douve, River, 56, 57, 131
Dove, Cpl., 101
Dozinghem Military Cemetery, 33, 43, 68, 128
Dragoon Camp, Ypres, 135
Dragoon Camp Cemetery, 34, 126
Drake, Cpl. A. G., 54
Dranouter, 34, 35, 64, 65, 108
    Dranoutre Churchyard, 34, 35
    Dranoutre Military Cemetery, 34, 35
Droogenbroodhoek Cemetery, 10
Duhallow Advanced Dressing Station Cemetery, 35,
    36
Dumbarton Lakes, 30, 45
Durham Cemetery, 85
Dwyer, Pte. E., 58

Eagle Trench, 142
Ecole de Bienfaisance Cemetery, 10
Edward, Prince of Wales, 8, 145
Edwards, Pte. W., 25
Eecke, Memorial to Adj. Armand van, 139
Eerneghem German Cemetery, 59
Eikhof Farm Cemetery, 124
Eiskellar German Cemetery, 108
Elsenwalle Brasserie Cemetery, 36, 104, 124
Elsenwalle Chateau Cemetery, 124
Elverdinge, 17, 25, 38, 42, 47
    Churchyard, 38
Eppinette Road Cemetery, 113
Esplanade Cemetery, 134
Essex Farm Cemetery, 36, 37, 38
Evans, Pte. A., 63
Evans, Cpl. D. B., 100
Eveleigh, Pte. A. E., 128
Everill, Pte. G., 94

1st D. C. L. I. Cemetery, 38, 39, 44, 59, 80, 112, 130
Factory Farm, 149
Feilding, Col. R., 51
Fellows, Pte. E., 6, 84
Ferdinand Farm Cemetery, 76
Ferme des Douze Bonniers, 100
Ferme Henri Pattyn-Vanlaeres Cemetery, 52

Ferme Olivier Cemetery, 25, 38, 142
Firth, Spr. S., 100
Fisher, Lce/Cpl. F., 69, 105
Fitzclarence, Brig-Gen. C., 69, 89, 147
Flanders Field American Cemetery, 108
Fortrie Farm Cemetery, 117
Fox, Lce/Cpl. J. S. V., 30
Francois Farm Cemetery, 76
Fraser, Pte. E., 85
Frelinghien Communal Cemetery, 61
French, Field Marshal Sir John (Earl of Ypres), 4,
    44, 145, 147
Frenchman's Farm Cemetery, 131
French Memorials
   32nd Infantry Division, 40
   45th Infantry Division (Les Joyeaux), 6, 7, 26, 27,
      34, 126
   87th Infantry Division (Les Peperes), 6, 7, 17, 26,
      27, 34, 126
   2nd Brigade of Light Cavalry, 63
   1st Battalion of Light Infantry, 28
   17th Infantry Regiment, 140
   23rd Infantry Regiment, 63
   4th and 12th Regiments of French Dragoons, 63
   2nd Regiment of Chasseurs d'Afrique, 142
   1st Zouaves, Driegrachten, 138
   Cross of Reconciliation, Steenstraat, 138
   De Klijte Church, 54
   Mont Kemmel, 140
   Ypres, 4
Frezenberg, 8, 20, 32, 148, 149
   Ridge, 32, 103
Friedhof XI Cemetery, 127
Fryer, Pte. J. W., 94
Fusilier Farm, 27
Fusilier Farm Cemetery, 76
Fusilier Farm Road Cemetery, 76
Fusilier Wood Cemetery, 35, 36

Garter Point Cemetery, 85
Gawler, Pte. R. W., 128
Geary, 2nd Lt, B. H., 58
Geddes, Col. A., 32
Geluveld, 44, 45, 46, 85, 108, 136, 137, 138, 147, 150
George V, King, 33, 58, 60, 111, 123
German Memorials
   46th Reserve Division, 141
   51st Reserve Division, 141
   52nd Reserve Division, 141
   2nd Westfalian Pioneer Battalion (Koln), 141
   24th Pioneer Battalion, 141
   15th Reserve Jager Battalion (Potsdam), 141
   18th Reserve Jager Battalion, 141
   52nd Reserve Infantry Regiment
     (Brandenburgisches), 141
   201st Reserve Infantry Regiment, 141
   202nd Reserve Infantry Regiment, 141
   203rd Reserve Infantry Regiment, 141
   204th Reserve Infantry Regiment, 141
   205th Reserve Infantry Regiment, 141
   206th Reserve Infantry Regiment, 141

   238th Reserve Infantry Regiment (Karlsruhe),
     141
   43rd Reserve Field Artillery, 141
   44th Reserve Field Artillery, 141
   Deutsche Christliche Studenten Vereinigung
     D.C.S.V., 141
   Deutsche Werschafte, 141
   Kyffhauserverband der Vereine
     Deutscherstudenten, 141
Gheluwe, 45, 46
Ghistelles Churchyard, 59
Ghukiere, Albert, 14
Gibson, Pte, D., 68
Girault, Memorial to Brig. Emilien, 142
Glencorse Wood, 45, 89, 107, 147
Glimpse Cottage Cemetery, 76
Godewaersvelde, 13, 39, 40, 72, 73, 103
   British Cemetery, 39, 40
   Churchyard, 39
Godezonne Farm Cemetery, 40, 132
Goode, Sgt., 103
Gordon Cemetery, 133
Gordon House Cemetery No. 2, 85
Gordon Terrace Cemetery, 112
Gore, Pte. F. C., 94
Gorle, Lt. R. V., 60
Gough, General Sir Hubert de la Poer, 149
Goumier Farm, 73, 126
Gower, Lt. W., 8
Great Wall of China Trench, 84
Green Hunter Cemetery, 129
Grenfell, Capt. F. O., 122
Grieve, Capt. R., 115
Grimbaldstone, Sgt. W. H., 26
Groenenberg German Cemetery, 79
Grootebeek British Cemetery, 21, 40, 41
Grosvenor, Capt. Lord H. W., 136
Gunners' Farm Cemetery, 24, 41
Guynemer, Memorial to Capt. Georges, 88
Gwalia Cemetery, 42
Gwalia Farm, 42

Hackett, Spr. W., 12
Hagle Dump Cemetery, 42, 43
Haig, Field Marshall Sir Douglas, 15, 44, 83, 104
Haldane, Dr. J. S., 7
Halfway House Cemetery, 84
Hall, C.S.M. F. W., 69
Hallebast Restaurant Crossroads, 41, 52
Hallowes, 2nd Lt. R. P., 10
Hamilton-Gault, Mjr. A., 101
Hammond's Corner, 75
Hampshire Farm, 56
Handzaeme German Cemetery, 59
Hans Kirchner German Cemetery, 85
Hanway, Col., 32
Harding, Gunner, 45
Haringhe (Bandaghem) Military Cemetery, 33, 43,
    68
Haringhebeek Cemetery, 124
Harris, Pte, T., 84

Hartells, Pte. B., 6
Hawker, Capt. L. G., 32
Hawkins, Pte. T., 17
Hazebrouck, 8, 10, 150
Hedge Row Trench Cemetery, 38, 44
Hellblast Corner, 137
Hellfire Corner, 15, 16, 33, 45, 86, 98, 118, 137
Hengebarte Cemetery, 129
Hewitt, 2nd Lt. D. G. W., 69
Hill 19, 142
Hill 60, 31, 39, 44, 57, 58, 59, 80, 98, 108, 130, 137,
    149
  Express, 98
Hill 62, 66, 107, 109
  Trench Museum and Cafe, 107
Hill 63, 12, 48, 57, 75, 99, 106, 108, 121, 136, 139,
    141, 148, 149, 150
Hill, Lt. G. B. W., 45
Hilltop Farm, 75
Hitler, Adolf, 14, 28, 135
Hoffman, Capt., 28
Hollandescheschur Farm, 28, 149
Hollebeke, 36, 59, 81, 108
Hooge, 8, 10, 15, 19, 44, 92, 107, 140, 149
  Chateau Wood, 45
  Crater Cemetery, 44, 45, 46, 107
Hooglede, 86, 143
  German Military Cemetery, 143
Hoogemotte Farm German Cemetery, 80
Hoogstade, 33
  Churchyard, 143
Hope Farm, 48
Hope (Hepple), Pte. R., 38
Hope, Pte. T., 12
Hop Store Cemetery, 46, 47
Hospital Farm Cemetery, 42, 47
Houthem-les-Ypres German Cemetery, 80
Houthulst, 81, 85, 88, 139, 142
  Churchyard, 139
  Forest, 38, 85, 105, 133, 139
  Forest Belgian Military Cemetery, 139
  Forest Chateau West Cemetery, 31
  Forest New Military Cemetery, 88
  German Cemetery, 85
Hughes, Pte. H., 48
Hutchison, Lt-Col. G. S., 72
Huts Cemetery, 47, 48, 84
Hyde Park Corner (Royal Berks) Cemetery, 12, 48
Hyde, Pte. J. J., 68

Iberian South Cemetery, 120
Iberian Farm, 120
Iberian Trench Cemetery, 120
Ichtegem German Cemetery, 59
Ijzer, River, 144
Imperial Trench, 59
Imperial War Graves Commission, 4, 61, 68, 92, 134
Impudence Trench, 59
Inderster German Cemetery, 80
Infantry Barracks Cemetery, 133, 134
Ingelmunster German Cemetery, 108

Institution Royale, 71
International Trench, 59
Inverness Copse, 30, 45
Irish Farm Cemetery, 76
Irish House Cemetery, 49
Iron Cross, 105
Ives, Cpl. F., 6, 84

Jam Row Trench, 107
Jeffries, Capt. C. S., 119, 120
Johnstone, Capt. W. H., 12
Jones, Pte. W., 64

Kandahar Farm Cemetery, 49, 50
Kansas Cross, 32
Kastlehoek German Cemetery (No. 61), 108
Keerselare, 88
  French Cemetery, 88
  West German Cemetery, 85
Keerselarehoek German Cemetery, 85
Kemmel, 36, 40, 49, 50, 51, 52, 56, 62, 66, 74, 82, 90,
    98, 103, 104, 112, 113, 114, 124, 131, 132,
    133, 139, 140
  Chateau Military Cemetery, 50
  Churchyard, 51
  Kemmelberg, 40, 50, 51, 62, 64, 90, 127, 139, 140
  No. 1 French Cemetery, 51, 52, 127
  No. 2 French Cemetery, 54, 127
Kerkhove Churchyard, 10
King, Pte. J., 117
King's Own Scottish Borderers Cemetery, 46
Kingsway, 112
Kink Corner Cemetery, 120
Kipling, Rudyard, 145
Kitchener, Lord Horatio Herbert, Earl of
    Khartoum, 145
Kitchener's Wood, 105
Klein Vierstraat British Cemetery, 52
Klein Vierstraat Cabaret, 52
Klein-Zillbeke German Cemetery, 108
Knight, Lt-Col. G. C., 105
Knowles, Capt. J. E., 26
Koekuit German Cemetery, 81
Koelenberg German Cemetery, 45
Kollwitz, Kathe and Peter, 144
Kortekeer Cabaret, 105
Kortekeer German Cemetery No. 12a, 108
Kortemark, 59
  German Cemetery No. 1, 59
Kortrijk, 136, 144
Kosmos, Hotel (Rodeberg), 74
Kriegerfriedhof des Reserve Infantry Regiment 248
    am Polygonwald German Cemetery, 89
Kruiseeke, 59, 135
  German Cemetery, 45, 108, 136

L.4 Post, 97
L'Abeele, 103, 140
L'Alouette German Cemetery, 108
La Basse-Ville German Cemetery, 113
La Belle Alliance Cemetery, 53

La Brique Military Cemetery No. 1, 53, 54
La Brique Military Cemetery No. 2, 53, 54
La Chapelle Farm Cemetery, 46
La Clytte Military Cemetery, 54, 55
La Creche Communal Cemetery, 55
La Laiterie Military Cemetery, 55, 56, 124, 133
LaLiberte, Pte. C., 94
Lamb, Driver A., 122
La Miterie, 76
   German Cemetery, 76
Lancashire Cottage Cemetery, 56, 113
Langemark, 6, 7, 20, 25, 26, 27, 32, 33, 34, 73, 76,
   81, 85, 86, 88, 104, 105, 109, 119, 120, 123,
   126, 140, 142, 143
   German Cemetery, 81, 140, 141, 142
   German Cemetery No. 7 (Toten Walchden), 85
   German Cemetery No. 8, 85
   German Cemetery No. 9, 108
   Line, 106
Lankhof Cemetery, 129
La Petit Douve Farm, 57
La Plus Douve Farm, 57
La Plus Douve Farm Cemetery, 57, 99
La Premiere Borne Cemetery, 135
Larch Wood (Railway Cutting) Cemetery, 26, 31,
   57, 59, 80, 112, 137
Lasnier, Memorial to Lt., 28
Latham, Cpl. G. W., 117
Lawrence Farm, 56
Lawrence, Pte. E., 133
L'Ebbe Farm Cemetery, 85
Leckie, Lt-Col., 105
Ledegem, 60, 150
   Churchyard, 60
   Ledeghem Military Cemetery, 60
Ledward, Sir Gilbert, 12
Leffinghe German Cemetery, 59
Le Bizet, 60
   Convent Military Cemetery, 113
Le Gheer, 56, 87, 113
Le Pelerin, 56
Le Romarin, 67, 77, 117
Le Roukloshille Military Cemetery, 72
Le Touquet, 21
   Railway Crossing Cemetery, 60, 61
Levi Cottage Cemetery, 120
Liddiard, Lt., 103
Lijssenthoek, 78
   Military Cemetery, 61, 62
Lille Gate, 3, 4, 69, 98, 99
Lindenhoek, 62, 82, 90, 131, 132
   Chalet, 62
   Chalet Military Cemetery, 62, 82
Linen Factory Cemetery, 117
Lizerne, 76, 138
Lloyd, Lt-Col. W. R., 105
Lloyd George, David, P. M., 56, 148
Loader, Pte. F., 103
Lock 8 Cemetery, 6
Loker, 8, 29, 34, 35, 41, 54, 63, 64, 65, 140
   Church, 63, 64, 65

Convent/Hospice, 63, 64
Locre Churchyard, 63
Locre Hospice Cemetery, 63, 64
Locre No. 10 Cemetery, 64, 65
Town Hall, 63
London, Bishop of, 65
London General Omnibus Company, 21
London Rifle Brigade Cemetery, 65
Lone Tree Cemetery, 65, 66, 92, 111
Loring, Lt-Col. W. L., 22
Ludendorff, Gen. E., 150
Lumley, 2nd Lt. R. J., 86
Lumm Farm Cemetery, 71
Lynn, Pte. J., 21, 41
Lys, River, 59, 67, 77, 80, 150

McBride, Cpl., 77
McBride, Rfmn. S., 48
McColl, Pte. C. F., 133
McCrae, Lt-Col. J., 36, 37
   Memorial to, 37
McFarlane, Pte. J., 78
McGee, Sgt. L., 119, 120
McGeehan, Pte. B., 94
McGuffie, Sgt. L., 22, 136
McKenzie, Lt. H., 69, 83
McKirdy, Cpl., 103
McLaren, Mjr., 105
Macintosh, Pte. G., 73
Mackenzie, Pte. J., 12
Maedelstede Farm, 149
Mahieu, Memorial to Freres, 80
Malakoff Farm Cemetery, 35
Malliavan, Memorial to Adj. Andre, 142
Mannekin Farm German Cemetery No. 3, 85
Manor Road Cemetery, 76
Maple Avenue, 107
Maple Copse, 107
   Cemetery, 66, 67, 98
Maple Leaf Cemetery, 67
Markhove German Cemetery, 59
Marengo Farm, 9
Martin, Lt. C. G., 11
Martin-Leake, Surgeon-Capt. A., 32
Maxwell, Brig-Gen. F. A., 133
Mellish, Capt. E. N., 22
Mendinghem British Cemetery, 33, 43, 67
Menen, 60, 83, 143, 144, 150
   Communal Cemetery, 107
Menen Road, 15, 23, 44, 45, 46, 67, 70, 85, 90, 100,
   101, 107, 109, 134, 134, 147, 149
Menen-Wald German Military Cemetery, 143
Menin Gate Memorial, 3, 4, 66, 68, 69, 70, 89, 99,
   101, 105, 113, 116, 119, 130, 134, 145
Menin Road North Cemetery, 70
Menin Road Pill-Box Cemetery, 46
Menin Road South Military Cemetery, 70, 101
Merkem, 113, 138
   Church, 138
   Town Hall, 138
Mesen, 13, 14, 22, 24, 50, 51, 56, 57, 65, 66, 71, 72,

75, 97, 99, 108, 111, 116, 128, 131, 132, 148, 149
Abbey of, 14
Church, 14
Messines German Cemetery No. 2, 108
Messines German Cemetery No. 3, 108
Messines Ridge British Cemetery, 14, 68, 71, 72
Museum, 14
New Zealand Memorial to the Missing, 68, 71
New Zealand Park, 71
Ridge, 13, 21, 23, 30, 57, 71, 99
Meteren, 72
Churchyard, 72
Communal Cemetery, 72
Military Cemetery, 72
Michael, Pte. J., 94
Middle Farm Cemetery, 71
Middle Prison Cemetery, 134
Military Cemetery at the Foot of Nightingale Hill, 121
Milnes, 2nd Lt. H., 119
Minty Farm, 73, 116
Cemetery, 73, 126
Mirfield Cemetery, 76
Mitchell, Pte. L., 54
Mitford, Lt. the Hon. C. B. O., 122
Moffat, Pte. M., 60
Moles, Pte. T. L., 133
Montgomery, Lt. B., 72
Mont des Cats, 39, 40
British Cemetery, 72
Indian Cemetery, 72
Monastery, 72
Mont Kemmel French Ossuary, 51, 139, 140
Mont Noir, 72, 74
Hotel du, 74
Military Cemetery, 74
Monts des Flandres, 5, 13, 47, 50, 54, 74, 77, 127, 150
Mont Vidaigne Military Cemetery, 52
Moon, Lce/Cpl. W. A., 8
Moore, Driver T., 69
Moorslede, 10, 108
Morris, Pte. H., 94
Morrow, Pte. R., 128
Motor Car Corner Cemetery, 61, 74, 75, 108, 113, 115
Motor Car Corner Cemetery German Extension, 108
Mottershead, Sgt. T., 8
Mound, The, 21
Mount Sorrel, 107
Mousetrap Farm, 20, 41, 109, 128
Mud Corner, 75, 87, 104, 115
British Cemetery, 75, 113
Mullin, Sgt. G. H., 83

Nachtegall German Cemetery No. 1, 113
Nachtigall German Cemetery, 85
Neubert, Lt. von, 136
New Irish Farm Cemetery, 20, 31, 53, 75, 76

New Zealand Memorials
Buttes Memorial to the Missing, 22, 23, 68, 71
Gravenstafel, 32, 119, 121
Messines Ridge Memorial to the Missing, 68, 71
New Zealand Park, Mesen, 71
Tyne Cot Memorial to the Missing, 68, 119
Nieppe, 77, 91
Communal Cemetery, 77
Nieuwekriuseeke Cabaret Cemetery, 46
Nieuwkerke,
Brewery, 77
Churchyard, 77, 78
North Cemetery, 131
Railway Halt Cemetery, 131
Town Hall, 77
Nine Elms British Cemetery, 78
Nisbet, Pte. J., 98
No Man's Cot, 116, 126
Cemetery, 76, 79, 117
Nonne Boschen (Nun's Wood), 147
Noordschote Churchyard, 143
North Bank Cemetery, 129
Norton-Griffiths, J., M.P., 149

Oak Dump Cemetery, 79, 80, 124
Observatory Ridge, 107
O'Neal, Sgt. J., 60
Onraet Farm Cemetery, 71
Ontario Farm, 149
Oostaverne,
Line, 80, 148
Wood, 80
Wood Cemetery, 80, 81, 109
Oostnieuwkerke German Cemetery, 120
Oostvleteren Churchyard, 143
Ormond, Mjr, 105
Otto Farm Cemetery, 119
Oudenburg Churchyard, 59
Ouderdom, 41, 103
Military Cemetery, 40
Oxford Road Cemetery, 81, 82, 89, 109
Oxford Road Cemetery No. 2, 81

Packhorse Farm, 82
Packhorse Farm Shrine Cemetery, 82
Padstow, Capt. W. G., 64
Pallingbeek Park, 26, 59, 80, 112
Papot Military Cemetery, 91
Paratonnier's Farm Cemetery, 76
Parry, Pte. A., 67
Passendale, 82, 83, 84, 85, 86, 119, 120, 121, 140, 149
Church, 84
Crest Farm Canadian Memorial, 84
New Military Cemetery, 83, 84, 120
Ridge, 83
Town Hall, 84
Pearkes, Mjr. G. R., 83
Peckham Crater, 111, 149
Perth Cemetery (China Wall), 84, 85, 86, 98, 108
Petain, Marshal Henri Phillipe, 140

Petit-Pont German Cemetery, 108
Pheasant Trench Cemetery, 26
Pheasant Wood Cemetery, 125
Phillips, Pte. L. R., 83
Picadilly Farm, 136
Pick, Sgt. J., 69
Pilkem, 76, 105, 108, 149
Pilkem Road Cemetery, 76
Pilkem Road German Cemetery, 88
Pill-Box Cemetery, 46
Pitts, Pte. A., 12
Ploegsteert, 24, 41, 48, 56, 57, 61, 65, 67, 71, 74, 75,
    86, 87, 91, 97, 99, 104, 108, 112, 113, 114,
    115, 121, 140
  Churchyard, 86
Ploegsteert Wood, 56, 75, 87, 97, 104, 112, 113, 115,
    129, 150
  Military Cemetery, 87, 104, 115
  New Cemetery, 113
Plumer, Field Marshal Herbert Charles Onslow, 1st
    Baron Plumer of Messines, 4, 68, 133, 149
Poelkapelle, 83, 85, 86, 87, 88, 89, 103, 139, 140, 142
  British Cemetery, 87, 88, 89
  Church, 88
  Communal Cemetery, 89
  East German Cemetery, 88
  German Cemetery No. 2, 85, 89
  German Cemetery No. 3, 85
  German Cemetery No. 4, 10
  Guynemer Memorial, 88
  New German Cemetery, 88
Pollinkhove Churchyard, 143
Pomern Castle, 149
Polygon Wood, 22, 23, 45, 77, 85, 86, 89, 90, 107,
    147
  Cemetery, 89, 90, 109
Pond Farm, 90
  Cemetery, 90
Pont d'Achelles Military Cemetery, 91
Pont de Nieppe Communal Cemetery, 91, 92
Pont de Nieppe German Cemetery, 9
Pool of Peace, 66, 92
Poole, 2nd Lt. E. S., 94
Poperinge, 5, 9, 18, 19, 25, 31, 33, 38, 40, 42, 43, 47,
    52, 61, 62, 68, 69, 78, 85, 92, 93, 94, 95, 97,
    102, 103, 123, 125, 128, 140, 143
  Berthinstraat, 92
  Communal Cemetery, 92, 93, 108
  Gassthuistraat, 92
  Grote Markt, 92
  Old Military Cemetery, 92, 93
  New Military Cemetery, 61, 69, 93, 94, 95
  Rue de L'Hopital, 92
  St. Berthin's Church, 92
  Skindles, 92
  Stanilas College, 92
  Sugar Refinery, 92
  Talbot House, 92
  Town Hall, 92, 93
Potijze, 5, 6, 33, 51, 95, 96, 135, 140, 148
  Burial Ground, 95

Chateau Grounds Cemetery, 95, 96
Chateau Lawn Cemetery, 95, 96
Chateau Wood Cemetery, 95, 96
Potsdam Redoubt, 32, 120
Poulton, Pte. E., 100
Povey, Cpl. G. H., 69, 130
Prison Cemetery No. 1, 134
Prison Cemetery No. 2, 134
Proven, 33, 43, 67, 68, 128
  Churchyard, 68
Prowse, Brig-Gen. C. B., 97, 129
Prowse Farm, 129
Prowse Point Military Cemetery, 48, 75, 87, 97, 104,
    113, 115, 129
Prowse Point Lower Cemetery, 113
Pryce, Capt. T. T., 12

Queensland Cemetery, 71
Queen Victoria's Rifles Cafe and Museum, 58

Rabschloss German Cemetery No. 64, 108
Rae, Memorial to 2nd Lt. T. K. H., 107
Raemdonck, Memorial to Gebroeders van, 138
Railway Chateau Cemetery, 97
Railway Dugouts Burial Ground (Transport Farm),
    86, 97, 98
Railway Wood, 5, 58, 100
Ramparts Cemetery (Lille Gate), 98, 99
Ration Dump Burial Ground, 85
Ration Farm, 57
Ration Farm (La Plus Douve) Annexe, 99
Ravine, The, 39, 130
Ravine Wood, 149
Ravine Wood Cemetery, 44
R. E. (Beaver) Farm, 132
R. E. Farm Cemetery, 100
R. E. Grave, 15, 100, 101
Red Farm Cemetery, 101, 102
Redmond, Mjr. W. H. K., 64
Remi Farm, 61
Rendle, 2nd Lt. A. E., 130
Reninge, 143
Reningelst, 40, 54, 93, 95, 102, 103, 123, 127
  Chinese Cemetery, 9
  Churchyard, 102
  Churchyard Extension, 102
  New Military Cemetery, 102, 103
Rest and Be Thankful Farm, 132
Reutal, 22, 32, 86
  German Cemetery, 86, 108
Richardson, Lt. R. F., 23
Ricketts, Pte. T., 60
Rickman, Pte. A. 122
Riddell, Brig-Gen. J. P., 106
Ridge Wood, 103
  Military Cemetery, 103, 104
Rifle House Cemetery, 104
River Douve Cemetery, 71
Roberts, Pte. R., 100
Roberts, Pte. W. W., 8
Robertson, Capt. C., 82, 89

Robertson, General Sir William Robert,
    Commander of the Imperial Staff, 148
Robertson, Pte. J. P., 83, 120
Robinson, Lt. E. W., 124
Robinson, Pte. J., 6
Rodeberg, 52, 63, 73, 74
Rodgers, Pte. J., 8
Roe, Pte. G. E., 84
Roeselare, 60, 134, 150
Ross, Q.M.S.M. V., 123
Rossignol German Cemetery, 85
Rossignol Heights, 121
Roupell, Lt. G. R. P., 59
Royal British Legion, 69
Royal West Surrey Cemetery, 13
Ruisseau Farm, 104
    Cemetery, 17, 104, 105

St. Armand, Church of, 8
St. Augustine Street Cabaret, 97
St. Charles-Potijze French Military Cemetery, 140,
    52
St. Eloi, 11, 21, 22, 27, 66, 71, 80, 81, 111, 112, 124,
    129, 136, 149
St. Franciscus Xaverius, 17
St. George, 2nd Lt. H. A. B., 137
St. Jan, 20, 31, 53, 73, 75, 76, 82, 84, 95, 116, 128,
    129
    Churchyard, 76, 89
St. Jans-Cappel, 74
St. Joseph German Cemetery, 86
St. Juliaan, 20, 26, 27, 73, 76, 79, 82, 88, 105, 106,
    140
    Church, 105
    Communal Cemetery, 86
    St. Julien Dressing Station (D.S.) Cemetery, 20,
        105, 106
St. Michael, Church of, 17
St. Quentin Cabaret Military Cemetery, 106
St. Sixtus Abbey, 33, 128
Sackville Street, 50
Salvation Corner, 4, 53
Sanctuary Wood, 44, 66, 70, 107, 108
    Cemetery, 92, 107, 108, 109
    Hill 62 Canadian Memorial, 107, 109
    Old British Cemetery, 46
    Trench Museum and Cafe, 107
Scherpenberg, 30, 54, 127, 128
Schier, Jacques, 107
Schrieboom German Cemetery, 86
Scottish Wood, 36, 103
Scotton, Pte. W., 69, 113
Seaforth Cemetery, 76, 106, 109, 110, 117
Seaman, Lce/Cpl. E., 120
Seymour, Pte. J., 35
Shrapnel Corner, 40, 51, 86, 98, 137
Shrewsbury Forest, 59, 137
Simmonds, Pte. W. H., 94
Skinner, C.S.M. J., 26, 123
Skrine, Memorial to Capt. H. L., 101
Slade, Pte. F. W., 17

Slijpskapelle Churchyard, 108
Small, Lt. F. G., 77
Smith, Pte. J. C., 50
Smith, Pte. W., 103
Snitchel Farm, 71
Solferino Farm, 110
    Cemetery, 35, 110
Somer Farm, 110
    Cemetery, 71, 110, 111, 133
    Cemetery No. 2, 133
Spanbroekmolen, 65, 71
    British Cemetery, 111, 112
    Mine, 65, 66, 92, 149
Spencer, Pte. V. M., 48
Spoilbank Cemetery, 59, 112
Spooner, Spr. W., 100
Spree Farm Cemetery, 76
Staden French Military Cemetery, 89
Staden German Cemetery, 120
Stedman, Pte. J., 94
Steenbeek, 25, 26, 73, 76, 149
Steenwerk German Military Cemetery, 117
Stevenson, Pte. R., 94
Stewart, Pte. S., 50
Stirling Castle, 45
Strachan, R., 146
Strand, The, 87, 112
Strand Military Cemetery, 112, 113
Strange, Lt. L. A., 77
Strudwick, Pte. V. J., 37
Strutt, Lt. A. H., 19
Strutt, Mr. G. H., 19
Suffolk Cemetery, 69, 113, 114

Talana Farm, 114
Talana Farm Cemetery, 114
Talbot, Lt. G. W. L., 92, 108
Talbot, Reverend N., 92
Tancrez Farm Military Cemetery, 61, 114, 115
Tattenham Corner, 4, 53
Taymans, Memorial to Adj., 139
Ten-Brielen Amerika German Cemetery, 81
Ten-Brielen Communal Cemetery German
    Extension, 59
Terdegem Churchyard, 108
Thompson, Pte. A. D., 6
Thourout German Cemetery No. 2, 59, 109
Three Houses German Cemetery (Hollebeke
    Cemetery No. 60), 81, 109
Tite, Pte. R. T., 94
Toc H, 66, 92
Torhout, 59, 144
Toronto Avenue Cemetery, 115
Torroken Farm Cemetery No. 1, 24, 116, 132
Totenmuhle, 88
Touquet-Berthe German Cemetery, 113
Tower Hamlets, 30, 46
Tower Hamlets Cemetery, 46
Track 'X' Cemetery, 20, 116, 117
Transport Farm Annexe Cemetery, 86, 98
Trench 127, 149

Trench Railway Cemetery, 86
Treurniet German Cemetery, 86
Triangular Wood, 79
Trois Arbres Cemetery, 117, 118
Tubb, Mjr. F. H., 62
Tuileries British Cemetery, 118
Turner, Pte. F., 10
Turpie, Pte. W. J., 128
Tyne Cot, 119
    Cemetery, 4, 32, 61, 68, 83, 85, 119, 120, 121

Underhill Farm Cemetery, 121
Union Street Graveyards No.'s 1 & 2, 16
Urquhart, Capt. E. F. M., 17

Vallentin, Capt. J. F., 66, 69
Valley Cottages Cemetery, 98
Vancouver Corner, 26, 32, 33, 88
Vanheule Farm Cemetery, 76
Verlorenhoek, 5, 32, 129
Veurne, 25, 134, 142, 144
Vidaignberg, 52, 74
Vierstraat, 30, 40, 52, 113, 114
Vieux-Chien German Cemetery, 85
Vijfwegen German Cemetery No.1, 89
Vijverhoek Brasserie Cemetery, 125
Villa Gretchen Cemetery, 34
Vince Street Trench, 107
Vinck, Baron de, 108
Vladslo, 144
    German Cemetery, 59
Vladslo-Praatbos German Military Cemetery, 120,
    144
Vlamertinge, 18, 19, 31, 41, 43, 46, 47, 85, 101, 102,
    122, 123, 125, 128, 129
    Churchyard, 41, 122
    Military Cemetery, 122, 123
    New Military Cemetery, 26, 122, 123
Volksbund Deutsche, 92, 141, 143, 144
Voormezele, 6, 21, 22, 28, 36, 79, 103, 123, 124, 125,
    129, 140
    Churchyard, 124
    Enclosures No.'s 1 & 2, 123, 124, 125
    Enclosure No. 3, 124, 125
    Enclosure No. 4, 125

Wall, Sgt. J. T., 94
Walleghem, Pastor van, 30
Wallemolen German Cemetery, 86
Ware, Fabian, 145
Warner, Pte. E., 69
Warneton, 39, 44, 56, 60, 71, 75, 87, 97, 113, 130
    Churchyard, 113
Warneton Sud-et-Bas German Cemetery, 59
Waterloo Farm Cemetery, 121
Waterloo Road, 126
Watkins, Pte. G., 38
Watou, 30, 125
    Churchyard, 125
Wavell, Mjr. A. P., 44
Weidendreft German Cemetery, 86

Welsh Cemetery (Caesar's Nose), 125, 126
Wendover, Viscount Lt. A., 5
Wervik, 59, 80
    Communal Cemetery and Extensions, 59
    German Cemetery, 136
Westhoek, 85, 101
    Ridge Small Cemetery, 46
Westhof Farm, 126
Westhof Farm Cemetery, 126
Westouter, 52, 127, 140
    Westoutre British Cemetery, 127
    Westoutre Churchyard and Extension, 127, 128
Westrozebeke, 84, 88, 89
    Church, 31
    German Cemetery No. 2, 86
Westvleteren, 33
    Belgian Military Cemetery, 143
    Churchyard, 142
Westwood, Pte. A., 17
White House Cemetery, 10, 53, 128, 129
Wieltje, 5, 106
    Farm, 129
    Farm Cemetery, 129
Wijnendale German Cemetery, 59
Wijtschate, 6, 21, 23, 24, 27, 28, 29, 49, 62, 64, 65,
    66, 71, 80, 100, 110, 111, 112, 113, 116, 12,
    133, 136, 140, 148, 150
    Wytschaete Military Cemetery, 49, 116, 132, 133
Wilde Wood Cemetery, 129
Wilhelm II of Germany, Kaiser, 136, 147, 148
Williams, Cpl. J., 49
Wilson, Lt-Col. G. C., 137
Wilson, Lt-Gen. Sir H. F. M., 65
Wilson, Pte. J. H., 94
Wimmereaux Cemetery, 37
Wipers Times, 69
Woesten Churchyard, 142
Wolfhoek British Cemetery, 74
Woodroffe, 2nd Lt. S. C., 69
Woolley, Cpl. G. A., 100
Woolley, 2nd Lt. G. H., 58
Woods Cemetery, 39, 86, 130
Worsley, Lord C. S. P., Bt, 135, 136
Worsley, Pte. E., 91
Wulvergem, 49, 50, 57, 71, 72, 82, 90, 99, 100, 106,
    108, 111, 130, 131
    Churchyard, 69, 130, 131
    Dressing Station Cemetery, 131
    Wulvergem-Lindenhoek Road Cemetery, 131,
    132

Y.M.C.A., 123
    Australian, 35
    hut, 87
York Road, 55
Yorkshire Cemetery, 76
Youens, 2nd Lt. F., 98
Ypres
    1914-1918 Ypres Salient Museum, 4
    Belgian Memorial, 4
    Belle Godhuis, 4

Benedictine Convent Grounds Cemetery, 135
Cloth Hall, 3, 4, 70
   Memorial to Earl Baldwin XI and Queen
     Margaret of Champagne, 4
   Memorial to King Albert and Queen Elizabeth,
     4
   Memorial to Our Lady of Thuyne, 4
   Memorial to the Sacred Heart, 4
   Memorial to the French Dead of 1914 - 1918, 4
Commonwealth War Graves Commission Office,
   134, 146
Eton Memorial School, 4
Fire Brigade, 69
French Memorial, 4
Grote Markt, 3, 70, 99, 134
Infantry Barracks, 133
League, 110
Lion Tower, 4, 99
Menin Gate, 3, 4, 66, 68, 69, 70, 89, 99, 101, 105,
   113, 116, 119, 130, 134, 145
Moat, 4, 99
Powder Magazine, 4, 99
Prison, 133, 134
Ramparts, 6, 69, 84, 85, 98, 99
Reservoir Cemetery, 92, 133, 134, 135
Reservoir Middle Cemetery, 133, 134
Reservoir North Cemetery, 133
Reservoir South Cemetery, 134
Rijselstraat, 4
St. George's Memorial Church, 4
St. John's Almshouse, 4
St. Martin's Cathedral, 4, 99, 133
   King Albert Memorial, 4
   Royal Air Force Memorial, 4
   British Expeditionary Force Memorial, 4
   5th (Princess Charlotte of Wales's) Dragoon
     Guards Memorial, 4

Memorial to the British Commonwealth Dead,
   4
Memorial to the French Dead in the Salient, 4
Munster Memorial, 4
St. Peter's Church, 4
Tourist Office, 4, 70
Town Cemetery, 44, 134, 135
Town Cemetery Extension, 135, 136
Ypres-Comines Canal, 6, 26, 39, 80, 112
Ypres-Ijzer Canal, 4, 138 134
Y Wood, 15

Zandvoorde, 44, 59, 107, 128, 135, 136, 140, 150
   Churchyard, 136
   Hill, 128, 136
   German Cemetery, 59
   Zantvoorde Military Cemetery, 22, 108, 135, 136,
     137
Zillebeke, 6, 10, 15, 26, 27, 38, 39, 44, 45, 46, 57, 66,
   67, 76, 84, 85, 86, 95, 98, 100, 107, 112, 118,
   128, 130, 137, 140
   Church, 118, 137
   Lake, 16, 98, 137
Zonnebeke, 6, 12, 15, 16, 22, 32, 33, 46, 85, 89, 95,
   96, 101, 105, 119, 120, 128, 129, 134, 140, 148
   Church, 32
   Streekmuseum, 32
   British Cemeteries No.'s 1 & 3, 10
   British Cemetery No. 2, 121
Zouaves, 114, 138, 142
Zouave Villa, 76
Zouave Wood, 107
Zuidschote, 138
   Church, 138
Zwaanhoek, 86
   German Cemetery, 81
Zwarteleen, 87

NOTES

NOTES